TUDOR DRAMA AND POLITICS

TUDOR DRAMA

CAMBRIDGE, MASSACHUSETTS 1968

AND POLITICS

A CRITICAL APPROACH

TO TOPICAL MEANING

BY DAVID BEVINGTON

HARVARD UNIVERSITY PRESS

© COPYRIGHT 1968 BY THE PRESIDENT AND FELLOWS OF HARVARD COLLEGE
ALL RIGHTS RESERVED

DISTRIBUTED IN GREAT BRITAIN BY OXFORD UNIVERSITY PRESS, LONDON

PUBLICATION OF THIS BOOK HAS BEEN AIDED BY
A GRANT FROM THE HYDER EDWARD ROLLINS FUND

LIBRARY OF CONGRESS CATALOG CARD NUMBER 68-17637
PRINTED IN THE UNITED STATES OF AMERICA

FOR ALFRED HARBAGE

ACKNOWLEDGMENTS

I have received much generous assistance in my work. A grant from the John Simon Guggenheim Memorial Foundation in 1964-1965 enabled me to devote a full academic year to the completion of a first draft. Thereafter, the University of Virginia provided a summer research grant and funds for secretarial aid. For assistance in research I am much indebted to the library staffs of the University of Virginia, the University of Chicago, the University of North Carolina, Harvard University, and Duke University; also the Folger Shakespeare Library and the Cleveland Public Library.

The first draft received careful inspection and compassionate recommendations from Professor Arthur Heiserman, of the University of Chicago, and Professor Clifford Leech, of the University of Toronto. Mr. Leech subsequently reviewed the revised manuscript, offering additional helpful observations. Professor David Underdown, of the Department of History in the University of Virginia, brought to the manuscript the much-needed perspective of a professional historian, and sent me to some important studies of Tudor parliamentary and economic history that I had heretofore overlooked.

En route to completion, portions of Chapters 2, 6, 9, and 13 appeared as articles in versions now somewhat revised. I wish to thank Professors George W. Williams and Samuel Schoenbaum, editors respectively of *Renaissance Papers* and *Renaissance Drama*, both for their generosity in first accepting and editing these articles, and for arranging permission for them to be used here. The articles were: "Political Satire in the Morality *Wisdom Who Is Christ*," *RenP 1963* (1964), pp. 41-51; "Is John Heywood's *Play of the Weather* Really about the Weather?" *Renaissance Drama*, 7:11-19 (1964); "Drama and Polemics under Queen Mary," *Renaissance Drama*, 9:105-124 (1966); and "John Lyly and Queen Elizabeth: Royal Flattery in *Campaspe* and *Sapho and Phao*," *RenP 1966* (1967), pp. 57-67.

From first to last, the manuscript of this book has been greatly improved by the editing skills and encouragement of my mother, Helen Bevington. My wife, Peggy, has participated critically and sympathetically in every

ACKNOWLEDGMENTS

aspect of analysis, writing, and revision. To Professor Alfred Harbage I owe a special kind of thanks: although he did not direct the writing of this volume as he did my first, he introduced me to the serious study of Elizabethan literature in its relation to history, and he has remained since then a mentor and friend.

DAVID BEVINGTON

MAY 1968

CONTENTS

TUDOR DRAMA AND POLITICS

It is enough for me (being in that state I am) to write of the eldest times: wherein also why may it not be said, that in speaking of the past, I point at the present, and tax the vices of those that are yet living, in their persons that are long since dead; and have it laid to my charge? But this I cannot help, though innocent. And certainly if there be any, that finding themselves spotted like the tigers of old time, shall find fault with me for painting them over anew; they shall therein accuse themselves justly, and me falsely.

Sir Walter Ralegh, *Preface to* History of the World

1 · INTRODUCTION: SOME APPROACHES
TO TOPICAL MEANING

Study of topical relevance in Tudor drama, especially in Shakespeare's plays, has a long history—much of it inglorious. Already in 1880, Swinburne was moved to lampoon the scholarly vogue, practiced *ad nauseam* by N. J. Halpin, Robert Cartwright, and others,[1] of equating dramatic characters with historical personages. Swinburne's facetious suggestion was that Romeo covertly represents Lord Burghley. The total dissimilarity of the two merely proves that Shakespeare was being obscure to escape the censor.[2] By 1930, Baldwin Maxwell was able to offer a more detailed parody, devastatingly true to type. Falstaff, he offered, is Robert Greene: licentious, surfeiting, on the verge of repentance ("Monsieur Remorse"), with a wife named Dorothy or Doll, ending his life broken and deserted. Most important, Shakespeare had a motive in responding to Greene's attack on "Shake-scene."[3] Well might Josephine Bennett write, in 1942, "Modern attempts to discover and interpret Elizabethan topical allegory have produced such absurdities at the hands of overzealous devotees, that a scholar who desires a reputation for sanity hardly ventures to touch the subject."[4]

Maxwell and Miss Bennett were reacting to a particularly energetic wave of publishing in the 1920's, inspired in part by the team of Manly and Rickert at Chicago. Triumphantly this school of criticism proclaimed its all-embracing theory of political usefulness in the Tudor drama. "What research is making continually clearer," wrote Miss Rickert, is "that in the sixteenth century the play and the masque did the work of the modern newspaper in guiding opinion." [5] Acting companies adopted the political viewpoint of their noble patrons, and churned out plays that were, despite their guise of entertainment, little more than propagandistic weapons of a continuing factionalism at court. The drama performed editorial rather than newsgathering functions, and was in fact a "review" in the style of *Punch*, caricaturing everyone in public life. [6]

At its extreme, such an approach was perhaps an unavoidable abuse of the philological quest for sources and background illumination. By no means all of its hypotheses were insane, and its contributions to factual knowledge were considerable. Nevertheless, the bulk of this scholarship has been written off as bizarre ingenuity, akin to Baconian or Oxfordian ciphering in its search for answers to a nonexistent mystery. [7] More serious, the approach implies a debased and contentious view of Elizabethan dramatic art. Too often it has reduced even Shakespeare to the ignoble status of polemicist and mere copyist from life. Hamlet's assertion that dramatists should offer "the abstract and brief chronicles of the time" (a phrase Shakespeare might well have expunged if he could have foreseen its critical consequences) has become twisted into a creed of banal usefulness that denies the integrity of the artist. [8] As Brents Stirling has shown, these critical heresies threaten to engulf the present-day student of Shakespeare's political meaning. [9] If he defends the theory of didacticism in Renaissance art, the student must not look upon "message" as the sole or dominant aim of artistic expression. Most of all he must avoid the common temptation to argue that Tudor politics are relevant to modern ideologies, from Marxism to rightist totalitarianism.

On the other hand, romantic hostility to topical meaning is capable of producing its own distortions, especially when applied retroactively to the civilization of the Renaissance. Our world tends to overemphasize the separation of politics and art, partly because of our distrust of ever-increasing state power over the minds of men. Yeats spoke for many modern intellectuals when he said, "We have no gift to set a statesman right," even if Yeats did not always follow his own advice. Auden, too, in eulogizing Yeats, argued that poetry "makes nothing happen." [10] Both men were speaking in a romantic tradition exemplified earlier by Shelley, who insisted that a poet "would do ill to embody his own conceptions of right and wrong, which are usually those of his place and time, in his poetical creations, which participate in neither." [11] Ben Jonson, however, who attempted to set many a statesman right, would have rejected the implied dichotomy between usefulness and poetic vision. He assumed, as did his contemporaries, that art could be both universal and didactic, and he did not hesitate to set forth his conception of right and wrong for his own time. Even if we view the decline of didacticism as necessary to the flowering of great Renaissance art, we should not pretend that didacticism was eliminated entirely in the late Elizabethan period. For this reason, it is a romantic exaggeration to suppose with A. F. Pollard that "no period of English literature has less to do with politics than that during which English letters reached their zenith; and no English writer's attitude toward the questions, with which alone political history is concerned, is more obscure or less important than Shakespeare's." [12] One can applaud Tucker Brooke's efforts to rescue Shakespeare from the narrow topicalists and still object to his wishful depiction of Shakespeare as "that entrancing, brilliant moss-back" who "must have been one of the last men in London with whom an up-to-date Elizabethan would have thought of discussing politics, or religion, or geography, or current affairs." [13]

Shakespeare, Jonson, and the best of their contemporaries did of course transcend mere pamphleteering. Yet their remarkable success in doing so cannot be measured without an awareness of the polemical norms of their day. Art as a weapon of propaganda was a commonplace in the sixteenth century, taken for granted by the politically active noblemen who provided the financial support for many of England's writers.[14] During the formative midcentury years, religious politics was virtually the whole substance of drama, inevitably creating a tradition both of political commentary in the drama and of various dramaturgic techniques by which ideology could be given maximum propagandistic effect. Without this background it is not easy to assess the nature of Shakespeare's problem as a writer of history plays. The historical materials he used were habitually employed in topical controversy comparing Queen Elizabeth with her incompetent predecessors John, Edward II, Richard II, and Henry VI. Shakespeare's use of these materials did not make him a polemicist, but it did oblige him to be conscious of latent meanings for his audience and for his government. Furthermore, there is no good reason to believe that Shakespeare and Jonson wished to shun the political preoccupations of their generation. However universal their vision, however much emancipated from the literal equations of some allegorists, they chose the political or courtly arena as a means of dramatizing their ideals about man in society. In a thriving commercial theater they fortunately achieved a fair degree of independence from ideological servitude, and they used their independence to look beyond the narrowly political. Hamlet's espousal of the "abstract and brief chronicles" is of course infinitely more than topical; it offers a transcendent rationale for the artist's depiction of life as he sees it.[15] Without the providential demise of "pure" political drama during the years of Shakespeare's youth, later Elizabethan drama would have been indeed sterile and utilitarian. Yet even if a study of Tudor political drama must accordingly be anticlimactic in structure, looking forward with relief to the emancipation of the artist from a constricting view of his social function, it nevertheless is paradoxically true that contemporary political awareness contributed greatly to the highest literary achievement of English civilization. Shakespeare and Jonson did not use their freedom to eschew political responsibility but rather to speak as public moralists. They still believed in the power of art to guide and reform. Political dramaturgy was an inescapable and major portion of their heritage, and as in so many things their generation managed to transform stern realities into momentary splendor.

Shakespeare's dominance on the Elizabethan dramatic scene ordinarily requires that he be treated at length or not at all. He is certainly the universally known poet on whom most criticism (good and bad) has centered, as this introductory chapter will subsequently illustrate. In order to chronicle a many-sided debate on law and order, however, I have given to Shakespeare a place more proportionate to his political contribution than to his poetical and dramatic genius. My discussions of Shakespeare lean heavily on specialists in his political thought, and I will refer the reader to such studies for more detail than my present scope allows. Although such a method limits opportunity for extensive analysis of individual plays, it reveals the overall pattern by which the dramatic art of the Renaissance became more sophisticated in the use of its secular environment. This large scope will enable us to see the later Elizabethan drama in relation to its political origins in the early Tudor period. Shakespeare's political ideas emerge from the comparison as those of an eminently thoughtful man who catered neither to a complacent view of official policy nor to the firebrand rebelliousness of a man like the Earl of Essex. Among his contemporaries Shakespeare was, in fact, an unusually brave, sensitive, and humane defender of a middle position rapidly losing credence in the extremist temper of Elizabeth's last years. The burning issues of the 1590's were relevant to Shakespeare's career as a dramatist, not in terms of individual identities but of principles.

Apart from setting the political ideas of late Elizabethan drama in a broad perspective, this study attempts to achieve literary insight into the growth of dramatic forms. My emphasis is not on social and political history for which plays might be used as illustrative documents, but on the plays themselves. Techniques of characterization, for instance, were intensely affected by the Elizabethan dramatist's quest for ways to transform historical models into artistic abstractions or social types. The escape from the narrow didacticism of polemical portraiture was necessarily achieved in the context of a political tradition. Handling of viewpoint and use of chorus or of choral characters are matters for which a determining of political auspices is often vital. The artist's conception of the genre in which he writes is frequently the product of his political intent. These are literary questions for which a knowledge of historical background is a subservient but essential need.

In order to avoid the pitfalls of many topical interpreters of Tudor plays, with their grasping at coincidental similarities between drama and historical event (analogies often constructed on internal evidence alone), we would do well to survey two approaches to topical meaning: first, the considerable amount of external evidence concerning political activity in the drama, and second, some of the hypotheses advanced to explain the "secret" meaning of extant Elizabethan plays. The approaches are too often worlds apart. Yet the reliable external evidence, however cautiously it must be applied to the plays, is significant and pervasive throughout the Tudor period. The habit of analogizing, in drama as elsewhere, was universal. As Miss Campbell, M. M. Reese, and others have abundantly illustrated,[16] history was studied and restudied for the light it cast on contemporary events. In Herodotus' account of the Greek wars against the Persians, for instance, Elizabethans could see a mirror of their own struggle with Spain. They eulogized Queen Elizabeth at her coronation festivities as Deborah the woman judge, or as Alexander, Diana, Phoebe, and Arthur. Mary Queen of Scots was flatteringly compared to Aurora, the Muses, Helen, Ceres, Juno, Lucrece, Pallas, Jove, Clio, Diana, Venus, Penelope, and the Virgin Mary; by her enemies she was likened to Circe, Clytemnestra, Dalilah, Jezebel, Medea, Pasiphae, Calypso, the Sirens, Medusa, and Duessa.[17] The commonest sources for such analogies were the Bible, English history and legendary history, and classical mythology and history.

In drama, this habit of mind is discernible in the earliest accounts of medieval street pageants and courtly disguisings.[18] A pageant celebrating the reconciliation of Richard II with the City of London (1392) compared Richard to Solomon, Troilus, Absalom, and Christ; in a particularly pointed allegory he was depicted as Ahasuerus, with Queen Anne as the godly Queen Hester who could appease her husband's unjustified wrath toward his people. The advice was sharply critical, for the Londoners knew they had won their argument and could welcome Richard back largely on their own terms. Lydgate wrote a pageant for Henry VI's entry into London (1432) celebrating the king as Aristotle, Euclid, Boethius, David, and Solomon. Henry VII's progress to York, Hereford, Worcester, and Bristol in 1486 brought forth encomiums to a resurrected Solomon, Noah, Jason, Isaac, Jacob, David, Scipio, and of course Arthur. Lydgate's courtly disguisings of 1425-1435 similarly gave Biblical and mythological dignity to politically important embassies. Mummings were so potentially dangerous that they had to be prohibited at times (for instance, in 1417 and 1418). According to some chroniclers, a mumming provided the occasion for an attempted overthrow of Henry IV in 1400. Politically motivated disguisings continued into the Tudor period, as at the marriage of Prince Arthur to Katharine of Aragon (1501).[19]

Well before the Reformation, Henry VIII encouraged political drama dealing with the international power struggle. On the occasion of the visit of Emperor Charles V in 1522, to cement an imperial alliance, the signatories witnessed a play by young gentlemen that expressed Henry's viewpoint in the negotiations. According to Edward Hall's *Union*, a group of allegorical figures named Friendship, Prudence, and Might, representing the signatories, undertook to tame a wild horse representing King Francis I of France.[20] In November 1527, after a characteristic shift in diplomatic ties, John Ritwise and the children of Paul's performed a Latin play before Henry and the French ambassador, needling the emperor and the Spaniards. Cardinal Wolsey is the hero of this piece of open propaganda. With St. Peter's authority, Wolsey unites England and France against the enemies of the church, bringing the emperor to his knees and freeing the two sons of the king of France. Also in the production are Religion, Ecclesia, and Verity, opposing Heresy, False Interpretation, Corruptio Scriptoris, and the heretic Luther and his wife. Wolsey and Henry are "Fidei Defensor." Hall reports drily that wise men smiled at the cardinal's vanity.[21] The next year saw a companion piece performed before Wolsey on the release of the pope from captivity.[22]

Not all political dramas of this early period favored the administration so tamely. John Roo wrote a play (1527) about Lord Governance, "ruled by Dissipation and Negligence, by whose misgovernance and evil order Lady Public Weal was put from Governance; which caused Rumor Populi, Inward Grudge, and Disdain of Wanton Sovereignty to rise with a great multitude" to restore Public Weal. Hall, a member of Gray's Inn, gives a first-hand account of this Christmas performance before lawyers who were evidently up in arms about Henry's "amicable loan" of 1525. Roo claimed that the play had been written at the end of Henry VII's reign, but Wolsey was sufficiently offended to send Roo to the Fleet and rebuke the young gentlemen who had acted in the play.[23] In 1537, at a May-Day play in Suffolk, the actors told "of a king, how he should rule his realm," and "one played Husbandry and said many things against gentlemen, more than was in the book of the play." [24]

With the Reformation, political drama took a more violent turn. A comedy appeared at court in 1533-1534 "to the no small defamation of certain cardinals." Even the pope heard that Henry "feist jouer ou permist estre jouées des farces dedans Londres fort ignominieuses." Chapuys, the Spanish ambassador, tells a grisly episode of Henry delighting in his own thirst for blood. In June 1535, Henry traveled thirty miles to Windsor

7

one evening, walking ten of those miles "with a two-handed sword, and got into a house where he could see everything. He was so pleased at seeing himself cutting off the heads of the clergy," that "he sent to tell his lady [Anne Boleyn] that she ought to see the representation of it repeated on the eve of St. Peter." [25]

Anti-Catholic drama and its opposite were staple in the reigns of Edward VI and Mary, and of the early Elizabeth. Official fear of political drama and its two-edged potency was bound to increase, however, and Elizabeth's attitude was complex. Her sensitivity, combined with her fascination for allegorical subtlety, inevitably altered the method of political allusion. She was especially alert to the question of her marriage or establishing a successor to the throne. Did she merely drive political allusion into more tortuous and obscure forms of expression, or did she succeed in persuading her courtiers that the subject was too dangerous to mention? The question is central to Lyly's plays among others, and will be debated at length in the ensuing chapters. We cannot doubt, however, that Elizabeth suspected a never-ending commentary in most plays she saw. In July 1564, Guzman da Silva wrote to his Spanish master, King Philip, about a comedy he had seen in Elizabeth's presence: "I should not have understood much of it if the Queen had not interpreted as she told me she would do. They generally deal with marriage in the comedies." Similarly in March 1565, de Silva witnessed with Elizabeth a debate between Juno and Diana, representing marriage and chastity. After Jupiter had given his verdict in favor of marriage, "the Queen then turned to me and said, 'This is all against me.'" In 1567 de Silva wrote, "The hatred that this Queen has of marriage is most strange. They represented a comedy before her last night until nearly one in the morning, which ended in a marriage, and the Queen, as she told me herself, expressed her dislike of the woman's part." [26] Late in her reign, John Harington could report that Elizabeth "utterly supprest the talk of an heir apparent, saying she would not have her winding sheet set up afore her face." [27] Yet she still expected at this date to receive unwelcome advice in her plays. After witnessing a play in 1595 appearing to favor Essex, Elizabeth retired with the comment that "if she had thought there had been so much said of her, she would not have been there that night." And Lord Burghley wrote in a letter that same year, "I think never a lady besides her, nor a decipherer in the court,

8

would have dissolved the figure [explicated the allegory] to have found the sense as her Majesty hath done." [28]

Were Elizabeth's endless suspicions justified, however, in each case? Burghley's testimonial suggests rather that Elizabeth was a reader of deep meaning beyond the talents of highly accomplished decipherers in her court. If a comedy ending in marriage offended her, how could any comedy hope to please? Her remarks to the Spanish ambassador may well have been calculated to titillate Philip; she could depend on de Silva to repeat what she had said, and was not likely to offer an undiplomatic gambit. Philip long fancied himself as one of Elizabeth's wooers, and she was strategically in need of flirting with him. What we are left with is evidence that feeling did run high concerning the marriage question and that allegorical lock-picking was a courtly pastime amounting to a disease. No writer in Lyly's situation could overlook it, as his many disclaimers prove.

There are, to be sure, palpable instances in which courtiers did offer allegorical tributes to their queen, begging favors that were sometimes granted. These entertainments were not regular plays, however, but took the form of masques or pageants on the queen's progresses. At Kenilworth in 1575, the festivities planned by Leicester included a show "in which tale, if you mark the words with this present world, or were acquainted with the state of the devices, you should find no less hidden than uttered, and no less uttered than should deserve a double reading over." [29] Leicester's audacity in urging his suit of marriage appears to have backfired, however, prompting a rejoinder in the entertainment at Woodstock that argues against unequal marriages for princesses. Later, in 1595, Arthur Throgmorton asked permission to present before Elizabeth a "masque of the nine muses," upon which occasion the sponsor planned to beg a royal favor. Thomas Churchyard tells of a sumptuous show by Sir Walter Ralegh and others "in which book was the whole service of my L. of Lester mentioned that he and his train did in Flaunders." When Elizabeth visited Burghley in 1593 "she was welcomed by a dramatic device in which it was suggested in the plainest terms that Burghley's mantle of councillor should be allowed to fall upon his son Robert." At Essex's pageant before the queen in 1595 "there was much guessing as to the meaning of the allegory." [30]

This topical method, however, applies solely to private masques and shows, which were by nature occasional pieces, paid for by an aristocrat with the specific aim of cajoling or placating the queen. Regular plays, on the other hand, whether for adult or juvenile companies, were financed by a theatrical audience. The patron offered nominal protection in return for sporadic services; he did not commission the work. For these reasons it is unsafe to assume that plays like *Endymion, Love's Labor's Lost, Troilus and Cressida,* or *The Merry Wives of Windsor* fostered individual campaigns of flattery and begging on behalf of certain courtiers, as did the courtly entertainment. And in fact no Tudor document exists to demonstrate such a condition of performance.[31] Conceivably, the goals of public repertory and of courtly flattery might be merged, allowing Shakespeare, for example, to fashion *A Midsummer Night's Dream* for a noble wedding with the added expectation of a successful run at the Theater. Such a play could combine a covert meaning for its aristocratic auditors and a broader meaning for the public. At the private theaters, hidden meaning (like that suggested for *Endymion*) might appeal even to a select paying clientele. Such conditions of performance are, however, purely conjectural. It cannot be overemphasized that the wealth of external evidence on topical relevance in the Elizabethan period relates chiefly to lost plays or to the tradition of masques and entertainments.

Apart from aristocratic struggles for the queen's favor, the subjects most often urged in topical interpretations of late Elizabethan drama are dynastic: the Scottish succession, Essex's challenge of the queen's authority, the threat of Spain. There is no dearth of evidence showing that such inflammatory issues were publicly aired, and that the authorities were disturbed. The drama was by no means the only outlet for extremist sentiment. The Lord Chief Justice, in the Star Chamber, November 1599, reported of Puritan activity that "the fashion of it has been to scandalize the queen, censure councillors, and write against all authority, and the purpose is to disgrace those in authority and cause disobedience and sedition, and bring all to confusion." [32] In that same year, preachers spoke impertinently of the government, tolled bells for Essex, or prayed for him by name.[33] Allegorical allusion served as an all-weather vehicle for purposes of disclaiming responsibility for seditious talk. In March 1600, the Bishop of Worcester, preaching at court, made many insinuations on behalf of Essex: "As he was understood by the whole auditory and by the Queen herself, who presently calling him to a reckoning for it, he flatly foreswore that he had any such meaning." [34]

Basic to covert criticism of the government was the historical method of Robert Parsons, a seditious Catholic whose diatribe of 1584, known as *Leicester's Commonwealth*, likened Elizabeth to Edward II, Richard II, and Henry VI, weak kings who had been supplanted by successful and sane usurpers. Leicester, in this analogy, epitomized the parasitical frivolities of Gaveston and the Spencers, Mowbray, or the Earl of Suffolk. Elizabeth and her courtiers could hardly be unfamiliar with the analogy, and its implications. Her closest counselors were anxious not to be viewed as favorites. As early as 1578, Sir Francis Knollys fretted that if Elizabeth did not heed wise counsel, she would soon find herself surrounded by sycophants willing to "play the parts of King Richard the Second's men." Lord Hunsdon employed the same phrase, saying "I was never one of Richard II's men." [35] It was in such a taut context that Elizabeth remarked of Essex's rebellion (February 1601), "I am Richard II. Know ye not that?" Essex's followers had ordered a revival of a play on Richard II, by the Chamberlain's men, on the very eve of the abortive rebellion. Whether the play was Shakespeare's cannot be ascertained, but it seems likely.[36] The analogy does not implicate Shakespeare and his company, who were exonerated by the queen's examiners, but it surely indicates the extraordinary atmosphere in which the play was written and performed. Sir John Hayward, whose *History of Henry IV* appeared in 1599, was not as lucky as the Chamberlain's men, probably because of his ill-timed dedication to Essex himself. Although Hayward argues respectably enough that deposing a sovereign is unlawful whatever the provocation, the detailed exposure of Richard's weaknesses was deemed seditious and Hayward was sent to prison.[37]

If Shakespeare's company successfully avoided prosecution for intentional slandering of the queen, despite their use of a Richard II play, where then are the dramas that actually did revile public authority and support Essex? Topical interpreters have claimed many, but again the external evidence of sedition relates to plays no longer extant. We know only that the government was continually alarmed, and purportedly even took countermeasures by directing its own propaganda in the theaters. The Earl of Derby may have been prompted by such a motive when he was reported, in 1599, to be "busy penning comedies for the common players." William Cecil threatened, apropos of a Star Chamber case having to do with cozening, that "he would have those that make plays to make a comedy thereof and to act it with those names." [38] Personal libel against men in authority was viewed as a danger to the state. As the Privy Council wrote in 1601 to certain justices of the peace of Middlesex: "We do understand that certain players, that use to recite their plays at the Curtain in Moorfields, do represent upon the stage in their interludes the persons of some gentlemen of good desert and quality that are yet alive, under obscure manner but yet in such sort as all the hearers may take notice both of the matter and of the persons that are meant thereby." [39] Acting could apparently convey meaning not specified in the text. Middleton's pageant *The Triumphs of Home and Industry* (1617) was not derogatory to Spain, but one of its actors, overdressed as a Spanish dandy, persisted in kissing his hands to the unpopular Spanish ambassador Gondomar, who was in the audience. According to a Spanish eyewitness, perhaps biased, the laughter thus provoked was unmistakable in meaning.[40] Abuse of the Scots by "the comedians of London" was so flagrant in 1598 that an English agent in Scotland wrote Burghley, "It is wished that the matter be speedily amended, lest the king and the country be stirred to anger." Even in Ireland, in 1603, it was common knowledge "that the very stage-players in England jeered at him [James] for being the poorest prince in Christendom." [41] Neither of these witnesses, however, was on the scene in London.

Since we lack the plays specifically implicated in these allegedly vivid abuses, we are hard pressed to judge the merits of the charges. Council members and magistrates were, like Elizabeth, predisposed to see plays in the most controversial light possible. We are still left, therefore, with an inadequate means of demonstrating intentional topicality in the extant drama of the 1590's. On the other hand, we have many eloquent testimonials from those who felt they were being unfairly accused of conspiratorial purpose. Samuel Daniel, in 1605, was brought before the Privy Council to answer charges of having shown a sympathetic picture of the Essex rebellion in his *Philotas*. Fortunately he was able to show that his first three acts had been read by the Master of the Revels and Lord Mountjoy in 1600, before the rebellion occurred.[42] Michael Drayton's changes in depicting Richard II in his *England's Heroical Epistles*

(1599-1600) reflect Elizabeth's touchiness and perhaps Hayward's troubles with the law; the *Epistles* were dedicated to the Earl of Bedford, an Essex supporter.[43] Fulke Greville, on the advice of friends, burned his *Antony and Cleopatra* (ca. 1600) because there were things in the play "apt enough to be construed, or strained to a personating of vices in the present Governor, and government." His *Alaham* (ca. 1600) had also awakened the suspicions of the Cecil clan.[44] Ben Jonson's *Sejanus* inevitably produced a confrontation with the authorities. In the dedication to *Volpone* (printed 1607), Jonson commented acidly that "application is now grown a trade." Satire of needless deciphering appears too in his *Poetaster* and in *Epigrams* 92. Nicholas Breton lamented, "Who doth not find it by experience That points and commas, oftentimes misread, Endanger oft the harmless writer's head?" [45]

Thomas Nashe was brilliantly caustic on the subject, in his play *Summer's Last Will and Testament* and in several pamphlets. Authors, he said, are like men at a Persian banquet: "if they roll their eye never so little at one side, there stands an Eunuch before them, with his heart full of jealousy, and his bow ready bent to shoot them through, because they look farther than the laws of the country suffer them." Again, "Let one but name bread, they will interpret it to be the town of Bredan in the low countries." If a writer fails to qualify and disclaim sufficiently, "out steps me an infant squib of the Inns of Court . . . catcheth hold of a rush, and absolutely concludeth it is meant of the Emperor of Ruscia, and that it will utterly mar the traffic into that country if all the pamphlets be not called in and suppressed, wherein that libelling word is mentioned." [46]

External evidence, then, indicates overinterpretation as much as conspiracy. Clearly the possibilities of allusion were on everybody's mind. Yet the evidence does not provide a clear mandate for discovering court scandal in *Love's Labor's Lost* or particular reference to Essex in the history plays. The best that can be said for modern decipherers is that they are playing a venerable game, such as was practiced by Elizabethan courtiers and magistrates and by Elizabeth herself. In order to obtain perspective on proper rules for conducting such inquiries, let us examine some theories of topical identification, noting the frequently wide divergence between hypothesis and the reliable evidence already summarized.

A constant theme of the decipherers is the relationship of Shakespeare and his fellow playwrights to the Earl of Essex. However far afield or utterly unrelated some of the theories may seem, they almost invariably reveal their origin in a consistent myth. It explains Shakespeare's entire dramatic production. His admiration for Essex is supposed to have begun early and to have been soon fostered by his closeness to the Earl of Southampton, one of Essex's men throughout most of the period. Southampton was Catholic; Shakespeare, according to the myth, sympathized with the old religion; Essex was tolerant of it (as he was of Puritanism). Both young nobles were inveterate playgoers and friends of the players. Essex was unquestionably the darling of the London populace, or at least a rowdy section of it. Both young men were chevaliers, anxious for glory, hawks in their advocacy of war. They were enemies of the Cecil faction, which Essex unfairly accused of favoring the claims of the Spanish Infanta and opposing James of Scotland. Essex believed in a union of the British Isles, brought about by James's accession to the English throne and a tolerant peace in Ireland. Essex has been interpreted as something much better than a rash malcontent: he was a true "liberal," champion of the common man, of modern economics, the supremacy of Parliament, religious toleration—a man ahead of his time and a martyr for the causes of science, reason, and liberty that were to triumph in the ensuing century.[47] These, according to the theory, were Shakespeare's politics as well, and as the crisis mounted he threw more and more of his dramatic energy into the earl's defense.

Nor was Shakespeare the only Essexian dramatist on the scene. Marlowe's *Tragedy of Dido,* according to one interpreter, compares the Carthaginian queen's maneuvers to keep Aeneas at court with Elizabeth's reluctance to send her favorites (Essex most of all) on dangerous expeditions. The implied flattery of Essex as the founder of his country's true destiny is momentous. In *Tamburlaine,* Marlowe supposedly satirizes Philip II for his arrogant claims of universal dominion and his maltreatment of other princes. Thomas Heywood, in his *Royal King and Loyal Subject* (debatably dated in 1600) portrays an Earl Marshal faithful to his sovereign but hated by the counselors who ultimately drive him into trial for treason and banishment. This typical story of ingratitude is of course parallel to Essex's disgrace, and hence the idealized ending must be a plea for Essex's restoration.[48]

Shakespeare's fascination for the earl supposedly began with his earliest dramatic efforts. An incidental reference in *The Comedy of Errors* to "the salt rheum that ran between France and [England]," joined to some comic discussion on Spain and the Netherlands, conjures up the expedition of Essex and Biron on behalf of Henry IV (III, ii, 118-145). *The Taming of the Shrew* is offered as an elaborate allegory berating Burghley (Baptista Minola) for auctioning off his daughters.[49] *The Two Gentlemen of Verona,* in a "transparent veil," attacks Essex's foe Robert Cecil in the false friend Proteus. Proteus' father and uncle are Burghley and Sir Nicholas Bacon. The unsavory Thurio is Lord Rich; Silvia and Valentine are of course Penelope Rich and Sir Philip Sidney. The affair takes place not at Milan but at Leicester's camp in the Netherlands, and the idealized ending describes the bliss that Sidney might have found with his true love.[50] *1 Henry VI* derives important details from the siege of Rouen in 1591-1592; accordingly Talbot's patriotism and his betrayal by the lords at home owe something to Essex's situation.[51] In *2 Henry VI* the unflattering account of Eleanor Cobham does no credit to the powerful Lord Cobham who later sided with Cecil and the Admiral's men.[52]

Love's Labor's Lost has exercised the ingenuity of investigators more than any other of Shakespeare's early plays, partly because its names of Navarre (Henry IV), Berowne (Biron, Henry IV's general), Dumaine (Du Mayenne, brother of the Guise), Longaville (Longueville, Governor of Normandy), and perhaps Armado (Armada) and Moth (Marquis de la Mothe, Henry's amiable diplomat) were unquestionably names in the news during the early 1590's. In 1591 Essex banqueted with Navarre, Biron, and Longueville. Mayenne, however, was fighting bitterly on the other side, in the Guisian wars. Furthermore, in 1593 Navarre turned from the Protestant faith. To allude frivolously to these matters after 1589, when Henry III had been killed by a crazy monk and Navarre had inherited his unstable throne, Shakespeare would have had to be contra-topical.[53] Yet still-prevalent theories assert that the play attacks Burghley in 1591 for urging one of his daughters on Southampton, or Oxford for his affectation of foreign mannerisms, or above all the "school of night," whose members had quarreled with the Essex faction around 1593–1595.[54] Other figures drawn into the supposed satire include Nashe and Harvey, Florio (Southampton's tutor), Lyly, the Fantastical Monarcho, Antonio Perez, Philip of Spain, Don John of Austria, Chapman, and Bishop Cooper.[55]

Saner criticism has given its attention to the court of Henry of Navarre at Nérac in 1578, where Henry was visited by Catherine de Medici, with her daughter Marguerite, to settle the sovereignty of Aquitaine. The famous *escadron volant* accompanied the queen and boasted a series of conquests. The social atmosphere was like that of Shakespeare's play. Navarre wrote love letters. Navarre's court had a reputation as a "safe" place to educate Protestant English gentlemen who wished to travel. Another visit occurred in 1586 at St. Bris, but without *l'escadron volant*.[56] European politics had not yet rendered such a setting woefully out of date and trivial. Social gossip from this never-never land would have suited admirably an imitative Lylyan comedy in the late 1580's, possibly for boys.

Equally fruitless have been the various attempts to link *A Midsummer Night's Dream* with various state weddings: Stanley-de Vere, Berkeley-Carey, or Thomas Heneage and the Countess of Southampton (the Earl of Essex's dowager-mother).[57] To be sure, Shakespeare does seem to have had in mind the spectacular entertainments of Kenilworth (1575) and especially Elvetham (1591) in his recollection of "a mermaid on a dolphin's back" and "certain stars" that "shot madly from their spheres," when Cupid was unable to wound "a fair vestal thronèd in the west." Elizabeth had participated in such a flattering device.[58] Nor have critics erred too greatly in detecting a distant compliment to Elizabeth in Theseus.

To suppose a closer and more political involvement of Elizabeth is, however, extremely hazardous. Miss Rickert has argued, in a classic article of the lock-picking type,[59] that Elizabeth should be identified as in other literary works with the Faerie Queene, or Titania. Her crossing the will of Oberon alludes then to Elizabeth's refusal to accede to the will of her father, Henry VIII. (Oberon is of course Titania's husband, not father, but some changes were needed to disguise a controversial topic.) Henry VIII had settled the royal succession after his own children on the issue of Lady Katharine and Lady Jane Grey. Lady Katharine had married the Earl of Hertford in 1561, much to Elizabeth's displeasure; their son was Lord Beauchamp, whom Elizabeth had declared illegitimate and refused to recognize as heir. Politicians of the 1590's, desperately looking for an English heir as alternative to James VI of Scotland, made much of Beauchamp's so-called "Suffolk claim." He is the "changeling boy," and Shakespeare's endorsement of his right is central to the playwright's presumed crusade for an established succession.

Accordingly, Elizabeth (Titania) is punished for her obstinacy in not settling the succession by receiving the attentions of an unwelcome lover (Bottom the Weaver). Who else but the aspiring, unlovely James VI? James had in fact courted Elizabeth, and his own poems compared himself to Pyramus. In August 1594, in a pageant at the christening of his son Prince Henry, a lion was to have drawn in a ship of state but was withheld for fear of frightening the ladies. James was notoriously timid and could not bear the sight of a drawn sword. He was laughed at in England for his countrified manners and his "humour for a tyrant"— his preoccupation with divine right. Elizabeth was deeply offended with James in 1595, and the Scottish king for his part was considering a plan to enter England in concert with Philip of Spain. Thus, Shakespeare had a motive and a license to discredit James in the person of Bottom, while he urged the Suffolk claim. Only later, after sensing that the Suffolk claim was no longer tenable, did Shakespeare come around to Essex's view that James was at least preferable to a Catholic claimant.

Although the allusions to Prince Henry's christening and to Elvetham may have been conscious, the rest of the allegory is clearly unacceptable —not merely because it darkens one of Shakespeare's brightest comedies, but because it implies outrageous treatment of Elizabeth. If she was increasingly sensitive to any mention of the question of succession, how little would she have enjoyed viewing herself punished for her stand, and grossly in love with James whom she then abhorred? Shakespeare's supposed concealment of the allegory will not serve, for if Elizabeth with her mastery of decipherment could not read the message it would fail of its purpose. The record seems clear that the play did not offend.

Romeo and Juliet and *The Merchant of Venice* have also been explicated as part of the Essex-Southampton program. Although Shakespeare drew upon Brooke's *Romeus and Juliet* for his source in *Romeo*, his immediate inspiration was purportedly the Danvers-Long feud of October 1594. The Danverses were Essex roisterers who managed to escape prosecution for murder only with the aid of Southampton. Thus Shakespeare wrote "not *in vacuo* but in an actual environment the events of which stimulated his imagination along with his reading and his memory." [60] Perhaps also he mirrored the major rival factions at court, with Capulet as Burghley, Montague as Leicester, and Romeo as Essex, who had incurred the Prince's (Elizabeth's) wrath for secretly marrying Sidney's widow in 1590.[61] *The Merchant of Venice* is supposed to have grown out of the conspiracy of Roderigo Lopez, the Jewish physician charged with a plot to murder Elizabeth and the Portugese pretender Don Antonio, in the interests of Spain. Essex brought the charge against Lopez and was an intimate of Don Antonio. Elizabeth herself appears in the play as the merciful Portia, Essex as Bassanio. The play reflects the excitement of the Cadiz expedition of 1596.[62] More farfetched still is the reading of Shylock as Philip Henslowe, the tightfisted entrepreneur who extracted many a pound of flesh from his underpaid writers, and who married an illegitimate daughter to Edward Alleyn (Lorenzo). Thus the play was a major attack in the Chamberlain's men's war on the Cecil-oriented Admiral's company, who had had so much success with *The Jew of Malta.*[63]

Not surprisingly, Shakespeare's histories are the heart of his supposed campaign for Essex. *King John,* for instance, does in fact tone down the anti-Catholic virulence of its chief source, *The Troublesome Reign of King John.* The Essex theory supposes that Shakespeare's reasons for doing so were partly his own tenderness for the old faith and partly his deference to the platform of Southampton and his leader. (Essex, though no Catholic, preached tolerance.) Shakespeare also virtually eliminated the role of "Essex" as one of the rebellious barons in his source. Both Shakespeare and the author of *Troublesome Reign* purportedly modeled Faulconbridge on Sir John Perrot, an illegitimate son of Henry VIII. Perrot was in danger of his life in 1591 for having spoken contemptuously to the queen, and died in the Tower in 1592. Essex took his part. This allegiance of Shakespeare to Essex would have predated his meeting with Southampton.[64]

We have already seen the analogy, familiar to the Elizabethan mind, that Elizabeth was Richard II and Essex Bolingbroke. Extremists of the Essexian persuasion would have us believe that Shakespeare wished to see the earl on the throne, and that Essex's military and pragmatic virtues are reflected not only in Bolingbroke but more especially in his son. A more temperate but still highly debatable interpretation is that

Shakespeare sympathized with the earl and his platform, but feared the rashness of the passionate young nobleman and did not approve of the dangerous tendency beginning in 1599 toward insurrection.[65] Either reading supposes that Shakespeare's censures of Richard II are highly critical of Elizabeth, as in Robert Parsons' infamous analogy. Miss Evelyn Albright goes so far as to assert that Bolingbroke's claims to his Lancastrian titles reflect Essex's own line of descent from Thomas of Woodstock. She believes too that Shakespeare had actually read Hayward's *History of Henry IV* in manuscript, and borrowed from it censorious anachronisms such as the forced "benevolences" and the general agitation over taxes. "Benevolences" were not known by name in Richard II's time; hence Hayward and Shakespeare were simply describing the condition of England after 1592.

Miss Albright sees correspondences to Essex and Elizabeth in every aspect of Shakespeare's treatment of Bolingbroke and Richard. The allusions to Richard's deafness to counsel and love of flattery capitalize on often-repeated charges against Elizabeth. Essex, like Bolingbroke, complained of "letting of the realm to farm." Essex openly courted the commons, vailing "his bonnet to an oyster-wench." Essex's Irish expedition was popularly regarded as political banishment.[66] Other analysts have suggested further corroborative details. The names of Percy, Blount, and Vernon, among others, glorify the ancestors of several prominent members of the Essex group. The reference in *1 Henry IV* to the ebbing and flowing of the moon (I, ii) implies the uncertainty of Elizabeth's favor. Gower's mention of "a beard of the general's cut" (*Henry V*, III, vi) signals the famous "Cadiz beard" worn by so many rufflers after the expedition of 1596. Henry V's mercy to the citizens of Harfleur, unsubstantiated in history, reflects Essex's mercy to the citizens of Cadiz.[67]

This line of reasoning has never won much support, chiefly because the plays themselves are so eloquent on the dangers of faction and instability. External considerations also militate against the theory. If Shakespeare's intent was visibly inflammatory to his audience, why did the Chamberlain's men escape censure in 1601? Why would the authorities have allowed the plays to go on at all, instead of excising a few scenes like that of Richard's deposition? Its offense was probably not the treatment, but the subject itself in such dangerous times. Shakespeare very probably did not know Hayward's work when he wrote *Richard II*, for Hayward testified that he began the history one year before its publication in 1599.[68] Shakespeare has long been thought to have spoken admiringly of Essex in the chorus to Act V of *Henry V*, but the tribute may instead have pointed to Charles Blount, Lord Montjoy, Essex's far more victorious successor in Ireland and a constant favorite of the queen's. The choruses give evidence of having been composed after the quarto of 1600. Essex was dangerously in disgrace almost from the moment he began his Irish campaign. Mountjoy in 1603, holding titles of "Lord Deputy" and "General," was safe and popular.[69] If Mountjoy was intended, we lose the one supposedly tangible proof in all his plays of Shakespeare's devotion to Essex.

It is as easy to argue that Shakespeare voiced disillusionment and fear of Essex in his histories. Similarity to Hotspur emerges from the aftermath of the Cadiz expedition, when Essex "claimed the ransom of his prisoners for himself when the Queen demanded them." [70] Essex was a rash warrior headed for disaster, a devotee of honor. Another line of analogy is to speculate on Shakespeare's boyhood recollection of the Northern Rebellion of 1569, prominently featuring the names of Northumberland and the Percies and conducting its operations more or less in Shakespeare's back yard.[71] This approach may contain some merit in suggesting Shakespeare's sources, although it must be granted that thirty years is a long time back for a theater audience to recall.

All of Shakespeare's festive comedies have yielded Essex clues. One of Malvolio's innumerable supposed counterparts in Elizabeth's court was Ambrose Willoughby, an enemy of Southampton, who as squire of the presence in 1598 felt he ought to keep the earl quiet at bedtime, scuffled with him, and was thanked by the queen for his zeal.[72] *Twelfth Night* thus stands on the side of Essex's roisterers and opposed to the cold sobriety of Burghley's faction. A passage in *Much Ado about Nothing* alluding to "favorites, Made proud by princes, that advance their pride Against the power that bred it" (III, i, 9-11) has suggested Essex's troubled relations with the queen—although whether in hostility to the anti-Essex faction barring the earl's entry to Elizabeth upon his return from Ireland in 1599, or in hostility to Essex's own challenge of the queen's power, is a matter for the individual reader to decide.[73] *As You Like It*, according to one literary sleuth, "undoubtedly" tells of

Essex's banishment from the court in the person of Duke Senior.[74] The tragedy of *Julius Caesar* also idealizes Essex in the insurrection of Brutus against tyranny and illegitimate rule.[75]

Hamlet offers a rich field for topicality, as for other critical approaches, and reveals perhaps most clearly the basic error of the lockpicking sleuth. One starts with the assumption that *Hamlet* provides "abstract and brief chronicles of the time" (since Shakespeare tells us so) and one searches the annals for a young nobleman whose father has disappeared under suspicious circumstances and whose mother has married the suspected criminal. In other words, one takes a legend of archetypal significance and sees if it will apply to real life. It needs no ghost come from the dead to predict that the legend will so apply, for that is the strength of its fiction. The error is essentially comparable to that imposed on Bolingbroke and Essex: Shakespeare was fascinated with the recurring phenomenon of rebellion in English history as it applied to virtually every generation before his time. Any contemporary reenactment of the pattern was bound to resemble the artist's creation.

In *Hamlet's* case history, three theories have dominated. The first is of Leicester and Amy Robsart, back around 1560. Leicester himself had died in 1588. But a rumor supposed that Leicester (then Sir Robert Dudley) had done away with Amy in order to marry Elizabeth—the "seeming virtuous queen." The guilty lovers hushed up the affair as best they could ("a forgèd process of my death") and may even have fixed the jury ("great command o'ersways the order"). Such bald criticism of Elizabeth could not have been staged until 1603.[76] This preposterous theory received short shrift from H. H. Furness, who objected that Shakespeare had no motive to attack the dead Leicester, that the audience would not have cared for Shakespeare's opinion on this old scandal, that Cecil would not have permitted it even after 1603, that Shakespeare had probably allied himself with Leicester's players, and that *Hamlet* was surely staged while Elizabeth was still alive.[77]

A closer correspondence, but just as uninviting, concerns James of Scotland—Essex's white hope for the succession. James's mother Mary had been deeply involved in the scandal of James's father's death, and had married Bothwell, the supposed murderer of Darnley. Bothwell was a heavy drinker, like Claudius. Rizzio (Polonius), the meddling counselor, had been murdered in the presence of the queen (though not by James)

21

and had been disposed of "hugger-mugger" by means of a staircase. James, in 1600-1601, was a melancholy, retiring, and vacillating prince (his sanity was doubted by some), interested in learning. Shakespeare was at this time deeply committed to the Essex strategy of Scottish succession. Alternatively, Hamlet's hesitation in killing Claudius might reflect Elizabeth's delay in executing Mary of Scots. Significantly, these theories are not even discussed by J. E. Phillips in his thorough book on literary treatments of Mary.[78]

The only interpretation still given serious attention is that Hamlet reflects the plight of Essex himself, or, more broadly, Shakespeare's gloom occasioned by Essex's disgrace.[79] Essex's family history contained the necessary closeted skeleton. Rumor had it that Dudley (Leicester) had poisoned Essex's father to live in sin with Essex's mother, Lettice Knollys (who, parenthetically, is supposed to have been the "little western flower" of *A Midsummer Night's Dream*). Essex was moody, brilliant, unstable, a procrastinator, ill-fated, a hater of women (especially the queen), one who affected black in his costume. He scorned Burghley, whom many critics have seen as a model for Polonius.[80] Burghley was charged with being a master spy and tyrant's ear, a prosy busybody, tedious in his loyalty to the Establishment, hostile to the stage and stingy to poets, wealthy and frugal, affected in style and famous for his worldly-wise precepts left for his son Robert, complacent to studied insolence. Again, it should be argued that historical fact is perhaps merely reflecting Shakespeare's art rather than the reverse. If Hamlet were Essex, the Chamberlain's men would have been deeply involved in sedition. Fortinbras says of Hamlet, "For he was likely, had he been put on, To have proved most royal." The espousal of Essex as heir apparent was treason, before or after his death.

Traces of Essex have been found everywhere in the play. The "little patch of ground" calls up the siege of Ostend in the summer of 1601. Laertes' demagogic summons to the mob reflects Essex's public appeals at St. Paul's cross in 1601.[81] Other speculations have run to the extremes of ridiculousness. If Hamlet is Sir Philip Sidney (why not?) then Horatio is Herbert Languet, Marcellus is Fulke Greville, Bernardo is Edward Dyer, and Francisco is Gabriel Harvey. Old Norway is Sir Francis Knollys, the poison is *Leicester's Commonwealth*, and the incestuous marriage naturally is that of Katharine of Aragon.[82] Sober consideration requires one to ask, however, whether the political situation in *Hamlet* is even remotely parallel to that of Tudor England, or whether Shakespeare deliberately chose a constitutional framework that could not be analogized. Even if Hamlet is presumptive heir to the Danish throne, did an elective system make it possible for Claudius to be king legally? The English throne, however much subject to disputed succession as in the case of Henry VIII's will, would not countenance the displacing of a mature crown prince by his uncle. Perhaps topical politics are simply irrelevant to Shakespeare's most popular play.[83]

Essex's ignoble end can be used to explain the mood not only of *Hamlet* but of Shakespeare's problem comedies. *Troilus and Cressida* bequeaths a plague to both factions; Shakespeare had never liked the Cecils, but was bitterly disillusioned by the extremists in his own cause. Essex's sulkiness and irresponsibility can be seen in Achilles, whose relationship to Patroclus is not unlike that of Essex to Southampton. Shakespeare speaks through Ulysses, deploring the frivolity and divisiveness of his own tarnished heroes. Shakespeare had in mind Chapman's dedication of his *Homer* "to the most honored now living instance of the Achilleian virtues eternized by divine Homer, the Earl of Essex." Alternatively, one can read Shakespeare's Trojan debacle as still pro-Essex, lamenting the demise of a noble band ground under by superior force and guile. Shakespeare blames not Elizabeth for the death of his champion, but the Cecils.[84]

All's Well that Ends Well can also be considered critical of the Essex camp, for Bertram's dutifulness toward his mother and his reluctance to marry call back memories of Southampton and Elizabeth Vernon. If Parolles is Pearse Edmonds, a minion of Southampton's and hence a rival of Shakespeare, the motivation for Shakespeare's soured disposition becomes clear.[85] In *Measure for Measure*, however, we catch a brighter glimpse despite the play's moral complexities. With James's accession to the English throne, Essex's party was obviously back in favor as reward for its martyred leader's efforts in behalf of the Scottish succession. The Chamberlain's men received the title of King's men in recognition not only of their talent but of their pro-Scottish dramatic activity. Shakespeare did not even bother to eulogize Elizabeth—a fact noticed unfavorably by his countrymen. Elizabeth had been guilty of Essex's death and Southampton's imprisonment. The figure of the Duke in *Measure for Measure* is supposedly Shakespeare's first tribute to his new ruler, who like Vincentio shunned crowds of people and scoffed at Puritans like Angelo. James was notoriously sensitive to slander; hence the punishment of Lucio. Shakespeare probably read *Basilikon Doron* and set its theories into practice as homage to a new hero.[86]

Even later plays have been related to Essex and Scotland. *Macbeth*, according to Henry Paul and others, was written especially for performance before James, as a defense of the new king against the attacks of the private theaters.[87] Purportedly the play reflects the hysteria of the Gunpowder Plot, Scottish witch trials, and James's theories on divine right and on curing of the king's evil. As in *Measure for Measure*, Shakespeare voices his gratitude for an end to dynastic uncertainties. Such an interpretation tends, unfortunately, to read much of the play as flattering intrusion rather than as relevant thematic material, or to minimize Shakespeare's independent political philosophy concerning obedience due an evil king.[88] *King Lear* supposedly recalls Mary Stuart's treatment of Darnley, repulsing him when he rode with a train to follow her, giving orders to the Earl of Murray's wife not to receive him, depriving him of servants, and turning him out in inclement weather to seek refuge in a hovel on the wild heath.[89] *Coriolanus* attacks Ralegh for his contempt of the plebeians, in contrast with the popular Earl of Essex. The earl is portrayed directly in *Timon of Athens'* Alcibiades, or in Timon himself.[90]

The investigation of this book ends, however, with the deaths of Essex and Elizabeth. If space permitted, the story might well go on into the ample material available on Jacobean political activity in the drama. Yet the year 1603 serves as a convenient stopping point, for an era was ending in drama as in politics. No longer did the stage represent the many voices of political conflict. In the impasse brought about by James's confrontation with the Puritans, drama gravitated to the court and so lost its popular base. Although plays still appeared at public theaters after 1610, most drama became attuned to upper-class opinion only, and came to be despised by the average London citizen. Plays reflected the movement toward civil war only negatively, in their satires of shopkeepers and Puritans and in their increasingly patrician pursuit of refined emotion. Even Shakespeare laid aside his history plays. We are interested in the years of debate before 1603, when even the more moderate Puritans were still clamoring to be heard through drama.

I hope it is by now apparent that I am skeptical of topical identification of historical personages and particular events. Let me assure the reader at the start that I offer few if any new historical equations of this sort, and tolerate few of those already proposed. Even less am I concerned with non-political identifications supposedly arising from personal or literary feuds, such as Justice Shallow and William Gardiner, Slender and William Wayte, Malvolio and John Marston or William Ffarington, Falstaff and Florio, Fluellen and Captain Roger Williams, Holofernes and Chapman, Thersites and Marston, *Hamlet's* Lamord and Sidney, *Endymion's* Sir Tophas and Stephen Gosson, *Fair Em's* Mandeville and Robert Greene.[91] My study hopes to prove that politics is germane to a remarkable percentage of Tudor plays, but in terms of ideas and platforms rather than personalities. Even the allusions to kings or queens, although obviously referring in many cases to the reigning monarch, pertain to the office instead of the man. Granting then that we are dealing with a drama of conventional type rather than of historical verisimilitude, the Tudor drama is nonetheless sharp in its delineation of issues. How should men come to authority? By what means are the various pressure groups of which Tudor society is composed to obtain their wishes from the central authority? What role are church officials to play, or nouveau riche courtiers, titled nobility, merchants, apprentices? To what extent may the populace demonstrate about just grievances? How far may powerful counselors enforce their "advice" on the monarch? What voice is Parliament to have in naming a successor in the absence of an undisputed hereditary heir? Who determines policy about war with Spain, the execution of Mary Stuart, exposure of Catholic plotting, influx of cheap immigrant labor, rent inflation, pensions for disabled soldiers?

These are questions on which every Englishman wished to be heard, and conversely on which the government, when it was not divided among various factions, wished to implant its own formula. The impulse for debate and criticism was no less than that for official propaganda. Not that the two concepts were always opposed to one another. At its best, Tudor political playwriting supported Tudor policy in essence while maintaining a noble spirit of free discussion. Again, this is a framework in which our investigation properly ends with the death of Elizabeth.

It will appear that I have used the term "politics" broadly, though I hope not loosely. To me it connotes the wide range of activity in which men argue over the structure and method of decision-making in government. It embraces economic and social conditions, but only in the context of formulating and administering law. Interclass marriage is not in itself a political issue, but attitudes toward dueling and private revenge can bear importantly on conceptions of the state's authority to punish crime. Satire as a neoclassical genre does not concern us, but as a controversial weapon for reviling public authority it became centrally involved in an Elizabethan debate on law and order. In matters of religion we are interested not in doctrinal controversy but in the ever-present implications of political and dynastic revolution. Such an approach necessarily eliminates or minimizes some of the finest plays of the Tudor period. I hope no reader will presume that I offer a complete reading of even the most avowedly political play, much less of the masterpieces with which the century ends. I apologize for the distortion that sees more matter for discussion in *Respublica* than in *Doctor Faustus,* but I trust that, if read in correct proportion, this book tells a story which the Tudor period itself would have recognized as central to its literary and political development.

A part from the early masques and disguisings mentioned in Chapter 1, medieval drama reveals few traces of political activity. In part this is because most religious drama concerned itself simply with the soul of the ordinary man or priest. Biblical drama did comment anachronistically on contemporary life, as in the *Second Shepherds' Play*, but only to stress the timelessness of regeneration. Yet Dante proved overwhelmingly than a historical allegory of Guelphs and Ghibellines was not incompatible with literal, moral, and anagogical levels of meaning. Probably there was more political drama in this vein than has survived. In fact one clear instance is extant, dating well before Dante. In about 1160, at Tegernsee, a *Play of Antichrist* staged a confrontation between Haeresis, Hypocrisis, and Antichrist on the evil side and Misericordia and Justitia on the good. This satire is directed against a corrupt worldly church. The villains are the pope, aided by the king of France, and the secular clergy, who are apparently subverting Emperor Frederick I and the true Ecclesia.[1]

Just as medieval religious drama engendered vernacular writing, rustic comedy, and other "realistic" dramatic elements long supposed to have been hostile to its liturgical origin, so too religious drama was the first great sponsor of political dramaturgy. The impulse was natural and inevitable. Political concern was not at first a worldly antithesis of true religion, or forward-looking "secularization," but an expression from within the church of a desire for reform.

Perhaps the first play to show this impulse in England is the late fifteenth-century *Wisdom Who Is Christ* or *Mind, Will, and Understanding*. Its focus is on worldly political activity by the religious and the obviously related phenomenon of defection from the monasteries. The author probes the dilemma of monastic life with its overemphasis on withdrawal, and searches for a balanced life that will recall clerical politicians from their ambition, sharp dealing, and venery. To what extent should the church allow its members to serve Caesar? The problem concerns us because it questions how men should come to authority in early Tudor government. *Wisdom* foreshadows a series of studies on the role of the typical churchman-bureaucrat under Henry VII and Henry VIII.

Significantly, *Wisdom* is a morality. Biblical cycles had evolved a nonpolitical tradition; the morality was vastly more flexible. Its simple plot of soul-struggle and triumph could be localized in any setting, especially in retailing the contemporary abuses that drive the average man into sin. Broad homiletic advice prevails at the beginning and end of moralities, but descriptions of temptation and life in sin invariably propel the dramatist toward the events of his daily world. Accordingly, *Wisdom's* opening scenes give no hint of political motive. Although Wisdom enters in royal panoply with ermine hood, "imperiall crown," and "regall scheptur," he is no earthly monarch. Wisdom exists outside of time and human imperfection, and is known as "Everlastinge Wisdom" to "hem that in erthe be" (ll. 3-4).[2] He instructs Anima, the soul of every man, in orthodox theological explanations of man's fall from grace and hence the susceptibility of man's Mind, Understanding, and Will to the wiles of Fiend, World, and Flesh. This epistemology, interspersed with Latin chant, applies timelessly to each auditor and to the collective soul of mankind in its infancy. Even Lucifer speaks at first as though he were about to tempt man for the first time, through envy of man's favor in God's sight. The audience is prepared for a reincarnation of man's original fall in the eternal drama of human salvation. A third of the play passes thus in the realm of universal Christian allegory.

When Lucifer turns to his specific task of subversion, however, he does so not in his devil's array but as a "prowd galonte," or courtier. His temptations suddenly take on topical significance. He addresses himself to the monastic clergy, suggestively describing the limitations of their "contemplatyff lyff." Monastics, he argues, are guilty of idleness, since they eschew honest toil and family responsibilities for the luxury of "prayer and es of body" (l. 411). Christ himself, as an example to men, devoted his life variously to labor, to suffering, and to conversation with both holy men and sinners. Continued abstinence, asceticism, and prayer lead inevitably to bodily frailty, feebleness of wits, and thence to "fondnes," despair, and madness (ll. 431-439). "Singler devocions" are particularly susceptible to pride and hypocrisy (l. 452). By such arguments, Lucifer urges the religious to become a part of their contemporary world and use its pleasures. He repeatedly scoffs at their "nice chastite" (l. 476). Such temptations must have been painfully appropriate to clerics at a time when apostasy in the monasteries was a serious problem.[3]

Just as Lucifer has turned courtier, Mind, Understanding, and Will are now something quite different from the generic attributes of the rational soul. They are three representative monastics who have espoused a life of "hard living and going, with discipline dew," who "kepe silence, wepe, and surphettis eschewe" (ll. 434-435). They are evidently dressed at first in monastic garb, like their auditors, for they later reenter after their penance "all in here first clothing, her chapplettis [prayer beads] and crestis" (l. 1068f). Meantime, during their fall from grace, their costuming is a painfully visible manifestation of their waywardness. They boast of their jolly new garments, cultivate noble kindred, speak knowingly of the "gyse of Frawnce," are conversant with "govell [extortion] and simony," and aspire in all things to be "curtely personys." These three new gallants are not mere secular courtiers. They are clerics no longer content with a life of poverty, chastity, and obedience, the prototypes of men like John Morton, Cardinal Bourchier, and later Thomas Wolsey. The allusions here almost surely refer to the type rather than to any individuals, but the satiric portrait is clearly contemporary.

The crux of the political commentary concerns the fifteenth-century evil of "maintenance" and its corruption of the legal process through bribery and perjury:

> MIND. Maintnance is now so mighty;
>   And all is for mede.
> UNDIRSTONDING. The law is so coloryde falsly
> By sleyttis and by perjury;
> Bribys be so gredy,
>   That to the pore, trowth is take right nought a hede.
> WILL. Wo gett or loose, ye be ay winnande;
> Maintnaunce and perjury now stande;
> Ther wer never so moche reynande
>   seth Gode was bore.   (ll. 674-683)

Maintenance, in view of many late fifteenth-century observers, was the chief legal abuse of the age. It came into being largely through the breakdown of central authority in England. The medieval peers were trained to violence, and still enjoyed considerable autonomy in their feudal domains. The monarchy had not yet succeeded, as it was to do under the Tudors, in reducing the power of the nobility by attainder, by financial pressure, and by diversion to more peaceful service to the throne. Demands for military service in the civil wars added to the ascendancy of the barons. Factions became all-powerful in the see-sawing struggle between Lancaster and York, until followers of each feudal band came to look upon their respective leaders for ultimate protection and legal redress. Identified by their various liveries, the factions soon learned to flout common law by interference with courts and juries on their own behalf. In return for service, the chief lords of the realm "maintained" their liveried retainers against legal action by any power alien to their interests. Under this systematized protection racket, small landowners had no alternative but to seek dependence upon some influential lord. Bribed juries and perjured testimony were commonplace "all the londe hidyr and thedyr" (ll. 735, 763). Abuses were so rife that Richard III, and then Henry VII, moved strongly against livery and maintenance.[4] The danger to civil authority was as great as that of foreign interference, and it was only by incessant action against maintenance that the Tudor dynasty was ultimately successful in establishing itself.

As clerics of newly-acquired political power, Mind, Understanding, and Will reveal themselves as veritable coney-catchers in the art and terminology of legal shystering. Their topical references become lively and specific. They operate at Westminster, at the "parvise" (porch) of St. Paul's and at large in "the cite," frequenting its "lanys and weys" and of course "the stews" (ll. 792-804). They "engross" the purses of unoffending citizens, make false arrest, enforce forfeiture unjustly, indict persons without cause on one day and acquit them on the morrow "iff nede were" (ll. 808-815). They propose to blackmail an unsuspecting victim by means of spiritual authority until he "quak for very fere." Their protection is clerical immunity from the law: "With the crose and the pill I shall wrye it, That ther shall never man discrey it" (ll. 862-863). Although many of the nobility were guilty of similar malpractices, the playwright emphasizes repeatedly that he is concerned with the behavior of churchmen.

Appropriately, Mind, Understanding, and Will are each followed by a band of liveried retainers. The names are abstractions, suitable for a familiar Christian allegory of the seven Deadly Sins grouped into three categories of devil, world, and flesh. Mind's followers are all sins of the spirit; Understanding's are children of "the fadyr of us, Covetise"; and Will's are all "for the flesche" (ll. 719-759). Yet the immediate emphasis is topical,[5] and the language is that of the system of maintenance. "Here entur VI disgisyde in the sute of Minde, with rede berdis, and liouns rampaunt on here crestis, and yche a warder in his honde" (l. 695). This "meny of meyntement," who bear up falseness "and maintene it at the best," are reckless spenders and proud, insolent men defying all reformers who would cross their path (ll. 712-717). They flaunt their garish liveries. Understanding's six Jurors appear "in a sute, gownyde, with hodis abowt her nekis, hattis of meyntenance therupon viseryde [visored] diversly" (l. 727). Will's retainers are also "in sut . . . with wondyrfull visurs conregent" (l. 755). Inevitably the appearance of their rival bands leads to a quarrel. The whole effect is a parody of the maintenance system, emphasizing through its ludicrousness that the church has no business in such affairs. The playwright exercises a richly varied vocabulary in alluding to liveried bands: "thow that longe to ower retenaunce," "thow that ben of min affiance," "your resort," "in a sute," "thes meny of maintement," and the like (ll. 689-727).

Following a pattern established for him by the conventional allegory, the playwright examines and criticizes three facets of corruption in the church of his day. The first, spiritual pride, represents the lordly ambitions of the clergy to enjoy political rank, income, and dress equal to that of the nobility. To such a churchman, maintenance is important chiefly as a means of self-glorification. Men must sue to him for his friendship, and he in turn protects those who are loyal (ll. 632-638). Such a feudal relation is the source of his "worschippe" and earthly fame. When he spends recklessly, it is in the image of the beneficent lord bestowing liberality on his retinue. Covetousness and sensuality are complementary to pride, different in method but contributing to the total villainy of the worldly churchman. A covetous cleric is expert in usury, perjury, bribery, simony. His underhanded devices are all aimed at the amassing of personal wealth, through which he can buy power and honor or fleshly pleasure and French fashion (l. 770). Thus, despite the seemingly contradictory behavior of the three worldly types, they are all aspects of a composite portrait. The details are commonplace, but the occasion is topical. Rather than attacking three particular churchmen of his time, the playwright is probably drawing a generic caricature.

To fifteenth-century audiences, the caricature surely represented a familiar and persistent abuse. Indeed, as late as 1516, John Skelton was still able to satirize the type of churchman-bureaucrat in terms almost identical to those of *Wisdom:* spiritual pride, extravagant dress, aping of the nobility, extortion and bribery, fleshly overindulgence.[6] A contemporary illustration for Skelton would have been Thomas Wolsey, although Skelton's portrait in *Magnificence* is based on generic commonplaces rather than on biographical detail. Wolsey was perhaps the greatest of a long line of churchmen-turned-politicians; his method of self-advancement was, by 1516, common. The cause of such practices, as with maintenance, was in part the political chaos of the Lancastrian-Yorkist wars. The church owned much property, and in seeking to retain its titles in a time of uncertain loyalties it was forced into the game of political bargaining. Princes in these troubled years often could not trust their noble counselors, and hence preferred to elevate clerics to high office, accelerating a tradition of clerical advisers and bureaucrats that extended centuries back to Lanfranc, Roger of Salisbury, and Thomas à Becket. Furthermore, many of the greatest nobles were casualties of the long years of warfare. The clerical men who replaced them in government frequently came from families of no name. Efficient, well-educated, owing everything to a royal master, they were the bureaucrats of their age. Small wonder if a man's head should occasionally be turned by such sudden acquisition of power. Nor is it surprising that the clergy as a whole, especially in the monasteries, should dramatize their anxieties for correction of abuses. The reform is of a conservative nature, not zealously "protestant," but the tone is insistent because of constant increase in the abuse.

The idealized ending of *Wisdom* offers only the conservative solution of self-reform by each erring individual priest, submitting himself once again to "yowur modyr, holy chyrch so mild" (l. 986). Such a sinner is not asked, however, to practice an extreme renunciation of the world. The playwright (probably of the Benedictine house of St. Edmundsbury) evidently belonged to a school of thought, active in the fifteenth century, that was in revolt against the arid extremes of scholasticism. This school included Richard Rolle of Hampole, Walter Hilton, Henry Suso, Bonaventura, and St. Bernard of Clairvaux, many of whose writings served as sources for *Wisdom*.[7] Such men preached a doctrine of burning love that accepted the orthodox creed of the church but shifted emphasis away from rite and ceremony. They sought a balance between other-worldliness and the active life, like that celebrated in St. Augustine's *City of God* (Book 19, Chapter 19) or in the "active" and "contemplative" figures on the north portal of Chartres Cathedral. They even allowed political activity within reasonable limits.

Accordingly, the playwright insists first of all that penance cannot be wrought by outward forms of prayer and self-castigation unless the sorrow of heart is genuine. He is suspicious of reliance on mariolatry and the intercession of saints, and is also wary of crusades and of such military violence in the name of the international church (ll. 1027-1029). Consistent with these attitudes is the author's distrust of excessive self-punishment, especially flagellation. Repeatedly he adjures his audience to do good works of pity and charity, to suffer reproof with patience, to speak forbearingly; all these are far more worthy than walking with bloody feet, or fasting for forty years, three days in the week, on bread and water, or "than [if] thou discyplinyde thi body with peynys greve" (ll. 1020-1022). The overall impression is of a man who, though no

Lollard, seriously urges his clerical auditors to restore their practice of Christianity to the "primitive" virtues of good works, to live at peace and perform their humble calling simply, and conversely to eschew formalistic practices of saint-worship and asceticism. It was in fact through his lampooning of self-discipline (ll. 429-436) that Lucifer was able to tempt Mind, Understanding, and Will into rebellion against their clerical life. Extremes lead only to extremes. The playwright ultimately argues for a *"vita mixta"* (l. 428) in which the cleric's life is indeed like Christ's, both contemplative and active in a meaningful way, functioning usefully in the world and yet rendering unto God that which is God's.[8]

Although the playwright appears to be addressing himself primarily to the church, he offers advice for a larger audience as well. The play is designed for performance in a number of different localities. Even if it was acted entirely under clerical auspices, its audience would probably include lay persons. The pedagogical explanations of the sacraments, original sin, and the like are appropriate for a general public.[9] Thus the political satire must also have been offered as a general warning to fifteenth-century society. It urges all members of the church, both lay and clerical, to reconsider the role of the church in the light of its basic teachings. Simultaneously spiritual and secular in focus, *Wisdom* provided a practical model for the nascent political morality play, demonstrating how the morality could retain its popular and homiletic function while adapting itself to the fascinations of political conflict in the early Tudor regime.

Obviously, the early morality play could search out topical crusades other than the correction of political abuses. Though the late fifteenth century was a time of church decline, it was also a time of fervent espousals of various reforms. Heresy was abroad, and some churchmen-dramatists feared a decline in the authority of the clergy among the general populace. Some looked with alarm upon growing skepticism concerning the transubstantial miracle of the mass itself. Clerics in London or the provinces exercised themselves on the godlessness of apprentices or peasants, the spiritual apathy among young people that every self-questioning generation believes to be its own unique problem. This phenomenon, succinctly labeled by Arthur Heiserman as the "now-a-days" *topos*,[10] is the social framework of several popular early moralities.

As in *Wisdom*, homiletic generalities are illustrated in the specific locale of fifteenth-century England, especially in the scenes of temptation and fall from grace. A brief examination of some nonpolitical topicality may help to define what we mean by politics, and help also to show that political relevance in the religious drama was merely one part of the large process by which drama evolved an interest in contemporary life.

In contrast to the grand archetype of moral plays, *The Castle of Perseverance* (1405-1425), virtually every late fifteenth-century morality can be identified with some timely program of reform. *Perseverance*, although alive with incidental topical satire, is thoroughly diversified in its castigation of sinfulness. All classes of men are guilty of failing to tithe, underpaying servants, selling by false weights, wearing extravagant clothes, practicing adultery, and slackening in religious worship. Though the author attacks simony and extortion as in *Wisdom*, he does not limit his attack to monastics. This lack of any particular reforming program is especially evident in a comparison of *Perseverance's* ending with that of the later and better-known *Summoning of Everyman*. The situations are alike: the protagonist is unprepared for Death, sin-ridden, deserted by friends, his worldly treasure, and his heirs, and so deficient in good deeds that he must depend solely on God's mercy. All these similarities emphasize, by way of opposites, what is so dominant in *Everyman* and so lacking in *Perseverance*: the role of the clergy in man's salvation. *Perseverance* presents no figures of religious instruction, like Knowledge or Confession, without whom salvation cannot be achieved. The sacraments of the church receive scant attention for a play about the path to universal redemption. In fact the mass is mentioned only in a satirical context (e.g., l. 1215) and Mankind receives nothing symbolically equivalent to extreme unction. Unlike Everyman, he is miserably alone at his death. To be sure, the author's piety and respect for the church are orthodox. His admonitions to attend religious service and to perform deeds of mercy are plain enough, even if Mankind scrapes by without them. When the author of *Perseverance* fails to stress the role of the clergy, it is probably because he takes its benefits for granted.

Everyman (late fifteenth century), on the other hand, reflects a church on the defensive. Despite its well-deserved reputation as the most successfully timeless of morality plays, *Everyman* is designed for a crisis. The play is related to a particular continental reform movement of the fifteenth century, just as its atypical text appears to have affinities with drama of the Low Countries.[11] Several of *Everyman's* most striking doctrines and insights arise from the moral climate that also produced Thomas à Kempis' *Of the Imitation of Christ*.[12] Most distinctive, perhaps, is the play's affirmation that priests are "above aungelles in degree," possessing this greater power because with five sacred words they may consecrate God's body in flesh and blood, and thus reenact life's greatest miracle in their very hands (ll. 735-748). As Thomas à Kempis proclaims:

Grand is this Mystery; great too is the dignity of the Priests, to whom hath been granted that which is not permitted to Angels.

For none but Priests duly ordained in the Church, have power to celebrate this Sacrament, and to consecrate the Body of Christ.   (IV, v)

From this doctrine emanate other of Thomas' major beliefs, especially those of Book IV, "Concerning the Sacrament." The priest is above all men as well as angels, for in his hands are the sacraments and the Holy Scriptures, which are the two keys to human salvation (IV, xi). The priest as teacher must interpret them to his parishioners. The sacraments, especially the eucharist, are good works and must be performed frequently and regularly (IV, iii). It follows that the priest must be in continual exercise to purify himself for his monumental task: "O how clean ought those hands to be, how pure that mouth, how holy that body, how unspotted that heart, where the Author of purity so often entereth!" (IV, xi). Much of the earlier portion of the *Imitation* instructs priests, both regular and monastic, in a discipline of simple life. Fasting and penance are continually essential. A holy person must, like Everyman, learn to renounce "all riches, dignities, honors, friends, and kinsfolk" (I, xviii).

Similarly, the second half of *Everyman* is dominated by the presence of spiritual counselors who must provide the institutional means to the protagonist's salvation. Everyman must perform contrition, confession, satisfaction, and absolution under guidance of Confession, a "holy man" dwelling "in the hous of salvacion." He receives chastisement and scourging in remembrance of Christ's passion with "strokes of punisshinge" (ll. 539-540, 616). Spiritual Knowledge is equivalent in power to Good Deeds; allegorically the two are sisters (l. 519), and the way to redemption requires both. The Priest oversees and unites these two functions as teacher and as celebrator of the blessed sacraments. As teacher he has the exclusive responsibility to interpret the Bible for laymen: "To us holy scripture they do teche" (l. 733). Yet for the author of *Everyman*, as for Thomas à Kempis, it is the administering of the sacraments that raises priests to their indescribably awesome authority.

> There is no emperour, king, duke, ne baron,
> That of God hath commicion
> As hath the leest preest in the world beinge.
> For of the blessyd sacramentes pure and benigne
> He bereth the keyes, and therof hath the cure
> For mannes redempcion.   (ll. 713-718)

Everyman's brief diatribe on sinful priests (ll. 750-764), aimed at the selling of sacraments and living of unclean lives, shares Thomas' concern for straitness of life among those who "handeleth his Maker bytwene his hande." Its very digressive nature betrays concern for such vexing fifteenth-century questions as the spiritual efficacy of the sacraments when administered by corrupt priests. It is addressed particularly to priests, like much of Thomas' *Imitation*, and offers no solution to the existence of corrupt clergy other than "I trust to God no such may we find" (l. 764). This answer is not an evasion. It is an urgent plea for reform directed at those who alone have the power of reform: the individual priests. By exalting and spiritualizing their function, *Everyman* exhorts priests to live up to their rank in the spiritual hierarchy of existence. It also presents lay audiences with potent reasons for submission to the church and for avoidance of facile anticlericalism. Even more than *Wisdom*, *Everyman* is the supreme example of a timeless play that nevertheless had a mission to fulfill for its immediate society.

Another play (a miracle play, not a morality) of the late fifteenth century that addresses itself to lay and clergy alike, and faces a timely ecclesiastical crisis no less acute than that of *Wisdom* or *Everyman*, is the Croxston *Play of the Sacrament*. Its staging is designed for performance in various churches, perhaps at the end of the Matins service.[13] Miracle plays at this time were often the coordinated effort of monastic and regular clergy, with monks serving as playwrights.[14] The bishop's concluding sermon and celebration of the sacrament of baptism are profoundly ritualistic, deliberately confounding the distinction between dramatic performance and religious service in the manner of the ancient liturgical drama. The bishop bids "all ye peple that here are" to march "to chyrch with solempne procession," following him until all "shall entre the chyrch and lay the Ost upon the auter" (ll. 730, 757, 786). Priests in the audience or congregation are warned directly to beware of leaving their churches unlocked (ll. 844-847), of drinking, and of condoning the selling of the sacrament (as in *Everyman*).

The basic issue addressed to this religious and clerical audience, as in Book IV of Thomas à Kempis' *Imitation,* is the nature of the eucharist. *Sacrament* confronts the challenge of increasing skepticism concerning transubstantiation in the mass, and the despairing confusion or "wanhope" that so afflicted those religious men and women who lost their sure faith in the miracle of Christ's presence. The play is a test case. Jonathas and his fellow Jews want to determine "iff the Sacrament wer flessh and blode." The answer, for laity and clergy, is supposed to be a settling of doubt.

The emphasis on doubt versus faith can be seen in the author's characterization of the Jews. He has no interest in them as a race, as usurers, as social outcasts, or as perpetrators of hideous cabalistic massacres of Christians, despite the popularity of tales in the vein of Chaucer's Prioress. Jonathas the Jew is not at all unlike his Christian counterpart, Aristory the merchant, with whom he is on very civilized terms. Jonathas is simply a type of skeptic who considers the Christian dogma of the mass to be rationally indefensible. Thus his membership in the race of men who crucified Christ is important only as a historical analogy to contemporary life. He must reenact that passion in a profane parody of the Last Supper (ll. 313-324), inflict the sacred bread with the five wounds of Christ (hence the symbolic need in the play for five Jews), and nail the sacrament to a post. More important, however, Jonathas must suffer Christ's torments, echoing the Master's words with "ther is no more. I must enduer" (l. 440). The suffering is not retributive but cleansing, for the pilgrimage of satisfaction Jonathas undertakes leads to absolution and baptism by the bishop.

With so few if any Jews living in England at the time (none officially), the problem of their faithlessness was scarcely at issue. Rational skepticism among Christians was more serious, and evidently widespread— especially after Wycliffe's attacks on the doctrine of transubstantiation in 1381, which may have encouraged the writing of several "conversion" plays of this sort by way of counter-argument. A graphic example in the early sixteenth century of heterodoxy among even the regular priest-hood is that of John Bale, who, while still Prior of the Carmelite order at Doncaster (ca. 1531), taught one William Broman that Christ was not really present in the sacrament of the altar.[15] Controversy within the church itself over the real presence was especially active at Cam-bridge. The playwright of *Sacrament* argues by analogy that any man who doubts the real presence is in essence a pagan, be he Jew or nominal Christian. The Jews are men, like the Jews of the passion story, who knew Christ in the flesh and yet denied his immortality and power to open Heaven's gates to them. Their crime is not that they murdered Christ but that they denied faith. The Jews must be sympathetic and recoverable if they are to be protagonists of a "conversion" play.

The play's aim, then, is to re-kindle faith in a miracle that is explicitly nonrational. The *trompe d'oeil* theatrics used to "prove" the real pres-ence may strike a modern reader as naive and apt perhaps to induce disbelief of what is after all only stage illusion. Hands are removed from bodies, the Host must bleed in plain view, an oven must rive to reveal the speaking image of the Savior. In his stage directions to his clerical actors, the clergyman-author is explicit about the ingeniousness with which these wonders are to be brought off. Acceptance of such "proof" would seem to require a mightier faith than the abstract acceptance of transubstantiation. These stage methods are nevertheless thoroughly traditional in liturgical drama and are related to the nature of the mass itself. In the earliest Easter ceremonies, clergymen-actors displayed the sepulcher cloth as visual demonstration of Christ's having risen. Christ was there, and now he is not; what more could logic ask? The ac-ceptance of dramatic miracle in the *Sacrament* play is therefore syn-onymous with the acceptance of the doctrine of transubstantiation, not abstractly but vividly and immediately. It is in this largest sense that the *Play of the Sacrament* is conceived as a liturgical experience, a timeless act of worship restated in the later fifteenth century to meet the exigencies of a contemporary "wanhope."

Popular drama for lay audiences in the early Tudor period also de-veloped a topical program. It dealt locally with social unrest. *Mankind* (ca. 1471) is the work of a country clergyman living near Cambridge,[16] whose aim is to speak to his people in their own rough language. As the names of his *dramatis personae* suggest, his topical satire is aimed chiefly at the abuses of "Nowadays" and "New Guise." This emphasis is nowhere to be found in *Mankind's* source poems, unless *Piers Plowman* served as a general guide.[17] Except for the diabolical Tityvillus ("Totus Vilus," all things vile), the Vices are satirical types rather than abstractions. Their fashions in worldly vanity are eminently suited to parochial life rather than the court: highway- and church-robbing, horse stealing, jail breaking, and especially designing of clothes. The jacket "after the new gyse," which they fashion for Mankind by abbreviating his farmer's cloak, provides no defense against the cold. Mankind must also strut with long and conspicuous sword, break the Sabbath in the ale-house, and above all throw over obedience to his parish priest and to his agricultural way of life.

Mankind is a delver, both as a son of Adam and as a fifteenth-century worker of the soil. He is a farmer like many of his audience, and to the decently old-fashioned author of this play, the essence of "nowadays" is disaffection with one's lot in life. It is "smart" to mock the honest labor of the lower classes and to crave the fast life. Tityvillus tempts his victim by way of the normal but maddening frustrations of a farmer's existence: the soil is stiff as a board (literally, in this case, since Tityvillus has inserted a board), tools disappear, seed is lost, bodily functions assert their demands at awkward moments. Anger leads to restlessness, producing in turn idleness and the inevitable appeal of the new guise. Against this general moral decline, the author's spokesman, Mercy (who is a priest), shores up his defenses as best he can. He asks only for the possible, conveying his admonitions in pithy imperatives. Do good works, persevere, do not place faith in the transitory, avoid temptation. The author especially insists he does not ask for ascetic denial. "The good new gyse nowadays I will not disalow. I discommend the vicious gyse" (ll. 177-178). "Mesure is tresure" in the use of ale and wine; "I forbid yow not the use" (l. 230). This distinction between contentment with traditional country life and covetousness after excess is a matter of common sense. The milieu of the entire play suggests peasant restiveness, of which there was plenty in 1471 despite the fact that the common people had not suffered much from the Wars of the Roses.

Mundus et Infans, Hickescorner, and *Youth* (ca. 1508-1520), three popular Henrician plays of a similar stamp, show the continuing spread of hooliganism, especially in London, and the church's growing alarm at the utter lack of respect for the clergy among the young set. The gay young protagonists of these plays, Manhood, Youth, Freewill, and Imagination, display the evils of increasing social mobility and resultant disruption of moral values. Their conversation is rife with humorous allusions to Holborn, Westminster, the stews of Southwark, Eastcheap, the Pope's Head Tavern, Newgate, Tyburn, the Lombards, purse-snatching, highway robbery. Conversely, the authorial spokesmen (who are obviously clerics) uphold the simple dignity of the priestly calling. Suffering derision and even physical degradation in the stocks, these patient men ultimately persuade their adversaries to a life of practical piety. The church announces its campaign to shackle wildness and to reform it by simple preaching. *The Interlude of John the Evangelist,* although published much later (ca. 1550?), is yet another pre-Reformation homily on roistering and the need for rudimentary instruction in the meaning of the Catholic service. Criticisms of the church are concerned with personal morality, not dogma, and are answered by the example of the priestly central figure.

In its defense of priesthood and of transubstantiation, or in its concern with churchmen in politics, peasant restiveness, and London immorality, early Tudor drama of ecclesiastical and popular auspices proved itself highly conscious of contemporary problems. The stances were orthodox, the solutions conservative. From this background of broadly social and religious awareness we can turn to Chaplain Medwall, a man relatively sophisticated and well-connected at court. The transition ought to provide a sense of the enormous contrasts in the early Tudor church.

3 · CHAPLAIN MEDWALL AND THE
NEW TUDOR RULING CLASS

In its battle against maintenance and feudal autonomy, the Tudor monarchy introduced new criteria for political success in England. No longer supreme was the military warlord with his chivalrous pursuits, his hawks and his hounds, and his armed retinue. The man now prized at court was an eloquent speaker, canny adviser, tireless administrator of public policy, and above all well educated. This new emphasis was part of a conscious Tudor program to achieve a national rather than a feudal political control, and to counterbalance the authority of the old nobility. Other things being equal, the doctrine of rank still asserted that a nobleman deserved more respect and place than one of lesser birth; but the nobility was now more on its mettle, obliged to prove its "gentilesse." Noblemen demonstrated their concern by sending their children to the schools and universities in unprecedented numbers, sufficient to crowd the commoners.

These defensive maneuvers suggest how sensitive aristocrats were to the competition of the "new men" at court—persons from lower social backgrounds now in positions of high authority. Partly because the aristocracy had been decimated by the Lancastrian-Yorkist civil wars, partly because Henry Tudor preferred not to cater any more than was necessary to baronial privilege, certain fortunate commoners began to play an unusually dominant role in the royal administration. The process of elevation of the nouveau riche into the governing elite was by no means new—the de la Poles of the fifteenth century had been busy purchasing land from unthrifty noblemen—but the trend had accelerated. The aristocracy could no longer be assured of the truly important offices of state, or of a fixed proportion on the Privy Council. Social fluidity among the well-to-do, both upward and downward, became more active during the Tudor reign than in any other period prior to the nineteenth century.[1]

The extent of aristocratic displacement from the center of power during Henry VII's reign can be sampled in a comment later offered by Henry VIII. "Touching the beginning of our reign," he wrote, "there were but two worthy to be called noble, the one the treasurer of England, the other the high steward of our houshold; others, as Lord Marney and Darcy, but mean born gentylmen, ne yet of any great landes, til they were promoted by the king our father of most noble memorie, and by us, and so made knightes and lordes. The rest were lawiers and prestes, saving the two bishoppes of Canterbury and Winchestre."[2]

This is not to say that the aristocrats became mere hangers-on at court, nursing their wounded pride with a lavish display of their wealth, as has been too often alleged. In fact they displayed an astonishing resiliency, pursuing industrial and commercial ventures, managing their estates, turning to peaceful endeavors that were to be the pride of the ruling class in the eighteenth century. If they were excluded from the innermost councils of the monarch, they were almost invariably chosen as military commanders, ambassadors, lords lieutenants, and magistrates. In their regions they remained supremely important, and as leaders of society they converted newcomers to their patrician outlook rather than bending to democracy. The rewards of office meted out to persons of lower birth did not bolster the status of the bourgeois as a whole, nor were meant to. This social class lacked as yet any cohesive political ambition, and the more fortunate among its membership simply aspired to join the elite. The family of Edmund Dudley, Henry Tudor's financial wizard, rose under Elizabeth to the earldom of Leicester.

Bourgeois representation in the House of Commons never grew to significant proportions under the Tudors. The "new men" learned to put their social origins behind them as quickly as possible.[3]

Notwithstanding, new concepts of "gentilesse" under Henry VII inevitably created an urgent sense of social competition. Advancement for talented parvenus could be meteoric, both in secular careers and in the clergy. The church provided an opportunity to be well educated and to display administrative talents where Henry might appreciate them. New men acquired vast holdings in land; and although they probably were not in fact less hospitable or more given to enclosure than their erstwhile superiors, their newness called special attention to their occasional wrongdoings. Moreover, these men inevitably had a special interest in the doctrines of humanism, and commissioned humanist writers to create a rationale for the new Tudor society.[4] The new order naturally endorsed hierarchy of order and degree, but placed novel emphasis on professional ability, literary training, and the innate qualities of "gentilesse" that might be found in untitled men as well as in nobility.

It is in such a context that Medwall's *Fulgens and Lucrece* (1497) takes on political meaning. The truism of "gentilesse" was of course not new. Pious teaching that nobility resides not in blood but in deeds, as expressed in Chaucer's moral ballad to "gentilesse" and his "Wife of Bath's Tale," was just the kind of notion that late medieval Europe could endorse without visible disturbance of the social order. Yet humanism gave the concept new meaning, and Medwall is patently responsive to the power struggle taking place in Henry VII's court. His protagonists are not abstract exponents of vice and virtue, but specific types of entrenched nobleman and new administrator.[5] Publius Cornelius is guilty of "open maintenaunce." He is of an old family, and practices a "proud contenaunce," "nise aray," "theftis and murdres," "riotous disportis and play," sloth, cowardice, and other excesses (II, 632-639). His sloth is a sign of the aristocratic idleness so much deplored in More's *Utopia* and other Tudor humanist tracts. Like the satiric types of *Wisdom* he uses maintenance, perjury, and lechery, but his background is feudal rather than ecclesiastical. Gaius Flaminius, on the other hand, is no simple commoner, but an active politician. Unable to claim descent from "gentilman of . . . kin or blode," he nevertheless is nationally prominent "now of late" and "Among noble gentilman playest checkmate" (II, 532-

535). Publius bitterly resents this intrusion of new men lacking family name into politics. He attacks Gaius' rise to power as both recent and sudden:

> His auncetours were of full poor degre,
> Allbeit that now within a yere or twain,
> By cause that he wold a gentilman be,
> He hath him goten both office and fee.   (II, 565-568)

Medwall's career explains his motive in taking such a stand. He was chaplain to John Morton, one of the great pluralists and administrators of his age. Such churchmen, even if their ecclesiastical status prevented them from becoming outright members of the rising gentry, profited from the mobility of the new order. Furthermore, their allegiance to Henry obliged them to carry out his orders against the old families. Morton was a member of the Privy Council for the last forty-five years of his life, except for his periodic attainders under the Yorkists, and had helped Henry VII to the throne. Henry chose him lord chancellor in 1487. Like his predecessors the Despensers, and his sixteenth-century successors Wolsey and Cromwell, Morton was resented by the older families not only for his sudden increase of power but also for his ruthlessly efficient administration. The derisive title used to caricature his fiscal policy, "Morton's Fork," though probably unfair to his memory,[6] attests to the hatred of those who were forced to pay his taxes. More than anything else, Morton was despised for his unaltering loyalty to Henry VII in implementing a calculated policy of the reduction of baronial wealth to manageable proportions.

Medwall himself was probably not a full priest but an acolyte, virtually a layman. He had the patronage of many offices of a semi-legal character: Prerogative Court, Court of Arches, the Commissary Courts of Canterbury and of Calais, and the like. These institutions were served by a multitude of recorders, registrars, and commissaries.[7] Medwall's church title and education were the means to bureaucratic power. At the same time, he was sincerely devout. His *Fulgens and Lucrece* combines Christian idealism and humanistic endorsement of the new Tudor gentry in a manner that is characteristically English and is absent in his Italian source.[8]

The Italian original, Buonaccorso's *De Vera Nobilitate*, like Medwall's play, pits a debauched aristocrat against a virtuous humanist, and clearly awards the palm to Gaius even if Lucresse leaves the final choice to her father Fulgeus (the correct classical spelling) and the Senate. The Earl of Worcester's English translation, by way of a French version, is close in spirit to Buonaccorso; Worcester was a great admirer of Italian humanism, and partly for that reason was not popular with most Englishmen.[9] Buonaccorso's declamation was too continental in its values for Medwall's purposes, too apt to give offense if left unsoftened by an English viewpoint. Medwall is accordingly less interested than Buonaccorso in rhetorical techniques of the *controversia*.[10] By reducing greatly the length of his two suitors' orations in proportion to the length of the play, Medwall shifts the emphasis from the rhetorical triumphs of neoclassical humanism to other virtues, such as Christian charity and performance of public duty.

Medwall seems especially anxious to avoid the defiant challenge of aristocracy by a self-made intelligentsia in the original. Fifteenth-century humanists in Italy occasionally wielded great power. Learning was venerated, yet printing was unknown and manuscripts expensive. Good neo-Ciceronians possessed one of the age's surest means to advancement. Suitably, Buonaccorso's hero is more scholar than civil servant. Although Gaius pictures himself as a naval hero and leader beloved of the populace, he scoffs at the frivolity of the court and prefers Horatian contemplation. He can tempt Lucresse with "poor lodging," quiet rest devoid of superfluous pleasure, and an inspiring library of both Latin and Greek books. She can choose idleness and unchastity at court or philosophy away from court. Medwall's interest, on the other hand, is in successful advisers to the throne. His Gaius is not embarrassed by rank and wealth, and accepts "both office and fee." Living moderately, he still intends to guarantee Lucrece's comfort. He offers her no classical library. He will persevere as a loyal servant of the state. Whereas Buonaccorso glorifies the humanist himself, Medwall self-effacingly transforms his hero into a politician who befriends humanism but is not primarily an intellectual.

In his use of anachronism and mode of reference to the past, Medwall further reveals himself as spokesman for useful public service in a Christian tradition rather than an aggressively humanistic neoclassical scholarship. Buonaccorso's declamations are laden with the names of ancestral figures, both of patricians who have betrayed their public trust and of poor men who have achieved immortality through their writings. History is for him a book that demonstrates the continual ascendancy of intellect over inherited rank. Buonaccorso is careful throughout to employ only pagan forms of imprecation. Medwall conversely allows his characters to swear anachronistically, as in popular English drama, "By cokkis bonis," "By cockis body," "by godis mercy," by Saints John, James, Mary, and Sim. Even in the serious plot, this use of anachronism is conscious and fundamental. Fulgens, in his opening speech, assures us it is Christian duty that impels him to honor his daughter's choice. Christian duty obliges every man to accept and to fulfill responsibilities imposed upon him by the Almighty (I, 202-288). Lucrece vows that she will never assent to the worldly enticements of Publius, "Allthough he had as grete possession As ony one man in cristen region" (II, 799-800). Medwall refers only once to an ancestor, "cipion [Scipio] of affrick," and that only in the blatantly anachronistic company of "The gestis of arthur or of alexandyrs life" (II, 474). Medwall, in sum, is suspicious of the arrogant and pagan self-reliance of the continental humanist, and bids the English new men avoid such Italianate extremes.

In making his plea for humanism at the English court, Medwall also tactfully disclaims any intention of condemning all the old families out of hand. Given a nobleman and commoner of equal merit, he of course prefers the nobleman.

> B.   Than I put case that a gentilman bore
> Have godely maners to his birth according.
> *Lucrece.*   I say of him is to be set gret store.
> Such one is worthy more lawd and praising
> Than many of them that hath their beginning
> Of low kinred, ellis god forbede!
> I will not afferm the contrary for my hede.   (II, 780-786)

If the new gentry are to be tolerated in positions of power, their claim to royal favor must rest solely on a superior Christian virtue that they must continually demonstrate. They must be able to say, with Gaius, "I have borne unto God all my daies His laud and praise with my due devocion . . . Loving to my frend and faithfull withall, And ever I have withstonde my lustis sensuall" (II, 672-678). Repeatedly, Medwall insists that he wishes to conciliate the ancient nobility and pay tribute to its merits, rather than proclaim an aggressive new social order.

Even so, the confrontation between Gaius and Publius clearly implies that aristocratic abuse is the chief concern, especially in matters of sartorial extravagance and attendant ruinous cost. Publius shamelessly offers Lucrece wealth enough for idleness and overly fancy clothes: "About your own apparell ye can do non excess In my company that sholde displese my mind" (II, 550-551). His boast gives substance to what otherwise might seem a wildly exaggerated account by Publius' servant "B." According to "B," his master spends not twelve pence but twenty shillings for a pair of hose. The cost is so high not because the hose are silk and gold, but because "ther is in cutting A new maner of fascion nowaday . . . They most be stripid all this way With small slipes of coloures gay" (I, 729-733). Codpieces must be large, gowns must not descend below mid-thigh even though they consume seven broad yards of material in the making. Most of this cloth goes into the sleeves:

> All that doth that fascion were
> They have whingis behind redy to fly,
> And a sleve that wolde cover all the body;
> Than forty plaitis, as I think in my mind,
> They have before, and as many behind.   (I, 746-750)

As we shall see in *Nature*, Medwall was preoccupied with this particular fashion as a sign of decadently conspicuous consumption. He may have been indebted for some details of the convention to Brant's *Narrenschiff*, a Latin translation of which was available in 1497.[11] Medwall turns the convention to a support of Morton and Henry VII in their campaign against livery and maintenance. Significantly, Publius (who practices maintenance) brings in a liveried crew of mummers, "Certain straungers fresshly disgisyd Att his own expens" (II, 120-121). Evidently Publius was costumed much as "B" describes him, and the contrast of his and Gaius' appearance would indicate symbolically what is not always conveyed through characterization. Their very codpieces would betray differing views of marriage as nocturnal pleasure or as lawful procreation of the species.

Medwall is continually wary of sartorial extravagance in all men. He satirizes fashions moving through the court so swiftly that "every man" models himself on the gentleman (I, 755). "A" and "B," in their roles as suitors for promotion, are not exempt from ambition for new finery. Actors ape the gallants so "That a man shall not lightly Know a player from another man" (I, 55-56). Medwall's strictures against family pride are combined with a warning to the new men to maintain the proprieties of their station. He does not object to a proper sumptuousness befitting one's rank, or to "largesse" in proper measure. Those to whom God has entrusted riches are custodians for the poor (I, 208-217). Henry VII himself believed in gorgeous appearance as a part of the mesmerizing panoply of office, and was a scrupulous practitioner of almsgiving.[12] The conspicuous waste of constantly changing fashion and reckless generosity, however, were another matter. Henry's instincts for frugality kept a cold watch on the men he elevated to importance. Yet his chief fear was baronial wealth, and accordingly the weight of Medwall's satire falls on Publius.

Even with Henry's presumed blessing, this satire directed against the barons required great tact on the part of Medwall (and of Morton, whose views Medwall probably shared). *Fulgens and Lucrece* may have been performed on an impressive state occasion, such as a banquet for the ambassadors negotiating the marriage of Prince Arthur and Katharine of Aragon.[13] The barons were doubtless present. Medwall's chief safeguard is his use of comedy. The famous double plot of "A" and "B" is motivated chiefly by the need for comic undercutting of political satire and for conciliation through laughter.

Modern readers tend to look upon the burlesque scenes as comic relief from a series of arid disputations in the main plot. Medwall's audience, however, would have found the central argument all too stimulating, not merely because Tudor audiences relished the medieval débat but because the political issues were immediate and potentially offensive. Medwall's device of *reductio ad absurdum* in the comedy anticipates that of John Heywood (see Chapter 5). Medwall deserves more credit as Heywood's teacher than he has perhaps received. In fact, "A" and "B" bear important resemblances to Merry Report of *The Play of the Weather*. All three emerge from the audience, helping to bridge the distance between spectators and a serious affair that concerns them.[14] All three have similar resemblances to such popular morality figures of vice as Tityvillus in *Mankind*, adapted (perhaps an original contribution of Medwall's) to the humanist interlude in which they are not malign tempters in a soul-struggle but mimics and troublemakers.

The chief source of dramatic value in "A" and "B" is their comic indifference. As "B" observes:

> How be it the matter toucheth me never a dell,
> For I am nether of vertue excellent
> Nor yet of gentil blode.   (I, 140-142)

Unaffected by the political rivalry, they are in a position to reveal its ludicrous side. Their motive combines personal gain with the spirit of innocent fun and satire. The outcome of Lucrece's marriage does not concern them (I, 378-379). They refuse to state a preference for Gaius or Publius, despite their nominal allegiance as servants. As comic trouble-makers in the popular tradition, they parody the mannerisms of wooing, chivalric punctilio, prodigality, political envy, clothes-consciousness, and gluttony of their social betters—even of the spectators (I, 3-4, 1418-1420). It would be easy for a Tudor audience to laugh at ambition and extravagance in this guise, and to view such antics as the satiric obverse of the serious debate. Comic indifference is essential to Medwall in establishing another and safer viewpoint. He can appear amused and impartial, like "A" and B," without sidestepping his basic moral commitment. The audience can see the mannerisms of political controversy as petty, although the issues are substantive.

The comic routines must be viewed ultimately as "Divers toyes . . . To stir folk to mirth and game," subservient to "the matter principall" (II, 22-26), partly indeed to content those weaker men who cannot fasten their minds to unalleviated instruction. Yet Medwall's chief hope is to conciliate and thereby to win the good opinion of "every resonable man in this place" (I, 135). Repeatedly he asks that there be no violence of disagreement. Lucrece forbids it in the declamations of her suitors, and she upbraids Publius for his insinuations and words of hate (II, 369-374, 536-538). That Gaius urges patient hearing and scrupulously follows a course of dispassionate reasoning is a principal reason for his success. Hot tempers in the court of Henry VII can only aggravate the inherent conflict between nobility and commoners.

Accordingly, Medwall's soothing instincts prompt him to be tentative, self-humbling. He does not force his conclusions on the audience. Lucrece protests that her choice will be "After mine own fantasie, it shall not extend To any other person" (II, 429-430); and she exits with an apology: "I pray you all sirs, as meny as be here, Take not my wordis

by a sinistre way" (II, 766-767). It is the satiric commentator "B,"
however, who most wittily points out the saving fictional distance between spectators and play:

> Wherfor I can think these folk [the spectators] will not spare
> After plain trouth this matter to procede,
> As the story seyth; why shulde they care?
> I trow here is no man of the kin or sede
> Of either partie, for why they were bore
> In the citie of Rome as I said before.   (I, 175-180)

This comic protestation, necessary only because the audience might think
otherwise, preserves dramatic distance even as it establishes the link to
contemporary society.

Medwall's *Nature*, although seemingly not designed for a specific state
occasion like *Fulgens and Lucrece,* was intended for patrician audiences
rather than popular. The play's second half is to follow "Whan my lord
shall so devise" (E2^v), presumably after a banqueting interval. It is
evening, with a comfortable fire at hand and seats for the players
(A^v-A2^v, F2, G). The spectators, gathered around the players, are members of a numerous household (G3^v, H2). Medwall speaks again to
counselors of the realm, and the tone of his political advice is shaped
accordingly. The topical approach demonstrates, in fact, the authorial
similarity of Medwall's two apparently dissimilar plays: the satire of extravagance in dress, the conciliatory pleading for an end to factionalism,
the insistence upon a sensible moderation avoiding extremes of prodigality and covetousness.

As in other early Tudor moralities, the timeless homiletic soul-struggle
in *Nature* contains within it topical *exempla* of sinful behavior. The
focus of political satire is the figure of Pride. He receives disproportionate
attention in the roster of the seven Deadly Sins, and he greatly exag-
gerates one aspect of the sin he is supposed to represent: a fondness
for expensive clothes. This attribute is of course a commonplace of pride,
but Medwall's characterization appears deliberately onesided. His Pride
is not the embodiment of disobedience or presumption. Moreover, Pride's
garments correspond in minute detail with those of Publius Cornelius
in *Fulgens and Lucrece*. Pride is thus more courtly type than abstraction,
unlike his fellow Deadly Sins.[15] He is of "noble progeny" and "all his
dayes hath worn gilt spurs." Pampered from birth, he is easily offended

at any imagined neglect of protocol (C2). He practices maintenance: the other Deadly Sins are referred to as "all the company of mine affiaunce," "kinnesmen," or "retinue" (D2ᵛ, D4). He garnishes himself for battle "as it had be One of the ryall blode" (H2). His garments are not only those of the court but exclusively those of the older, literally "vested" interests.

Pride's excessive finery is blameworthy on three counts: personal vanity, constantly changing French fashion, and unrealistic cost paid for by exploitation of commoners. No man ever suffered more for appearance's sake. Pride sets his long hair in curls at night so that "it crispeth and shineth as bright As any pyrled gold" (C2ᵛ). He wears both doublet "on-laced byfore" and stomacher of pure satin, although they are too warm for comfort even in the wintertime. Useless weapons—a dagger and "a sword or twain"—so encumber him that he is obliged to keep his own bastard son as attendant to carry them (C2ᵛ). He teaches his French-speaking son how to "Set out the better leg," and is annoyed to discover that his imported styles are aped by "every knave" two days after they first appear in court. All this fashion is of course outrageously expensive. The hose, like Publius', are costly not because of cloth-of-gold material but because they shall be "striped With corselettis of fine velvet," and below the knee "freshly gard With colours two or thre" (D2, D2ᵛ). Pride's own gown is winged for flight. It also features the titillatingly abbreviated midriff described by Publius' servant "B":

> Than have I such a short gown,
> With wide sleves that hang a-down;
> They wold make some lad in this town
> A doublet and a cote.   (C2ᵛ)

Thus is Medwall able to apply his church's precepts to the service of Morton's "Fork." By ridiculing Pride's fashions and exploitation of the poor, Medwall defends a governmental policy of heavy taxation on those who can afford to support the public weal.

The impulse toward satirical typing occasionally involves Medwall in contradiction within his abstract framework. Nowhere do these contradictions afford more amusing evidence of his political motive than in his depiction of Avarice. The subject was apt to be touchy in Henry VII's court—even, apparently, in an orthodox morality. Avarice is never caricatured as are the other sins. Yet the morality plot requires that Man finally experience the sin of old age. When the moment arrives, Medwall astonishingly delivers from the mouth of Liberality a warning not against penuriousness but against prodigality. Asked if Liberality would have Man give away all his worldly goods to atone for covetousness, Liberality is quick to distinguish between proper generosity and reckless giving:

> I mene not so, parde!
> For that is wast and sinfull prodigalite.
> Take the mid way, betwixt theym two,
> And fle thextremitees how so ever thou do.   (I2ᵛ)

Charity is an art requiring no mean skill. Improper giving may damn the giver as readily as covetousness. Those who give recklessly are usually those who have gotten wrongfully by oppressing the poor as Pride has done, and who hope to make a belated appeasement of their consciences. Medwall's favorite metaphor of the proper handling of wealth, in the words of Liberality as in those of Fulgens, is of a stewardship. In heaven Man must "geve a rekening Of all the goodys that com to thyn use," explaining how he has practiced alms deeds or other distribution, "Or how thou hast these goodys wasted or abused" (I2ᵛ, I3). The wealthy man is not asked or even allowed to give away all, for he is the purveyor of an estate entrusted to him by heaven. He must practice generosity, but with circumspection.

The specific advice in *Nature*, then, where it enlarges upon more conventional themes, makes sense in terms of Medwall's sponsorship and patrician audience. He does not require spartan denial of the world from his comfortable spectators. Indeed, he gives moral sanction to their position in society as overseers of the distribution of wealth and as the rightful wearers of a decorous yet appropriately sumptuous apparel. Medwall's concern with other shortcomings of humanity is perfunctory. Compared with his strictures on finance and apparel, his final warnings against the sins of the flesh are brief and inoffensive to his audience. What he labels "Abstinence" is actually an easy, non-ascetic moderation. The final moral in *Nature* is a mixture of the general and the particular: be a good Christian, practice the seven Cardinal Virtues—and give active support to the government's views on fiscal moderation, livery, and maintenance. Such wise counsel could not fail to please Cardinal Morton and his royal master.

The confrontation between new men and old inevitably grew more sharp during the early years of Henry VIII's reign. The young king's fiscal extravagance and penchant for foreign involvement encouraged the ambitions of more aggressive members of the new ruling class, causing dismay even among those humanists who were at first disposed to be optimistic. The antagonism of the barons, already disaffected, was more fundamental. Those members of the small administrative council who had run the government during Henry's first five years, laboring on policy while he basked in his own popularity, found themselves increasingly shouldered aside after early 1514 by Wolsey. In succeeding years, the families of the Percys, Talbots, Stanleys, and Howards were forced to acknowledge the ascendancy of a new administrative caste, and to react defensively to it.[1]

Into the battle stepped John Skelton, a poet of deeply conservative instincts. Although a man of considerable humanistic accomplishment for his time, who inculcated in his royal pupil Henry a belief in the ascendancy of virtue and classical learning over wealth and nobility of blood, Skelton's political values were those of the old nobility. Never close to the More circle, he placed relatively little emphasis in his writings on the education of women. His social vision is closer to that of Elyot's *Governor* than to *Utopia*.[2] He did not espouse Greek, as did the more advanced humanists; his Latin was less fluent than theirs. Erasmus praised him, but perfunctorily as Prince Henry's tutor. Grocyn, Linacre, and William Lyly were not warm toward him. Broad social reform under a philosopher-king did not appeal to Skelton. He was no antischolastic or critic of monasticism. He abhorred Lollardry and defended pilgrimages. In *Speak Parrot* he upbraids the New Learning.[3] His play called *Good Order* (existing now only as a fragment), ascribed to him by John Bale, is an earnestly devout and orthodox Lenten exercise on the virtues of abstinence and the superiority of vocal prayer to mental prayer.[4] These factors, though they do not lessen Skelton's humanistic achievement, help explain why his political stance was more cautious and scholastic than that of the More circle.

Responsive to the aristocratic claims of the old families, Skelton was not one to be overwhelmed by Tudor propaganda. Furthermore, as former tutor to the Prince of Wales who became Henry VIII, Skelton evidently felt privileged to speak plainly concerning a monarch who savored too much of his youth. In his satirical poems directed against Wolsey one senses the equation of two ancient prerogatives, that of the poet and that of the aristocrat, both warning against the self-interested baseness of sycophants. Skelton was poet laureate not of the crown but of the English nobility and educated men.[5] In 1516-1518 he was, like them, a disaffected survivor of a previous reign, a once-trusted counselor who saw his pupil turning to new masters.

Skelton's play *Magnificence* does not belong to the group of vindictive personal satires directed against Wolsey: *Speak Parrot* (late 1521), *Colin Clout* (1522), and *Why Come Ye Not to Court* (1522). These satirical poems formed a compact group chronologically, and produced swift reprisal requiring an "effusive humbling" by the poet.[6] *Magnificence* is notably earlier (perhaps as early as 1515 and probably no later than 1518)[7] and did not place Skelton in danger. Wolsey was not, in these earlier years, as unpopular among the nobility and clergy as he was by 1522; he still had a workable relationship with the old family of the Howards. Moreover, in its genre *Magnificence* is not personal satire but a *Speculum Principis,* comparable to Skelton's own earlier *Speculum* treatise for Prince Henry stressing the danger of unscrupulous lieutenants.[8] Literary commonplaces in this tradition amply account for the source of Skelton's themes. Conventions of the low-born conniving counselor, and the true prince as distinguished from the tyrant, were to be found in Hoccleve or in Barclay's *Ship of Fools,* and in the writings of Erasmus and More. The concept of "measure" owes much to the popular pseudo-Aristotelian treatise purportedly written for Alexander, *Secreta Secretorum.* Warnings against flatterers recall John of Salisbury and a host of *speculum* writers. The term "magnificence" is probably derived not directly from Aristotle but from Lydgate and Burgh's verse version of the *Secrees of Old Philosoffres.* In the popular drama were such commonplace prototypes of the tyrant as Antichrist, Herod, or Pride.[9] For these various reasons, critics have grown properly wary of simple equations between Folly and Wolsey, Sad Circumspection and the Duke of Norfolk, and even Magnificence and Henry VIII.

Nevertheless, criticism has swung too far toward a study of conventions when it denies any relevance to Wolsey or Henry.[10] Although the play deals with programs rather than with personalities, *Magnificence* studies a political crisis in the years around 1516. Quite possibly, in a situation not yet as irreconcilable as in 1522, Skelton castigated a nameless type of evil courtier and impressionable king in order to leave some room for questioning the extent to which Wolsey and Henry were irreclaimably of this type. Still, the chancellor and king were unavoidable points of reference—not as Skelton's models but as his focus of concern. Even if Skelton wrote with Hoccleve and Barclay as his sources, his occasion was topical. Skelton's great contribution to political drama was not observation from the life but a closer application of old techniques to new realities than had heretofore been attempted.[11] This distinction is apparent in the play itself, in its handling of viewpoint and of calculated response from a Tudor audience.

The protagonist Magnificence, although drawn from commonplace sources, is involved in a particular financial crisis. He must work out his salvation not in terms of spiritual after-life, but of fiscal sanity in this world. The danger is not hoarding, but extravagance. This advice does of course have its appeal to every man, but Magnificence is "a noble prince of might," of "noble port and fame," who confers knighthood, lives in a palace, and presides over a court. He is a newcomer to office. Who will counsel the new monarch? What will be his attitude toward the control of finance? These questions are greatly exacerbated by the fact that his predecessor has been notoriously frugal. The mood has been one of repressive fear (ll. 30-31), and the great danger now is that long and barbarous restraint will engender the opposite reaction of license. Temperate men blame the old order for creating the ominous imbalance. Significantly it is Wealthful Felicity who delivers the most acid appraisal of the penury now ending.

> Yet Measure hath ben so long from us absent,
> That all men laugh at Liberte to scorn.
> Wealth and Wit, I say, be so thred bare worn,
> That all is without Measure and fer beyond the mone.　(ll. 221-224)

The problem of the moment, however, is not so much to assess blame for the evils of niggardliness during the preceding reign as to forestall a swing of the pendulum.

These circumstances, not emphasized to such an extent in traditional *speculum* literature, were the burning issues of the years around 1516.[12] Men could still remember Henry's coronation in 1509, and the sense of change that had come with it. Henry VII had been fabled for his parsimony. Ageing, wary, trusting as few men as possible, he had devoted his last energies to securing the throne against rival claims and to enriching the royal treasury. His son was, on the contrary, openhanded, popular, a keen sportsman and capable scholar. Yet by 1516 the opposite danger of recklessness was apparent to everyone. The virtuous Wealthful Felicity makes clear that Skelton does not wish to be caught defending the niggardliness of the preceding regime. Fiscal penuriousness and excess are equally hazardous, but the topical problem of the moment is the new king's excess.

Skelton frankly acknowledges the glamorlessness of his stand against the appeal of seemingly innocent, fun-loving freedom. Magnificence cannot resist the boyish charm of Liberty in chafing against restriction. By contrast, the strictures and gloomy prophecies of Measure and Wealthful Felicity begin to sound uninvitingly dutiful: "Hem, Sir, yet beware of 'Had I wist!'" (ll. 211, 1395). Skelton combats such misplaced sympathies, however, by the conventions of the morality play. Tudor audiences expected virtuous spokesmen to be abstract and given to long sententious speeches. Skelton dared to make his villains more dramatically appealing, as Milton later did, because he was sure of his audience. Evil had to be outwardly attractive if one were to understand its fascination. Truth could not hope to be as exciting, nor did it have to be. Skelton knew he could capitalize on a stock Christian response to justify the apparent dullness of his virtuous characters representing the party of fiscal moderation. He chose the morality form because its guidance of moral response is unambiguous and polemical.

The character traits of the fiscal moderates are thus entirely conventional. Personal resemblances to Tudor Englishmen are extremely unlikely. Nor are there covert allusions to such events as Tournay and Therouenne, Henry's costly and inconsequential engagements in the French campaign of 1513. Skelton's popular audiences need have gone no further, in fact, than to suppose that King Henry needed the fiscal guidance of sane men. Personalities aside, however, there was a polarization of attitudes at court reflecting that of Skelton's play. Archbishop Warham and Bishop Fox resigned from the Privy Council in 1516, evidently wringing their hands at the cumulative follies of the French expeditions, the French marriage of 1514, and then the double reversal of policy prompting Henry and Wolsey to pay for Swiss mercenaries in the fight against Francis' successful Italian campaign in 1516. It was a year of crisis for Wolsey. The Emperor Maximilian deserted his English allies near Milan, the French king triumphed at Marignano, and at the treaty of Noyon (August 1516) the English were excluded. Henry's cost had been ruinous, his benefits worse than nonexistent. Far from containing or defeating French territorial ambitions, the English found themselves outnumbered by a new continental alliance. Yet in the battle of policy in the Privy Council, Wolsey prevailed. Already cardinal in 1515, he now became chancellor of England. His policy of costly involvement in continental politics, alternatively pro- and anti-French, continued to monopolize Henry's energies.

According to R. L. Ramsay's detailed analysis, the Duke of Norfolk is the leader whose policy most closely approximates that of Wealthful Felicity and Measure.[13] Such a suggestion of particular correspondence is misleading. Recent evidence reveals that Norfolk was able to work with the cardinal in 1515 and even as late as 1519, that he was not frugally inclined and may even have abetted Henry's excessive liberality, that his discomfiture in 1511-1512 was temporary and not the result of his strictures on finance, and that with Wolsey he took an active role in the Milan war effort and other international intrigues.[14] Although Skelton did look to the house of Howard for patronage in his *Garland of Laurel* (1523) and the earlier "Peregrinacioun of Mannes Life," [15] his attachment cannot be proven in 1515-1518.

If we concede that Skelton was not interested in personal resemblances in his *speculum* play, however, we can still see in Norfolk the type of older family who anathematized Wolsey and all upstart administrators. The Howard family had been shabbily treated by Henry VII, attainted for treason because they had fought for the reigning king, Richard, at Bosworth Field.[16] Henry VIII tardily returned the dukedom of Norfolk only after Thomas Howard's glorious victory at Flodden Field. Such rebuffs were no doubt galling to a family accustomed to highest public responsibility and baronial prestige. Rivalry with Wolsey was in evidence in 1512, when Howard was temporarily discountenanced by the king. "Wolsey thinks it will be a good thing if he were ousted from his lodging there [at court] altogether." [17] When Wolsey obtained his cardinal's hat in 1515, according to a contemporary report, "The hat was then placed in state on a table, with tapers around it, before an empty suit, and the greatest duke in the land was compelled to make a curtsy to it." [18] After Howard's death in 1524 his son Thomas (third Duke of Norfolk) took up the crusade, first against Wolsey and then against Thomas Cromwell. Whatever their temporary accommodations, Norfolk and Wolsey were at enmity when *Magnificence* was written. The necessary and distasteful compromises that prevented the Howards from breaking openly with the man they so hated may have suggested the alternative of underhanded attack by way of Skelton's invective, allowing the poet to take the risk.[19] As lord treasurer, Norfolk was naturally the aristocrat to whom alarmed traditionalists looked for guidance. *Magnificence* is, appropriately, intended for a nobleman's troupe, to be acted at home and on tour. One of the five actors is a professional fool.[20] Doubtless Henry did not submit himself to the crotchets of his old tutor; he seldom received professional entertainers at court not attached to his own household.[21] Lacking royal performance, *Magnificence* was probably sponsored by some conservative of Norfolk's persuasion, if not by the duke himself, as part of a campaign against Wolsey's fiscal and foreign program.

Skelton's attack on the "new men" at court deals in satirical types contrasted point by point with the virtuous and traditional moderates. Counterfeit Countenance, Crafty Conveyance, Cloaked Collusion, and the others, who insinuate themselves into the king's favor, are clearly not historical individuals but composite figures with certain features in common. All are dissemblers, intent on exploiting the new regime for personal gain. Virtually all are sycophants of lowly origin, making a rapid fortune, intoxicated with suddenly acquired power, and fond of lavish costumes. They resemble the worldly churchmen of *Wisdom,* and, except for their humble birth, are much like the debased aristocratic types in Medwall's satires. This paradoxical resemblance between political opposites is an indication of the extraordinary adaptability of conventional types: they can be polemically applied to either side. Courtly Abusion, for example, is a quarrelsome duelist, a sprightly dancer, and a dandy of the "new gyse" with elaborate slippers, bushy hair, and copious sleeves —all in all, a "mete man" for the court (l. 764). His extravagance in costuming is sinful not so much because it is vain but because of the cost, as with Medwall's Pride. Crafty Conveyance operates by influence peddling and petty bribery, like the figures of vice in *Nature* or *Wisdom.* Courtly Abusion is "A carlys sonne, Brought up of nought" (ll. 898-899). Crafty Conveyance has likewise risen to become both courtier and "clark" (i.e., churchman), and ruler of the king's treasury (l. 632). In their obscure past, some of the villains have been butchers or carters: "A knokylbonyarde will counterfet a clarke," and "A carter a courtier" who "with his whip his mares was wont to yarke" (ll. 480-484). These details sound biographical, and indeed were often charged against Wolsey (in Skelton's own later poems, and elsewhere); but they were conveniently available in Barclay's *Ship of Fools,* which scoffs at making "a bailiff of a butchers son." [22] The very device of choosing six villains to represent the new man at court argues composite portraiture. The only manner in which Wolsey fits the description is as dominant practitioner, in 1516, of an old game. Nevertheless this applicability was, for Skelton's more understanding auditors, an inescapable one. Skelton created an illustration of lowborn presumption and allowed his auditors to draw the necessary conclusion.

Ultimately, however, the most daring topical meaning in *Magnificence* is not foreshadowing of the later Wolsey satires but implied criticism of Henry VIII. This implication is to be found, once again, not in personal resemblances but in unavoidable similarity to the political situation of 1516. No matter how much Skelton exculpates his protagonist by concentrating on evil tempters, or portrays Magnificence as originally well-intended, the playwright must ultimately reveal in Magnificence a tyrannical loss of control. Granted the trait is commonplace in a depiction of tyranny, it nevertheless corresponded with the royal crisis uppermost in the mind of any Tudor spectator. Magnificence's great weakness is sensitivity to any suggestion of "pusillanimite." He must live up to the role of king, and so is persuaded that "measure" is too niggardly. He is prone to a "largesse" that is really prodigality. In his later actions he appears so changed in character that he is barely recognizable. He has lost every trace of tolerance, wisdom, patience in argument, willingness to listen. He cuts off the moderates with a curt "Tush! hold your peas; ye speke like a daw" (l. 1379). He flaunts his willfulness and is a shameless boaster. He is vain of his dress, hot-tempered, lascivious. No longer a mere dupe of the sycophants, he appears to enjoy the cruel sport of broken promises and corruption at court. He becomes an active participant in villainy, genuinely choleric and mean, aware all the while of what he is doing. He is especially vicious in his handling of foreign policy and in his abuse of trusted old courtiers.

Magnificence's strutting soliloquy, delivered at the height of his power (ll. 1457-1514), parodies the bellicose rant of a warmongering king. Magnificence is not content with the adulation of his subjects. He must be "prince perlesse" even in the roster of such great warriors as Alexander, Hercules, and Charlemagne. He dresses more richly than Julius Caesar, and fears no man. Here too, of course, the *speculum* tradition offered Skelton his models. Yet who in Skelton's audience was unaware of Henry VIII's desire to be another Henry V? Behind Magnificence's bluster lies a thinly veiled threat to the princes of sixteenth-century Europe:

> It wolde not become them with me for to mell;
> For of all barones bold I bere the bell;
> Of all doughty I am doughtiest duke as I deme;
> To me all princes to lowte man beseme.
>
> . . . .
>
> Nor no man on molde, can make me aferd.
> What man is so maisyd with me that dare mete,
> I shall flappe him as a fole to fall at my fete.   (ll. 1497-1507)

As in the instance of the upstart churchman and Wolsey, Skelton here permits the auditor of 1516 to measure Henry by the generic portrait of a tyrant. Unmentioned specifically are the frantic rivalry with Francis of France leading to the extravagant Field of Cloth of Gold in 1520, the support of mercenary soldiers, the bewildering succession of alliances, the preposterous attempt to bribe the electors for the golden prize of the Holy Roman Empire. Thomas More, too, in 1516, wondered aloud in his *Utopia* about "some king" and the folly of meddling in the affairs of other nations rather than governing peaceably at home. That such strictures applied to Francis I as well as to Henry did not lessen the topical urgency of England's own crisis. Skelton's satire reaches dangerous extremes, portraying Magnificence as a ridiculous bully. Characterization gives way to caricature. The calm, rational tone of the play's beginning yields to a frenzy of attack.

A meddling bully in foreign affairs, Magnificence is no less callow with the representatives of the noble families. The scene in which Magnificence plays a practical joke on Measure (ll. 1629-1725) hints at sadism and a genuine loss of emotional control. Coached in the art of double dealing by Courtly Abusion and Cloaked Collusion, the king learns how to rid himself of an unwelcome petitioner. The trick is to invent some displeasure and burst into a fit of rage:

> Then some occacyon or quarell ye must find,
> And frown it and face it, as though ye wolde fight;
> Frete yourself for anger and for dispyte,
> . . . .
> Then feyne yourself diseased, and make yourself seke.
> To stir up your stomake you must you forge,
> Call for a candell and cast up your gorge,
> With "Cockes armes! rest shall I none have
> Till I be revenged on that horson knave.
> A, how my stomake wambleth! I am all in a swete.
> Is there no horson that knave that will bete?"   (ll. 1600-1618)

The king is delighted with such schooling because, as he confesses, it accords with his own choleric disposition. He succeeds all too well in practicing this device on Measure. His anger, feigned at first, becomes real, and he is unable to quiet his beating temples after the hapless

Measure has retreated in confusion. Only the thought of more "polling and plucking" of royal subjects can temporarily appease his insatiable anger and greed. This grim spectacle must have seemed bitterly appropriate to the old families. It may represent no specific occasion, but it does indicate the humiliating position of the nobles, forced to deal through Wolsey in their attempts to reach the king.[23]

The lengthy conclusion of *Magnificence* returns to a more universal allegory of fall from prosperity, penance, and eventual restitution. The pattern is clearly idealized rather than historical. Obviously Henry suffered no such extremes of privation as Magnificence does, learning "to begge at every mannes gate," exchanging his pomp and finery for a bed of straw, unclean linen, and Job-like afflictions of disease (ll. 1981, 2005-2020). Though Magnificence's decline on Fortune's wheel appears to contradict the idea of causality in his misfortunes, the ending is notwithstanding integral to the play's *speculum* intent. As William Harris has shown, Skelton insists that an ideal king must be able to withstand prosperity as well as adversity in a world alternately governed by these extremes.[24] Fortune "dawnsyth variance with mutabilite, Now all in Wealth, forthwith in Poverte" (ll. 2026-2027). Earthly felicity is always unsure, but the truly temperate man can be tempted neither to worldliness by good fortune nor to despair by evil fortune. Idealized as it is, the ending still reflects Skelton's political faith. A king like Henry must beware of temptations inherent in his own extraordinary power and wealth. If he should fail, no human agency will undertake to correct abuses. All may be righted if the king can only admit his folly and recover the use of his innate wisdom, with God's help throwing off his sycophants and listening to conservative advice. Although Skelton's belief in a second chance for the king seems like wishful thinking, it is certainly genuine and loyal.

5 · HEYWOOD'S COMIC PLEADING

FOR RECONCILIATION

As the tone of More's *Utopia* suggests, in 1516 the liberal humanists shared Skelton's alarm at the imperialist aims of Henry VIII. Indeed, the humanists of the More circle found themselves increasingly in a cruel dilemma. Moderate reformers at heart, outspoken in their analysis of church abuses and of social problems like enclosure, they had little sympathy for baronial feudalism. Yet Henry and his new men demanded impossible loyalties. Henry's fondness for and reliance on More as his chancellor led inescapably to martyrdom. Wolsey too looked for encomiasts rather than critics. With the Reformation, new rulers such as Cromwell and Cranmer were constrained to break the Catholic humanists and to foster a new crop of more tractable apologists.

One writer of the More group dared to speak of political matters before his royal master, but did it self-mockingly in the guise of an allowed fool whose jibes may be attributed to childish folly. John Heywood was a professional entertainer who instinctively avoided giving unnecessary offense. Yet he was courageous enough to take his stand; according to John Harington, he escaped hanging for his involvement in the 1544 plot against Cranmer only by his mirth.[1] Greater than that of any other humanist was his wish to bring disaffected factions together at court by resolving their differences in sane laughter. His lightheartedness was not a frivolous dismissal of the humanists' most serious problems, but an attempt to cajole through comic distance and self-effacement. *The Play of the Weather*, written possibly as late as 1527 or 1528 when the More group was at the verge of its crisis, was a generous if futile attempt to soothe tempers before irreversible damage had been done.

The ploy of zany comedy in *Weather* is protective coloration, possibly deceptive to the modern reader. The first impression is of a *jeu d'esprit* on a trivial subject, revealing the playwright's skill in mere ingeniousness of debate and of farfetched comic situations. A. W. Pollard asserts that *Weather's* only moral is "the mess which men would make of rain, wind, and sunshine if they had the ruling of them." [2] H. N. Hillebrand states flatly that *Weather* is "not concerned with religious satire or contemporary life." [3] Kenneth Cameron is right, however, in theorizing that Heywood's intent is essentially political, and that the figure of Jupiter as peacemaker and judge among factions is an extended analogy to Henry VIII in his function as governor of the realm. Heywood flatteringly describes a method of political rule that he hopes Henry will continue to follow.[4]

Like *Fulgens and Lucrece*, *Weather* is an interlude to enliven a patrician evening banquet. It was seemingly performed by the Chapel children, and was consciously aimed at the rulers of England.[5] Viewed in such noble surroundings, the play reveals a pattern of dramatic irony that would otherwise escape attention. In the opening scene, for example, we find an actor, probably a boy, posing as the monarch of the universe —in the presence of the royalty and nobility of England. The prevailing tone of Jupiter's speech is one of allowed license, of mock elevation and usurpation, something akin to the saturnalian rule of the Boy-Bishop.[6] Jupiter is ruler for this night, and he does not hesitate to demand obeisance from everyone in the audience including the king (ll. 19-20). At his first exit, Jupiter retires with regal superciliousness worthy of an impudent boy king:

> And now, according to your obediens,
> Rejoice ye in us with joy most joyfully,
> And we ourself shall joy in our own glory!   (ll. 183-185)

His account of the war in heaven among Saturn, Phebus, Eolus, and Phebe is exaggerated into heroic bombast. The whole concept of the deux ex machina, of men's fate as ruled by the Olympian gods, of the microcosm and macrocosm, is designed to the scale of a classical epic. In the context of this ostensibly "trivial" entertainment, however, the heroic becomes mock-heroic. Jupiter's warnings of dire happenings on earth suddenly collapse into the banality of what appears to be a debate on the weather.

Heywood's elite audience would perceive at once this gentle parody of kingship in a familiar tradition of court entertainment. The satire, achieved by juxtaposing high seriousness and triviality, is directed against discord. The device of *reductio ad absurdum* recalls a similar bickering "parliament" in Chaucer's *Parlement of Fowles*. Heywood's mocking, disinterested observer Merry Report also resembles Medwall's comically deflating servants "A" and "B" in *Fulgens and Lucrece*.

As the embodiment of comic indifference, Merry Report is central to Heywood's viewpoint. Although called "the Vice," he is closer to an allowed fool, the forerunner of the Fool in *King Lear*. He is the jester of the king's retinue who may scoff at everything because his impudence is unpremeditated. Beneath his raillery and abusive obscenity shine perceptions of natural wisdom. He parodies everything at hand, and even apes his master Jupiter by scurrilously demanding obedience from his noble audience:

> Why, ye dronken horesons, will it not be?
> By your faith, have ye nother cap nor kne?
> Not one of you that will make curtsy
> To me, that am squire for goddes precious body?
> Regard ye nothing mine authorite?   (ll. 188-192)

He is openly critical of the Gentleman's life of sensual ease and implicates the women of the audience in his endless jests upon cuckold's horns and apothecary's glisters. The audience must accept the satire of courtly life without offense because it is offered zanily and without venom. Laughter sweetens the mock but it does not invalidate the picture of court life as giddy and vapid. The device enables Heywood to speak plainly and morally without sounding pontifical. The satire of the lower classes is no less cheerful and to the point, an indication of Merry Report's evenhanded justice.

He is far wiser than the individual petitioners, for he can tell from the start how their differences will be reconciled—as, indeed, any fool could tell. Totally unmoved by their quarrels, he can only chortle to see them competing uselessly with one another. His witty commentary is the perfect foil for Jupiter's wise judgments. As the moving spirit of the play Merry Report represents not discord but amity; his function is not to destroy or to shame, but to reconcile through laughter. The point of view is that of the simpleminded observer, used so effectively by Heywood's beloved Chaucer. The audience, recognizing in Merry Report the type of allowed fool, would appreciate the dramatic irony of a simpleton's wisely exposing the insanity of supposedly sane men. He is mad, but they are "more than mad." The spectators, who are indicted as well, are asked to examine their own ambitions and to laugh at the folly shown them by a fool.

The discord Merry Report satirizes arises from the political self-inter-estedness of the various estates making up Tudor society. Just as individual men desire particular kinds of weather for their narrowly-defined purposes, and accordingly must be forced to accept a mixed climate decreed impartially by the gods to satisfy all conditions of men, so must political factions concede the wisdom of a central power in ordaining that no one segment of society may dictate for the whole. This political reading of Heywood's light fable is plainly indicated in the text. As in earlier political dramas such as *Fulgens and Lucrece* and *Magnificence*, the various suitors represent a cross-section of English society: the knight, the merchant, the overseer of a forest, the small mill-owner, the lady, the washerwoman. It is indeed a "parlement," as Jupiter calls it; and if the representation is more democratic than one would expect of Tudor parliaments, the decorum of rank is still punctiliously preserved. Jupiter enjoins Merry Report:

> Here to receive all sewters of eche degre;
> And such as to thee may seme most metely,
> We will thow bring them before our majeste,
> And for the rest, that be not so worthy,
> Make thou report to us effectually,
> So that we may hear each maner sewte at large.   (ll. 168-173)

Merry Report carries out the order with precise and meaningful distinctions. The Gentleman is unhesitatingly granted audience with Jupiter. So is the Merchant. The Ranger's request for audience is refused, but his exchanges with Merry Report are at least respectful. The millers do not even get so far as to request audience. And so it goes. These distinctions have dramaturgic value, for they vary the staging of a potentially repetitive series of appearances.[7] Their chief function, however, is to observe precedence in a debate before royal authority. All estates may have equal claim to royal attention, but few are privileged to approach the throne directly.

Heywood does not, like Skelton and Medwall, choose sides between titled aristocrat and self-made new man. Instead, Merry Report ridicules the pretentions of both to disproportionate worth. Although the Gentleman is accorded first audience with Jupiter by virtue of his rank, the arguments of special privilege for those who govern are shown to be biased pleading. Heywood does not, on the other hand, categorically deny all luxuries of inheritance. Merry Report's device is satirical, probing. The nobility shall get what they deserve in relation to the other equally essential ranks of society. Similarly the Merchant is shown to be myopic in his view of economic self-interest. However logical his arguments for the speculative investment and adequate return for investors without which the English economy will achieve no "comen encres," however appealing to humanist writers his credo of profitable industry rather than indolent luxury, the Merchant is mercilessly exposed to deflating mockery. His manner is egregiously pompous: he engages in no badinage with the audience, and deplores digression of any sort. He cuts short Merry Report's impudent small talk peremptorily: "But let pas, Sir, I wolde to you be sewter To bring me, if ye can, before Jupiter" (ll. 333-334). It is a plain, blunt proposition. The Merchant is alone among the suitors in supposing that Merry Report will wish to be requited for his part in the deal. Merry Report is comically outraged to be taken for a bribable courtier. The dramatic device of the fool places the Merchant in a satirical perspective.

Even though the debate focuses at first on the rivalry of aristocrats and new moneyed classes, other groups are indispensable as well. No major group should be either pampered or slighted, not even petty bureaucrats like the Ranger, the type of shiftless hack who is fit only for carrying out routine administration and so grumbles at a system he cannot escape. No government can afford to ignore the restive demands of its minor officialdom. Nor can it overlook the problem of small entrepreneurs like the mill-owners, who most graphically illustrate the inherent conflict between closely rivaled factions. In their fratricidal and unreasoning desire to deprive each other and to overwhelm themselves with needless excess, Heywood documents his belief that the motivating force of ungoverned society is self-destruction.

The débat between the Gentlewoman and the Launder has no direct bearing on the men's world of economic rivalry. Yet their moral conflict is of parallel significance. The Gentlewoman speaks in the name of "all other that beuty have," whereas the Launder represents all those who "daily toil and labour" for the well-to-do. The debate quickly centers on the topic of idleness, a favorite concern of humanist writers in such works as *Utopia* and the play *Calisto and Melibea*.[8] Which way of life is more defensible, the parasitic frivolity of the court or the productive labor of the servant class? This polarity has affinities to favorite medieval debating topics, as in the *Owl and the Nightingale*: youth versus age, physical versus spiritual beauty, sensuality versus moral wisdom, body versus soul. As thus defined, the debate would seem to favor the Launder's position that true gentleness resides in the soul and not in the superficial accident of noble birth or beauty—a truism expounded in other humanist plays, including Heywood's. Yet the viewpoint in *Weather*, as seen in the attitudes of Jupiter and Merry Report, does not express a preference. The ideal seems to be a golden mean. Fleshly and spiritual beauty seem at odds, but in the truly temperate life they act in harmony. Just as the body politic reconciles warring factions in a mutually profitable union, the individual life blends many diverse impulses into one ordered whole. Joy and seriousness, amusement and instruction are most effective in combination, as in a farcical yet thoughtful play. In both political and ethical life, Heywood sees balancing of opposites as the definition of wisdom.

Heywood's ultimate view of political life, then, is that the parts of society can never understand the whole. Only the king can act as umpire between elements seeking continually to destroy one another. To do so he must have knowledge of the claims of each estate, and so listens to partial arguments without accepting the advice of any one counselor. The best course for every subject is to accept this overruling wisdom with gratitude and to wait his turn patiently for such favors as he deserves. The petitioners of the play do so with sincerity, pledging their fealty to the throne in a ceremony that includes the audience as well. The ending reflects a humanist rationale for Tudor absolutism as the only viable defense against feudal autonomy or other forms of divisiveness in political life. Moreover, in the taut context of 1527-1528, this genial resolution must be read as an explicit answer to pleaders for various factions. Heywood deplores heated argument, and warns through laughter against an immediately impending disaster. The implications for Henry are not merely flattering. Courtly life must eschew its tendency toward idleness just as the lower classes must beware of ambition. Most of all, the king must realize the folly of playing off one faction against another.

Not only does this topical interpretation define Heywood's political stance, it also reveals the artistry of his dramatic method. It shows, first, his approach to metaphor. *Weather* lacks the pictorial metaphors and conceits that enrich later Renaissance drama. Instead, Heywood borrows the device of extended metaphor from contemporary religious drama. The structure of his entire play is a single metaphor: just as each individual selfishly hopes for one kind of weather to suit his peculiar needs, so in society each estate seeks its private welfare to the exclusion of others. The interplay of meanings is the chief source of dramatic irony; for, as the audience perceives, the debate is at once trivial and significant.

Most of all, the topical nature of *Weather* shows its basic literary genre to be the mock-heroic. This grand debate, commencing as a war in heaven and encompassing the fate of humanity, ends as much ado about nothing. Merry Report gleefully announces the ultimate anticlimax:

Lo, how this is brought to pas!
Sirs, now shall ye have the wether even as it was.   (ll. 1239-1240)

This is the well-deserved *reductio ad absurdum* of all political, social, and even ethical conflict. The solution of tolerant acceptance and harmony is so simple that it requires a fool to point it out.

The irreverent gaiety of Heywood's *Four PP* (ca. 1520-1522) has similarly led to critical overemphasis on farce at the expense of serious purpose. Emile Legouis comments, for example, that Heywood "was original in avoiding morality-plays and in having no purpose but to amuse. He has no notion of ecclesiastical or theological controversy." [9] To C. W.

Wallace, popular farces like *Four PP* do not even belong in the Heywoodian canon because they "have no didactic purpose." [10] The bawdy stories and seemingly unintegrated slapstick are of course entertaining. Nevertheless, Heywood's social philosophy not only is topical but gives thematic unity to the apparently digressive material. As in *Weather*, Heywood insists that discordant competition is a grave threat to social harmony. The conflicts in *Four PP* are religious and domestic rather than those of class struggles, for Heywood's audience in this earlier play is not courtly. He speaks to ordinary Englishmen about a religious debate that was to become Henry VIII's most abiding political problem.

Although Palmer, Pardoner, and Pothecary are con-men and quacks, Heywood's dramatic spokesman maintains an attitude of comic detachment. Like Merry Report or Chaucer's genial *persona*, Heywood's Peddler views the three sham promoters of human welfare as amusing and to be tolerated (although their vices are not), a part somehow of the complex wonder of divine civilization. Out of their antagonisms comes harmony. The Peddler's function is to expose folly to laughter and to harmonize through appeal to tolerance of old forms. First and last, he distinguishes between corruptions in pilgrimage or pardoning and the essential Christian spirit of pilgrimage or pardoning.

Heywood is more doctrinaire than Chaucer in defending the idea of varying church practice. He had reason to be, in an age of more extremist reform. By 1520 Luther had published his famous theses, and Henry was fervently at work on his orthodox *Defense of the Seven Sacraments*. Heywood's farce is in harmony with the king's position as "defender of the Faith." [11] *Four PP*, for all its seeming anticlericalism, upholds not only true palmers and pardoners but almsgivers, friars, rich patrons of chantries, and charitable builders of public highways. All such activities are potentially equally valid ways to salvation.

> And so for all that do pretend
> By aid of Goddes grace to ensewe
> Any maner kind of vertue:
> As, some great almys for to give,
> Some in willfull povertie to live,
> Some to make hye-wayes and such other warkes,
> And some to maintain prestes and clarkes
> To sing and pray for soul departed.   (ll. 1158-1165)

The cause of error is not Catholic multiplicity of jurisdiction but individual impurity of heart. The Palmer who undertakes his pilgrimage "for love of Christ" (l. 1145) spends his time well. One who makes a fetish of punishing his body in hope of spiritual reward does so vainly and selfishly. He is a charlatan and apt to be a liar. The Pardoner must provide his indulgences "Unto your neighbours charitably For love of them in God onely" (ll. 1151-1152). Pardons will be efficacious only for those who have "ones had contrission" (l. 400). Heywood emphasizes the spiritual intent combined with the ritual and institutional act. He urges tolerance for religious diversity, not of doctrine but of occupation. This idea is equivalent to that of tolerant diversity in the commonwealth. Both church and state, Heywood warns, can be torn asunder by fratricidal rivalry.

> One kind of vertue to dispise another
> Is like as the sister might hang the brother.　　(ll. 1187-1188)

Competition is inevitable but must be held in check. As in *Weather*, Heywood's literary device is to expose combativeness to ridicule by focusing it on absurd topics of debate.

The seemingly diverse contests of *Four PP* are united by a theme of "maistry," as in *Weather*. In comically overinflated terms, each debater claims a disproportionate role in human salvation. Is it more efficacious to flagellate one's way toward heaven with the Palmer or to buy one's way thence painlessly with the Pardoner's piece of paper? One might as well assert, as the Pothecary brazenly does, that medicine performs an equally vital role in sending men to heaven, since it kills the body. These boastings, as well as the contest in lying, treat facetiously a serious idea of hierarchy and leadership.

> Man can nat prosper wilfully ledde.
> All thing decayeth where is no hedde.　　(ll. 426-427)

The itinerant jester, as peacemaker and comic moralist, refers all such questions of rivalry to the church and its moral code. Even "maistry" in the relationships of men and women, the subject of much apparently extraneous, scatological antifeminism (ll. 234-280), reveals the existence of inherent conflict and the need both for hierarchical authority and tolerant diversity.

The appeal to the audience is to live and let live patiently in marriage, as in all aspects of life. In religion the advice is even more particular and is aimed at curbing, not exacerbating, anticlericalism. The audience, having been invited to laugh at these charlatans, is urged to check its laughter in other circumstances. When the abuse of honesty is obvious as in this play, "and all other that ye know fayned," satirical laughter is in order.

> But where ye dout the truth, nat knowing,
> Beleving the best, good may be growing.
> In judging the best, no harm at the lest,
> In judging the worst, no good at the best. (ll. 1209-1212)

The ordinary Englishman, understandably alarmed by the selling of pardons and fraudulent pilgrimages, as well as by activities of friar, monk, and chantry priest, is asked not only to interpret always for the best, but to let the church administration weed out its own corruption. "But as the church doth judge or take them, So do ye receive or forsake them" (ll. 1215-1216). The alternatives of acceptance or rejection imply Heywood's sure faith that the church will reform itself before it is too late. As the closing prayer for the "church universal" indicates, Heywood's *Four PP* is a plea for the conservative reform of the Catholic humanists, and a defense of the ideal church as the arbitrator of social disunion—a function that the church shares in dignity and peace with the Tudor state. *Four PP* thus accounts for the estate of the clergy, which is missing from the spectrum of *Weather*.

Heywood does not always deal so earnestly in homiletic affirmatives. *John John* (1520-1523), if indeed it is Heywood's, employs standard anticlerical humor in the fabliau vein, without the mitigation of a moral viewpoint. The fight of cuckold and priest at the end is a standoff, signifying the total amorality of the jest. *The Pardoner and the Friar* (1513-1521) does end in virtuous triumph for parish curate and good Neighbor Pratt, signifying the positive religious ideals from which the Pardoner and the Friar so manifestly digress; but Heywood plays up feelings of religious nationalism, as did other writers like Erasmus in the days before the church seemed threatened. This play does not yet evince Heywood's fear of the impending Reformation.

The Play of Love (ca. 1520-1533), on the other hand, while nonpolitical in subject, reflects the pervasive Heywoodian metaphor of amity. *Love* uses the device familiar in *Weather* and *Four PP* of ingenious debate about nothing, of heated rivalry needing "some man indifferent" (A4ᵛ) as arbitrator, ultimately proving the perfect balance of conflicting claims. To be hopelessly in love is to suffer intense pain and pleasure; to be free of emotional commitment is to know peace of mind. There is a balance in the nature of things by which all men achieve equal satisfaction. "Affeccion unbridled" may cause us to think ourselves wronged, but reason assures us that ultimately there is no partiality. All four debaters concede finally that "mine estate right wel contenteth me" (E3ᵛ). As it is with them, so with society at large, of which they are a microcosm.

> Thus, not we four, but al the world beside
> Knowledge themself or other in joy or pain,
> Hath nede of contentacion for a gyde.
>
> · · · · · · · · · · · ·
>
> Be we content, wealth or woe.   (E3ᵛ)

Heywood's basic optimism and desire for reconciliation enabled him to hope for the best in Henry VIII's administration. Men like John Rastell were not so sure of that hope.

Among themselves, the humanists of More's circle were given to speculating about England's social and political ills in terms of radical alternatives: election of rulers, elimination of inheritance, common ownership of property. Such ideas were of course not new. Jean de Meun's *Roman de la Rose* was a favorite source of iconoclastic diatribes against entrenched privilege. Medieval sermons could be bluntly satirical. Boccaccio, Vincent de Beauvais, Chaucer, and John Herolt spoke of gentilesse as superior to noble rank.[1] The humanists were careful not to offer such familiar radical notions as a blueprint for popular insurrection: More wrote *Utopia* in Latin as a semiprivate and fanciful dialogue among learned men. Its implicit criticisms of England were nonetheless serious and generally agreed upon by both conservative and radical partners to the debate.[2] Utopian answers were necessarily visionary, but the questions remained in force. Erasmus rebuked idleness of the aristocracy and disputed the rationale of their preeminence over shoemakers and plowmen.[3] Colet and Vives were frequently drawn into discussions of common ownership, based on practices of the early church.[4] Reginald Pole, in his dialogue with Lupset (ca. 1534), argued the theoretical advantages of the election of rulers and church officials, and the elimination of primogeniture, although conceding the impracticality of such reforms for the current state of England. In 1549 and afterwards, radical social agitation was inevitably associated with the preaching of Robert Crowley, Thomas Lever, and members of the "Commonwealth party"; many of these reformers were obliged to disclaim the practical consequences of their Christian idealism.[5] However commonplace in medieval satire, such criticisms were of profound immediacy to the More group in the 1520's.

A particularly zealous student of reform was Heywood's son-in-law, John Rastell. Lawyer and publisher, interested in education and social betterment, he crusaded for a better informed populace. In his *Abridgement of the Statutes* he condensed and simplified English law so that "the people might sone without gret difficulte have the knowlege of the same lawes." [6] He grew up in the restive and mercantile atmosphere of Coventry, and may have entertained heretical religious views as early as 1507. Ultimately he broke with the More group on the religious question and became an anti-papist publisher for Cromwell. Overly idealistic and tactless even for the Reformation administration, Rastell ended his life destitute and in confinement.[7] While Catholic humanists recoiled at the break with Rome and so turned their energies to fighting heresy, Rastell anticipated a new generation of Protestant humanists who, in their rationalizing of new policies and leaders, "forged a link between the social thinking of the middle ages and the seventeenth century." [8]

Of Gentleness and Nobility (ca. 1523-1529) seems to reflect Rastell's blunt sincerity. He published the play, stating in the colophon that *"John Rastell me fieri fecit."* Whether this much-debated phrase means that Rastell caused the play to be printed, or to be composed by another, or to be performed on his Finsbury stage or elsewhere, can scarcely be resolved by the language itself.[9] Heywood, whose name does not appear in the text, is chief contender for authorship. Technical and thematic affinities to plays like *Weather, Witty and Witless,* and *Love* are numerous: the emphasis on Socratic logic, the paucity of stage movement, the balancing of *ad hominem* arguments, the themes of true gentleness and of economic rivalry among the various estates. Yet these techniques and themes are humanist trademarks, not exclusively Heywoodian. Joint authorship is by no means out of the question. Rastell collaborated with the More group on translations.[10] Even so, can a characteristically Rastellian program be discerned in this and other plays attributed to him? The question depends on handling of dramatic viewpoint and of tone. *Gentleness* seems more downright and preachy than Heywood's known plays. It touches upon more radical issues, even if it declines finally to endorse them.

Crucial to an understanding of viewpoint is the role of the Ploughman. If his radicalism has authorial blessing, the play too is radical. Such a view is attractive to modern democratic sentiment, but is critically dangerous. A debate can be onesided, as in More's later rejoinders to Tyndale—a calculated imbalance prompted by More's reaction to heresy. More's *Utopia,* however, and the Heywoodian norm, suggest the benefits of multiple viewpoint in debate. Kenneth Cameron has argued, accordingly, that the Ploughman's boastful assertions of self-sufficiency resemble inordinate claims of social usefulness by the Knight and the Merchant, that the Ploughman's boorishness and penurious living imply the author's condescension, and that the very humor of the play is the deflation of class quarreling in each estate.[11] Such a reading would bring the play close indeed to Heywood's amicable vision.

In *Weather,* however, boasts of social indispensability from each suitor are offset by the iconoclasms of a witty, independent spokesman and are arbitrated by impartial authority. In *Gentleness* the comic voice is that of the Ploughman, who is hardly disinterested. His abuse of the Knight raises problems of moral allegiance in the spectators, not objective satiric deflation. Though it is funny to see a peasant strike a nobleman and call him abusive names, the laughter has parricidal overtones. Landuser turns on landowner, responding violently to the oldest of economic rivalries. The author provides no referee to jibe at the Ploughman's presumption. The Knight and the Merchant of course protest, but they are merely arguing for their own privileges.

Another vital departure from the Heywoodian norm is the absence of lighthearted fable. This play does not purport to discuss a frivolous matter like weather or the role of apothecaries in salvation. The topic is "A dialoge . . . who is a verey gentilman and who is a noble man, and how men shuld come to auctorite," making no nonsensical attempt at allegory. Confrontations are embarrassingly direct. Two open quarrels end in physical abuse. The contestants battle it out, agree in part to disagree, and are driven at last to submitting separate opinions to the audience. The result is not *reductio ad absurdum,* but a cogent debate on the issues.

The debate is, moreover, not threesided as it might seem at first. The Knight and the Merchant soon join forces against peasant daring. This realignment pits lower-class poverty against all upper-class privilege, and inevitably raises questions of a revolutionary nature. It is this dichotomy between old guard and radical that gives such preponderance to the Ploughman's social philosophy. Admirable or not, his is the new creed that must be answered.

The Knight and the Merchant naturally have their differences. The Merchant, explicitly nouveau riche, resents the fact that his artisan forbears were exploited by the nobility (ll. 50-64), and is now in a position to challenge the Knight for control of the Establishment. "I am able to bye now all the land That thou hast, and pay for it owt of hand," he boasts (ll. 25-26). Early Tudor statutes limited the amount of land merchants could buy, because the demand was great enough to arouse patrician resentment. Yet to the Ploughman, this new man is but old aristocrat writ large. The Merchant naturally endorses inheritance now that he is rich. Indeed he aptly illustrates the tendency of aspiring Tudor commoners to become absorbed entirely into the landed aristocracy, adopting its values while leaving behind all bourgeois identity, converting capital into land at a considerable sacrifice of profit in order to buy prestige. Both the Merchant and the Knight attempt to justify themselves by what they were, not what they are (ll. 217-226). Accordingly, the focus of *Gentleness* is not on the rival claims of these two factions, but on lower-class complaints about the entire power structure. The Ploughman is always on the offensive, raising questions that cannot always be answered. He becomes the gadfly, like Hythloday in *Utopia.* Because he prescribes the substance of the debate, he is protagonist even if he is not authorial spokesman. In this sense he seems to be "having the best of it." [12] The very fact that he wins an equal hearing constitutes in itself a kind of victory.

The Ploughman's character is like that of Hythloday. No simple farmer, he is well read in the lessons of history and able to quote Latin to the purpose. He is a believer in "naturall reason" and a foe of scholasticism ("these fond clarkes that go to scole"), a crusader for education and for the equality of teachers with churchmen and government officials in the power structure of society (ll. 795, 839-855). He is at times more humanist intellectual than peasant, and his special interest in "new learning" corresponds with John Rastell's *idée fixe* in the *Play of the Four Elements*. This distortion of dramatic character for ideological effect, at the expense of credibility, is again more characteristic of Rastell's drama of ideas than of Heywood's professional entertainment. The Ploughman represents a fusion of the exploited agrarian worker and the idealistic intellectual.

As a type, the Ploughman is not without flaws. His fellow rustics are proverbially lazy, prone to petty theft, lax in attending divine service, and lecherous (ll. 692, 934). Compelled by lack of wealth to live simply, the Ploughman deserves little credit for his plainness. Nevertheless, his contentment is self-conscious. Though he has no choice, he still extols the advantages of virtuous poverty. Peasant crimes are petty; gentlemen "Use mych more vice and iniquite" (l. 700). If one takes seriously the goal of chastening worldly vanity, the Ploughman is willy-nilly closer to that goal and the rich man spiritually imperiled by what is at best a social necessity. No one accuses the Ploughman of disobedience to authority, and he forswears political agitation. He typifies his class, however exaggeratedly, as content with self-sufficiency and wanting only to be left alone to enjoy the modest benefits of healthy labor. By contrast, rich men of new families and old are obsessed with pride of raiment at excessive cost, indolence, and *droit du seigneur*. Their depravity must bring the whole issue of hierarchy into serious question. "How men shuld come to auctorite" is here a more radical topic than that of defining true gentleness because it examines systems alternative to monarchy.

In his analysis of the origins of hierarchy, the author of *Gentleness* is plainly fascinated with theories anticipating social contract. No debater, not even the Knight, relies on analogies to hierarchy in the plant and animal kingdoms or in the heavenly host. The hidden assumptions throughout are rational. Society evolves in response to its own fears of disorder in the natural state. The Knight explains that hierarchy first arose from the need for laws to curb the "gret stryf and debate" among individuals coveting each others' property. "Then such as mine auncestours were that were wise Did studi to make laws how the people might

be Liffing togedyr in pease and unite" (ll. 590-592). In return for
this protection, the populace were content to pay their lords, first in
kind and later in cash.

The Ploughman accepts the postulate of an anarchic natural state,
but applies the assumption to his radical theory of history: exploitation
of the masses by those ruthless enough to seize power. "All possessions
began furst of tyranny." Those who at first took the ascendancy did so
not to prevent anarchy but to promote their own "idleness." They seized
"by violence" the property of others. In the second stage of this supposed civilizing process, the oppressed had to yield up part of their
production in return for a portion of land: "So possessions began by ex-
torcion." The third stage was codification of usurped ownership into the
perennial monopoly of inheritance.

> And when such extorsioners had oppressyd
> The labouring people, than they ordeinyd
> And made laws mervelous strait and hard,
> That their heir might injoy it afterward.
> So the law of inheritaunce was furst begon,
> Which is a thing agains all good reason.   (ll. 616-622)

Patterns of history yield present realities. The Knight and the Merchant demonstrate in their lives the heritage of grasping for power.
The Merchant desires not opportunity for all but economic monopoly
for himself; his pious protestations about "free" competition are mere
hypocrisies. Notoriously uncharitable toward the indigent, merchants are
as a class unfit for public office: "when any of them be Promotyd to rule
or auctorite, They disdain all lerning, law, and reason" (ll. 681-683).
Aristocrats are no better, rationalizing enclosure of land with the pre-
tence of profit for the commonwealth. "If any land like them that lieth
nye them Of their pore neghbors they will distroy them" (ll. 659-660).
As in *Utopia*, no one can question the fact or the evil of enclosure.

Because he pointedly neglects to exclude monarchy from this analysis
of exploitation, the Ploughman brings it into question as well. Monarchy
is not, as in *Weather*, an adjudicating force independent of the nobility;
in origin, it is the apex of extorted privilege. It is preeminently prone,
therefore, to the three basic evils of inheritance: monopoly of wealth,
incentive to idleness and vice, and restriction of the privilege of rule

to those who have no proven qualifications and who by the nature of their luxurious upbringing are overly inclined to willful insensitivity toward the poor. The Ploughman sees little likelihood that a spoiled child of a monarch, suddenly invested with undeserved power, can hope to resist flattery and temptation to self-indulgence.

> Oft times they shuld rule that have littill wit,
> Or disposyd to be proud and covetous,
> Or to life after their lustis voluptuous
>
> .   .   .   .
>
> Where justice shuld be, there wold be tyranny;
> Where peas shuld be, warr, debat, and envy.
>
> (ll. 819-825)

The familiar pattern of corrupted will leading to royal tyranny and the dangers of war echoes the humanists' deepest concern for their own generation.

For all its acrid intemperance, the debate finally reaches a degree of consensus. The Knight and the Merchant have orthodox answers against "election" of rulers: as a system it usually produces "Men of evill consciens that grete tyrauntes be" (l. 1043). The Ploughman, however, has already conceded this defect. Republicanism is governed by "drede, mede, and affeccion." The Ploughman maintains sympathy of viewpoint by freely allowing his inability and unwillingness to correct the wrong. Contentment teaches him the doctrine of passive obedience to evil rule and reliance on the wisdom of the Almighty (ll. 1006-1010). Moreover, the Knight and the Merchant at last willingly concede the opposite but equal danger of tyrannical men, who, fearing neither God nor man, "Without councell or advise folow their own will" (l. 1048). The estates need one another. The final position, on which all disputants and the choric Philosopher agree, is close to that of *Weather*—indeed, it could hardly be otherwise. The route by which that conclusion is reached is, however, far more caustic. Unless it can reform itself, the system of hierarchy is simply the lesser of two evils when compared with republicanism. If the system is to be allowed to muddle on, it must thank the forbearance and pious conservatism of the commoner. Like *Utopia*, *Gentleness* examines English society from an exaggeratedly iconoclastic viewpoint. The debate is intellectually playful and does not "prevaile the weight of a fether For the helping of any thing that is amis" (ll. 1019-1020). Nevertheless, its moral intent is entirely serious.

Gentleness shares with two other plays often attributed to Rastell a predilection for a device of viewpoint not found in any of Heywood's plays: the serious choral spokesman who appears only in prologue or epilogue to speak directly for the author. Rastell could have appended such choric passages to the work of other authors with whom he perhaps collaborated,[13] but in each case the sentiments do reflect substantive issues in the plays themselves. In *Calisto and Melibea* (ca. 1516-1533), for instance, the central topic is aristocratic idleness as contrasted with virtuous poverty. The heroine, Melibea, rejects the improper advances of the wealthy, indolent Calisto, together with the *carpe diem* sophistries of the bawd Celestina insinuating that the only true "idleness" in nature is denial of worldly pleasure (ll. 567-568). The servant Parmeno, a fervent proponent of "joyfull poverte," dares to rebuke his master Calisto for licentiousness. This emphasis on the dangers of idleness is dramatically excessive,[14] reflecting the humanists' penchant (especially Rastell's) for using drama as an ideological sounding-board. It is not to be found in Fernando de Rojas' original, from which the play was adapted. The program of the play is close instead to Vives' *De Institutione Christianae Foeminae*.[15] Such a didactic social view does explain, in any event, the relevance of Danio's seemingly intrusive concluding oration on the true nature of idleness.

Danio is more formal apologist than character in the play. He does not even refer to the Roman personalities of the love story just concluded. Instead, he anachronistically spells out a contemporary and political application of the fable. Nevertheless, his theme is not an afterthought, but a disquisition on the recurrent theme of idleness. Danio preaches bluntly, as Rastell preferred to do, seeking at the cost of obviousness to avoid ambiguity. Idleness and poverty are momentous social problems "in this region," requiring not only parental caution in the training of children, but a new approach to the penal code. The cause of most stealing, he explains (though there has been no stealing in the play), is economic need.

> That many of them compellyd be
> To beg or stele by very necessite.

> But if there be therefore any remedy,
> The hedys and rulers must furst be diligent
> To make good lawes, and execute them straitely,
> Uppon such maystres that be necligent.   (ll. 1070-1075)

The masters are to blame, not the servants. Laws and social reform must seek out the roots of crime, not merely treat the symptoms. Law must "prevent the cause before." To punish men after they have offended is not only socially unjust but ineffectual. This view of crime is astonishingly advanced when compared with criminal practices of the day, but it is in wholehearted accord with the brilliant analysis in *Utopia*—an analysis endorsed by all parties to the debate. As a lecture on aristocratic idleness, *Calisto* is close in spirit to the idealistic social speculations of Hythloday and the Ploughman.

Similarly, in *The Interlude of the Four Elements* (ca. 1517-1518), the Messenger's prefatory lecture is dramatically excessive, even though it touches upon themes basic to a treatise on "natural philosophy." This lecture is at once a humanist manifesto extolling new learning at the expense of scholasticism, and a glorification of the intellectual rather than the decadent aristocrat as reformer of society. Viewpoint is frankly authorial. The attitude confirms that of the Ploughman, and of the Philosopher whose lecture brings *Gentleness* to a close. As the Messenger sees it, English humanists have a service to perform for which they are uniquely qualified. They are able to read Latin and Greek, unlike "divers pregnaunt wittes" of England, "As well of noble men as of mean estate" (A2ᵛ). The condescension toward many of the aristocracy sounds pedantic here, entitling the humanist perhaps to be a schoolmaster but not governor. Yet as schoolmaster, Rastell envisions a power over man's social institutions recalling that of Buonaccorso and other Italian intellectuals. The philosopher's opportunity for moral leadership comes about largely by the default of the nobility.

> But what divilish mind have they which, musing
> And laboring all their liffes, do no nother thing
> But bring riches to their own possession,
> Nothing regarding their neighbours distruccion.   (A3)

As the Ploughman also insists, all wealth ultimately stems from the Supreme Maker and from the laboring class who produce goods. The rich have the keeping of this wealth, yet deserve no praise for having taken what "by other mennys labour it is got before." Sharp-witted men can easily gain wealth at the expense of their consciences, of the poor, and of the commonwealth. Such autocratic power is exploitation and not leadership.

The true Philosopher, though clever enough to make his fortune, chooses instead to serve public morality. His reward is to be accounted "but a daw" in the eyes of the worldly. Yet he alone "for a commyn welth bisily Studieth and laborith, and livith by Goddes law" (A3). He and not the nobility acts "To releve pore people with temporall goodys," "to bring People from vice and to use good living," and to bring "them to knowledge that ingnorant be" (A3^v). The Philosopher does not administer law, of course, but his humanistic functions of writing, publishing, establishing schools, and the like bring about more actual social good than political organisms. Because the legal and administrative apparatus of government is manifestly imperfect and likely to remain so, leadership of society must devolve upon the moralist. The responsibilities of such leadership entitle the intelligentsia to public respect and even modest remuneration. Similarly, the teacher in *Gentleness,* along with bishops, judges, and other commonwealth leaders, is to receive lands for term of life.

The Philosopher in *Gentleness* is perhaps Rastell's most unabashed spokesman. In him we see that, whatever the author's impatience with the inequities of a political system, he is not ready to turn his back on politics. Even though the intellectual may be in actual danger from an envious court, he risks engagement. He has made Thomas More's choice to advise a king, bluntly when occasion demands.[16] The Philosopher offers far-reaching proposals, arguing that all rulers must be subject to law and that all save the king must be subject to impeachment and dismissal for malfeasance.

The king must perforce be exempt, since he cannot be challenged without royal election and all the attendant perils of republicanism. Vengeance for tyranny in this case must be God's alone. In all other cases, however, true gentleness must be regarded not as a pious abstraction but as a workable criterion for selection and continuation in office.

> Then these hedys, rulers, and governours all
> Shuld come therto be cause of their vertue,

> And in auctorite they ought not continue
> Except they be good men, discrete and wise.
>
> (ll. 1138-1141)

Specifically, term of office for lesser officials must always be "But certain yeris and than to be removyd" (l. 1172). If they offend before the expiration of normal term, they must be punished and deprived of office. Rastell's bluntness and lack of whimsy are everywhere apparent in the speeches of his choric apologists.

7 · ROYAL DIVORCE AND SUPPRESSION
OF THE MONASTERIES

As the crisis of the Reformation neared, liberal Catholic humanists and those of Skelton's more aristocratic persuasion joined against the common foe. Even the More circle could no longer afford to urge church reform with events moving so swiftly. In the new order of the 1530's, loyal Catholics inevitably became the spokesmen for reaction. Skelton died in 1529, before the worst had come, but his program of antipathy to new men lived on. The Pilgrimage of Grace (1536-1537) was a characteristic northern rebellion that brought into alliance the religiously conservative peasant and the feudal baron. The chief aims were preservation of the old religion and removal of lowborn types from public office. When the Duke of Norfolk dared to suggest that only noblemen should administer the West Marches, the Privy Council replied: "If it shal please his majesty to appoint the meanest man . . . to rule and govern in that place; is not his graces aucthoritie sufficient to cause al men to serve his grace under him without respect of the very estate of the personage?" Henry endorsed this missive signed by Cromwell and Cranmer, noting further: "For surely we woll not be bound of a necessitie to be served there with lordes. But we wolbe served with such men what degre soever they be of as we shall appoint the same."[1] Perhaps with a certain grim humor, Henry turned the humanists' arguments of true gentleness against the old faith that most of them upheld.

All the sentiments of those who were being forced into a reactionary stand can be heard in *Godly Queen Hester* (ca. 1527-1529). The play is loyal to the Catholic Queen Katharine, to monasticism, and to systems of personal charity and hospitality. It deplores lowborn counselors, with obvious reference to Wolsey. At the same time, this Skeltonic program is joined to a humanist defense of the ideally educated woman, as elaborated by More and especially Vives.[2] Skelton has been posited as author, but his capitulation to Wolsey in 1523 argues against the possibility. An even less likely suggestion is William Roy, author of an attack on Wolsey in *Read Me and Be Not Wroth*.[3] Authorship must remain conjectural.

As political drama, *Hester* attempts new and sophisticated techniques in the allegorizing of biblical narrative. The story of Hester (Tudor Vulgate spelling) or Esther (Authorized Version) had old political connotations, having been used as early as 1392 in the pageant of Richard II's reconciliation with the city of London.[4] Richard was compared to King Ahasuerus as the unwitting persecutor of his people, because he had surrendered authority to wicked men. Esther (Queen Anne) won the sympathy of the London citizens as the virtuous consort who could supply tactful counsel once the hated sycophants were banished. The analogy became well established. In 1536-1537, during the northern rebellion on behalf of the monasteries, Friar John Pickering of Bridlington wrote a poem comparing Thomas Cromwell and Haman; and in 1572, a member of the House of Commons applied the character of Haman to the Duke of Norfolk, with Hester as Queen Elizabeth.[5] Although *Hester* follows a tradition, its own scope of allegory is nevertheless unusually ambitious. It faithfully adheres to the outlines of the scriptural account: Esther's Jewish blood, the rivalry between her kinsman Mordecai and the vengeful counselor Haman, Esther's brave intervention to save her people from Haman's plot of mass execution. To find anachronistic correspondences for all these unalterable facts of the story required some ingenuity. The devout author could not abuse sacred texts for the benefit of his comparison. Sacred history is less flexible than the kind of archetypal fable that Heywood used in *Weather* or the adaptable frame plot of the morality. Moreover, biblical allegory imposes the further difficulty of a substituted rather than a simultaneous meaning. The author's prime motive is to explicate not Jewish sacred history but an English political crisis. History is not his subject but a device of viewpoint, used to elicit a guided moral reaction to current problems, as in Dryden's *Absalom and Achitophel*.

Hester's political bias plainly appears in its non-scriptural themes. The first such emphasis is in repeated warnings against surrender of royal power to unscrupulous lieutenants—a consideration of no relevance to the biblical Ahasuerus, who is never criticized for kingly negligence or favoritism and is seemingly an Eastern potentate with unlimited power to elevate or destroy as he chooses. Conversely, the play's monarch must be lectured on "justice personall." Like Solomon, a king should watchfully administer in his own name; he alone is impartial, and only his continual diligence can guard against the selfish interests of subordinates. This pointed advice proves all too necessary and yet unavailing. The king does in fact delegate authority to Aman, of whose character little is known, appointing him "chauncelour" (a term not in the Book of Esther) "without meanes of intercession"—with no pre-established term of office or procedure for impeachment. Even if the king does so with no willful malice, and maintains the right to resume personal rule by dismissing his chancellor, the king has ignored the advice of his own counselors. He has also violated the most fervent precepts of humanists in the late 1520's, and has precipitated a crisis of manifestly topical relevance.

Hester's role in this moment of danger bears more relation to that of Katharine of Aragon than of the biblical heroine. She becomes an ideal woman of learning, administrative talent, and compassion for the poor. These facets of character need not be regarded as exclusively biographical of Katharine; indeed, the playwright's more generic intent is to fashion a model of behavior for the "vertuous matrons and women kind" of his audience. Nevertheless, the topical application to England's queen is predominant. Unlike the biblical Esther who replaces the divorced consort Vashti (a circumstance uncomfortably close to that of Anne Boleyn), this Hester is the king's first, legal, and loyal spouse. Vashti is simply not mentioned. The king is "comfortles for lack of a queen" (l. 117), and concerned "least default of issue" should threaten his dynasty. Hester too is evidently marrying for the first time. These repeated assertions of legitimacy were a necessary discretion at a time when Katharine's first marriage was being used as an argument against her nuptial contract with Henry.

Esther's appeal in biblical story is physical. She is supreme among the king's concubines, going to him one evening after having been purified with myrrh and oils for a twelvemonth. Each woman thus summoned returns to the keeper of the concubines, and "must come in unto the king nomore, except it pleased the king, and that he caused her to be called by name" (Esther 2:14).[6] Esther's spectacular success in pleasing the king and thereby becoming royal consort is naturally expurgated from the Tudor play. Hester attracts the king not by appearance but by other, rarer qualities of maturity, wisdom, and modest demeanor.

> But ye, fair damsell, of the highest stature
> And of most ripe age, as should seame
> Of all this company of most finest nature.
> Tell us your linage.   (ll. 230-233)

Katharine, as Arthur's widow, was older than her second husband, and she was not petite. The playwright "tries to turn a clumsy compliment on the disparity."[7] Also, her Spanish background had taught her to look on marriage as a virtuous duty rather than a physical pleasure.

Hester obtains favor because she is pure, gentle, demure, well read in literature, and eloquent as a speaker. The king asks for a sample of her wisdom upon "Some problem of hye dubitation," and it is her oration —entirely absent in the Bible—that wins the day. Her subject, deeply imbued with the teachings of Vives, is a tactful defense of Katharine's position in England. Hester knows, as Mordocheus (Mordecai) has taught her, that her first loyalty is not like the biblical Esther's to her minority race, but to her king and his entire people; the playwright is anxious to insist that Katharine is truly English and not merely a Spanish woman defending her country's interests in hostile territory (ll. 177-184). Accordingly, Hester explains, a queen complements true majesty but does not challenge its superior authority. She holds her position solely by marriage; the king owns "the jurisdiction of the whole province" without question (l. 275). Yet as the embodiment of those soft, merciful graces needed in a true prince, she may offer counsel and must be educated to act as the king's substitute in cases of emergency.

> But eftsons it may chaunce at sundry season,
> The king with his councell most part of all
> From this realm to be absent, when warre doth call.
> Then the quenes wisdom sadly must deal,
> By her great vertue, to rewle the common weal.
>
> (ll. 282-286)

The biblical Esther had no such ambitions. Katharine actually administered the realm in 1513, when Henry was chasing the French in the chivalric but profitless siege of Therouenne and the Battle of the Spurs. She saw to her responsibilities well, and could justifiably claim some credit for the decisive victory over the Scots at Flodden Field.

In her role as intercessor for the poor and as patroness of charity (the sources of Katharine's enormous popularity during her years of trial), Hester is concerned lest "Goddes service and hospitalitie" should decay, especially that which supports the indigent. This patently non-biblical allusion to English monasticism warns not against total suppression, but against unequal distribution of monastic wealth, providing temptation for some opportunist (ll. 318-322). When all wealth "is gathered together on a heap," the imbalance threatens the entire system. Poorer houses must be allowed to continue their modest programs of charity. Hester has no sympathy for "efficiency" reforms. Like Katharine, her way of dealing with poverty is the medieval one of almsgiving; she has no systematic vision of social improvement, and wants her beloved institutions to continue as they have done.

The villain who fulfills Hester's prophecy of raiding the smaller houses of hospitality is of course Aman. Suddenly and capriciously elevated to power, marching about "with many men awaiting on him" (l. 129), he becomes the familiar type of worldly lowborn churchman satirized in *Wisdom* and *Magnificence*. Indeed, the playwright invokes abstractions from the morality tradition to characterize Aman's universal malevolence. In an entirely separate action (ll. 338-580), Pride, Adulation, and Ambition congregate to lament the worldly successes of Aman, who has so far surpassed any abstract concept of evil that the three personifications declare themselves superseded by him. They bequeath to Aman their detestable qualities and depart. However lame theatrically as a means of conveying characterization, this direct editorial comment enables the playwright to overcome the factual limitations of his source and to speak anachronistically through the medium of abstraction.[8] Ignoring for the moment his biblical setting, he can rail openly at a "Divine" who practices "pluralite" and controls "the nomination of every good benefice," violates the statute of apparel, and buys up enough cloth to serve ten towns. This churchman employs sycophants to spy, to bribe, and to reduce the clergy to poverty. Even more topical are the references to foreign policy. Aman's vacillation imperils the nation "if warre should chaunce, either with Scotland or Fraunce" (l. 479). "In peace he is bold, but in war he is cold" (l. 352). He urges mobilization so that he can tax the commons and force them into beggary, but is a coward and "will not fight." This game of extortion under pretense of foreign campaigns was not new with Wolsey; but the financial crisis of the 1520's, brought on by years of extravagant posturing, was more acute than anything known under Henry VII. The dramatist's longing for fiscal moderation and a cessation of imperialist aims is close to that of both Skelton and the More circle.

Hester's chief concern, nevertheless, is the wrecking of the monasteries. Here Aman's role is most pointedly historical. He attacks "Ordinances and foundation" responsible for providing poor relief (l. 461). Whereas beggars earlier "had they releef, both of bread and beef," without having to beg from door to door, now "the dore standes shet" and Aman "eatith up all their food" (ll. 471-477). What with unemployment, military demobilization, and monastic suppression, the plight of the poor is bitter indeed.

The situation, as described by the abstractions and by Hester, is not the wholesale suppression of all monastic establishments under the Reformation measures of Thomas Cromwell. Aman is guilty not of disestablishing the Catholic Church but of personal aggrandizement under the guise of administrative housecleaning. Occasional suppression of this sort was not new. Earlier, William of Waynflete had eliminated two priories to endow Magdalen College, and in 1497 the Bishop of Ely similarly dissolved a nunnery to found Jesus College at Cambridge.[9] Wolsey began such activities as early as 1522, but only after receiving in 1524 a bull from Clement VII to found Cardinal College (later Christ Church) at Oxford did he suppress a number of smaller monasteries. The move was highly unpopular in the countryside, and "at Bayham, a Premonstratensian house in Sussex, the country people, disguising themselves, put the canons in again for a time—an outrage which, of course, was duly punished." [10] A ballad called "An Impeachment of Wolsey" appeared in the 1520's, and Skelton's *Colin Clout* (ca. 1523) depicted religious turned from their houses and forced to wander.[11] (Aman complains specifically to the king about such "rimes" and "railinges so farre set abrode," l. 597.) Wolsey was viewed not as a heretic but as an extortionist, destroying the church from within.

Reformation may not yet be at hand in *Hester*, but the hour is late. Aman has poisoned the king's mind against the Jews and has set a date for their extermination; only the miracle of Hester's intervention can persuade the king to issue a last-minute reprieve, countermanding his own order with a public explanation (ll. 1110-1153). Hester's bravery in speaking for the Jews is remarkable, since she is made more vulnerable to Aman's attacks by associating her cause with that of an unpopular religious minority. She chooses to defend the persecuted by making public and emphasizing her attachment to their faith. Although divorce is not mentioned, the attempt to "destroy" Hester suggests a date after 1527, perhaps very shortly before the cardinal's fall.[12]

Aman's campaign against the Jews centers upon the heated English problems of separate monastic wealth and of monastic impunity from the king's law—the old contention of ecclesiastical jurisdiction. The playwright is at pains to prove the correctness of the traditional stance of his church. Aman, on the other hand, though motivated solely by persecution mania, employs arguments against Roman jurisdiction that were soon to become the rationale for a break with the papacy. Wholesale suppression, he argues, will yield a tremendous financial windfall (l. 757) —unlike the biblical purge, the costs of which will be borne by Aman himself at considerable self-sacrifice (Esther 3:9).[13] Simultaneously, Aman will rid the kingdom of a seditious minority, "within themself dwelling, desevered from our nation," governed by their own laws and beyond the reach of civil authority. The Jews openly proselytize and "draw unto their conversation, And unto their ceremonies and faction, Of our people as many as may be" (ll. 731-735). Aman attacks their religious group not for its doctrine but for its "factious" recognition of a law higher than the king's, which sets an example of disobedience that will prompt "Your subjects to rebell in hope of like liberte" (l. 743). Such disloyalty is all the more dangerous because "their possessions be of substance So great and so large" that they have the power to wage successful civil war against the monarch. This non-biblical emphasis on civil danger (see Esther 3:8) reflects the playwright's view that Wolsey, even while bargaining for papal favor, was opening the door to Reformation by encouraging nationalistic resentment of monastic exemption from common law, and by exploiting Henry's sensitivity to the danger of civil disobedience during his divorce proceedings.

Hester's most urgent mission is to convince her royal husband of the groundlessness of Aman's charges, including his assertions that the Jews (monastics) do "Not feed the poor by hospitalite" but prefer to live voluptuously among themselves (ll. 943-946). She stresses the antiquity of the hospitable institutions and their divine sanction (ll. 950-954), arguing that God alone can dissolve the household that He established on earth. No institution, of course, is free from the need for occasional correction, and Hester readily concedes that if the king's administration contains malefactors so too may the monastic houses. In place of Aman's edict, she urges that privy counselors be sent throughout the realm to investigate religious abuses.

> And if any have the law abused
> Of all the Jewes within your comon weal,
> Let them not spare correction to deal,
> And straightly constrain them self to address
> To observe that law God gave them by Moses.
>
> (ll. 1091-1095)

Her definition of the balance between civil and clerical law is significantly ambiguous, for it seems to give the king authority over the clergy and yet consigns them to the obedience of their own prior and separate law. The Reformation was soon to rule on this matter that had not been entirely satisfactory since the time of Henry II and Becket. Yet the playwright hopefully supposes that the present relation of church and state is not unworkable, given a mutual forbearance and correction of abuses on both sides. Extreme forms of suppression destroy what is fundamentally good along with what is superficially bad. Monasticism, on balance, is holy and devoted to public welfare: "And al the whole realm for them fares the better" (l. 1102). The crisis of church and state is not really as momentous as it seems, but is the cruel work of opportunists. The basic problem is not decay of charitable houses but improper delegation of authority.

The conventional idealized ending, with the death of Aman and the ascendancy of Hester's virtuous counsel, is prophetically hopeful like that of *Magnificence*. It seemingly precedes the fall of Wolsey, for that event brought no relief to Queen Katharine. The ending serves to offer Henry an easy way out of his dilemma in 1527-1529 by laying the blame on Wolsey. The king need only tacitly admit his misjudging of the cardinal. If even this modest concession was too much to ask of Henry, the playwright (and Katharine) saw no other possible hope. To make accommodation even more feasible, the ending promises that no general vengeance will follow a restoration of monastic security. Unlike the biblical Jews, who carry out a nationwide massacre with the king's consent (Esther 8:11f), Hester and her kindred are content to forgive and rule wisely. Only Aman's blood is shed, for he bears the entire responsibility.

That the play failed of its purpose can hardly surprise anyone with historical hindsight of the king's personality. Indeed, one wonders if Henry saw a performance of *Hester*. The surroundings seem consciously feminine and cloistered. The playwright speaks to "vertuous matrons and women kind," eschewing bawdry. The occasion is more religious than entertaining. Referred to as "this congregation," the audience is dismissed with a benediction. Ritualistic phrases in Latin are not translated. The stage may have been an actual chapel, with "many maidens" at hand and chapel singers in attendance on Assuerus in his curtained pew.[14] Perhaps *Hester* was written specifically for the queen's own chapel, to encourage and console her with a scriptural vindication of her cause. *Hester* is permeated with a dignity and earnestness befitting quiet bravery in time of peril.

A manuscript fragment called *Albion Knight* (ca. 1537) appears to represent a continuation of the Skeltonic conservative viewpoint during the first troubled years of the Reformation. The historical occasion is probably the Pilgrimage of Grace, for the tortured negotiations of that northern rebellion are summarized in detail in the play.[15] The Commons and Principality (the monarchy) have reached a nearly fatal misunderstanding. The monarch believes the people have ungratefully risen against him "In time of need" when he went to them for financial support. The people conversely suspect him of using tax money for his favorites and as his personal lucre rather than for defense. Accordingly the rebels are egged on to issue ultimatums, refusing to fulfill their duty of taxpaying "Except like duetie be ministred on his parte" (l. 297). This impasse is the work of troublemakers seeking "To make of an old grudge a new frenesie" (l. 331)—that is, to awaken old resentments in the name of the Reformation now in progress. The lords temporal, who have long held it their right "To have the governaunce about Principalitie" by virtue of their inherited dignities, are incensed by new clerical men who "wolde rule all" (l. 303). Thus it is that a tax-oppressed peasantry and a slighted nobility join forces, as they actually did in the Pilgrimage of Grace, to demand an end to favoritism at court and the increasingly radical administration of lowborn counselors. Though placing the blame chiefly on new men, the playwright is also visibly alarmed at willful tendencies in the monarch himself.

Catholic sentiment for Queen Katharine and the nobility evidently gave a new and dangerous perspective to some of the great mystery cycles of the northern counties.[16] In the N-Town apocryphal "Death, Funeral, Assumption, and Coronation of the Virgin," for instance, the envy of bishops and princes toward Our Lady prompts the threat of popular uprisings. These civil dangers menacing the state in the event of Mary's execution, although related much earlier, may have seemed newly appropriate to Henry's problem in disposing of Katharine.[17] Katharine epitomized to embattled Catholics not only the old faith but also matronly virtue and charity. Quite possibly, the administration's campaign against the cult of the Virgin was inspired not only by Protestant antipathy to shrines and saints but by the hazards of political analogy. Similarly the Becket shrine, a particularly hated icon, may have offended in part because of the potent "mirror" of Becket's ecclesiastical triumphs in the name of clerical impunity from king's law.

The Northern Rebellion of 1536-1537 made clear that Henry's Reformation and the influx into government of an ever-increasing number of lowborn Protestants were by no means popular everywhere. Conversely, the Reformation encouraged the outspokenness of those who desired even more radical changes. On May Day in 1537, a dissident play presented "a king, how he should rule his realm," in which one actor "played Husbandry and said many things against gentlemen, more than was in the book of the play."[1] Anabaptism made its dreaded appearance on the continent. The party of victory in the 1530's, composed of zealous episcopal reformers such as Cranmer and ambitious politicians such as Cromwell, rapidly discovered the need for strong propagandistic countermeasures against their opponents to right and left—especially at first to the right. Henry was constrained by the intensity of conservative opposition to give the new activists his support, whatever his personal disinclination toward plainness in religion.

The new drama engendered by this crisis was conducted largely or perhaps entirely under government sponsorship—not under Henry directly, but under his reforming ministers. The fragment *Temperance and Humility,* for instance, may have appeared shortly before the major dissolution of the monasteries in 1536-1537, as a part of Cromwell's campaign to prepare the nation for the event. The play satirizes rebelliousness "in every order" and excessive wealth masquerading as "Due Prosperity" in court, country, and convent. Because Disobedience is so wealthy, he must be starved into submission. Unless the religious can practice obedience, Temperance warns, they will soon "stand in drede." The intended effect of the lampoon is clearly not to offer a reconciliation but to win popular support for removal of the houses.[2] There had been much widespread passive resistance to the Act of Succession barring Mary Tudor from the throne, and to Henry's assumption of the title of supreme head of the church.

Thomas Wylley, vicar of Yoxford in Suffolk, wrote for Cromwell a play (now lost) "against the Pope's Counselors," radical enough to have earned Wylley the enmity of many fellow priests who "will not receive me into their churches to preach."[3] His strictures against Virgin-worship and "a Rude Communalty" were probably inspired by the Pilgrimage of Grace. Thomas Kirchmayer dedicated his Latin *Pammachius* to Cranmer in 1538.[4] The archbishop's genius for inspiring literary propaganda in the drama was no doubt supplemented by Cromwell's genius for production and distribution. As a skillful anti-Catholic reinterpretation of history, *Pammachius* was enormously influential. John Bale, on Cromwell's payroll, translated the play and incorporated its practices into the recasting of his own *King John* (first written around 1531-1534).[5]

Since they were commissioned directly by the Reformation government, such plays naturally reflect official policy in detail. Bale's *Three Laws* (ca. 1530-1538), for instance, does not content itself with recounting historically the moral crimes of the Catholic Church, like sodomy, legalism, and superstition. Bale's program systematically touches upon the points of rite, doctrine, and church government that were being suppressed by ecclesiastical visitations to the English parishes: paxes, images, ave marias, crossings and kissings, censing, candles, ear confession, beads, rings, cream, oil, relics, transubstantiation, justification by works versus faith, purgatory, masses for the dead, pilgrimages, pardons, simony, monasticism, and the like. Bale particularly urges clerical marriage in order to avoid children's graveyards behind the convents, stews in Rome of both sexes, and such lurid abuses as papal homosexuality or fornication behind the altar during confession. Similarly, Bale's fragment of a mystery cycle in *God's Promises, John Baptist,* and *The Temptation of Our Lord,* intended to replace the Catholic cycles in popular esteem, stresses salvation through faith rather than Pharisaical ritualism and portrays Christ as supreme exemplar of virtue rather than as vicarious bloody sacrifice.

This propagandizing for reform continued at a feverish rate until Henry's reversal of policy in 1540. With the execution of Cromwell, the erstwhile official dramatists of the Reformation were driven into exile. Official as their connection may have been, however, they were no sycophantic mouthpieces. Though in need of Cranmer's and Cromwell's support, they wrote as they believed, heralding the millennium and tolerating no delays. They must in fact have been a tricky lot to handle. Bale was perhaps the most tactless and independent. While still a Catholic prior, he had scoffed at transubstantiation. He married immediately upon leaving the order and gave reason to suspect that a young lady named Dorothy had something to do with his change of faith.[6] His congregation in Thorndon, Suffolk, accused him of radicalism when he fulminated against the Pilgrimage of Grace; and Henry, looking for a few scapegoat heretics, might have sent Bale to the stake but for Cromwell's intervention. Cromwell, characteristically indifferent to Bale's personal life and ideals, recognized and exploited the apostate friar's gift for invective. Together they chose the popular morality play, acted on tour by a small troupe, as the obvious genre for maximum exposure. Cranmer joined Cromwell in active support of Bale; *King John* was performed at Cranmer's house in the Christmas festivities of 1539.[7] Under these men, Bale was intensely loyal to the administration. After Cromwell's death, however, Bale was disillusioned by Henry's retrenchment and by the political uses being made of confiscated monastic wealth. Bale did not hesitate to voice his disapproval in the revised ending of *King John.*

Bale's devotion to the new order and his irascible independence are thus both evident in *King John.* Intrepidly he finds fault with everyone: with Rome of course, with the English clergy considered as a group, with the recalcitrant nobility and the superstitious commons, with civil authority, later with the Anabaptists, with the historical John for having yielded to Catholic importunity, and even with the present Imperial Majesty for condoning or ignoring papist backsliding. Bale finds the world hostile to truth. Widow England, representing the spirit of her country, cannot elicit the support of any segment of the English people. Her sole champion is an idealized king-figure whose beliefs and personality are, in spite of the play's presumed historical setting, those of neither King John nor King Henry VIII but of a forthright Protestant moralist. Bale uses historical analogy to argue that King John adumbrated a heroic type: the Reformation saint. Bale implies that King Henry at least partially incarnates the type, more successfully than his ancestor. Yet the portrait of Bale's champion is drawn not from the current ruler of England but from Bale's own temperament and creed. Both John and Henry are judged in relation to Bale's vision of the perfect ruler, who most nearly resembles Bale himself.

To bring about this daring innovation in viewpoint, Bale makes freer and more sophisticated use of dramatic time than his predecessors. Elastic time, freed by abstraction, permits Bale to draw upon the events of the thirteenth and sixteenth centuries and yet to occupy a fictional world of his own creating. This world is particularly dominant in the play's opening confrontation. The historical personages of Stephen Langton, Pope Innocent III, Pandulphus, and Simon of Swinsett are reserved for much later. King John's name is mentioned briefly in the first sixteen lines, but thereafter for nearly one quarter of the play's considerable length no allusions to the thirteenth century appear. An essentially nameless English king faces the recurrent backsliding of his people, nobility, and clergy.

Accordingly, the objects of this king's wrath are timely for a Reformation audience, even though not limited exclusively to the sixteenth century. The king berates "Latin howrrs, serimonyes, and popetly playes," pardons, "halowed belles and purgatory," "relickes, confession, and cowrtes of bawdry," and the like (ll. 416-425). Although some of these abuses (such as "popetly playes" and Latin ceremony) were actually of no concern to the historical John, Bale artfully implies that the English monarchy at its best has always detested ecclesiastical decay. Bale invokes a cumulative spirit of reform never entirely absent from the Middle Ages. Even more significant, he implies that the present monarch, famous for his attack on Rome, is especially zealous in his opposition to all the abuses catalogued here. A Tudor audience, hearing a generic English king decry "trentalles" and "scalacely messys," would inevitably attribute the sentiments to their own anti-Catholic ruler. Without having to specify that Henry did in fact deplore aural confession and the mass—assertions that Henry would no doubt have resented—Bale throws the weight of England's king behind every item of Cromwell's and Cranmer's reform program of the 1530's.

The same unspoken equation suggests that Henry, like his virtuous forbear, can rely but little on his aristocracy, local gentry, or populace. The defiant clergy, secure in their independence from criminal prosecution, enjoy a life of sexual aberration in monastery and bishop's palace, and export England's wealth to the pope at an alarming rate. Yet noblemen and secular authorities do nothing, unwilling to brave the church's displeasure. Commonalty too cannot be trusted to break with long-established superstition. This reactionary alliance, which exploded in the Pilgrimage of Grace, was of serious concern to Cromwell and Cranmer. The anger of Bale's king-figure at such traitorous recalcitrance would suggest to any Tudor audience that their king had weighty reasons for displeasure in 1536-1537. Bale's analogous interpretation of the northern rebellions is opposite to that of *Albion Knight*. Unbendingly, Bale justifies Henry's harsh treatment of the rebels on that occasion. Imperial Majesty's hoodwinking of Sedition (ll. 2421f) is very like Henry's false cordiality toward Robert Aske, who came to beg on behalf of the rebels that Cromwell be dismissed. Aske received offices and royal bounty, only to find himself a few months later sentenced to be hanged and quartered.[8] In Bale's view, Sedition and Aske got what they richly deserved. Once more, without having to say so, Bale implies that Henry is architect of a stringently Protestant policy.

The implied equation of the idealized king-figure with Henry is most daring in Bale's revelation of the king's personal qualities as a ruler. Unlike the tyrannical and gullible king-figures of *Magnificence* and *Hester*, Bale's Reformation prince is always in the right and always self-possessed. He chivalrously comes to the aid of a woman in distress, being ordained by God to "help such as be desolate" (l. 174). His godliness sustains him even when all his subordinates desert the true cause. Subject to no generic soul struggle, this prince seems to have been born old and wary. Unassisted, he lays down firm rules for reform of the clergy. Conversely, no one need warn him of carrying the Reformation too far; he will retain all dutiful bishops (after all, Bale was a reforming bishop). The king's universal distrust of his counselors is not paranoia but due caution, for the actions of Civil Order and the rest justify his anger. Able to rule wisely without counsel, he will not appease his enemies even though he must stand alone against thousands. Yet he desires to recover all his wayward subjects to the true religion.

Can this king-figure be Henry VIII? Temperate, firm, divinely instructed in Protestant zeal? Not precisely—Bale has never said so, and has in fact named him King John. If pressed to confirm the exact meaning of his analogy, Bale can protest with Chaucer's Nun's Priest that "Thise been the cokkes wordes, and nat mine." Yet the implications are of course highly flattering to Henry, and portray him as solely responsible for the glorious aims of the reforming party in Henry's government. Henry himself, if he saw the play, might well have appreciated the complete dominance of the king's role, even though the playwright causes the king to speak a language more befitting a saint than a ruler.

"Avoid, lewd person! for thy wordes are ungodly," the king accosts Sedition (l. 45). The strident tone and characteristically reforming diction (not unlike those of Jonson's Zeal-of-the-Land Busy) are here directed not at disloyalty but at the use of unseemly language. Sedition has employed the comparatively colorless oath of "by Jesus" and has gabbled about "'bichery." The king is not amused. Although he allows himself innocent recreations—"Thow canst with thy mirth in no wisse discontent me, So that thow powder it with wisdom and honeste"—he will not tolerate profane or salacious talk and never descends to such depths himself. The king's diction is similarly that of the reforming saint in his attacks on the "rabyll Of Latin mummers and sectes desseivabyll," and on "Belles prystes, Living by idolles, yea, the very Antichristes!" He will have none of "yowr traysh, yowr ringing, singing, and piping" (ll. 427-428, 1355-1356, 1389).

The king is also no mean theologian. In rapid succession he alludes to biblical accounts of Solomon, David, Mary and Joseph, Jehosephat, Ezekias, Maccabees, Dathan and Abiram, Susanna, and Balaam, as well as to the Book of Ecclesiastes, Revelation, the Epistles of Saint Paul, and the Gospels (ll. 1344-1526), in order to prove doctrines of contemporary politics like the subservience of church to state in secular matters. He is at the same time sarcastic about Catholics' attempts to twist the texts for their sinister purposes (ll. 53-54, 451-456).

Bale was of course adept at such biblical gymnastics; and by crediting the king with these accomplishments, he both flatters Henry and invests his king-figure with the personal attributes of a Protestant saint. The sources of Bale's characterization are his own spiritual preoccupations. The unfaltering vision, the distaste for profanity, the obsession with the sex life of the monasteries, the perverse delight in being right when everyone else is wrong, the anticipation of martyrdom, and above all the irascible text-splitting biblical scholarship, though they proceed from the king's mouth, are the viewpoint of Bale and men like him. Bale's ideal king, similar at times to John and Henry, is essentially an authorial spokesman.

Bale's handling of the monarchy in *King John* is symptomatic of the zealous Protestants' dilemma after the Reformation. They were obliged to depend on an absolutist monarch as the only force capable of bringing about the millennium in the face of widespread apathy and entrenched corruption. Yet by expecting so much of the king, they doomed themselves to frustration. The necessity of cooperating with Machiavellians like Cromwell was equally trying; Bale has no place in his vision of saintly rule for Cromwell's *realpolitik*. Bale's fictional king is thus not simple flattery of Henry but a potential standard for criticism. Bale specifically endorses Tudor divine right (l. 103), but insists that God's instrument on earth must take firm charge of God's Reformation.

To succeed, the ideal Protestant king-saint must learn important lessons from the past. The historical analogy of John and the thirteenth century, with which the play is chiefly concerned, offers an edifying sermon on the tenacity of Catholic duplicity. Bale's philosophy of history, even if patently biased, discerns a theme in the evolution of late medieval Europe. Bale insists that his Reformation is the reaffirmation of something begun long ago. "For three hundred yers all Englond shall it rewe," boast the prescient schemers of John's undoing (l. 771). Their tactics of interdict and Catholic alliance with England's neighbors on all sides were indeed to plague Henry as they had John. In questions of jurisdiction and diplomacy there was a repeated (if intermittent) pattern of conflict between nascent centralization of national power and declining pan-European ecumenism.

The political world of Bale's play, then, is plausible as a composite portrait of England's international crisis over the centuries, even if it is manifestly anachronistic in its details. Pope Innocent, King Philip Augustus, Stephen Langton, and the thirteenth-century Inquisition directed against the Albigensians (ll. 976-979) are early manifestations of a current struggle. So too are export of annates and tithes, licentious living in the monasteries, and the struggle between crown and church over power of appointment in the ecclesiastical hierarchy. Most of all, Bale's portrayal of European alliances follows a pattern provided by the continuing late medieval norm. The danger, for Henry as for John, was Catholic league among all or most of England's neighbors. The traditional enemy, France, had done rather well against both John and Henry, and in the play John's clergy do not miss the chance for some pointed sarcasm at military failure (l. 561). Even in the British Isles, Ireland is superstitiously obedient to the church and hence a tinder-box of sedition (l. 986). Scotland actively prepares for invasion under King Alexander (l. 1622). Under papal interdict and excommunication, which not only absolve John's subjects of obedience to him but encourage Catholic princes of Europe to carry out the pope's denunciation, John suddenly finds himself literally surrounded by enemies: French to the south, Spanish to the southwest, Easterlings, Danes, and Norwegians to the east (ll. 1622-1629).

England's timeless insular fears of Catholic league and invasion are epitomized in the act of excommunication. The actual ceremony, performed on stage, is a lampoon of the ritual with kneeling and knocking of breast (ll. 1034-1052), intended to dramatize the absurdity of such a superstitious little man actually claiming to remove the king from "His eternall light." [9] Bale's most potent weapon, however, is hysteria. Think what might happen, he says in effect, if England were to be invaded in Henry's reign as she was in John's.

> The burning of townes, the throwing down of buildinges,
> Destruction of corn and cattell, with other thinges;
> Defiling of maides, and sheding of Christen blood . . .
>
> (ll. 1724-1726)

Abbeys will be re-entered by clerics eager to make up for lost time and completely free from civil jurisdiction. Kings will be poisoned, and

true men condemned in ecclesiastical courts for their faith. Publication of
the play after Mary's reign, with inserted references to Elizabeth and
to "our late King Henry" (l. 1102), would add obvious point to the
warnings against recusancy. England's subjects are invited to see themselves as living in a still dangerous but happier time than that of John,
if they heed the lessons of history.

The image of John as martyr to a lost cause, maligned by his detractors and yet steadfast in his vision of truth, is clearly one into
which Bale projected a great deal of his own lonely battle against the
Antichrist. The malevolent attempts of Catholic chroniclers in all ages
to destroy the memory of good deeds must call forth champions of
holiness. King John is "like to rewe it sore Whan ye write his time, for
vexcing of the clargy," predicts Nobility (ll. 580-581), and so it proves.
The clerical Polydore Vergil typifies the slanderer. John Leland is one
of the chosen few who "witness a trewth" (l. 2151). Tyndale, who specifically praised John as an opponent of Rome, may have given Bale the
idea of attacking the Catholic chroniclers.[10] The figure of Verity, as
Bale's mouthpiece, pronounces a restorative evaluation of John's true
worth and warns that the godly will always be willfully misunderstood
by the wicked. "Report what they will, in their most furious madness,"
the insinuations of the enemy must be rejected by an act of faith.

The idealized ending of *King John* moves avowedly out of thirteenth-
century time and approaches the millennium. Imperial Majesty, patently
King Henry, is "supreme lord of the church." Yet the ending, presumably
from a later version of the text, also reflects the new dangers of Henry's
policy of religious retrenchment in the 1540's. Sedition is back, no longer
Stephen Langton but boasting of his recent successes in the Northern
Risings. Parliament is not as firm as one could wish, and the king must
receive plain warning:

> In your parlement, commaunde yow what ye will,
> The popes ceremonies shall drown the Gospell still.
> Some of the bishoppes at your injunctions slepe.

> (ll. 2475-2477)

Curates are lax in their duties, and churchmen continue to persecute
true Protestants.

> First of all, considre the prelates do not preach;
> But persecute those that the Holy Scriptures teach.

And, mark me this wele, they never ponnish for popery,
But the Gospell readers, they handle very coursely.

(ll. 2493-2496)

Imperial Majesty listens wisely but does not commit himself to Gospel-preaching.

Bale's party of reform, so frustratingly close to success, is on the defensive. It experiences attack from both flanks: subsequent developments on the religious left ironically force Bale, in another inserted passage, to conclude an anti-papist play with repeated warnings of "The Anabaptistes, a sect new risen of late" (l. 2579). Queen Elizabeth must be especially alerted to this threat. The dramatic afterthought typifies the dilemma of zealous episcopal reformers like Bale or Cranmer, who never conceded and perhaps never realized that their anti-papist propaganda encouraged extremism from whatever corner it might appear. The danger detracts considerably from the idealized vision with which Bale had hoped to end, but does not lessen the energy and inventiveness of his bilious propagandistic art.

After his reversal of policy in 1540, Henry saw no more Protestant drama. In fact, he saw little drama at all, turning instead to sumptuous reveling as a respite from official cares and poor health. From 1540 to 1546, the court enjoyed sixteen masques and perhaps one or two plays.[11] The sole extant morality fragment of the period, dramatizing *The Four Cardinal Virtues and the Vices Contrary to Them* (printed ca. 1541-1547), pointedly warns against those who climb too high. Justice, Temperance, and Prudence, on behalf of "this realm," subdue Willfulness and reclaim Disobedience from his rebellion. Religious arguments are notably absent. Prayer is offered for the intercession of Christ's mother (ll. 18-19). The lesson, confirmed by a concluding prayer to Henry and the young heir Edward, is one of obedience and decorous conciliation.[12] Grimald's *Christus Redevivus* (Oxford, ca. 1540) is also notably noncontroversial.[13]

Elsewhere in England, the government suppressed reforming polemicism as it had the Catholic cycles. Bishop Gardiner objected to Kirchmayer's anti-Catholic *Pammachius* as "so pestiferous as were intolerable."[14] Under the Act of Six Articles, the Keeper of the Carpenters' Hall at Shoreditch was prosecuted for sponsoring performance of an interlude "wherein priests were railed on and called knaves." One Spencer, an ex-priest turned actor, was burned at Salisbury for having performed "matter concerning the sacrament of the altar." [15] In 1542 Bishop Bonner of London forbade performance of all plays in churches. An Act of Parliament in 1543 made illegal scriptural interpretations in drama "contrary to the doctrine set forth or to be set forth by the king's majesty" —with the government itself to decide at any time what constituted proper doctrine.[16] A city proclamation of 1545 put new controls on the places of performance and posting of public advertisements. Interludes were to be presented only in noblemen's houses or under the watchful eye of sheriffs, mayors, aldermen, or head parishioners. Accordingly, in 1546 the Earl of Bath's servants were committed to the counter for "playing lewd plays in the suburbs of London." [17] Actual licensing of performance and publication was not yet in force, but the state, having discovered its power to create a drama of topical ideas, now extended its power to curtail those ideas.

Liberal Protestants naturally chafed under this retrenchment, and loudly insisted that Protector Somerset unleash the drama in 1547. Bale, sanguine once again, characteristically updated the ending of his *Three Laws* to greet "Tu puer propheta, elected of the Lord, King Edward the Sixth, to have godes law restored." Coronation festivities, in which Edward himself acted, were evidently anti-papal. So were many other revels of this reign.[18] Edward was easily led by Somerset's program of active reform. Cromwell was gone, but Cranmer still carried on, aided by a host of returning exiles. The new government repealed the Act of 1543 regulating "interpretation of Scriptures."

The result was predictably explosive. Plays were so widely suspected of being used for political agitation that playwrights and actors were occasionally burned or otherwise punished for their activities; and in fact it was at a play, according to Holinshed, that the ringleaders of Kett's Rebellion (1549) successfully exhorted the crowd "to enter further into their wicked enterprise." [19] Ultimate return of control was necessary for public peace: in 1549 all plays were banned for a period of two months, and in 1551 a government proclamation required licensing for all professional troupes of actors, even in the house of their patron.[20] No talk was to touch upon "his majesty, his council, magistrates, justices, officers, or ministers," and the signature of the Privy Council was required for publication. These stringent measures were of course not uniformly effective, and indeed seem to have been used chiefly against Catholic activities.[21] Virulent Protestant drama, however closely controlled, remained a staple to the end of Edward's reign. Nevertheless, freedom of speech in Edward VI's first years had the paradoxical effect of tightening state control over the drama in the subsequent years of the Tudor period.

Not surprisingly, then, extant plays from Edward VI's reign tend to be polemical. One understandable impulse was to analyze causes of failure during the years of Henry's religious retrenchment. Such an attempt is evident in the fragment, *Somebody, Avarice, and Minister,* or *The Spoiling of Lady Verity* (ca. 1547-1550). The danger here is not international meddling and inquisition by Rome and Spain, as in early Elizabethan analyses of the more violent Counter Reformation from 1553 to 1558 (see Chapter 10). Lady Verity's foes espouse false doctrine, but their corruption is domestic. The pleasure-loving Minister has long chafed at the restrictions of his virtuous taskmistress, and gladly turns to the embraces of Simony. Old abuses of penance and absolution, synodals, and pardons are quickly restored. Oppression and burning are the fate of those who speak against avarice and soft living. For "many yeres" the English people will give ear to "the fals prophetes of Antechrist," but Verity promises eventual recovery. England's clergy are to blame, and her people gullible for having accepted false appearances. Similarly, the lost *Old Custom* (ca. 1547-1550) attacks Insolence and "Old Blind Custom" in the name of Hunger of Knowledge.[22] The hero of Grimald's *Archepropheta* (published 1548) is John the Evangelist, type of Gospel preacher and foe of hypocrisy, luxury, courtly flattery, and the curtailment of free speech. Edwardian unleashing of such frank discussion may also have encouraged the radical *Love Feigned and Unfeigned* (existing as a fragment), an argument for Anabaptist doctrines of burning love, abolition of rank, and communal ownership of property after the practice of the early church fathers.[23]

Assessment of blame in Henry's late reign had to be balanced with more constructive proposals. Official propaganda was not all vituperative; it had to consolidate Protestant gains among the mass of perplexed Englishmen. R. Wever's *Lusty Juventus,* ending with a direct appeal to Edward VI and the Protector, reflects both the zeal and the responsible caution of an erstwhile opposition now in power. The author, although not as strident of voice as Bale, details nevertheless his contempt for unclean sexual practices, superstition, popes, vestments, hermits, friars, pardoners, beads, brooches, and the like (B4ᵛ-C1). He speaks of "cov-enaunts" and "the lamb," and paraphrases the psalms; he argues that works should be performed only as "fruites of true repentaunce" (A3-B1). The way to truth is a narrow path depending less on sacraments than on the art of extempore prayer (A4). Dress is to be in the plain style, a fashion apt to provoke sarcasm from the unrighteous. Good Christians must become used to this vitriol.

Yet Wever is equally concerned that Protestants temper their own extremist tendencies toward "preciseness" and censoriousness. Speaking for a government that must now win wide popular support, he stresses that pride in one's Bible-learning leads to faction and thus plays into the hands of the papists (D2). If plainness is allowed to become a fetish, ordinary Englishmen will soon learn the game of mere outward compliance. The protagonist Juventus, struggling valiantly to discover true faith, is an easy prey to this cynical response because of the popular notion that zealous Protestants are too "curious." Hypocrisy instructs him in ways to deceive the quarrelsome reformers by putting on a semblance of fanaticism. Juventus must ostentatiously inveigh against "old popish priestes" and carry his holy book where it easily "may be spied," in his girdle or bosom (D1-D1ᵛ). If he does these things, he may live as licentiously as he wishes. To the extent that some extremists have invited this parodying of mannerisms, says Wever, Protestantism itself contributes to indifference, disaffection, mere lip-service among the mass of believers, and accordingly to the fleshly backsliding shown by Juventus in this play. Possibly Wever implies that extremism contributed in part to the setback of 1540-1547. Despite its anti-Romish cast, Wever's play speaks from the position (very different from Bale's) of having achieved most of the ritual reforms desired by the moderate Protestants. These reforms must not of course be relinquished, but the average parishioner must be taught that essential Christianity need not be joyless. Wever's play typifies the Edwardian popular morality in its heavy emphasis on the political aspects of religious change.

Choir boys' plays at court during Edward's reign tended also to be polemical, giving contemporary bias to an academic tradition of Plautus and Terence that had heretofore preferred a safe distance from theological controversy. Even after the break with Rome, in Henry VIII's late years, schoolboys' drama had focused on themes of instruction and entertainment for the young scholar. Gnaphaeus' *Acolastus* (1529), the fragmentary *Prodigal Son* (printed in 1534), and John Redford's *Wit and Science* (Paul's boys, ca. 1539) are devoid of polemical slant; they are innocently and totally involved in a boys' world of education, tedium, and the need for relaxation. *Thersites* (1537), probably by Nicholas Udall, concludes with a prayer for Henry, Queen Jane Seymour, and the newly-arrived Prince Edward, to whom Udall offered his Protestant allegiance, but the play is otherwise free of political involvement. The humor refers familiarly to Purgatory, Rome, and lying Pardoners (A4^v, C1) in the spirit of Heywood, but without doctrinaire alignment.[24] Some courtly playwrights were themselves Catholic, unable to engage in controversy and yet free to write for the traditionally nonpolitical drama of the boys. Such a person was Heywood, close to the Catholic princess Mary Tudor, and probably associated also during these years with Redford.[25] As a group, Henry's choirmasters and purveyors of children's dramas were religiously either conservative or moderate, enjoying a safe refuge from the Protestantizing trend of the times.

The continual proximity of the court and its politically influential spectators, however, exerted an influence on choir boys' drama that was not to be resisted under the Protectorate reformers. *Jacob and Esau*, although nominally concerned with schoolboy themes, succumbs to the temptation to be political. Licensed in 1557-1558, the play is too early for Elizabeth's reign and too Protestant for Mary's. Most probably it dates from Edward VI and illustrates how even the staple tradition of schoolboy drama could be shaped to specifically Protestant use. As in *Hester,* the anonymous author[26] of *Jacob and Esau* is less concerned with informing his audience about Old Testament history than with seeing the original story as a type of current history. He is a zealous Calvinist engaged in his favorite task, discovering new "truths" in Scripture that dictate a pattern for contemporary society.

The biblical account (Genesis 29) [27] is puzzling to most Western readers today, and evidently was no less so in Tudor England. On its surface at least, Jacob's ruse in taking away his elder brother's birthright seems unethical even if it is not illegal; and the irreversible nature of father Isaac's mistakenly bestowed blessing seems equally legalistic and harsh. The midcentury Anabaptist play *Love Feigned and Unfeigned* equates the guile of Jacob and Rebecca with ancient Catholic falsehood (ll.

211-212). Shakespeare too captures a Christian sense of bewilderment in the corollary tale of Jacob and Laban's sheep, told by the Jew of Venice with obvious non-Christian relish as proof that such shystering tricks profit a man—so long as they are within the "bond" or letter of the Mosaic law.[28] Jacob, as admired by Shylock, becomes the type of unreconstructed pre-Christian. The author of *Jacob and Esau,* on the other hand, transforms Jacob's dubious behavior into unassailable Protestant virtue.

The play's topical bias is everywhere evident in the contrast of the brothers Jacob and Esau. The established, corrupted authority of the elder is being challenged by the virtue of the younger. Jacob hesitates to seize power against the rule of primogeniture (a moral nicety not observable in the biblical Jacob) but does so under compelling edict from the voice of God. Divine sanction justifies what may appear at first to be a revolutionary usurpation. In Calvinist terms, the brothers typify two irreconcilable factions of humanity, one destined to triumph over the other after a long and undeserved captivity. Their mother Rebecca observes:

> I remember, when I had you both conceived,
> A voice thus saying from the Lord I received:
> Rebecca, in thy womb are now two nations
> Of unlike natures and contrary fashions.
> The one shal be a mightier people elect.
> And the elder to the yonger shall be subject.
> I know this voice came not to me of nothing.
>
> (ll. 226-232)

The contrast between Jacob and Esau predates their birth. "Jacob was chosen, and Esau reprobate." Man's will or merit to be saved has no bearing on the divine covenant. As St. Paul explains, it is "in Gods mercy who choseth whom He will" (Prologue). Even education cannot save Esau, for he has been given the same advantages as Jacob. Despite the outward resemblances to school drama, then, this play is more interested in demonstrating the fundamental "ill inclination" of the corrupt old guard than in extolling the benefits of pedagogical training. Esau's neighbors have given him over as a goat who cannot become a sheep (ll. 184-186).

Esau gives every evidence of being beyond grace. He is a "ruffler." His hunting is interpreted (in a novel departure from the Bible) as a wildly irresponsible pastime, like dicing. He expresses contempt for his conscientious, sober, stay-at-home brother, and for the pallid daily labor of his neighbors. He does not care what his mother thinks of him, and he presumes on his father's dotage. Although there could easily be an attractive side to this Charles Surface, in contrast with his mild-mannered and scheming brother, the author does everything he can to prevent any sympathy for the wastrel. Esau is not generous. He plagues his servant with long hours and short rations, and most cruelly refuses to feed the servant after he, Esau, has sold his birthright for a mess of pottage. In a somewhat florid exhibition of savagery and cannibalism, he is seen as ready to devour his hunting dogs, his own arm, or his hapless servant to allay his hunger. His willingness to sell his birthright is heinously worldly: "It were sinne not to sell ones soul for such gear" (l. 749). He has succumbed to his temptation in the wilderness, and is unrepentantly prepared to fall again tomorrow.

Esau's ungodly behavior places Jacob in a dilemma of considerable interest to the sixteenth-century "elect." For if Esau is reprobate, he is still tolerated by his father, and is entitled to his position by sacred privileges. Isaac says:

> The title of birthright, that commeth by descent,
> Or the place of eldership, comming by due course,
> I may not chaunge nor shift for better nor for wourse.
> Natures law it is, the eldest sonne to knowlage.   (ll. 430-433)

Isaac concedes that "The Lord after His way" may "chaunge thinheritance," but insists that human agency may not initiate such a change. His argument is respected and conservative, passively accepting corrupt privilege so long as it is duly constituted. Jacob's problem, like that of the Protestant elect, is to see where action is necessary. Jacob anticipates radical questions, soon to be posed by John Ponet, Christopher Goodman, and John Knox, as to "How Superior Powers Ought to Be Obeyed." Passive obedience will not always serve. Since God will surely cleanse all evil in His good time, when and how do the elect know that they are to become instrumental in divine destiny? They know they are elect, but they are prone like Jacob to bear with evils that are sufferable rather than to violate long-established precedents (a truism aptly expressed by another Protestant society in the American Declaration of Independence). In these terms, *Jacob and Esau's* chief ideological purpose is to justify seizure of power, and to insist that the seizure is reluctantly undertaken. The author explains actions already taken by English Protestantism, but his theory dangerously sanctions any rebellion when divine command may be taken to oversway established order.

Rebecca's voice from the Lord goes to the heart of the epistemological question in Protestant theology as well as religious politics. The authority of God's word is to be determined by the individual to whom He speaks, not by an established government or religion. In *Jacob and Esau,* the truth of divine revelation through Rebecca is unquestioned, even by those who would prefer to leave things as they are (Isaac) and by the reprobate (Esau). Rebecca knows her course because God has spoken; the truth is self-evident. "God who, by His word and almightifull decree, Hath appointed thee Esau his lord to be, Hath appointed some way to have it brought about" (ll. 250-252). Rebecca too is loath to offend God's majesty by overthrowing tradition merely for the sake of change, "But by me (I doubt not) to work He doth intend." It follows that Rebecca's subsequent plans to steal away Esau's blessing by "policie" are also inspired by direct revelation:

> So that by policie he may beguiled be,
> I shall devise how for no ill intent ne thought,
> But to bring to pass that I know God wil have wrought.
>
> (ll. 898-900)

Rebecca is assisted in her holy machinations by an eavesdropping, thrown in her way by Providence, enabling her to understand the drift of Isaac's intention toward Esau (III, ii). God's hand also delays Esau in pursuit of the deer that is to elicit Isaac's blessing, allowing Jacob to get there first; Esau blasphemously ascribes the frustrating prolongation of his hunt to "luck" (l. 1416).

Jacob's deserving of power is attested to by all the characters in the play, and by his own intense struggles of conscience. He is both deeply aware of the appearance of fraud and guiltless of it because God has ordered him to perform a distasteful business. Isaac, bowing to God's will, commits Esau to the governance of the younger brother, an act "predestinate" and standing "in force of necessitie" (ll. 1490, 1509). The churlish Esau, after threatening tyrannical reprisals once he recovers his "place of succession" (l. 1457), miraculously accepts Jacob's virtuous authority and is reconciled. This idealized ending is both non-biblical and flatly contradictory to the play's theme of predeterminate reprobation; but one can easily see the political necessity in Edward VI's reign. Now that the older power has fallen, with its bluster of recrimination and violent threats, the great need is for persuasion and unity "that with one accord We may all with one voice sing unto the Lord" (ll. 1773-1774). The Opposition may be reprobate as a class, but some individuals in society are reclaimable.

Nice Wanton (ca. 1547-1553) is a similar boys' play with a Calvinist slant, although the political analogy is muted and the play retains traditional themes of education drama that are lost in *Jacob and Esau*.[29] Once again, children of a single family are alternately elect or depraved. Barnabas is another Jacob, aware that "Man is prone to evil from his youth" (l. 27), and that education is the only hope to turn man from his "naturall wont evill" (l. 11). He chides his rebellious brother and sister for their truancy, and demonstrates that the new religion depends on the persuasive powers of mere individuals rather than on a corporate sacramental tradition. His clothes and deportment are soberly modest. He endures the taunts of the ungodly, as the elect must learn to do. Church and state are closely interdependent in the process of reform. The nemesis figure of Daniel is sent to do "the kinges majesty justice," and resists attempts at bribery "As I owe to God and the king obedience and awe" (ll. 344, 365). The Prologue too urges "An honest quiet life, correspondent always To Gods law and the kinges" (ll. 7-8). Despite the predeterministic bias that seems to remove any hope of educability in the wayward Ismael, *Nice Wanton* does envisage a crucial role for education in the Protestant millennium at hand. Corrupted individuals of the old order must be reclaimed by the new; the fallen sister repents at the last moment and is saved through Christ's mercy. *Nice Wanton* demonstrates the ubiquitous presence of Protestant and pro-administration sentiment in even the most traditional forms of dramatic entertainment allowed by the government of Edward VI.

9 · ENGLAND RETURNS TO CATHOLICISM:
HOW FAR?

The government of Queen Mary, coming to power after a reign of increasingly headstrong Protestantism, was faced with a propaganda crisis. Mary's assumption of power found a great deal of popular emotional support, but it naturally antagonized the more zealous Protestants both in and out of government who, tutored in large part by Cromwell's propagandistic techniques, were organized and experienced in the art of mass persuasion. In the summer months of 1553, spontaneous demonstrations of affection for Mary gave way in London to angry Protestant demonstrations at St. Paul's Cross, directed chiefly at the Catholic mass.[1] In these tense months, drama was certain to be viewed apprehensively by the government as a two-edged weapon. Old cycle plays were resuscitated for public performance. Conversely, Protestant drama continued surreptitiously, necessitating on August 18, 1553, a governmental warning against all plays and books of a factional nature.[2] In 1556, after the queen's marriage to the hated Philip of Spain, a touring company wearing the livery of Sir Francis Leke uttered "very naughty and seditious matter touching the King and Queens Majesties."[3] Mary found that she had to continue and augment the policy of control begun under her younger brother.

Apart from simple revival of older dramatic forms, new explanations were needed to meet the country's uneasy mood. How far did Mary intend to go in restoring the ancient faith? What Protestant offenses would be punished, what pardoned? Perhaps must crucial, what sort of restitution of seized property and wealth would be required? Would this restitution extend as far as the enormously wealthy lands of abbey and monastery?

Mary was subject to intense pressure on the subject of restitution of church lands, and her own feelings were equally strong. Her simple wish was to restore the church to its former splendor and wealth. Few of her most loyal counselors agreed. The nation's newly wealthy men had prospered chiefly at the expense of church property. Mary could hardly have purged all of them without jettisoning the English ruling class. Many who accepted or even welcomed Mary's Catholicism could not tolerate the prospect of losing landed property. Among the populace, traditions of anticlericalism militated against anything approaching a complete return to the ecclesiastical wealth of Henry VII's era. Too much time had elapsed since the dissolution of the monasteries. Yet Mary, deeply pious, emotional, impractical, was determined to do what she could.

In this uneasy situation the anonymous author of *Respublica* had to exercise great tact. The play is intended for boys' performance at court, during the Christmas season of 1553. The issues are accordingly those of courtly politics rather than theology or ritual. There is no discussion of pilgrimages, saint worship, papal authority, and the like. The playwright's specific delicate task is to reconcile Mary's courtiers to her program of restitution, and at the same time to caution the queen gently about extremism in punishing or disenfranchising minor offenders. He wishes also to assert Mary's right to rule her counsel, not be ruled by it as Edward had been. In doctrinal and ritual matters, the author avoids inflammatory recriminations. Mary herself, for all her religious zeal, was sensible of the explosive emotional issue involved, and agreed to a plan of discreet restorations of rite where possible without public notice. Protestantism as such is called no names in *Respublica*, in fact is hardly seen to exist other than as a rationale for a few greedy men.

By implying that there is only one church, the playwright avoids the danger of labels and pre-set attitudes.

Politically, however, the author makes no attempt to hide his disapproval of the Protectorate ministries just ended. Although he speaks "as it were in figure by an allegory" (l. 18), he is at pains to specify the years 1547 to 1553. Queen Mary, appearing among the cast, is "our most wise and most worthie Nemesis" whom Heaven has sent "To reform thabuses which hithertoo hath been" and to restore Respublica "from hir late decay" of precisely five to six years' duration (ll. 46-53). The Cotswold rustic, People, complains that "Vive or zix year ago chad vowre kine to my pail"; now he prospers once again, but "I wis ich cowld not zo zai these zix yeares afore" (ll. 1021, 1601). Respublica sighs, "O Lord! how have I be used these five yeres past" (l. 1777). The entire play is a representation of Edward's reign and the first few months of Mary's reign, ending at the very moment the play is presented. No idealized vision of the future is necessary as in *Magnificence* or *Hester*.

The playwright finds fault not only with the Protectorate ministers but by implication with Henry VIII in his role as Protestant king. At the commencement of the play (obviously 1547), Respublica is already "sore decayed through defalte of Policy," and wealth has "been bard from me a great while" (ll. 484, 490). The Vices realize they are victimizing a lady who "is left almost desolate. Hir wealth is decayed" (ll. 238-239). Indeed, Henry's resumption of a policy of continental alliances and foolhardy military campaigns in 1541-1542, when he acted as his own chief minister after the downfall of Cromwell, had contributed to disastrous inflation, debasing of the coinage, and economic malaise. Respublica willingly accepts the newly proffered administration in 1547 because she is already in dire straits. For a recollection of true plenty comparable to the promise of Mary's reign, People is obliged to think back past "these yeres twise twenty" (l. 723).[4] *Respublica* everywhere expresses Mary's longing for the pre-Reformation years of her orthodox and financially solvent grandfather.

However exact its sense of time, *Respublica* is abstract in characterization. Even though the evil counselors arriving some six years prior to 1553 obviously point to Somerset and Northumberland, personal similarities are nonexistent. Leonard Magnus has searched, confessedly in vain, for four historical individuals who might correspond one-to-one with

Avarice, Adulation, Insolence, and Oppression.[5] He gingerly proposes that Adulation may represent Sir William Paget or Sir William Cecil, or both, since they like Adulation were forgiven their relatively minor crimes of acquiescing to Protestant rule. The hypothesis is unrewarding because it is circular in reasoning. No doubt the Marian courtly audience would have drawn its private conclusions as to which courtiers deserved pardon according to the play's view of justice. Perhaps they would have concurred in a verdict. Artistically, however, Adulation draws his inspiration from conventions of the morality. Even less do Henry VIII and Edward VI appear as personalities among the Vices; however blameworthy they may have seemed in Catholic eyes, and however much they may be implicated by the chronology of Respublica's ill fortunes, they were Mary's blood relatives. As with Wolsey in *Magnificence*, the Protectorate ministers here provide the motive and occasion but not the dramatic materials for the satiric characterization of the four evil counselors. Conventional abstractions of type are employed even when the author might have been more cutting.

The total absence of king-figures in the first four acts suggests that there was no real monarch, after all, from 1547 to 1553. *Respublica* ponders the evils of the power vacuum created by the historical accident of a minority kingship. Its conclusions are that the counselors of the realm cannot be trusted to rule dispassionately. Coming forward at a time when England needed most to rely on her ruling elite, since a form of regency or protectorate was mandatory, Edward's counselors reverted (in the dramatist's view) to the darkest days of the Wars of the Roses. This stark prospect of takeover, and the implicit assault on all royal prerogative, were still crucial in 1553 and afterwards. Although Mary was no minor like Edward, she was a woman whose presumed weaknesses as such encouraged more assertions of upper-class power (both of aristocracy and gentry). Religious debate gave added incentive to the challenge of her authority. Elizabeth, as a young Protestant woman, inherited this struggle between throne and ruling class, and had to do battle with domineering advice in a play like *Gorboduc* (see Chapter 11). Throughout midcentury, English monarchy was fighting for its ascendancy, and the outcome was by no means assured. Thus *Respublica's* attack on the corrupt advisers of Edward's reign concerns not only religious establishment but the theory of royal absolutism.

Respublica views the so-called "Reformation" as nothing more than one manifestation of lust for power by the ambitious elite. The villains are motivated not by heretical desire for simplified service or English scriptures, but by an age-old corruption in the guise of revolutionary zeal. As in *Hester*, Protestant Vices behave exactly like the worldly churchmen of pre-Reformation drama; conventions of the morality allow its types to be applied to both sides of the controversy. If the four evil counselors of *Respublica* correspond with the Protectorate ministers, they also recall Mind, Will, and Understanding. Avarice is chief among the evil counselors, not because he most nearly resembles the historical figure of the Protector but because avarice is the root evil, the source of corrupted power. Nor are his struggles to obtain mastery over his peers (I, iii) biographically significant; Vices always behave so in morality drama. In a timeless pattern of worldliness, the evil courtiers seize monasteries for their own profit, enclose farm land, deliberately inflate prices through their ability to monopolize commodities, serve as absentee landlords or pastors, and practice simony and usury. Their only distinction from earlier practitioners of such villainy is their specious cry of reform. Even when their misdeeds are most explicitly satirical of the Protectorate ministers—exporting strategic metals, devaluating coinage, cutting down valuable forests[6]—the generic nature of the allegory permits the author to see Somerset and Northumberland as nothing more than the latest in a succession of intriguers against the throne. The power-seeking impulse is the essence of "Protestantism," never named.

Politically, then, *Respublica* is an attack not only on the counselors of Edward's reign, but on the very system yielding power to men of their class. Even their advice is dangerous. Strong, unquestioned single rule can provide the only safeguard. The queen-figure in Act V of *Respublica* is no umpire, as in Heywood's *Weather*, who listens to all estates impartially. The nobility or merchants are represented by no abstractions in the closing scenes. Nemesis (Mary), who is herself a goddess, listens only to the voice of divine guidance. The insistence on royal absolutism sanctioned by providence is thus a political deterrent to the theory of rule by human counsel. Subsequently, Mary's sister Elizabeth was to cultivate this myth as a weapon in her struggle against powerful advisers.

Respublica does of course have one virtuous friend representing humanity during her tribulations and eventual triumph, but People does not qualify as an adviser. His numerous complaints reach Mary's ears, and in the final scene he is awarded custody of Insolence and Oppression. Nevertheless he is no Ploughman of *Gentleness* or John the Commonweal of Lindsay's *Satire of the Three Estates,* invited to participate in a thorough redistribution of political responsibility. People is as powerless as Respublica herself. His agrarian attachment to a feudal idea of kingship is thoroughly in accord with such backward-turning protests as the Pilgrimage of Grace. Decisions must be made for him. The attitude toward him is humorously condescending; he speaks in homely fashion for "we ignoram people," splitting his tongue on highfalutin words like "imagination" ("madge mason," l. 656). He has the countryman's dislike of courtly behavior, and it is his ingenuous viewpoint that the author usually employs for satire of social climbing. The evil counselors appear especially unattractive in their contempt for People. By contrast, his simple, gnomic wisdom commands respect. The dramatic portrait skillfully catches Mary's own attitude toward the commons, of paternalistic (or maternalistic) fondness, of desire for popularity achieved through good works of charity like those of her mother Katharine, of endearing concern for a populace that is supposed to know its place and respond with affectionate loyalty to a strong, compassionate leadership.

Correspondingly, the economic argument of this play is backward-turning. The author has no awareness of the long-range economic problems during midcentury before which the Protectorate ministers, and Mary herself, were essentially helpless: constantly rising prices, an agricultural population expanding beyond the capacity of the land under cultivation, and widespread conversion of arable land to pasture (the evil of enclosure) to feed an unrestrained expansion of the wool industry, which had collapsed in 1551 creating severe unemployment. When People grumbles at his lot, he speaks for an agricultural proletariat caught in the squeeze of inflation and lagging wages for day-labor. The author's solution is to accuse the previous administration of profiteering, and to propose essentially feudal remedies that are only palliative but are unavoidably necessary in any pre-industrial society. With so much underemployment and so much of the population existing at bare subsistence levels, the privileged few of enormous wealth must constantly be prepared to provide charitable relief on a large scale, particularly during periods of national catastrophe and famine.[7] The author's plea for a return to the system of monastic hospitality is essential to his (and Mary's) unconstructive but charitable program of poor-relief.

In chastising "these your late governoures" (l. 1825) who have betrayed Respublica, Nemesis does not bid Respublica to find new counsel. Instead, Nemesis herself undertakes the correction of abuses with the advice of four sisters, Mercy, Truth, Justice, and Peace. These abstractions are spiritual entities, unlike the four debased social types (Avarice, Adulation, Insolence, and Oppression) whom they have replaced and to whom they correspond in balanced antithesis of good versus evil, female versus male. A divine government replaces an earthly one, and Nemesis or Mary is its new head. As a divinity she is self-sufficient, embodying qualities of both clemency and rigor, infinitely compassionate but still formidable when finally aroused. The author is intent upon justifying the queen's belated moves against her more dangerous enemies, yet at the same time urges temperate handling of minor offenders.

All the abstractions agree, however, that no accommodation can be allowed on the question of restitution. Avarice must pay back all: "There is no remedie; powre itt owt in my lappe" (l. 1737). Since "only Avarice made us all to fall" (l. 1837), it is only just that each sinner return all that he has illegally obtained.

> *Nemesis.* People, take this felowe . . .
> That he maie be pressed as men doo press a spounge;
> That he maie droppe ought, tevery man his lotte,
> To the utmoost ferthing that he hath falslie gotte.
>
> (ll. 1903-1906)

Nemesis' divine commission authorizes her, furthermore, to exact penance "in all eastates" (l. 1791), not merely the corrupted governors of the realm. This sweeping promise, together with a specific endorsement of the hospitable mission of the older religion—when "they had their livinges, men were both fedde and cladde" (l. 1070)—points to a sizable renovation of religious houses. Mary did in fact attempt such renovation among the friars of Greenwich and other places, willingly foregoing the profits of many revenues that her father had enjoyed and spent. Doing so cost more than her government could afford; her dream of renewed wealth for the church was as financially impossible as it was emotionally unacceptable to the majority of her people. And although Mary stood ready to impoverish herself for the church, her courtiers who held church lands did not. What seemed so easy and so just in the concluding scenes of *Respublica* proved out of the question.

Mary's reign saw other pro-Catholic plays, such as the lost *Anglia Deformata and Anglia Restituta* performed at Trinity College, Cambridge, and probably the lost morality *Genus Humanum* at court in 1553 or 1554.[8] The sole surviving popular morality of her reign, *Impatient Poverty,* is actually a revision of a much earlier text, with its Catholic emphasis on the necessity of formal penance and ecclesiastical courts (ll. 1038-1039, 1053-1055) even though the system is frequently abused. Just as old cycles were revived, pre-Reformation moralities could be adapted to the 1550's with little difficulty. For the most part, however, Queen Mary preferred not to confront her problems too intensely in dramatic form. Increasingly the revels at court turned to entertainments and elaborate masques, as in Henry VIII's late reign. When an actual play was chosen, it was apt to be Plautine comedy.

The fact that Udall's *Ralph Roister Doister* stresses in its prologue the value of mirthful recreation may be no political coincidence. Formerly assigned to Udall's Eton period around 1538,[9] the play is now generally thought to have been composed shortly before the appearance in January 1554 (or perhaps 1553) of the third edition of Thomas Wilson's *The Rule of Reason,* containing *The Art of Logic,* which quotes the mistakenly pointed letter of III, iv as Udall's.[10] Wilson, an old pupil of Udall's and likely to have been in touch with Udall's latest work, does not use the letter in earlier editions of 1550-1552. The closing prayer in *Roister Doister* to the queen is probably not much help in dating the play, since epilogues of this sort were frequently updated for printing.[11] Queen Mary's fondness for Udall is well established, despite his earlier service to Protestantism. He has been suggested as the author of *Respublica.* In 1555, he composed for Mary a court masque, now lost. Mary took part with Udall in a translation of a paraphrase of the Gospel of St. John in 1549.[12] In any case he had been close to the court ever since 1541, writing under the patronage of various noblemen after his dismissal from Eton. Under these circumstances it appears most likely that Udall wrote *Roister Doister* for Mary's entertainment shortly before or after her coronation, to be performed by choristers rather than public school boys. The actors may have been the boys of Bishop Gardiner's school at Southwark, engaging in a full ecclesiastical revels celebrating the Lord of Misrule.[13] Appropriately, Christian Custance's story of feminine courage, charity, and firm maternalism is calculated to warm Mary's heart. Although Christian Custance is no allegorized alter ego for Mary, she defends a system of values that Mary had cherished from the beginning of her Catholic and conservative childhood.

As Udall's didactic heroine, contrasted point by point with Roister Doister throughout the play, Christian Custance has no Plautine counterpart in the *Eunuchus* or elsewhere. Her confrontation with Roister Doister is essentially a battle of the sexes, reminiscent of the division between female virtue and male vice in *Respublica*. Christian's household is predominantly female: Madge Mumblecrust, Tibet Talkapace, Annot Alyface. Roister Doister's forces, on the other hand, include Dobinet Doughty, Harpax, "two drummes with their ensignes," the two-faced Merrygreek, and the like. The caricatured names emphasize the distinction between pert "talkapace" maidservants and "daughty," brusque young men. Roister Doister himself typifies all the noisy bravado that so annoyed the ladies in *Respublica*. He is a ruffler, a disturber of the peace, divisive and importunate, crass. The maids live in quiet, gay harmony, love their mistress, and are inspired by her bravery that is so lacking in flamboyance.

The basic contrast between Christian and Roister Doister is in the management of their respective households. Roister Doister bullies his servants, sends them on endless rounds of senseless errands, issues conflicting orders. Dobinet Doughty mimics his master in exasperation:

> "Go bear me this token!" "Carrie me this letter!"
> Now, "This is the best way"; now, "That way is better!"
>
> (ll. 572-573)

Roister Doister is a bad disciplinarian, and earns as reward the scarcely-concealed contempt of his servants. They scoff at his wooing, and complain of the long, late hours so potentially injurious to the health of a schoolboy chorister: "Up before day, sirs, I charge you, an hour or twain!" Later, "Then up to our lute at midnight, twangledom twang" (ll. 574, 583). They object to his use of profanity, and characterize him as setting the servants to spy on one another in constant fear of treachery (ll. 578-579). He manages to create dissension even in Christian's household, but his shallow ruses merely give Christian an opportunity to display a patient, warm, and somewhat condescending control of her innocent helpers.

Tibet and the rest are indeed much like the ingenuous People of

Respublica. They want to please their mistress, but they require detailed, repeated instructions and a good deal of forbearance. The mistress is the wary one, patiently aware that her servants have heeded Roister Doister's blandishments through simpleness rather than malice. She dismisses the offense with a warning and a moral tag: "I shall make all girles by you twain to beware . . . Good wenches would not so ramp abrode idelly, But keep within doores, and plie their work earnestly" (ll. 744-751). In its positive aspect, the play is a courtesy-book for young women rather than for scholars.

Udall's acute perceptivity about feminine psychology seems more apt for Mary's court than for the juvenile monasticism of Eton. Christian is thoroughly complex and admirable as a character. She is blessed with a sanity that dismisses Roister Doister's pranks lightly: "This will prove some foolish matter in the end" (l. 765). Her view of love is a sane one that allows her to sleep at night (l. 821). She has so little curiosity about Roister Doister's importunate letter that she doesn't even bother to open it. She even welcomes Matthew's reading of the letter as amusing "sport," and returns honest answers to Roister's bluster with no attempt to humiliate. She dismisses Roister Doister and Merrygreek with the forbearing "No, God be with you both, and seek no more to me" (l. 1123). She wishes only to avoid strife.

At the same time she is very much a woman, loyal to her betrothed Gawin Goodluck, and on the verge of tears when the seemingly minor irritation of Roister Doister's courtship threatens to blacken her reputation before the world and Gawin. The lesson of prudence in maintaining appearances becomes a serious Christian duty.

> O Lord! how necessarie it is now of dayes
> That eche bodie live uprightly all maner wayes;
> For lette never so little a gappe be open,
> And be sure of this—the worst shall be spoken.
>
> (ll. 1864-1867)

Christian is a heroine protected by the same Providence that guarded Mary Magdalene, Susanna, and Queen Hester—a figure associated in court drama with Mary's mother, Katharine. The daily world, dominated by men who go "jetting up and down" with their "lustie bragge" (ll. 1004, 1006), is a world of slander and treachery, in which women must move cautiously. Yet God will protect them. Christian's victory over Roister Doister is therefore not one of Amazonian "maistry"—for Christian is loyally subservient to Gawin's proper masculine authority—but an assertion of the feminine values of concord, domesticity, and forbearance similarly advocated in *Respublica*. The harmless ending in a banquet suggests the social reconciliation that Mary so earnestly desired.

Religious motifs in *Roister Doister* reinforce the hypothesis of courtly performance under Mary. The celebrated parody of the Catholic service for the dead (1. 936f) would have sat strangely with the Protestant advisers who saw *Jacob and Esau*. The tone is light and friendly; the satire is directed not at the service itself but at the comic discrepancy between Roister Doister's ineffectual melancholy and the seriousness of "*Requiem aeternam.*" The technique is that of Skelton's "Philip Sparrow," with its tradition of the medieval Venus mass or mass of the birds. The voices of the choristers are lovingly familiar. The mock-heroic rite follows Catholic liturgy rather closely, progressing from the visitation of the sick to the vespers for the dead (*"Placebo dilexi"*), matins (*"Dirige"*), mass (*"Requiem aeternam"*), and burial service (*"In Paradisum"*).[14] There are no malapropisms as in Bale's savage lampoon of excommunication in *King John,* no duckings and crossings, no blasphemies or references to the pope.

No play expresses better than *Jack Juggler* (ca. 1554)[15] the sense in which Plautine comedy could attempt escape from the weight of responsibility. The playwright, aware that his innocent fun may be forced into topical meaning and his disclaimers cynically ignored, nevertheless offers an antidote to fear and the divisive emotions of politics. He has consciously avoided hidden, serious meaning:

> for higher things endite
> In no wise he wold, for yet the time is so quesie,
> That he that speakith best, is lest thank worthie.   (ll. 66-68)

The old comedy can be enjoyed for its own sake. Of course no author in the Tudor period can refuse to pay lip-service to the dogma of moral usefulness, and the ancient writers accordingly furnish "mutch wisdom and teach prudent pollecie" (1. 54). Still, this wisdom is "not worth an oyster shel, Except percase it shall fortune to make you laugh well" (ll. 62-63). The essence of *Jack Juggler* is a trifle.

> Therfore, sith nothing but trifles may be had,
> You shall hear a thing that onlie shal make you merie and glad.

And such a trifling matter, as when it shalbe done,
You may report and say ye have heard nothing at all.   (ll. 69-72)

Comedy of relaxation had precedents both in old comedy and in English drama, especially in *Thersites* and *Gammer Gurton's Needle* (perhaps as early as 1550). Yet these plays were intended for public school or university, where they could take advantage of the ivory tower. The defense of pleasure is unusually vociferous in *Jack Juggler* because it appears against a political background in which "the time is so quesie." The playwright looks upon boys' drama as the last refuge of innocence in which political considerations are both a comfort-killing intrusion and an artistic indecorum: "For this maker shewed us that such maner things Do never well besime litle boyes handelings" (ll. 76-77). Plays like *Jacob and Esau*, the prologue implies, force upon the boys a political maturity ill-suited to their specialized talents. Why should choristers plead like Calvinists? The tradition of "pure" boys' drama has been all but forgotten in the grimness of a Reformation court.

The attitude of courtly irresponsibility appears throughout the play of *Jack Juggler*. The plot is one of mistaken identities, engineered by the fun-loving Jack Juggler in "as mad a pastime this night As you saw this seven yers" (a span of time comparable to the five or six years of Protestant corruption bewailed in *Respublica*). Jack's victim is Jenkin Careaway, whose name connotes his comic irresponsibility. Jenkin has dawdled in conveying a message to his mistress in order to play at dice with the "bucklers" of London, where he loses all his money, and has stolen the apples of a street vendor. For these acts, treated as heinous social problems in the moral drama of the period (such as *Impatient Poverty* or *Juventus*), Jenkin is never punished. His master reprimands him for dilatoriness, not for theft, and Jack's viewpoint is one of amusement at Jenkin's discomfiture.

If the play suggests any relevance to current social norms, the suggestion is one of a modest courtly hedonism. Some details are not evident in the source play, Plautus' *Amphitruo*. Jenkin's master and mistress enjoy a life of idle pleasure, dining and dancing, tennis, kissing "gentilwomen two or three" (l. 261). In a tale to beguile his mistress that Jenkin concocts out of the events of his daily life, he speaks of "Gorges dames of the corte and galaunts also, With doctours and other rufflers mo" (ll. 272-273). The mistress, who is "As denty and nice as an halpeny worth of silver spoons, But vengable melancolie in the aftirnoons" (ll. 221-222), longs for more social activity. Jenkin supposes she will not be unwilling to hear of a would-be gentleman caller who desires to send love tokens and make a visit in the master's absence. None of these dissipations is viewed with moral revulsion in the play, and none merits retribution. Sympathy lies with youth, "sport," intrigue, and harmless disrespect for authority. Much of this is of course Plautine; but the applicability to Catholic courtly society, wearied of Protestant sobriety, is explicit and new.

Protestant morality in its turn found this view intolerable, and asserted its opinion in a later postscript to *Jack Juggler*. An unidentified spokesman follows Jenkin Careaway on stage to deliver a conventional moral ending at once so jarring in tone and so simply irrelevant that it is surely an Elizabethan addition for publication in 1564. The epilogue could not be the work of the playwright who has so heatedly denied topical meaning, for it openly indulges in allegorical sleuthing. Rejoicing that "no tale can be told But that sum English may be piked therof out" (ll. 1145-1146), the epilogue deplores "the fashion of the world now a dayes" in which innocents are deluded and "shamefullie abused" to their "gret harm"—as if Jenkin were innocent or had suffered any serious punishment. The most outrageous abuse is that men are made "To belive and say the moun is made of a grene chese" (l. 1155), a metaphor presumably allegorizing Jenkin's hapless loss of identity into Catholic thought control. As B. J. Whiting observes, the reader is alarmed to discover that *Jack Juggler* has suddenly become a satire on transubstantiation.[16] "Darest thou affirm to me That which was never sene nor hereafter shalbe, That one man may have two bodies and two faces, And that one man at one time may be in two placis?" (ll. 899-902). Ironically, an Elizabethan publisher has foisted this retrospective interpretation on a play that urgently pleads for a courtly drama innocent of political motive. Catholic entertainment becomes Protestant polemic. By the early 1560's, English society had sufficiently recovered its senses to know that plays must omit no opportunity, however strained, to castigate "Force, strength, power, and colorable subtlete," which "Doth oppress, debar, overcum, and defeat right" (ll. 1158-1159). Jenkin Careaway has been somehow transformed into a hero from Foxe's *Book of Martyrs*. The struggle for political control of drama as an organ of religious settlement had not yet ended.

Queen Elizabeth handled the political drama of her early reign with a finesse that baffled both critics and admirers. Her method was of a piece with her foreign and domestic policy, avoiding inflexible positions, countenancing secret propaganda even while she publicly cajoled and temporized. During her first year, in the exuberant days of Protestant reascendancy, she actually witnessed an anti-Catholic mumming "of crows in the habits of Cardinals, of asses habited as Bishops, and of wolves representing Abbots." [1] Yet her court was not to continue open defiance as Edward's had done. Acting in part on Spanish complaints, she issued stern proclamations in April and May of 1559 warning magistrates not to license performers "wherein either matters of religion or of the governance of the state of the common weal shall be handled or treated." [2] Political drama continued active, either in spite of these proclamations or with the government's tacit approval. Count de Feria, not convinced by Elizabeth's protestations of concern, reported that Cecil was actually directing the efforts of certain playwrights as Cromwell had done.[3] The satire was venomously personal: the Venetian ambassador reported in 1559 that the actors "brought upon the stage all personages whom they wished to revile, however exalted their station, and amongst the rest, in one play, they represented King Philip, the late Queen of England,

and Cardinal Pole, reasoning together about such things as they imagined might have been said by them in the matter of religion." [4] Publication certainly went on apace: *Juventus* and *Nice Wanton* were registered in 1560, *Three Laws* in 1562-1563, *Cruel Debtor* in 1566, *The Longer Thou Livest the More Fool Thou Art* in 1568-1569. A disheartened Bishop Quadra sent home in 1562 certain portions of Bale's satire on Philip of Spain, "As I was tired of complaining to the Queen of the constant writing of books, farces, and songs prejudicial to other princes, and seeing that notwithstanding her promises no attempt was made to put a stop to it." [5]

Elizabeth was certainly playing a double game with the Spanish. Yet the polemical drama she allowed was carefully circumscribed. It could speak of political matters such as the international menace of Catholicism, but had to be more discreet on doctrinal hairsplitting. Elizabeth had no intention of allowing her "settlement" to be discussed after she had settled it. By and large, early Elizabethan drama reflects her genius in finding a religious consensus for her strife-torn nation. The Elizabethan compromise began and ended as a state of profitable tension between antagonistic viewpoints. Her solution was to leave as much as practicable to individual conscience, provided that causes of conscience not be permitted to "exceed their bounds and grow to be matter of faction." Obviously the solution demanded an end to quarreling over individual points of dogma and ritual. At least until the dangerous arrival of Mary Stuart in 1568, Elizabeth attempted to win over England's Catholics by gentle persuasion. Nothing better reveals her statesmanship and personal courage than her defense of a broad and tolerant policy against the occasionally intense pressures from both houses of Parliament and even from her Privy Council. Elizabeth herself probably had a certain fondness for religious formalism. Stories were whispered of her "honourable sentiments" for saints and her private chapel garnished with tapers.[6] When the Dean of St. Paul's ventured, in 1565, to digress on the subject of images, alluding presumably to the crucifix kept by the queen in the royal chapel, "Leave that," she exclaimed, "It has nothing to do with your subject, and the matter is now threadbare." [7] The extreme vulgarities of Protestant controversy were not "altogether to her private taste." [8]

Even the external Catholic threat needed to be placated and postponed because of England's division and military weakness. With France showing hostile intent in Scotland and (after 1562) against the Huguenots, England could ill afford to alienate Spain and thus unite two great continental powers against her. Later, in the pre-Armada years, anti-Catholic propaganda would again prove useful. At the moment, every consideration urged judiciousness. As controversy waned, the drama turned from theology to economic and social problems, and especially to external (hence unifying) problems such as the threat of cheap foreign labor.

As in the earlier Protestant return to power of 1547, a natural impulse of drama in the 1560's was to search out reasons for the backsliding of the Catholic years just ended. Most such analyses are surprisingly mild. An exception is Nathaniel Woodes's *Conflict of Conscience* (ca. 1570). Probably not officially sponsored or even performed, its untypical bitterness may have been caused by the new dangers around 1570 of Mary Stuart, the Northern Rising of 1569, and the excommunication of Elizabeth.[9] Even this play, however, is not aggressively factional in the spirit of Bale. Woodes is anti-Catholic but not Puritan.[10] He examines not the Elizabethan settlement but the continuing threat of Catholic takeover through English weakness. He pointedly asks what may happen when typical English Protestants again have to face a papal inquisition like that afflicting Woodes's protagonist, Philologus. Will they, like him, break under questioning and despairingly renounce the true faith? Can they find answers for the existence of so much evil in England, and the perseverance to endure it?

Woodes exchanges the Italian setting of his chief source, Francisco Spira's autobiography, for a northern English locale where conservative religious tendencies were unusually pronounced. The papist priest Caconos, who informs against Philologus to the Cardinal, grossly endorses every form of image worship and traffic in relics or pardons. Woodes's satirical indictment of this superstitious northerner is fierce, but the central issue is still Philologus' inability to withstand Caconos' treachery. The ascendancy of Catholic inquisition is a divinely meaningful affliction, designed to test the constancy of the elect and to purge away their carnal lusts. (Woodes here echoes a commonplace explanation of the Marian Counter Reformation as expressed by Miles Coverdale, Roger Hutchinson, John Marbeck, and others.)[11] Philologus, as a rightminded

Protestant clergyman, grasps the significance of his temptation in the wilderness and yet succumbs to worldly considerations. Such a fall is infinitely more horrible than the sinning of the ignorant. Woodes's play is, therefore, a sobering object lesson in the insidious perils of religious relapse, addressed chiefly to clergymen. The author candidly admits that not all victims of Catholic terror are as superhumanly heroic as they appear to be in Foxe.[12]

An anonymous play similarly fearful of backsliding is *King Darius* (printed 1565), which, as Bernard Spivack observes, "is a reaction to Elizabeth's obscure course in religion during the first years of her reign, and . . . is filled with Protestant anxiety over the chance of a Catholic restoration."[13] Preachers of the Gospel are roughly handled and temporarily expelled by the bullying papal Vices, who turn anew to defrauding the poor and living licentiously (ll. 285-610). These unregenerate villains refuse all spiritual counsel, and are finally driven off to perdition along with the flattering counselors who have attempted to mislead the king.

The anonymous *New Custom* (ca. 1563) better exemplifies Elizabeth's policy of moderation and gentle recovery of wayward Catholics. Although memories of the Marian Counter Reformation are still keen in this play, Romish practice is on the defensive. The villains cringe at the prospect of certain overthrow: "For the matter so standes, if we look not well about, That we quite perish all out of doubt" (C^v). Perceiving that their Latin mummery is failing to convert English worshipers, the villains turn in desperation to crude violence. Jailings and burnings are earnestly topical: "here in England," and more specifically, "in the daies of Queen Marie" (C3^v). The author cites a particular case of martyrdom in 1557 from Foxe's *Book of Martyrs*.[14] Avarice and Cruelty reflect the bankrupt policies of Mary and Philip, although without personal resemblance. They are easily defeated, leaving Light of the Gospel in control.

In this mood of quiet jubilation, *New Custom* temperately concerns itself not with settling old scores but with determining the shape of the new era and justifying the change. A major problem, as in the Edwardian *Juventus*, is education of the English public to the true nature of Protestantism. It must be seen not as revolutionary but as "primitive constitution," the restored church of Christ's first apostles. "New Custom" is actually a pejorative term, foisted on the elect by those who would claim antiquity for themselves.[15] Most of all, Protestants must eschew vituperation and must not seem lacking in patience toward their less devout brethren. Although the play castigates the reactionary habit of doing "as thy fathers have doone before thee" (D), and Calvinistically allows that there will always be those whom God has rejected (D2ᵛ), the protagonist is after all a benighted papist who finally sees the light of the Gospel. Such conversions are seemingly possible, and are infinitely preferable to repressive alienation and thus abandonment of practitioners of the old faith. The playwright welcomes the assistance of the Protestant state, believing that its rulers "earnestly studie that fault to amend" (B1ᵛ). Their virtuous intentions, of reclaiming the great mass of Englishmen by means of a flexible and gradual program of reform, deserve the support of those elect who might otherwise prefer a more thoroughgoing change; some compromise may be necessary. The playwright, for example, would personally like to see more plainness in religious vestments than is currently allowed, but he accepts the prescribed sumptuary regulations in recognition that "wise princes" have commanded "the clargie in such sort to be clad" (D3ᵛ). The author is thus a moderate Protestant willing to work with the authorities—the only sort of Protestant, presumably, whose dramas might ordinarily be performed. Lewis Wager's *The Life and Repentance of Mary Magdalen* (ca. 1558) similarly pleads for a drama that will "teach true obedience to the king" (prologue), and will offer examples of non-controversial, simple faith such as Christ himself demonstrated when subjected to inquisition at the house of Simon the Pharisee. As *New Custom* insists, a return to the primitive gospel of the early church is not revolution, but a wholesome means of ending dogmatic rivalries.

Both extant plays of William Wager (possibly related to Lewis Wager), *The Longer Thou Livest the More Fool Thou Art* and *Enough Is as Good as a Feast*, focus on the problem of what to do with England's wayward Catholics in the early 1560's. The scene is not disguised: it is England and London (*Longer*, ll. 1016, 1021), when "of late dayes this canker pestilent" is "Corrupting our realm to our utter decay," presenting the spectacle of "the Brethren . . . burned with fire, the child with the mother" (*Enough*, Bᵛ). The protagonists of these two plays, Moros and Worldly Man, are naturally reprobate men who can feign

Protestant virtue but who quickly seize oppressive power during the Marian regime. As men who "are like to come to dignitie and promotion," they typify a corrupt ruling class and even relate indirectly to Philip II.[16] Yet they are also ordinary Catholic fools whom Fortune has capriciously elevated for a time to prove the mettle of the persecuted elect.

A staunch Calvinist, Wager accepts the division of mankind into elect and reprobate. Nevertheless, as spokesman for the new order, Wager must urge an endless patience with the wayward. Figures like Heavenly Man and Discipline explicitly represent the power of the reformed state as well as the church. Piety considers it one of his highest responsibilities to:

> teach you your dutie to kinges,
> To rulers and majestrates, in their degree,
> Unto whom you must be obedient in all thinges
> Conserning the statutes and lawes of the countrie.
>
> (*Longer*, ll. 431-434)

Accordingly, the virtuous place great emphasis on education, which must begin early with the child. Moros and Worldly Man are "past cure," like too many Englishmen who have been brought up in the old ways of matin bells and idolatry. Moros' comic mimicry is a sad reminder of Catholic education by rote; now he can learn a new pattern, but superficially as before. Protestant humanism, although partly hobbled with the dogma of predestinate depravity, still clings to the truism that "While a plant of a tree is yonge and tender, You may cause it to grow croked or right" (*Longer*, ll. 527-528). The compromise, looking forward to a new generation to be raised under Protestant aegis, all but gives up on the old.

Yet Wager can justify the abandonment and punishment of Worldly Man and Moros only after all attempts at recovery have failed. Heavenly Man actually brings Worldly Man to pious life for a time. Discipline and his fellows argue patiently with Moros long after they have concluded unlikelihood of success: "For the love that we owe to mankind, And chiefly unto Christianitie, We will prove to alter his mind" (*Longer*, ll. 182-184). Aware of the "vitious infection," they go softly at Moros with the power of retaliation held in check but plainly evident.

If with any lewdness I chaunce him to take,
I shall minister to him such correction,
As shall make his flesh tremble and quake.

(*Longer,* ll. 560-562)

This time-honored governmental policy of the threat of force withheld urges patient forgiveness of Catholic Englishmen as far as public safety permits.

It is in attacking general social evils rather than religious doctrines, however, that Wager most successfully turns away from the divisive polemics of the previous generation.[17] Worldly Man is a Catholic, but the methods of his evil are simply mercenary—underpaying his servants, demanding exorbitant services from his landed tenants, and especially charging high rents for his London dwellings. (The play fragment *Cruel Debtor* [ca. 1565], by one of the Wagers, similarly attacks usury as forbidden by Matthew 18.) The elect in these plays are content with "enough as good as a feast," a philosophy that stresses plainness but does not prevent them from seeking a decent prosperity. They deplore especially the commercial inroads of foreigners—immigrants to the London area who pay whatever rents are asked and so price native Englishmen out of their dwellings. The Cotswold-speaking Tenant charges landlords:

And they are not zo covetous to ask nother, ich beleeve,
But a zort of vooles are as ready to give;
And espetially straungers, ye, a shameful zort,
Are placed now in England, and that in every port,
That we, our wives and children, no houses can get
Wherin we may live, such price on them is zet.   (*Enough,* E^v)

With such a scapegoat conveniently at hand, English popular drama of the late 1560's and 1570's was prepared to soft-pedal the domestic religious question.

This commercial resentment against foreigners, although sharply on the rise after the disastrous wool crisis of 1551, was only the extension of traditional hostilities. The pre-Elizabethan *Wealth and Health* (S. R. [Stationers' Register entry], 1557) attacks the Flemish as drunkards and opportunists deserving to be expelled so that "Englishmen shall live the better daily" (l. 762); the Flemish Hans speaks a thick Germanic stage dialect soon to become familiar in the early Elizabethan theater.[18] Resentment of aliens was prominent in the "Ill May Day" riots of 1517, and Wolsey was later the object of attack for allowing his diplomatic maneuvers to interfere with cloth export. *A Discourse of the Common Weal* (1549) vehemently insisted that all loyal subjects should "buy English" to discourage traffic in imported trifles, and that the government should avoid international agreements contrary to the interests of English trade. Generally, however, arguments for restriction went unheeded while cloth exports continued to expand rapidly under Henry VIII. This expansion gave the appearance of prosperity to the English cloth trade, but profits were in fact being undermined by an accelerating inflation and by an ever-widening depreciation in the rate of exchange. England's excessive reliance on a single product and on the single market of Antwerp made her vulnerable to unpredictable fluctuations in demand. When the overexpanded wool industry finally collapsed in 1551, economic distress was severe. A glutted market produced widespread unemployment, especially among the laborers of the wool industry. Xenophobia, dormant before, now demanded compulsory restriction of output and competition. Spanish meddling in the Netherlands further cut off vital export markets, and after 1567 accelerated the wave of Flemish and Walloon refugees expert at fashioning new and lighter cloths needed for a more diversified market. The Hanseatic League, long resented for the favorable trading rights it obtained from the English crown in the thirteenth century and again from Edward IV, faced temporary suspension of its privileges in 1552 and ultimate expulsion from its famous Steelyard location in London (1598).[19]

Anti-foreign sentiment accordingly increased in tempo in the social moralities of the late 1560's and 1570's. The Vice of *Trial of Treasure*, Inclination, is adept at mimicking the French and Flemish ("Ick en can ghene english spreken vorwaer," C\u1d5b) who support his program of violence and greed. Ulpian Fulwell's *Like Will to Like* satirizes Flemish servants who "will quass and carouse, and therin spend their gain" (B4), like Philip Fleming or Hans, who enters "with a pot," tongue-tied with alcohol. Ludicrous as they are with their dancing "as evill favoured as may be devised," Hans and Philip are harmful dissipaters of England's wealth. George Wapull's *The Tide Tarrieth No Man* and Thomas Lupton's *All for Money* take up the crisis of the forced evictions brought about by grasping owners of rented dwellings. As in *Enough*, the underlying problem is foreign labor ready to pay double rents in the port cities. The honest Neighbor in *Tide Tarrieth* is particularly bitter about the shabby lack of patriotism manifested by English landlords:

> For among us now, such is our countrey zeal,
> That we love best with straungers to deal.
> To sell a lease dear, whosoever that will,
> At the French or Dutch church let him set up his bill
> And he shall have chapmen, I warrant you good store.
> Look what an Englishman bids, they will give as much more.
>
> (ll. 496-501)

Concern for economic rivalry rather than religious doctrine led to the satirical exposure of domestic villains as well as foreigners. The themes are identical with those of contemporary pamphlets such as Philip Stubbes's *The Anatomy of Abuses* (1583), Edward Hake's *A Touchstone for the Time Present* (1574), or Francis Trigge's *An Apology or Defense of Our Days* (1589).[20] "Coney-catching" insights into the London underworld, so frequent in later Elizabethan literature, repeatedly expose the purse-snatcher or cheating merchant: Grim the Collier, Cuthbert Cutpurse, and Pierce Pickpurse in *Like Will to Like*, Snatch and Catch in the morality *Wit and Wisdom*. Tudor audiences are told how to guard their wealth as well as how to live by more honest means. Usury becomes an obsessive target of satire. The interest racket is set forth in plentiful detail, and with a realism derived not from conventional types but from observation.[21] Taking of interest had been forbidden in 1552, but was by implication permitted to a limit of ten percent by "an act against Usury" in 1571.[22] The spendthrift Courtier in *Tide Tarrieth* discovers to his sorrow that he can borrow money only at ruinously high rates for short terms, because so many financial middlemen are involved in the transaction (ll. 980-985). The most heinous form of "usury," curiously, is the forcing up of prices in time of short supply.

The Protestant moralists of these plays today appear reactionary in their views of social change and commerce, but these views were at least shared by the government and the nation. Manipulating the market in terms of supply and demand was widely regarded as "excessive gain"; financial restraint and public relief in times of distress were supposed to be the merchant's charitable duty enjoined by God. Paternalistic Tudor social legislation attempted to compensate for the vast and misunderstood problems of inflation and unemployment by dictating "just" prices. The Parliament of 1597-1598 concerned itself with abuses that had long vexed the crown: forestalling, engrossing, and regrating, various devices to "corner" the market in times of dearth or to buy and sell merely for profit-taking. Usurers and other middlemen, although tolerated in times of prosperity, were the inevitable scapegoats in times of economic malaise; the government cracked down on taking of interest intermittently as the country's mood changed. Only later in the century was the interference of the paternalistic state in free competition challenged. Most Englishmen agreed with the economic philosophy of the popular dramatists, who sought a decent compromise of prosperity and virtue not so much by legislation as by the moral guidance presented in their own plays.[23]

Uneasy about the newer modes of finance, these dramatists amply demonstrate a typical Protestant antipathy toward idleness and an addiction for religious morality as a guide to daily life—what L. B. Wright has called the "Hebraic conception of the profitableness of well-doing." [24] Even *Trial of Treasure*, illustrating in rather wooden allegory the truism that lust and treasure turn to dust and rust, hesitates between rejection of all worldly vanity and the modest rewards of a temperate life on earth. The other plays inculcate practical holiness without apology. They denounce financial abuses not to foster otherworldly contemplation but to assure adequate plenty for the industrious. The aptly-named Virtuous Living in *Like Will to Like* insists on the tangible rewards of sober effort:

> For vertue and fortune be not at strife.
> Where vertue is, fortune must needs grow;
> But fortune without vertue hath soon the overthrow.   (D2)

Faithful Few in *Tide Tarrieth* readily allows the propriety of a modest profit (l. 1559). *All for Money's* central thesis is that good things like money may be abused, and that responsible craftsmanship of the artisan class in particular is basic to economic prosperity (l. 174). These plays, written largely for working and mercantile audiences in a period when (in spite of general inflation and a bad depression in the 1550's) some fortunate Londoners were able to achieve prosperity, breathe an optimism in the very acerbity of their tirades against abuses of the system. Though they are occasionally impatient with a government that condones interest rates, they nonetheless rely generally on the civil administration to carry out the conservative reforms of everyday morality that they urge.

That social moralities of this type could also convey a growing sense of restiveness in their lower-class London audiences, and imply more searching criticisms of the establishment, is evident in *The Peddler's Prophecy* (ca. 1561).[25] Another violently anti-foreign play, it inveighs against an uninterrupted flow of immigrants, shortage of renting space, inflated prices, and a mongrelized population (ll. 824-827). The author is dissatisfied with the manner in which the authorities are handling such crises, and permits the lower-class figure of the Peddler to castigate clergy and judiciary unsparingly. The tone and program are similar to those of the reforming preachers associated with the agrarian social radicalism of 1549, so much resembling Anabaptism in the minds of fearful public officials. Like the early apostles, the Peddler is an ignorant man preaching to his betters of hell-fire lying in wait for the socially decadent. He is abused for his plain speaking, just as Christ would be despised if He returned to earth (l. 1357). The Peddler is the prophet of divine punishment: "I think God hath revealed to him things to come, To the ignorant" (ll. 1042-1043). Speaking in parables of Ilion and Tyre because his criticisms of clergy and justices might be construed as talk "of the state of this region," "of the queenes majestie, and of the councell" (ll. 1451-1452), the Peddler insists that it is right for men to "rail upon authoritie." He goes so far as to suggest that princes themselves, although good in heart, are unable to stop moral decay and will be punished at God's hands for their subjects' crimes (ll. 1459-1460). The figures of authority who hear this jeremiad impugning their competency are aggrieved "To have a tinker or a cobler to minister to us" (l. 1339).

The author of *The Peddler's Prophecy* grudgingly admits at last that his radical doctrines are visionary and that the evils he cites must be left to "the administration." The queen and her council must be acknowledged as infallible. Except for the monarchy, however, the Peddler insists that he and his fellow moralists be permitted to impeach corrupt officialdom. They may not punish, but they will accuse; and their hostility toward magistrates as a class is scarcely alleviated by their loyalty to the throne. The Peddler, as folk hero and critic of the upper classes, anticipates the viewpoint of much heterodox London drama of the 1580's and 1590's (see Chapter 15).

No play serves better than Robert Wilson's *Three Ladies of London* (early 1580's) to summarize the thematic preoccupations of the Elizabethan late morality play, and to indicate new directions in the London drama after 1576. Like the Peddler, Wilson is impatient with magistrates and clergy. Their correction must be left to the Almighty, whose prophet is the angry moralist of lowborn sympathies. Yet Wilson's conservative and jingoistic program supports the policies of Elizabeth and Burghley on such matters as ordnance manufacture and the restriction of non-essential imports of spices, silks, and wines.[26] Wilson was, after all, a member of the Earl of Leicester's (Dudley's) men who received special favor from the queen in 1574 to perform in London regularly on weekdays, and who established themselves at James Burbage's Theater in 1576.

Wilson's detestation of foreigners exceeds even that of popular drama in the 1570's. His attitude bespeaks increased danger from the Catholic league, and indicates the willingness of Londoners to anticipate some kind of showdown. A generation of peace under Elizabeth has brought new strength. As the Italian Mercatore laments, Parliament exhibits an unexpected toughmindedness: "I tink some skall knave will put a bill in da Parlament, For dat such a tings shall not be brought here" (B3). To be sure, many craven Englishmen collaborate with the enemy in their midst for financial gain, but the government is alert to the danger.

The alien threat is no longer simply one of inflated rents and trade competition for English artisans, but of undermining England's preparations for war. Flemish and French are joined by new villains from Italy. Mercatore, with his marked Italian accent, combines the evils of Roman international conspiracy and Venetian usury. With mercenary intent he exports English strategic goods—bell-metal, leather, meats—to adorn gentlewomen (B2^v). He is disloyal not only to England, but to his own nation: "Me will a forsake a my fader, moder, king, countrey, and more den dat" (B2^v). The type of Machiavel, he gleefully exports bell-metal "for ordinance, yea, and ordinance itself beside, Dat my cuntry and oder cuntreys be so well furnisht as dis cuntry" (B3). Any nation, not just Italy, is invited to arm itself for the merchantman's profit.

In addition to fostering the perils of armament competition, alien activity undermines the home front by demoralizing the honest English worker. Mercatore is again to blame for inflating rents in the port cities, for he has learned (like the extortionists of *Enough* and *Tide Tarrieth*) to exploit the combination of scarce housing and the willingness of poorer immigrant families to crowd themselves together (C3^v). The Englishman's typical sense of decency is being used against him; he refuses to live in squalor and must yield to those who will. Similar humiliations prevail in the domestic arts. Honest English craftsmen, squeezed out of decent profits by the underpaid shoddy work of the Flemish, are scarcely able to feed their families. "For there be such a sort of straungers in this cuntry, That work fine to please the eie, though it be deceitfully" (B3^v). Too many customers refuse to patronize English goods only, even though Wilson insists it is their patriotic duty. Worse for artisans than privation is the temptation to offer shoddy goods in competition with foreign-made items, cutting corners to eke out an acceptable profit. Usury is also on the increase: the incident in which the courtier begs for the pardon of Usury, who has come from Italy to undo English hospitality, pointedly satirizes the repeal of the usury ban in 1571.[27] All of these abuses, though fed by English pusillanimity, originate in a foreign conspiracy.

Just as Wilson adumbrates the trend of the pre-Armada years to "busy giddy minds With foreign quarrels," [28] and thus to deemphasize England's internal difficulties by a display of outward-turning patriotic zeal, he also foreshadows a new breed of dramatist needed for an expanding commercial theater. Wilson's sympathy for the increasingly dominant audience of London tradesmen is combined with his own viewpoint as religious teacher and intellectual. He is not a simple cleric, like many playwrights in the 1560's and 1570's; he is a professional man of the theater and a member of an acting company. Yet he also anticipates the University Wits of the 1580's and 1590's in his concern for the economic distress of well-educated men in search of a rewarding career. Like *All for Money*'s virtuous but impoverished scholar named Learning Without Money, Wilson's figure of Sincerity is a university-educated authorial spokesman who finds that his arduous theological training has left him a bitter legacy of profitless parishes and ungrateful patrons. Such men in the late 1570's are already facing the problem of writing for an increasingly commercial theater. Wishing to guide that theater as moralists and yet dislocated themselves by the demands of show business, they identify their economic quandary with that of the London citizenry.

Yet Wilson, for all his sympathies for university men, is clearly of the old stamp by the early 1580's. His tastes in drama are homiletic, and he finds himself in a hostile new dramatic environment of revenge motifs, stage battles, mythological nonsense, and above all romance:

> We search not Plutos pensive pit, nor tast of Limbo lake;
> We do not shew of warlike fight, as sword and shield to shake;
> We speak not of the powers devine, ne yet of furious sprites,
> We do not seeke high hilles to climb, nor talk of loves delights.
>
> (Prologue)

Not only his own tastes, but those of a sizable portion of his audience, are old-fashioned. Wilson speaks for reforming moderates who as yet objected not to the theater itself but only to abuses of it. Stephen Gosson was another such man, a participator in the drama until the vogue of *Common Conditions* and similar plays forced him into opposition.[29]

Romance, with its staples of tyrant kings, exile and reunion, and love marriages between princes and commoners, was to exploit lower-class sentiments in totally unreal and escapist dreams of glory (see Chapter 15); but men like Wilson increasingly refused to countenance sensationalism and mere entertainment. With Wilson's era begins the struggle that was to end with Puritan disavowal and then suppression of the London stage. The building of Burbage's Theater, an enterprise with which Wilson was associated, was the prime occasion for the first attack. Wilson's attempts to utilize the new London theater for conservative and didactic aims, and to retain the allegiance of London's more sober citizens, were to continue fitfully until the end of Elizabeth's reign. Nevertheless, as Wilson's defensiveness attests, the effort at compromise was a rear-guard action from the moment that Italianate romance first asserted its powerful spell.

J ust as Elizabeth succeeded during her first twenty years in turning the zeal of popular drama to outer dangers rather than to inner conflicts, she deflected the energies of a dramatic tradition at court long used to choosing sides in political controversy. This chapter will investigate four early and middle Elizabethan plays often thought to be political in intent, in order to trace the developing struggle between a resourceful queen and those who felt privileged to make suggestions. One of the earliest and best known is *Gorboduc,* presented by the gentlemen of the Inner Temple before the queen at Whitehall Palace, January 18, 1562.

Overshadowing the specific question of royal succession in *Gorboduc,* which has perhaps been too narrowly interpreted, is the larger issue of royal will versus the authority of England's chief counselors. As we have seen, the greatest threat to political stability in midcentury England was the attempted ascendancy of the governing class in a time of minority or feminine rule, disputed line of succession, and religious conflict. Henry VIII had abetted patrician autonomy by granting exemptions to the ban on maintenance and livery for friends whom he could trust as a check against the barons; Mary had resorted to the same tactics. The result was something approaching the revival of aristocratic military power. Northumberland's strength in 1550 was considerable. The fortifications of Buckingham (before 1521), and later of Leicester at Kenilworth, were well-equipped with munitions and sufficient to withstand an extended siege. Elizabeth inherited a situation that had degenerated badly since 1547, and was in fact as ominous as anything since the fifteenth century. She had to employ stern measures, preventing the renewal of the northern fiefdoms of the Stanleys, Derbys, Talbots, and Shrewsburys, and turning instead to a reliance on the squirearchy and gentry.[1]

Disputed succession added to the danger. Henry VIII, despite his personal popularity, had with his marital difficulties nearly subverted the strong monarchical system of his father. According to one religion or the other he had illegitimized and disinherited in turn all three of his children, thereby encouraging the possibility of "election." He had enlarged the number of possible candidates by specifying in his will the succession (in default of lawful grandchildren) of his niece, Lady Frances Brandon—who became the mother of Lady Jane and Lady Katharine Grey. Other possible claimants included the Earl of Huntingdon, an earnest religious reformer. These options gave to powerful advisers an initiative that was quickly abused. When Henry VIII provided a regency for his son Edward, the Duke of Somerset managed instead to have himself chosen Protector, in a move frighteningly reminiscent of Richard Duke of Gloucester's Protectorship of Edward V. The political struggle of 1547 to 1553 centered not on the figurehead position of king but on the actual authority of the king's chief "adviser." The winner, Northumberland, thought nothing more natural in 1553 than to conceal news of Edward's death until a coup had brought the duke's tractable young relative, Lady Jane Grey, to the throne in Mary's stead. Mary's dramatic success in outmaneuvering Northumberland accounts for her hostility to the counselors in a play like *Respublica* (see Chapter 9).

The prospect of Elizabeth's accession to the throne was no less uncertain until the last moment in 1558. Once achieved, it seemed a fragile victory for Protestants and for all those who hoped to reestablish a strong monarchy. Not a few of the older families were still Catholic in sympathy, ready to plot with Elizabeth's nearest relative and potential heir, Mary Queen of Scots, and with continental powers, for Elizabeth's overthrow. Elizabeth's serious illness from smallpox in 1562 heightened the atmosphere of crisis. The situation awakened the latent ambition of the nobility to prevail as they had in the fifteenth century. Perhaps equally disturbing, however, was the determination of the gentry and squirearchy, some of them Puritan in outlook, to control England's political destiny in Parliament. Their clamors for a Protestant successor of their own approving were as much a threat to monarchical supremacy as was Catholic reaction. No one knew better than Elizabeth the dangers of unsettled succession; and yet, in her canny way, she knew also that marriage or announcement of her heir in her precarious first years must fatally yield the balance of power either to an internal faction or to a foreign opponent. Her availability as a spinster, with its potential reward for the fortunate wooer, became her trump card. Keeping her own shrewd counsel, she soon made it plain that the sort of blunt advice proffered in *Gorboduc* was not to her taste. She berated a Parliamentary delegation in 1566 for urging settlement of succession, and denied the Commons free discussion of the issue.[2] She was especially outraged at the parliamentary device of incorporating a royal promise to marry in the preamble of a money bill. By 1581 the so-called "Statute of Silence" made discussion of the rights of any heir punishable by death.[3] Although the Inns of Court prevailed once upon her to witness a play like *Gorboduc* in 1562, they were not to do so in the future. With its openly critical and Parliamentary message, *Gorboduc* is the last of its obvious type.

The gentlemen-lawyers who wrote *Gorboduc*, Thomas Sackville and Thomas Norton, joined forces (as did the upper and lower houses of Parliament) on the issue of royal succession. Both men were close to Edward Seymour, Earl of Hertford, who in 1560 had secretly married Lady Katharine Grey—the heir presumptive according to Henry VIII's will. Sackville was a friend of Hertford, Norton a former tutor.[4] Yet the two authors were significantly diverse in background and interests.[5] Sackville became in time a very distinguished peer, first Lord Buckhurst and then Earl of Dorset. In 1562 he could already look forward to a courtly and literary career. Born to a landed family and of some kinship with the queen, his politics were conservative and nationalistic, neither Catholic nor Puritan. He later participated in negotiations for the marriage of Elizabeth to the Catholic Duc d'Anjou. Norton, on the other hand, was related by marriage to Cranmer, and fanatical enough as a Puritan to suffer Elizabeth's wrath later in life. As chairman of a Parliamentary committee in 1565-1566 pressing petitions on Elizabeth, he was in the thick of the battle not simply for Protestant succession but for Parliamentary prerogative. Later he turned against the stage. His defensive attitude toward royal authority is evident in his portion of the text. The quarto of 1565 assigns him the first three acts; perhaps he also collaborated in the concluding scene of Act V, containing the most avowed polemics on the issue of succession.[6]

Whereas Acts IV and most of V depict the tragic struggles of the royal protagonists, and the efforts of the nobility to regain order in their kingdom, Norton's viewpoint is exclusively that of the gentry in council and Parliament. Sackville's Dukes of Cornwall, Albany, Logris, and Cumberland make their belated entrance in Act V somewhat awkwardly, for heretofore Gorboduc's kingdom has been run entirely by untitled advisers. The lengthy speeches of these commoners dominate the play, in actual number of spoken lines and in thematic emphasis on the importance of good counsel, the obstinacy of princes, the distinction between a true adviser and a parasite, and the like. Ferrex and Porrex are seldom seen; instead, counselors like Dordan and Philander file detailed reports on the deteriorating situation, debate what to do, or lament the folly that their betters have committed. Eubulus, as architect of the plan to suppress rebellion and as explicator of the ultimate political lesson to be learned, is actually the spokesman of the play. Norton's heavyhanded choruses and dumb shows, indulging in unambiguous editorializing that merely paraphrases the sententiousness of Norton's mouthpieces, reinforce the impression of domination by counsel.

It is Queen Videna who first focuses responsibility for the welfare of Britain not on kings but on their subordinates. Monarchs like Gorboduc are (somewhat condescendingly) expected to come up with erratic decisions; but Gorboduc cannot perpetrate his royal whimsy without the "assent Of all his counsell to his fond device."

> There resteth all. But if they fail thereof,
> And if the end bring forth an ill success,
> On them and theirs the mischief shall befall.

(I, i, 54-56)

144

Civil strife is the inevitable result when trusted counselors, "To please the present fancie of the prince, With wrong transpose the course of governance." Accordingly, as Videna predicts, the opening debate of the play is one of crucial choice, with power in the hands of the advisers. Arostus and Philander are needlessly and culpably anxious to conciliate Gorboduc, despite the fact that he acknowledges their decisive function "whereby yet I reign" (I, ii, 6) and enjoins them "without all wrie respect Or poisonous craft to speak in pleasing wise" (ll. 29-30). The king does not resent Eubulus' plain speech, and might seemingly have been swayed by a unanimously courteous yet firm opposition. With a majority catering to his whim of a divided kingdom, however, Gorboduc is largely exculpated for proceeding as he does.

Once the wrong decision has been made, the fate of Britain still rests chiefly in the hands of powerful advisers. In the antithetical soul-struggle between their good and evil advisers, Ferrex and Porrex are virtually pawns; the long, schematized speeches center not so much on the person choosing as on the techniques and ethics of persuasion. The play's interest in rhetoric signifies the exploration of language as a useful public art. True counselors favor talk, diplomacy; parasites are for sudden, expedient action. True counselors recoil in horror at Machiavellian statecraft; parasites espouse an opportunist view of fate in which "lust of kingdomes hath no law" (II, i, 143).

The power of virtuous parliamentary counselors must withstand not only royal whimsy, but the nobles' inveterate tendency to exploit Britain's division and lack of royal line for their personal gain. As Duke of Albany (Scotland), Fergus represents the threat in the 1560's not only of Scottish and Catholic invasion in the name of Mary Stuart, but the reactionary stand of England's old families, especially in the north. A leading peer with enormous wealth and private armies at his disposal, Fergus is the specter of neo-feudal "maintenance" in a time of unsettled monarchy.[7] His fellow peers, although seemingly loyal to the throne, are bent on violent annihilation of the rebelling commons. Only the quietly heroic Arostus and Eubulus can prevent further bloodshed, by persuading the commons to return home peaceably and warning the lords against seizure of unlawful self-aggrandizing authority when they "shall vanquishers return from field, And find the princely state an open pray To gredie lust and to usurping power" (V, ii, 139-141). If they will only "all with one assent forbear Once to lay hand or take unto yourselves The crown" (ll. 153-155), they can peacefully convene in Parliament and proceed to the election of a new prince. For in such national emergencies Parliament is the law of the land, the great middle force that alone can forestall anarchy and feudalism. It is prepared to defend the monarchy against commons and barons alike, but only on condition that Parliament now settle the affairs of state so woefully mismanaged by the reigning family.

Not all criticisms leveled against Gorboduc apply literally to Elizabeth, of course. She, after all, did not have two sons. The carefully preserved pseudo-historical setting, with its pagan cosmology of "the gods," is a "mirror" and not allegory for the contemporary scene. Yet Gorboduc's division of the kingdom is disturbingly close to Elizabeth's refusal to settle the succession or to marry. Unlike Gorboduc's counselors, who delayed too long, Parliament must take matters in hand now, before the crisis of challenged reign erupts.

> No, no; then Parliament should have bene holden,
> And certein heires appointed to the crown,
> To stay the title of established right.   (V, ii, 264-266)

Furthermore, they must choose according to specific criteria congenial to the interests of both Sackville and Norton. The right leader must be English-born and constitutionally designated:

> Right mean I his or hers upon whose name
> The people rest by mean of native line,
> Or by the vertue of some former law,
> Already made their title to advaunce.   (V, ii, 165-168)

Mary Stuart is eliminated from consideration; Katharine Grey, provided for in Henry VIII's will, is the likeliest choice.[8]

Norton and Sackville naturally disclaim any heterodoxy. They insist that subjects must obey the prince, and must not even condemn his actions in their thoughts. The authors do not justify rebellion as do their contemporaries John Ponet and Christopher Goodman. Nevertheless, Norton especially insists on momentous prerogatives for Parliament: the right not only to offer specific proposals on succession, but to discuss all such matters freely since Parliament has a duty to restrain willfulness in princes. These were the precise issues upon which Elizabeth and her Parliaments disagreed, for example in 1563 and 1566; and later even her Privy Council, including Burghley, favored a plan to appoint Parliament and the council as an interregnum government in the event of Elizabeth's untimely death, empowered to choose a successor to the throne by an act of Parliament.[9] Elizabeth's anger need not be imagined, for she gave vent to it on many occasions.

Boys' plays at court, if they touched on the question of succession at all, were of necessity far more circumspect. John Phillip's *Comedy of Patient and Meek Grissell* (S.R., 1565), from approximately the same period as *Gorboduc,* has been called a play of topical reference.[10] Yet the proof is tenuous, and rests chiefly—as in several later Elizabethan examples—on the dangerous ground of extended analogy. Phillip omits allusive clues or statements of didactic meaning, such as abound in Act V of *Gorboduc.* Before accepting a hypothesis of hidden political meaning, presumably obscured in deference to Elizabeth's increasing sensitivity to the guessing game of court allegory, we must ask if the dramatist has significantly altered his sources in a way most suitably explained by topical motive.[11] Without such evidence, the analogy may be nothing more than coincidental—life imitating art, as it so often does.

The Griselda story, like that of Hester, was not new to Renaissance politics. William Forrest's long nondramatic verse narrative entitled *The History of the Second Patient Grissell* is avowedly an allegorical defense of Katharine of Aragon, written for Katharine's daughter Mary during her reign—despite the obvious inapplicability of Griselda's low birth to Katharine's royal lineage, or of the happily restored marriage to Katharine's sad end. To compare Prince Gautier's marriage problems with those of Elizabeth would require scarcely more ingenuity or wresting of the text. The reversal of sexes was easy; Elizabeth had a fancy for calling herself "prince" or "king" rather than "queen." [12] Gautier is a prince whose people urge him to marry and bear children in order to avoid the dangers of unsettled succession. He does so unwillingly for their sake, stipulating only that the choice of queen be his. Elizabeth's reluctance to marry was well known, and yet candidates for her hand existed in abundance: the Archduke Charles of Austria, Philip of Spain, the Earl of Arundel, Sir William Pickering, and—most significant—Lord Robert Dudley, later Earl of Leicester.

Dudley was, like Grissell (again reversing the sexes), of considerably lower station than the prince. In 1560 Elizabeth was toying with a bill to raise Dudley to the peerage; she finally destroyed the bill for the time being, and in any case steadfastly refused to consider the possibility of Dudley as king. Rumor of foul play to Dudley's wife destroyed Dudley's hopes, and by the summer of 1561 the crisis was past. Nevertheless, a play before 1561 could be pleading for a marriage of love conquering rank, thereby both justifying the queen's choice and extolling the virtues of Dudley as worthy of the marriage.

The difficulty with such a reading, of course, is that it casts Elizabeth in the unsympathetic role of hard-hearted tester during the major concluding portion of the story. Is Griselda's unbelievable patience to signify Dudley's plight as rejected wooer? If so, the play would offend Elizabeth and thus fail tactlessly in its presumed intent of softening her heart toward Dudley. The narrative elements of separated children, threats of death, and reunion are extraneous in any case. Elizabeth might well prefer to identify herself with Grissell as an enduringly popular type of feminine virtue, in a "mirror" of harmless political flattery. Moreover, the seemingly topical themes are already present in Boccaccio, in Petrarch's Latin translation, and in Chaucer: the plea for stable succession, the prince's insistence on personal choice.[13]

Nevertheless, Phillip's version does offer significant emphases not to be found in earlier treatments. The first part of the story, potentially the most topical, receives extended treatment. The narrative up to the birth of the first child occupies nearly half the play, whereas in Chaucer the proportion is more like one fourth. In this long exposition, Gautier's attitudes toward marriage are examined with particular care. A model prince loved by his people, receptive to criticism, he is aware of the cogency of his subjects' fears about succession. The specific warning that in time of disputed royal line "every man in lordlie state doth covit for to raign" (l. 181), missing in Chaucer, reflects *Gorboduc's* preoccupation with the dangers of an ambitious aristocracy. Another notable change is Gautier's veneration of chastity, as praised by Saint Paul (ll. 171-175), surely an unusual attribute in a knight of worldly honor. Love of chastity is Gautier's sole reason for having remained single, and he is accordingly vulnerable to the Vice's distasteful insinuations about marriage: that partners almost always fight (ll. 187-194), and even more repellingly that marriage is apt to be an impulsive union of lechery. "I hard many a one say, That the first daie for wedding all other doth excell" (ll. 183-184). Politic Persuasion, epitomizing stubbornness and self-indulgence, is contrary to the public good and must be overruled by Gautier as an example of "vertues scool." *Grissell* urges every prince to do likewise, even while it concedes the attractiveness of a longing for chastity. These special considerations found only in the play of *Grissell* certainly resemble those of the virgin queen contemplating marriage. Moreover, they can be documented plentifully in the exchanges between Elizabeth and her impatient Parliaments. She repeatedly asserted her intent to marry, albeit against her personal inclination, and actually conducted serious negotiations in 1563 with the Archduke Charles of Austria after the Dudley affair had passed; Parliament, while conceding her the right to choose her consort, was unrelenting in its agitation for a solution.[14]

Equally original in the play are the Vice's attempts to turn the nobles against the prince's choice of partner. Politic Persuasion harps on Grissell's being a stranger to the court, of inferior rank, and apt to produce an heir of common stock. He plays on the courtiers' very real fears that an upstart consort may in fact prove tyrannical (ll. 371-385). If these machinations reflect courtly fears of Dudley's lowborn ambition to be king and father of a new dynasty, then the playwright's answers are politically momentous. Griselda proves to be the embodiment of dutiful self-effacement. She is unambitious for rule. The marriage was not her idea. Indeed, she urges Gautier to make another choice of more equal rank (ll. 670-671). Such disclaimers naturally pull the teeth of any criticism concerning ambition. The relationship of Gautier and Grissell also dismisses any insinuations of royal lust or premarital affairs (l. 650) —like those the rumormongers had spread about Dudley and the queen.

The special object-lesson of Phillip's version, then, is the groundlessness of fears about a prince's unequal marriage, from the viewpoint of both prince and wary counselors. The edifying result is a triumphant unity in which the courtiers accept the prince's choice and discover that he has chosen better than they could have hoped. Resentment or slander, as embodied in the Vice, is a deplorable tendency that must be expunged. Whether these themes applied especially to Dudley or simply to any of Elizabeth's non-royal suitors, their relevance in the early 1560's gave special piquancy to a play that also appealed to a timeless portrait of feminine virtue. The analogy pertains chiefly in the first half, and is not the sole purpose of the play. Nevertheless it served, with *Gorboduc,* to put Elizabeth further on her guard against unwelcome advice in the plays she saw at court.

The potential affront in a play like John Pickering's *Horestes* (printed 1567) was still more serious than that of *Gorboduc* or *Grissell.* If it was the "Orestes" acted at court during the year-end revels of 1567, probably by Lord Rich's men, it may have seemed peculiarly appropriate to the inflamed Scottish situation.[15] That very year, Mary Queen of Scots had been forced to depose herself in favor of her infant son James, with Murray as regent. Mary was widely suspected of complicity in the death of her husband, Darnley, in order that she might marry the Earl of Bothwell. This sordid triangle resembles that of *Horestes,* in which Queen Clytemnestra kills her husband Agamemnon to live with Egistus. It might follow, then, that Horestes' revenge upon his own mother despite the pleadings of "Nature" is intended to justify the execution of Elizabeth's blood relative, Mary. Such a program would have found favor among Elizabeth's ministers—Cecil, Leicester, Throckmorton, Bedford— who supported the Scottish nobles against Mary and wished to keep them out of the French camp. If Elizabeth had gone along with her ministers at this time, Mary would almost surely have died.[16] Yet Elizabeth was furious at the deposition. She had never given up hope of some sort of rapprochement with Mary. Paramount in her mind was the danger of encouraging her subjects to a similar rebellion. Clearly, in late 1567 she was in no mood to receive advice on the wisdom of Mary's execution. Just as clearly, her exasperated ministers were doing everything they could to keep up the pressure.

In this delicate situation, Pickering's advice to the throne is couched in the most general terms. The biographical parallel is itself not conclusive. It is derived from Pickering's source, Caxton's translation (from the French of Raoul Lefevre) of *The Recuyell of the Historyes of Troye,*[17] and is in any case an archetypal pattern of murder and adultery. In several details the parallel is misleading. Horestes is engaged in civil war to regain his own kingdom; Elizabeth had no plans to invade Scotland, nor was she its ruler in exile. Horestes is avenging his father; Elizabeth had no interest in defending Darnley's name. More important, Horestes is impetuous, having to be restrained by counsel, whereas Elizabeth urged temporizing.

Pickering's topical thesis is to be found not in biographical resemblances, but in political truisms regarding the difference between a true prince and a tyrant. For such a method he could model himself on a wealth of classical and biblical "mirror" plays of the period—*Cambises, King Darius,* and the like (see Chapter 12). Virtually all of his alterations of his source move in this generic direction. Whereas Caxton's *Recuyell* approaches the acts of civil war and matricide as those of personal satisfaction, the play insists that such acts must be justified by codes of princely conduct. In Caxton, Horestes proceeds to war without listening to counsel, enlists the support of other princes (such as Forensis) who hate Egistus for personal reasons, gives no opportunity to the city of Mycoene to surrender peaceably, and disposes of Clytemnestra in the following garish manner:

> In the morn Horestes did his moder Clytemnestra be brought to fore him all naked, her handes bounden. And as sone as he saw her, he ran upon her with his naked swerd and cutte off her two pappes; and after slew her with his handes and maad her to be drawen to the feldes for the houndes to ete and devowr, and to the birdes.[18]

Pickering transfers these bloody impulses to the Vice, whose urgings of "cruell revengment" must be offset by the counsel of Nature. Any true prince must strike a balance between justice and mercy. The advice is implicitly flattering to any ruler like Elizabeth who prided herself on her humane conscience.

The ideal prince must be restrained by human counsel as well as abstract "Nature." Unlike Elizabeth, whose caution toward Mary was opposed by her ministers, Horestes is naturally impulsive: "Oh, how my hart doth boil in dede, with firey perching heat!" (l. 251). Imploring his uncle Idumeus for assistance "without delay," Horestes is gently rebuked with a plea for caution. "Stey there a while, Horestes mine, till counsell do decree The thing that shall unto your state most honorabell bee" (ll. 306-307). The figure of Counsel, weighing the issues, concludes that Horestes may proceed not in a vindictive spirit but as an officer making wholesome corrective example: "but rather shall it be a fear to those That to the like at any time their cruell mindes dispose" (ll. 313-314).[19] These admonitions might apply generally to Elizabeth's handling of all forms of opposition to her throne, Catholic or otherwise.

Other lessons in military statecraft inculcated by Idumeus do not apply at all to the Scottish situation, since England was not at war with her neighbor, but do apply to the education of the ideal prince. When battle approaches, Idumeus teaches the young man how to comport himself in the eyes of true fame, "for to obtain the victorey and praise That lasts for aye" (ll. 555-556). Men are not to be thrown recklessly into the front line without a "pollicy." "For over rash in doing ought doth often damage bring. Therefore take councell first" (ll. 579-580). Be liberal and gentle with the men, prove a brave example of leadership. The enemy too deserves respect, particularly in a civil war when all combatants are native-born. In direct contrast to his prototype in Caxton, Horestes offers amnesty to Mycoene and commences the siege only when his offer is refused. Horestes' words at the gate are substantially those of Henry V before Harfleur (ll. 810-855).

Pickering's manner of depicting Egistus and Clytemnestra can also be explained by his thesis of true prince versus tyrant. The lovers are in every respect the opposites of Horestes, and as such are edifying public examples of wrongdoing. "For, lo, the universaull scoll of all the world we know Is once the pallace of a king, where vices chefe do flow," as well as virtues (ll. 631-632). As types of evil rulers they are appropriately irresponsible and fleshly. Clytemnestra wantonly submits Mycoene to siege rather than yield honorably. Furthermore, because she is not an anointed queen as Mary was, but a simple murderess withholding the throne from the legal heir apparent, Horestes is not guilty of regicide. He punishes malfeasance but does not tamper with the succession.[20]

Obviously, these broad considerations of true prince and tyrant might permit an Elizabethan audience to apply such truisms to England's most agonizing political issue of the moment. Scottish propaganda had in fact equated Mary with Clytemnestra, and by 1570 Elizabeth's ministers were covertly sponsoring anti-Marian pamphlets. In the Parliament of 1572, Richard Gallys compared Mary to Clytemnestra as "a killer of her husband and an adulteress."[21] Whatever conjectures his auditors may have entertained, however, Pickering never accommodates his sources to an overt allegorical parallel. He follows the safer custom of discussing the universal attributes of all wise rulers, allowing Elizabeth to interpret as she saw fit.

The author's most avowedly didactic statements urge an end to dissension rather than further bloodshed. However much vengeance may be necessitated "after extremite," it tends to produce reprisals (l. 1093). Even the seemingly irrelevant comic scenes, not in Caxton, enforce themes not of violence to an anointed monarch, but of political amity and an end to civil discord. Menelaus' eagerness to revenge Clytemnestra's death is sobering proof of the evils of violence, and prompts the weary Nobles to ask only that they "may now live in pleasaunt state, sartain, Devoid of wars and civill strifes, while yet your grace doth raign" (ll. 1341-1342). The commons agree.

> A kingdom kept in Amite, and void of dissention,
> Ne dividyd in himself by aney kind of way,
> Neather provoked by wordes of reprehention,
> Must nedes long continew, as Truth doth say.

(ll. 1371-1374)

In the 1560's public audiences as well as Elizabeth's court could well applaud these sentiments as an allusion to political and religious divisions now hopefully in the past.

Even after Mary's execution in 1587, great tact was necessary in treating any subject that might allude to her death. Elizabeth had agonized over the decision for years, despite the open dangers of excommunication and the Babington conspiracy of 1586; she had even tried to persuade Secretary Davison to have Mary killed privately. Once the deed was done, Elizabeth had little appetite for reminders of her feelings of guilt. When the gentlemen of Gray's Inn wrote *The Misfortunes of Arthur* and presented it before Elizabeth in February of 1588, they accordingly exercised a restraint missing from the earlier *Gorboduc*. Experience had taught these lawyers the wisdom of speaking in distant parables about true prince and tyrant, in the vein of *Horestes*, with no open references to Parliament or succession. The parable of Arthur and Mordred is a mirror for princes, of course, but does not spell out its contemporary application. Only in the handling of their sources do Thomas Hughes and his fellow authors reveal topical intent, and even here any specific allusions to Mary and Scotland are most oblique.

Extensive similarities to the *Horestes* story offer suggestive but entirely misleading hints as to the nature of topical meaning. As in Pickering's drama, a prince (Arthur) returns to his homeland to find his wife adulterously living with a usurper, and so must wage distasteful civil war and proceed in vengeance against his own flesh and blood. The search for extended analogy, or "coincidence" theory of interpretation, naturally equates Queen Guinevere with Clytemnestra and Mary, Mordred with Egistus and Bothwell, and Gorlois' ghost with Agamemnon and Darnley.[22] This detailed correspondence, so far satisfactory, breaks down in the identification of Arthur. James VI did hate Bothwell, to be sure, but was neither his father nor his nemesis.

Like Pickering, Hughes is not pursuing a one-to-one analogy. Instead, he pairs and contrasts his figures for the purpose of defining tyranny and its opposite.[23] Mordred is an adulterer, so ambitious that he cannot tolerate superiors or peers, a believer in blind chance and in opportunism, one who rejects advice and places his private good above common weal (I, iv and II, ii). Arthur is wise, a powerful orator, devout, concerned for his people's welfare. Especially as the great ancestor of mythological Tudor genealogy, Arthur foreshadows the attributes of Elizabeth (V, ii). This flattery is conventional. What is unusual about Arthur, however, in comparison with source-figures of the king, is his emphasis on lenity. Whereas Geoffrey of Monmouth and Malory depict Arthur as eager to do battle with Mordred, Hughes makes a point of Arthur's reluctance to kill a blood relative.[24] His counselors must repeatedly remind him that "A king ought alwaies to preferre his realm Before the love he beares to kin or sonne . . . No worse a vice than lenitie in kings" (III, i, 45-62).

Compunction is a necessary quality in the ideal Christian prince, but the overabundance of it is a defect—as explicated, for instance, in Elyot's *The Governor* (II, vii) or the *Homily Against Disobedience and Willful Rebellion*.[25] The definition of a true prince will explain Hughes's divergences from his source. Yet Hughes's disproportionate emphasis on Arthur's compunctious attitude suggests a defect in the prince to whom he offers the mirror. Elizabeth seemed for years to place her kinship with Mary ahead of public safety. Like Mary, Mordred is Arthur's heir to the throne, and would have proved "the hope of all your realm, Had not his lust to rule prevented all" (V, i, 96-97). Arthur's grief, displayed at length, is a tactful complement to the author's sterner message: the dangers of indulgent lenity, such as King David unwisely showed toward Absalom. Yet one need not specify Mary alone to explain the topical viewpoint. The entire Catholic conspiracy of the 1570's and

1580's, decried by Gorlois' ghost as the work of "rebelles, traitors, and conspirators, The semenary of lewd Cateline, The bastard coovie of Italian birdes" (an alternate speech for V, ii), is sufficient grounds for Elizabeth's tender concern and her counselors' warnings of the need for firmness.[26] Elizabeth had been greatly troubled in signing the death warrant of her cousin, Thomas, fourth Duke of Norfolk, in 1572, for his major role in the Northern Rebellion of 1569—especially since his was the first such execution of her reign. Members of the Parliament of 1572, in urging Norfolk's execution, employed the same arguments and biblical citations against mercy to kinsmen as they applied to Mary; in the Book of the Covenant in Deuteronomy, for example, they explained, "Here you may perceive that God willeth his magistrates not to spare either brother or sister or son or daughter or wife or friend." [27] Francis Bacon, one of the contributing authors of *Misfortunes*, supported the program of Burghley and Walsingham for tough action against the Catholic danger.[28]

Although seemingly topical, then, *Misfortunes* avoids extended analogy or equation of dramatic figures with real persons. The adulterous triangle is a misleading clue, and is in any case too universal in human nature to prove useful as a specific proof of topicality. Parallel situations of this sort were dangerously libelous, and hence were far less satisfactory than Senecan truisms about the ideal monarch.

An unmistakable phenomenon in the 1560's and 1570's is the vogue of "mirror" plays exploring the nature of tyranny and the proper attitudes of subjects under its cruel sway: *Cambises, Appius and Virginia, Virtuous and Godly Susanna, Jocasta, Promos and Cassandra,* and *Damon and Pythias.* These plays do not employ analogy to particular events such as *Gorboduc's* parliamentary concern with succession, and in fact seem deliberately to have chosen historical and legendary examples far afield in order to avoid more overt forms of political equation. They obviously dare not hint at dictatorial abuses in Elizabeth herself. Instead, they implicitly or explicitly flatter Elizabeth by the contrast between her and the conventional tyrant. These plays define the qualities of the ideal prince negatively. Their very willingness to discuss the evils of tyranny, as More and Erasmus had done before the Reformation, bespeaks a return of hope for political stability. Dispassionate analysis of evil rule is scarcely possible in times of royal obstinacy, minority kingship, or inquisition. These plays, in a series of historically remote settings, test the nature of monarchy in its most unendurable forms.

Despite the lack of direct analogy, these test cases in tyranny were by no means purely hypothetical in the 1560's and 1570's. Puritan manifestos such as Knox's *Monstrous Regiment* (1558) openly encouraged disobedience toward women rulers; and although Calvin hastened to assure Elizabeth that reformers would make an exception for her and would "tarry for the magistrate," [1] the ouster of Mary Queen of Scots in 1567 was a sobering precedent. Similarly the Catholic position, after the Northern Rising of 1569 and the excommunication of 1570, defiantly proclaimed that all heretical kings were undeserving of allegiance, and were tyrants or usurpers offensive to God no matter what their blood descent from previous monarchs.

The Elizabethan establishment, thus on the defensive against extreme arguments from left and right, countered with the absolutist theories of passive obedience and the supreme authority of king as head of the church. Cranmer, Tyndale, Lever, Hooper, and many others, bolstering their claims with biblical citations, argued that even a pagan ruler merited civil obedience.[2] Accordingly, the choice of a pagan setting in these "'tyrant" plays is politically more relevant than it seems at first. If an oriental despot like Cambises is to be endured in passive obedience, then no duly constituted monarch closer to home can fail to deserve as much. These plays test extremes to define the rule that no exception to obedience is allowable. The illegitimate authority of a usurper is of course another matter, not touched upon in these plays. Here, the issue is simply one of extraordinary misbehavior in a lawful king.

Only God could dispose of an evil yet legitimately established monarch. Since God might choose to inflict an evil ruler on a wayward people for their punishment, rebellion against His scourge would only increase divine wrath. Yet the faithful could expect prompt relief. The doctrine of passive obedience asked not endless submission to slavery but faith in God's deliverance. *Cambises'* protagonist, for example, reigns less than two years (although the period is much longer in Herodotus), clearly a sign of God's unwillingness to tolerate abuses (ll. 31-33). In the words of *Cambises'* immediate source: "This exemple testifieth that God woll not long suffre tyrantes to reign." [3]

In precisely what fashion, however, would God's will be accomplished on earth, and by what indirect use of human agency? As we have seen, in *Jacob and Esau* the will of God could prescribe means as well as ends for Protestant apologists of revolutionary change (see Chapter 8). By what historical process will God end an evil reign? The logical consequences of such thought have always proved disturbing to monarchical conservatives. Even Dr. Johnson, in a later century, though maintaining stoutly the absolutist principle of monarchy, allowed that in extreme cases "there is a remedy of human nature against tyranny." This nature, acting as a kind of immutable law unto itself, will at last rise to correct the abuse. Johnson refused to specify the means of organizing such a movement, or to specify justifiable grounds, for to do so might set a precedent for human action.[4] In a variety of manifestations these Tudor "tyrant" plays offer the same necessarily vague assurances and unwillingness to follow the ramifications.

The example offered in Thomas Preston's *Cambises* seems edifyingly simple. The tyrant's reign is short, and his "accidental" self-inflicted sword wound is divine retaliation for Cambises' sin. "What mesure the king did meat, the same did Jove commence" (l. 32). No human agency is involved. Yet the chief emphasis in the play is not on this satisfactory retribution, but on the living evil of tyranny and the complex rules of conduct demanded of its sufferers. Preston defends passive obedience, but he also defends outspoken criticism within the limits of obedience. True subjects must not simply endure, but must stand up bravely to royal incompetence or whim. Only those who risk their lives merit deliverance.

Thomas Preston was evidently one of those numerous zealous Protestants who inclined to continued reform but who looked to Elizabeth as their best hope. His source, Richard Taverner's *The Second Book of the Garden of Wisdom*,[5] had been written under Cromwell's aegis as an instrument of anti-papal support for Henry VIII. Preston was very probably the scholar of King's College, Cambridge, later Master of Trinity Hall, who in 1564 received the queen's favor and pension as her "scholar."[6] However unsuited to an accomplished Latinist *Cambises* may at first seem, it is in fact replete with scholarly allusions (e.g., ll. 1-24) and consistent political philosophy. In his other works Preston wrote against Rome and the Catholic Northern Rebellion of 1569. *Cambises* briefly compares its evil protagonist to Bishop Bonner, the hated pontiff of London under Mary (l. 1141). If written, as seems probable, for Dudley's (later Earl of Leicester's) men at court in 1560-1561, the play was sanctioned by Elizabeth's then favorite minister and leader of the progressive anti-Catholic party. Correspondingly, the play defends the free speech of loyal advisers even as it warns against sedition.

Cambises' typed portraits of tyrant and true prince resemble those of *Horestes* and *The Misfortunes of Arthur,* except that they are somewhat oddly incorporated in a single person. The protagonist's sudden shift from virtuous to vicious behavior ("his one good deed of execution, after that many wicked deedes and tyrannous murders") is psychologically unexplained by Taverner or Preston. As a thematic device, however, it enhances the contrast of good and evil rule. Cambises is for a time praised by Lord and Knight. As a "puisant king" seeking true praise, he asks and receives from Counsel approval for the Egyptian war so long as it is conducted for "martiall feats and kingly sport," not in a riotous manner. The king willingly hearkens to advice: "Speak on, my Councel, what it be, you shal have favor mine" (l. 47). As in *Gorboduc,* the king's advisers share responsibility for the decision to appoint Sisamnes. The king's punishment of his corrupt lieutenant is both swift and just. Even Sisamnes' grief-stricken son concedes the benefit of viewing his father's "vile" death: "O king, to me this is a glass; with greef in it I view Example that unto your grace I do not prove untrue" (ll. 469-470).

The essence of tyranny in Sisamnes and the later Cambises is that they consider themselves above law and counsel. Sisamnes boasts, "Now may I abrogate the law as I shall think it good" (l. 117). Cambises turns intractable when criticized for his drinking; his heinous deed of shooting an arrow through the heart of Praxaspes' son stresses not so much the evils of alcohol as the developing persecution complex accompanying Cambises' violent reaction to advice. The arrow is Praxaspes' reward "For councel given unto the king" (l. 580). A similar fate befalls the king's brother, Smirdis, and the king's young cousin-german he incestuously marries, both of whose wholesome criticisms are maliciously interpreted as sedition. Like all tyrants, Cambises feels himself surrounded by enemies, especially those with claims to succession. His frantic quest for security leads him to destroy all his allies and hopes of dynasty. In the last stages even his most flattering counselors desert him and look upon his death with relief.

Preston is concerned not only with exemplifying tyranny but also with dramatizing the stance of courageous martyrs to truth. Praxaspes and Smirdis are his heroes, and their grievances call forth his most eloquent passions. Clearly Preston does not mean to imply that these men should have contented themselves with appeasement. Counselors must be willing to satisfy God's wrath by their own correct lives and by their uncompromising opposition to royal decadence. They die that others may live in peace. To be sure, the wavering and irresponsible commons must learn to avoid the facile temptation of seditious talk, urged on them by the Vice, Ambidexter. In the disease of fear which has spread even to the marketplace, Hob and Lob turn hysterically on each other and even go so far as to wish the king were dead (ll. 780-781), until they are reconciled by the virtuous Marian-May-be-Good and by their own common-sense spirit of forbearance. Other comic scenes similarly convey the susceptibility of the commons to demagoguery and to the licentious example of their betters in time of corrupt rule. These dangers of peasant restiveness do not mean, however, that men of authority must countenance the evils of tyranny with silence or fawning. Although tyrannicide is forbidden, refusal to obey criminal orders (such as those given to Smirdis' two murderers) is clearly incumbent upon every just man. Mere waiting is not the only recourse. God will sooner deliver those who uphold an absolute moral code. Thus, while Preston eschews rebellion, he is deeply aware of the role of human agency in resisting tyranny.

Two anonymous hybrid moralities of the 1560's offer more ambiguous and suggestive answers to Dr. Johnson's paradox about "human nature" rising to end tyranny. In both *Appius and Virginia* and *The Comedy of the Most Virtuous and Godly Susanna,* punishment figures who pass judgment on chief magistrates hover unsubstantially between abstraction and human type, so that an audience cannot surely ascertain the extent to which human agency is responsible for the correction of princes. The skillful avoidance of clarity on this delicate issue is illuminating in a hybrid drama of transition from moral abstraction to Senecan and neoclassical tragedy. As the drama turned to secular subjects, how was it to find a human causality for retributive justice heretofore administered by homiletic abstractions? The punishers of these plays almost, but not certainly, act as citizens reproving or supplanting their own supreme lord.

Both plays offer didactic contrasts between virtuous and tyrannical behavior, in settings that are anachronistically updated from their Roman or Apocryphal originals. Virginia and her parents are models of passive obedience and chaste affection, worthy of imitation by both wedded ladies and virgins in an Elizabethan courtly audience (ll. 22-26). Confronted with Judge Appius' "filthy lust," suborning of witnesses, and other abuses of his power of office, Virginia's family never consider an act of reprisal (unlike Livy's heroic plebeians, who openly threaten the decemvirs with armed rebellion). No authority exists to whom they can appeal, other than the "trump of good fame" that will forever proclaim their virtues and the divine wrath that will destroy Appius. As in *Cambises*, their passive obedience means not catering to Appius' whim but a willingness to die for the ideals of chastity and duty. Similarly, the marriage of Joachim and Susanna is offered as a mirror of forbearance for "you wives" and "your husbandes" in the audience (*Susanna*, ll. 161-162). The marriage illustrates the themes of chastity, right reputation, and God's deliverance of the helpless (ll. 8, 28). Outmaneuvered by the evil judges who lust for Susanna and threaten to prevail over her with their entrenched power of wealth, office, and falsely deserved reputation, Joachim and Susanna are seemingly at the mercy of an unjustly applied law.

Yet the deliverance upon which the heroines of both plays must rely is not solely divine. However otherworldly in origin, it must operate through human agency and human institutions. Thus, when Judge Appius calls upon Justice and Reward to carry out his vile edicts against Virginia and her family, he addresses the two as officers of the state at his disposal. "Come, Justice, then; come on, Reward, when Judgment now doth cal" (l. 1062). Like Counsel and Execution in *Cambises*, they are abstractly named but seem in fact to be ordinary servants of the chief magistrate. Appius is therefore understandably surprised when Justice and Reward turn on him in the name of a higher law. "We both are ready here at hand to work thy fatall fall." "O gorgan judge, what lawles life hast thou most wicked led!" (ll. 1065-1067). Still, he is not actually being arrested by his own lieutenants in a palace revolution. Justice and Reward have taken refuge in their abstract natures; despite the predominantly secular setting of the play, they are instruments of God, not specifically human agents. (In Livy, the emphasis is on a well-coordinated political movement aiming to overthrow the decemvirs by violence and reestablish tribunician rule; and even Chaucer's Physician's Tale describes a throng of people who rescue Virginius and condemn Appius by mob action.) True justice cannot be bent to the practices of tyranny. Yet insofar as Appius possesses all the machinery of justice for whatever use he wishes, the dilemma remains unresolved. What human hands would dare touch the king and elect Virginius in his stead? The hybrid morality, by bringing in abstractions at this point, only intensifies the puzzlement of those who would know how a tyrant can actually be deposed without human rebellion.

In *Susanna,* the resort to otherworldly redress is also ambiguously balanced against the need for human agency. Once the evil judges have prevailed at law against Susanna and are about to punish her, "God raiseth the spirit of Daniell." This stage direction, paraphrasing the Scriptures, is baffling as a guide to production (the play may never have been acted) and as a definition of legal and political authority. This Daniel preempts the role of the magistrate who has heretofore mismanaged the case. Following legal rules of evidence, Daniel shows how the trial should have been conducted, and so arrives at a second and superior judgment. The actions of Daniel are derived from the Apocryphal account, but the thematic focus on theories of jurisprudence is new. Daniel is concerned not merely with justice after this life but with legal safeguards in this world. Witnesses must be cross-examined separately to determine if their stories confirm the circumstantial evidence. The display is edifying and correct in law, but what is Daniel's constitutional authority so to intervene? He is a spirit sent by God, yet as in *Appius* he takes charge of human affairs in a manner that can be assumed only by human agency. Again, the playwright avoids the direct question of challenge to legal authority by taking refuge in abstraction.

The authorial spokesman, Daniel, is a reforming moralist who places civil authority under the guidance of divine law, and who comes close to justifying some kind of human intervention in the name of that higher law. The nature of the intervention, however, remains vague. Ultimately it cannot take a more specific form than advice to the magistrate, urging him to amend his own fault (ll. 1122-1125). Having illustrated the true course of justice, Daniel correctly resigns the power of sentencing to the rejuvenated authority of the state (l. 1204). The reformer will tarry for the magistrate, but only after having shown him how to perform his duty. The assertion of the moralist's rightful influence in the actual conduct of law is not entirely concealed in *Susanna* and *Appius* by the evasions of abstract characterization.

A more orthodox solution to the problem of tyranny appears in George Whetstone's *Promos and Cassandra* (1578). Judge Promos is, like Cambises or Appius, an abuser of his power for the sake of bodily lust. Also as in *Susanna*, the villain has "strict law" upon his side. Bonds are forfeited, houses seized by extortion—all in the name of legality. These evils demand from their sufferers moral courage and a patient faith in deliverance. Yet the cleanser of evil is no divine abstraction, but the king himself as God's appointed deputy on earth. He is as free from taint as the spirit of Daniel or the abstractions Justice and Reward. Whetstone avoids the problem of conflict between earthly and divine justice by presupposing "the perfect magnanimity of a noble king" (title page). Unlike Shakespeare's Duke Vincentio in *Measure for Measure* (based in part on Whetstone's play), who must be held responsible as ruler of a festering city, Whetstone's King Corvinus is merely the overlord of Promos' city of Julio and so is above the daily process of administration that has grown corrupt. He has never winked at moral decadence. He does not share man's innate tendency to sin. His "searching judgment" can assess all secret wrongs (Part II, II, v), and his subjects mention his name with hushed reverence.

Above all, he is a champion of social justice, especially for the poor (Part II, I, viii). Justice must treat rich and poor alike, but the rich do not require special help. The intimidated poor dare not complain for fear of reprisal by the rich. Hence a true monarch must actively seek out complaints and offer protection to those who testify. "First, if any person, officer, or other, hath wronged any of his true subjects, by the corruption of bribes, affecting or not favoring of the person, through usurie, extortion, wrong imprisonment, or with any other unjust practice, his majesty willes the partie so grieved to repair to Sir Ulrico, one of his highness privie counsell" (Part II, II, ii). The bravest and most admired figures of the play are those who risk defiance of "lawful" authority to make such an appeal: the Jailer who substitutes a dead prisoner's head for Andrugio's, and Cassandra who risks open shame and reprisals by confessing her relationship to Promos.

Whetstone's play does not solve the dilemma of corruption in a supreme ruler. Though he implies flatteringly that such a situation does not pertain to Elizabethan England, Whetstone does join *Cambises, Appius,* and *Susanna* in supporting a measure of lawful resistance to tyranny at any level short of the throne. All these "tyrant" plays insist that tyranny cannot receive the cooperation of the moralist or philosopher-poet. Ways must be found within the monarchical system to alleviate social distress. Either the king must be willing to impeach unjust magistrates within his jurisdiction, or some vague and partially divine assistance must rescue those brave enough to endure tyranny rather than capitulate to it. Even English neoclassical translations of this period such as Gascoigne's and Kinwelmershe's *Jocasta* reveal, in the translators' marginalia and prefatory material, a preoccupation with defining the "tyranny" of Creon and the laudable resistance of Antigone, in seeming disregard for the play's original theme of conflict between a religious code and the needs of a secure state. Cumulatively, these "tyrant" plays represent an early Elizabethan debate on the limits of obedience to a potentially corrupt civil authority.

The most comprehensive statement of these limits, from the viewpoint of an intellectual at court pondering the advisability of endorsing a political administration, is to be found in Richard Edwards' *Damon and Pythias.* Performed by the Chapel children before the queen in 1565, this play is deeply concerned with the philosopher-poet's freedom to observe and criticize, and conversely his obligation to remain free of political entanglements or financial reward. Edwards returns to the problem much discussed by earlier humanists in *Utopia, Of Gentleness and Nobility,* and other of their works. After the unsettling years of mid-century, the intellectuals are once again seeking a means to influence the center of power and to mold a new leadership in their own image. Are the courtier and scholar compatible types? Edwards argues that they have much to learn from one another only if they remain as separate in function as possible.

Edwards' setting is distantly removed from England, as in all such "tyrant" plays, and the author is quick to affirm in speaking of Dionysius' court that "we mean no court but that" (Prologue). Dionysius is no Elizabeth; the advice is tactfully indirect. Yet the lessons of history are useful in testing the proper stance of the philosopher-poet under extreme conditions. Dionysius would appear to be as unregenerate a tyrant as history can offer. Plato had in fact used the example of Dionysius to prove his point that a philosopher at court will be dragged down to its Machiavellian level instead of raising the court to his ideals.[7] By choosing this notorious case, Edwards deliberately heightens the miraculous nature of Damon's and Pythias' influence over the king.

Yet Edwards also insists that the king's conversion is credible. In this interpretation, Dionysius is not without virtuous impulse. He has ruled through fear and hate only because he has been shown no other way, and is himself a terrified victim of his paranoid nightmares (ll. 934-937). Increasingly isolated by flattery, he is the prisoner of a courtly system from which he is dramatically rescued not through political counsel but through the example of the virtuous life led by the two Christian philosophical brothers. Such, in Edwards' view, is the proper role of the intellectual at court—and it is a role that can decisively alter the course of political history.

To be sure, philosophers can succumb to the courtly way if once they begin to compromise with the system. Aristippus is Edwards' model of "a philosopher of late" who professes now "the courtly philosophie: To crouch, to speak fair, myself I applie To feed the kinges humour with pleasant devises" (ll. 20-22). By trying to succeed at the game of Carisophus the parasite, Aristippus throws away his fine university training for worldly friendships, intrigue, disappointment, rejection by the king's changeable mood, and finally despairing self-denunciation, until the examples of Damon and Pythias teach him how to recover himself. He illustrates negatively what Damon and Pythias have long maintained: the necessity of complete objectivity. In Pythias' words, philosophers must be the "lookers-on," viewing the world as a stage, discerning the good from the bad in the manners of all nations (ll. 397-400). The value of their assessment depends on breadth of view—"A wise man may live everywheare"—and on total freedom from restraint in their utterance. Even if their openness of speech places them at the seeming mercy of vindictive tattletales like Carisophus, they must never yield to the promptings of caution. Damon and Pythias are delivered from tyranny by the strange power of truth. If they had begun to fear for their personal safety and so held their tongues, Dionysius would never have come to know himself. Philosophers must believe that honest criticism will never lead to their destruction because the Almighty will defend them. The play is above all a plea for the absolute freedom of the inquiring mind.

The philosopher must be permitted, indeed encouraged, to evaluate the contemporary political situation. He is not, however, to take action or recommend practical reforms. Damon and Pythias observe tyranny and denounce it because it is wrong; thereupon their responsibility ends. "Fame reporteth strange thinges of Dionysius. But kinges matters, passing our reach, pertain not to us" (ll. 487-488). Their attitude toward corruption is the correct one, as in *Cambises*, of passive obedience to a tyrant. "My friend, the goddes forbid so cruell a thing That any man should lift up his sword against the king . . . Whom to rule on earth the mightie goddes have sent" (ll. 495-498). They never tell Dionysius how to run his government, but offer proof in their own lives of the power of friendship. What they offer rises above politics; to learn their lesson, Damon tells the king, "you must forget you ar a king, for friendship stands in true equalitie" (l. 2152). Yet the effect on Dionysius redounds to the health of the common weal.

The crucial importance of the philosopher does not mean that good courtiers are unnecessary. On the contrary, since Damon and Pythias are nonpolitical and uninvolved, the patient pragmatism of Eubulus the counselor is commendable. Like his namesake in *Gorboduc*, Eubulus is a brave man, daring to question Dionysius' whims. He points out to the king the element of mere surmise in the charges against Damon and Pythias; he argues rule by mercy and love. In one of the play's most didactic passages, he lectures Dionysius on tyranny and the lessons of history (ll. 903-912). At the same time Eubulus is a man of compromise—in his view, meaningful compromise. "Who deals with kinges in matters of great waight, When froward will doth bear the chefest sway, Must yeld of force" (ll. 1874-1875). Strongly disapproving of Dionysius' continued wrath toward Damon and Pythias, Eubulus can only wring his hands and hope for better luck next time. Damon's and Pythias' triumph through Christian love is outside his experience of cloakroom maneuvering. For all his virtue, Eubulus is wrong in yielding even slightly to worldly wariness. Dionysius sees and emphasizes the theme of the philosophers' victory over even the best of courtly ways: "O noble friendship, I must yeld! At thy force I wonder . . . This sight hath brought this about, Which thy grave counsell, Eubulus, and learned perswasion could never doo" (ll. 2125-2129).

Edwards' play is thus uncompromising in its insistence on philosophic detachment and candor. Courtiers must learn virtue, but even in their finest hour they must rely on the intellectual's purity of philosophical vision. The viewpoint clearly reflects Edwards' own humanist bias, added to the old story of perfect friendship. Edwards' vehicle is tragicomic art, a rhetorical form more persuasively moving than abstract argument in council.[8] For Norton and Sackville, the parliamentarian was the hero to protect the nation against a faltering king; for Edwards, the hero is the artist of Christian learning. A new group of humanists was at hand for Elizabeth. Their concern for better and more widespread education was unquestionably welcome, but the zeal with which they viewed their mission at court presented the politician queen with a problem in tact. In the 1580's and afterward, she studied ways to receive their praise and preserve their loyalty, while at the same time seeking to curb their insistence on free speech and criticism. She had success enough to ensure an effective degree of unity in the drama of the 1580's, as England approached her great showdown with the Catholic powers of Europe.

The flattering courtly play of the 1580's is a new and distinct genre. Borrowing heavily from native traditions of débat, masque, and pageant, and exploiting classical literature for refined sentiments, language, and dramatic structure, this new fusion of Renaissance art is essentially topical in its focus on the image of Queen Elizabeth. Complimentary effusions about her are no longer perfunctory afterthoughts, but the nucleus of dramatic meaning. This ornately decorated drama begins with flattery as its motive, expressing through fanciful analogy a national spirit of cultural awakening embodied in England's monarch. Elizabeth becomes the controller of human destiny, superior to the Olympian gods and goddesses, the leader of a new society explicitly contrasted with the foibles of men in ancient legend or romance.

Guided as much by her canny instincts for national solidarity as by mere vanity, Elizabeth encouraged this triumph of devotion and determined that it should not lapse into critical advice on her own domestic arrangements. Even when her most powerful courtiers entertained her on her official "progresses" at their noble residences, in costly spectacles less under her control than regular plays at court, she could strike back at effrontery. Leicester's blunt advocacy of matrimony in the entertainment at Kenilworth, 1575, prompted the rejoinder of Woodstock in which the Faerie Queene herself persuades the heroine against an unequal marriage (see Chapter 1). Private appeals for office or gratitude for restitution of royal favor were, however, occasionally permissible in a privately sponsored presentation. The most suggestive is Sir Henry Lee's Woodstock entertainment of 1592, described by Thomas Churchyard. An old knight is in a perpetual sleep, openly emblematic of Sir Henry's faithlessness to his trust with Anne Vavasour, and can be awakened only by the relenting Faerie Queene. Clearly the sleep is royal disfavor; the knight confessedly has failed to guard the pictures left in his care. By 1590 Elizabeth had recalled Lee to favor despite his open cohabitation with Anne in that year.[1] Such dramatic spectacles, extolling the queen's bounty, might serve the dual purpose of flattery and begging. Yet regular plays at court did not necessarily partake of the inherently occasional nature of these entertainments on royal progress, when the queen was being feted by a particular courtier and was inevitably asked to consider her relationship with him. At court, the Master of the Revels could and frequently did amend performances intended for Elizabeth's amusement.[2] The central critical question, then, is whether regular court drama of the 1580's, especially Lyly's, included private topical meaning as well as praise for England's queen.

Elizabeth's emergence as *deus ex machina* in courtly drama began early in her reign with an entertainment optimistically intended to celebrate a meeting of reconciliation between Elizabeth and Mary Stuart at Nottingham Castle, 1562—a meeting that never took place. The elaborate plans for the entertainment reveal how keenly Elizabeth desired a rapprochement. Her dramatic spokesman, Pallas, presides over a masque symbolizing the expulsion of Prepensed Malice and the exalting of Prudence, Temperance, and Peace. Both real queens are present in the audience and are spoken to directly by the abstractions.[3] In the epilogue to another spectacle written specifically for a state occasion, *Sapientia Solomonis* (1566), Elizabeth and her royal visitor the Princess Cecilia of Sweden are compared to Solomon and the Queen of Sheba. Solomon's merciful judgments and building of the temple, dramatized in the play itself, are but tokens of Elizabeth's triumphant propagation of the true faith. Similarly, in the epilogue of *Liberality and Prodigality* (ca. 1567-1568), Elizabeth subsumes the qualities of Lady Virtue and so oversees the bestowal of rewards with which the play ends. She is the deified representative of Liberality, a quality the author tactfully and flatteringly wishes to urge upon this sometimes parsimonious monarch.[4] A fourth such instance is the ending of *The Rare Triumphs of Love and Fortune* (1582), in which Love and Fortune reconcile their claims of supreme influence over the affairs of men by acknowledging Queen Elizabeth's ascendancy over them both. She is explicitly a corrective to the violence and ingratitude of the story just ended; only her intervention can establish a new moral order, transcending pagan eroticism and instability of fortune. In each instance, analogy to Elizabeth is the essence of the occasion, and performance would be impossible without her presence.

George Peele's *The Arraignment of Paris* (published 1584, probably acted at court 1581-1582) is the culmination of this flattering device. The well-known tale of Troy had been commonly used as a device of Tudor flattery in poetry and painting since the time of Henry VII. The play has no formal sources other than court pageantry and the currently fashionable pastoral.[5] (Peele's *The Hunting of Cupid,* of which only scattered fragments remain, was evidently of a similar type.) Peele's father had been a writer of pageants, and *The Arraignment of Paris* bears the imprint of that semidramatic tradition. Its elaborate and costly stage edifices, schematized color symbolism and bestiary lore, and festive ritual are all designed to the scale of a royal entry. The conspicuously large cast and elegant costuming are lavished on a single performance, requiring Elizabeth's presence and meaningless if repeated without her. Even the second plot of the shepherds adumbrates the function of the anti-masque. *Arraignment* is in short an "entertainment" for Elizabeth, disciplined into the form of a five-act play on a classical theme but nonetheless celebratory in occasion.

Appropriate also to the tradition of aristocratic entertainment is the series of debates structured in configurations of three, with Elizabeth as final arbitrator surpassing the pagan gods. She receives the apple or ball of gold for which ancient Troy burned, and reconciles the factions of Juno, Venus, and Pallas by subsuming all their immortal qualities into her own godlike person. She is the leader of "a second Troy" tracing its mythological lineage from Aeneas but avoiding errors of the past. Hence the deliberately jarring revision of Paris' trial, with its second and more exalted judgment, is no mere poetical "conceit" but an affirmation of order and Christian morality. Venus may no longer sport with Mars in "a net or else a cloud"; Jupiter may not play the ranger "in every open grove" (ll. 371, 379). The ruler now is one who "honor[s] Dian for her chastity, And likes the labors well of Phoebe's groves" (ll. 1244-1245). She is more peerlessly regal than Juno, more fair of person than Venus, more famous for her deeds and wisdom than Pallas. By her victory over the fatal powers of Clothos, Lachesis, and Atropos she signals an end to the caprice of fortune as demonstrated in ancient Troy and Mount Olympus. She is thus not only a resolution of all the debates but the focus of the play's elaborate structure. In its surprising artifice, Peele's device convincingly expresses an artistic and political national purpose daring to rival and even exceed that of ancient civilization.

Almost exactly contemporary with *Arraignment*, John Lyly's *Campaspe* was performed at Blackfriars in 1583 and at court "before the queen's majesty on New Year's day at night" in 1584. Although not a one-performance "entertainment," *Campaspe* is a celebratory drama structured on two interwoven debating topics: the relationship of a great monarch to his nation's philosophers and artists, and the proper attitude of a monarch toward love and honor. As royal patron of the arts and conqueror of erotic love, King Alexander is (like the goddesses of *Arraignment*) a prototype of Elizabeth—lesser than she, but worthy of comparison. The flattery is tactfully indirect and avoids the dangerous immediacies of the marriage question. Nonetheless, contemporary analogy in broad terms is basic to Lyly's artistic intent. The central design of *Campaspe,* which cannot be attributed to the heterogeneous sources in Pliny, Diogenes Laertius, and Plutarch,[6] grows from the author's awareness of his position at court.

Just as the earlier *Euphues* relates the fortunes of a young scholar moving from Athens (the university life) to Naples (the court, the world of intrigue and advancement), *Campaspe* debates at length the role of the learned man in a society of courtiers and soldiers. Lyly had himself only recently come down from Oxford, seeking not only to prosper but to justify himself in the world of practical deeds. Yet only the occasion is topical; Lyly's materials and sources for the debate are commonplace. His polarities are truisms: the contemplative versus the active life, vanity of ambition versus fulfillment in this world. The philosopher, pondering as in *Damon and Pythias* whether or not to counsel a king, can willingly embrace service as Aristotle does, or seek Plato's careful balance between philosophic vision and worldly activity, or insist upon the absolute detachment of Diogenes. The extreme of independence is, significantly, the most challenging alternative. Diogenes can offer Alexander, or any monarch wishing to be immortal, a perspective on himself unattainable through compromise. The king has the world at command, the Stoic philosopher can "Unlearn to covet." As in most Renaissance views of Diogenes, he is here a positive figure, spokesman for an essentially Christian disavowal of worldly vanity, a scabrous wit but incisive corrector of manners.[7] His resolute refusal to worship kings "Because they be no gods" (II, ii, 128) is a salutary deflation of Alexander, one that this rare king welcomes in an effort to know himself. Diogenes argues for much the same unmovable virtue as Damon and Pythias, and is perhaps more responsible than any other external factor for the king's final self-mastery in love. Even when the king has proved himself totally self-sufficient as warrior, statesman, and friend, Diogenes' rejection of worldly acquisition continues to mock Alexander's restless search for new conquest. The ideal king still remains limited by earthly achievement, all his strivings meaningless in the world of the spirit.

Despite the appeal of this philosophical independence, Diogenes is not Lyly's authorial spokesman. The play demonstrates, as G. K. Hunter points out, that Lyly wanted to be both humanist and courtier.[8] The position of Diogenes is one extreme of the composite man. The ideal monarch, as the epitome of the courtier, makes an equally valid contribution, whose only limits in fact are the vanity of worldly achievement as defined by the Stoic philosopher. Alexander's court is clearly a model of greatness, because of the king's resolution to "have as great care to govern in peace as conquer in war; that, whilst arms cease arts may flourish, and joining letters with lances, we endeavor to be as good philosophers as soldiers" (I, i, 80-83). Lyly's intent to praise Elizabeth's encouragement of the arts is unmistakable. Alexander is himself both captain and philosopher, just as Elizabeth is here analogously commander of an invincible loyal people and mistress of a bright new literary circle (I, iii, 60-62). Without at least this analogy between ancient Greece and Elizabethan England, the applicability of this play about intellectuals and rulers would be meaningless. Lyly both flatters and urges a continued place for intellectuals in Elizabeth's favor. Even the warlike Hephaestion agrees that "It is better to have in court a wise man, than in your ground a golden mine," although he stipulates that "They were not philosophers if they knew not their duties" (I, iii, 53-99).

Limits must be imposed, however, on the extent to which kings may hope to become philosophers and artists (or the reverse). In searching to define the place of the learned man at court, Lyly insists upon specialized talents that cannot be acquired by amateurs. Alexander's greatest quality is his recognition of Diogenes' wisdom and its inaccessibility to himself. The king turns back to the world as his inescapable milieu. Similarly the king acknowledges the talent of Apelles the artist, after trying himself to draw.

> *Alexander.* Nay, if all be too hard or soft, so many rules and regards that one's hand, one's eye, one's mind must all draw together, I had rather be setting of a battle than blotting of a board. But how have I done here?
>
> *Apelles.* Like a king. (III, iv, 108-112)

Learned men must be regarded as professionals. Art and wisdom are not mere adornments but are needed to give perspective to the immediacies of politics. It follows *per contra* that learned men must know the limits of their involvement in state affairs. If Lyly is asking to be a courtier too, it is with a difference—not as administrator or soldier, but as of equal value to the nation and hence an integral part of the court. The play insists that Lyly cannot hope to be both Diogenes and Alexander; and whereas one need not go to either extreme, the learned man and the ruler are still separate entities who must learn from each other but never coalesce.

The applicability of these typed portraits to the court of Elizabeth is central to Lyly's artistic purpose, but involves no personal resemblances whatever. Lyly is no Diogenes, and Elizabeth is no more Alexander than is any monarch who aspires to learning and liberality. Elizabeth after all had not returned from the wars in 1583, nor was she about to embark on a new series of conquests. The same lack of personal equation applies to the analogy of love versus honor, *Campaspe's* second major theme. Alexander's triumph over carnal affection is appropriate to a virgin queen. Yet the debate of love and honor is commonplace.

The analogy need not and indeed cannot be related to a biographical incident.

Alexander's passion for a commoner offers at first a tempting parallel to Elizabeth's various possibilities of marriage, especially Dudley's (Leicester's) suit in which the issues of unequal rank and ambition had been much in people's minds. The reversal of sexes needed for such an allegory, hinted at in *Patient Grissell* (Chapter 11), would have seemed all the more suitable in view of Elizabeth's fondness for comparing herself to Alexander and Caesar.[9] Campaspe is "born of a mean [middle] parentage" (I, i, 72) and scarcely worthy to be consort. Yet she speaks as though marriage and coronation are within her grasp if she accepts Alexander: "a distaff is fitter for thy hand than a scepter" (IV, ii, 12-13). Campaspe's temptation is not to commit fleshly sin (a prospect that would require no inner struggle for this virtuous maiden) but to desert Apelles for ambition: "Ants live safely till they have gotten wings, and juniper is not blown up till it hath gotten an high top" (ll. 13-15). Conceivably, then, the king's magnanimous surrender of Campaspe idealizes Elizabeth's final position toward Leicester and the Countess of Essex, whom he had secretly married, thereby incurring the queen's intense displeasure.[10] The seeming parallel is especially suggestive because Alexander's triumph over passion anticipates that of the queen figures in *Sapho and Phao, Galathea,* and *Endymion.*

Yet any such hypothesis encounters insuperable difficulties in *Campaspe.* Alexander's tyrannical behavior under the influence of passion is unattractive. He will "conquer as he list" and refuses advice. "No more, Hephaestion! In this case I will use mine own counsel" (II, ii, 103-113). To fall "from the armor of Mars to the arms of Venus" is debasing enchantment, conventional enough but hardly flattering if applied specifically to Elizabeth. More offensive still in any allegorical meaning, Campaspe is in love with Apelles and finds the king's advances unwelcome. However much Leicester may have wished to defend his choice of the Countess of Essex, Lyly was certainly in no position to imply that Queen Elizabeth had lost out to another woman, or that men generally found her less than irresistible. Moreover, parallel love situations, such as Hephaestion's for the captive Timoclea, are manifestly variations on the theme of love versus honor.

Surely, Apelles is not drawn from the life story of some court lady who beat Elizabeth in the game of love. His existence as a rival suitor fulfills the requirements of a debate like that of *Fulgens and Lucrece:* impoverished true love versus wealthy importunity. Such a familiar confrontation leads Campaspe to describe the love of kings in graphically unfavorable terms:

> O Apelles, thy love cometh from the heart, but Alexander's from the mouth! The love of kings is like the blowing of winds, which whistle sometimes gently among the leaves, and straightways turn the trees up by the roots . . . They place affection by times, by policy, by appointment. If they frown, who dares call them unconstant? If bewray secrets, who will term them untrue? If fall to other loves, who trembles not if he call them unfaithful? In kings there can be no love but to queens; for as near must they meet in majesty as they do in affection. It is requisite to stand aloof from king's love, Jove, and lightning. (IV, iv, 20-33)

The advice is generalized, like Laertes' to Ophelia; it scarcely does justice to Alexander, and is disastrous if applied to Elizabeth. Yet as a truism about royal unapproachability it is, paradoxically, flattering to England's queen. She may not, as unvalued persons do, carve for herself. In these large terms the play celebrates the lonely self-sacrifice of a maiden queen who is not rejected in love but who decides herself against unequal entanglement. Just as the ideal monarch becomes enamored of philosophy but must stop short of contemplative withdrawal, so that monarch tastes the deepening passion of love only to conclude that it too is incompatible with the monarch's unique role. Nevertheless the monarch is made more complete by these contacts with the intellectual and emotional experiences of other men. Elizabeth is at the center of this fusion of the two themes of *Campaspe.*

Sapho and Phao, written very shortly after *Campaspe* and "played before the queen's majesty on Shrove Tuesday [March 3, 1584] by her majesty's children, and the boys of Paul's," also touches upon the theme of the scholar in a court famed for learning. Queen Sapho is renowned for attributes not to be found in usual accounts of the poetess of ancient times: "fair by nature, by birth royal, learned by education, by government politic, rich by peace" (I, ii, 7-9).[11] She is certainly not short and dark, as Ovid describes her. Moreover she can, like Alexander, command the services of wise men such as Pandion, recently arrived from Euphues' own Athens and bemused about the conflicting values of court life and philosophic study.[12]

Whereas these familar debating themes establish a connection between Sapho's court and Elizabeth's, the dominant interest is in the love story and the enormous social inequality separating the title figures. Phao is a ferryman, free and contented with his physical labor, happy once again at the story's end to resume his life of the oar. The maiden Sapho conquers her love for this commoner as a passion unbefitting her lofty station. The facts here are derived from legend. Do they also apply to any of Elizabeth's courtships? Phao is made extraordinarily handsome by Venus, but is also by nature reluctant to yield to any woman's love. As a type of male chastity he is well suited to be Sapho's platonic admirer in the play's happy ending. Yet his coyness in wooing, if applied topically, would make Elizabeth the aggressor. Love's tyranny is unflattering, as it was for Alexander. At the extremes of her passion, Sapho is quite desperate for Phao. She is presented in bed attended by her ladies (IV, iii) more dead than alive, waspish about her bed-linen, mercurial of mood, concealing the truth from her women. These clinical and disparaging symptoms are certainly too commonplace to need biographical explanation.[13]

The ending in which Phao contentedly worships Sapho from a distance, "My loyalty unspotted, though unrewarded," aptly describes the attitude Elizabeth wished to encourage in all her courtly entourage. Conversely, it is ill suited to boosting the claim of any particular suitor. Phao surrenders all claim not only to Sapho's person, but also to a comfortable life in her proximity. He is not, like Endymion, one of the queen's admiring and ever-present courtiers. He leaves the country —as, for instance, did d'Alençon[14]—but wishes no more than the rustic life to which he was born. If this play was written in behalf of a particular one of Elizabeth's suitors, such as Leicester,[15] it has failed to ask or to achieve any tangible benefits. If, on the other hand, Lyly was expressing his resentment of a French match and his joy at d'Alençon's departure,[16] he has given a strangely sympathetic portrait of the ugly little duke in Phao.

Sapho's rival for Phao's affection is Venus, and any historical allegory would have to suppose her (like Tellus in *Endymion*) a beautiful woman in Elizabeth's court vying for the attentions of the favored suitor. Such an equation is, however, inconsistent with Venus' generic attributes as goddess of erotic love. Her first wish is to compel Sapho to be passionate for Phao, to bow the neck never bowed in love; only later does Venus herself fall in love with Phao. No waiting-lady of the court would have any motive to force Elizabeth's attention on some man. To the goddess Venus, on the other hand, Sapho's reputation for transcending carnal affection is a galling affront, one that intimidates even Cupid. Sapho's Diana-like power must be made to yield to desire. Hence the flattering of Elizabeth is undeniable, but is mythologically indirect. Elizabeth is, like Sapho, the goddess-like vanquisher of Venus' sensual power, in herself and in her courtly circle. Like Alexander the queen has tasted human passion in order to overcome it. The biographical circumstances are too delicate to portray accurately. The rival is certainly no mortal woman but the erotic impulse itself: "Shall not I rule the fancies of men, and lead Venus in chains like a captive?" (V, ii, 66-67). As in *Arraignment*, Venus and all Olympus yield their pagan qualities to a new morality. Sapho will direct the affections of men as well as of women; in this sense Phao's platonic submission is emblematic of all men in Elizabeth's society rather than of a particular man.

As with Alexander, Sapho's regal unapproachability is at once a personal self-sacrifice and a necessary definition of her greatness. Lowliness is Phao's sole disqualification. Having aspired to "build thy nest in the sun," he struggles virtuously against an ambition that is blasphemous (II, iv, 4). Conversely, Sapho discovers the pain of stooping too low (III, iii). Her dream, a fanciful allegory that might seem to require particular application,[17] tells of a stockdove nesting in a tall cedar and losing his feathers so that he falls to the ground. The dreamer can condemn neither the tree, troubled with burrowing ants and caterpillars, nor the bird, which grows more feathers and seems on the verge of rising again. Sapho wishes the tree might bow, but then awakes; descent is impossible (IV, iii).

The meaning of her sorrow, flickering hope, and final resolution is plain enough. The caterpillars are more enigmatic, suggesting courtly parasites (as in *Richard II's* "caterpillars of the commonwealth") and hence a possibly covert allegory of political conniving not elsewhere implicit in the play. Yet as the emblems of faction, ingratitude, and envy (see *Endymion* II, i and V, i) they need not be inconsistent with an allegory of disturbing rivalry in love at Elizabeth's court. As in *Patient Grissell,* a chief danger of Elizabeth's marriage with a commoner was the resentment of disappointed wooers. Such disturbing alienations are the afflictions of Sapho's noble mind until she triumphs over passion. By refusing one lover, she accepts all as platonic admirers. The force of *Sapho's* topical allegory pleads for a universal disclaiming of all marriage pretensions. Sapho's dream is generic, like the dreaming experiences of her ladies: love ending in death or false prattling of a friend, love yielding to gold or ending in marriage. The infinitely varying edifice of love, a favorite theme of Lyly in his later plays, has at its apex the example of queenly love and self-mastery. Lyly's philosophic interest in the platonic ladder of human affection combines with his courtly intent to extol Elizabeth as the fulfillment of man's quest for the divine.

In *Endymion,* written some four years later for performance "before the queen's majesty at Greenwich on Candlemas Day at night," 1588, the enspherement of Elizabeth reaches its culmination. No longer enervated even briefly by passion as in *Campaspe* and *Sapho,* the regal figure of *Endymion* is unapproachable from the start and is adored by a courtly follower who concedes the hopelessness of his longing. Cynthia is unaware of love's sorrow, puzzled by Tellus' vindictiveness, pleased but surprised to hear of Endymion's worship of her. Even more openly than its predecessors, *Endymion* apotheosizes a queen for whom marriage is unthinkable. Her courtiers are enjoined to harmonious, platonic affection without rivalry for special favor.

Because of Cynthia's total lack of erotic entanglement, topical hypotheses based on the marriage question have proven uniformly unsatisfactory. Leicester, most often chosen as the queen's wooer,[18] was not in Elizabeth's good graces after his insubordinate behavior in the Low Countries during 1585-1586, and his increasing identification with the Protestant extremists. Besides, Lyly's patron the Earl of Oxford was no friend of Leicester and his protégé Sir Philip Sidney.[19] Although Endymion's involvement with Tellus might conceivably be a parallel to Leicester's secret marriage against the queen's wishes, Elizabeth did not like to be reminded of that disloyalty. She barred all talk of her marriage, most of all Leicester's old suit. Even less would she hear of the subterfuges of Mary Queen of Scots, urged by R. Warwick Bond as the true meaning of Tellus' rivalry. Mary did set her cap for Leicester while in prison; but she did not marry her jailor as Tellus does, and the play gives no hint of Scottish, French, or papal topicality. Leicester would not have welcomed such formidably dangerous insinuations of his alliance with Catholic sedition. Many of these arguments also nullify Albert Feuillerat's hypothesis that Endymion is James VI of Scotland abandoning his mother for Elizabeth, while Mary (Tellus) plots with the papists (Dipsas) to control her Protestant son.[20]

More plausible, because it avoids the marriage question entirely and sees *Endymion* as an expression of gratitude for restitution of royal favor (analogous to Sir Henry Lee's entertainment at Woodstock, 1592), is Josephine W. Bennett's interpretation on behalf of the Earl of Oxford, Lyly's patron. Oxford was in disgrace from 1581 to 1583 for suspected Catholic activities and for having purportedly fathered a child on Anne Vavasour. Mrs. Bennett sees the play as an argument for Oxford's innocence and continued loyalty to the queen, and a commemoration of the pension bestowed on Oxford (the kiss) in 1586. A parallel is found also for Corsites in Sir Henry Lee, who had custody of Anne Vavasour in the Tower and later became her lover.[21] This reading justly accounts for Lyly's motive, and would be consonant with an intent to flatter Elizabeth for her merciful bounty. However, many of the positive arguments against topical identification in Lyly's earlier dramas apply here as well.

Endymion's sleep is not, as in 1592 at Woodstock, an unmistakable sign of royal disfavor. Far from being wrathful, Cynthia is at first unaware of Endymion's tribulations; once she hears of her courtier's sad absence, she resolves compassionately and pragmatically to relieve his distress. She need hear no arguments of Endymion's innocence before he can be recalled. His mind has been solely fixed on her, to the neglect of the flesh; Earth can exact the penalty of withered limbs, by holding futilely on to the corrupting body, but is unable to move the virtuous spirit from its heavenly devotion. "From this sweet contemplation if I be not driven, I shall live of all men the most content, taking more pleasure in mine aged thought than ever I did in my youthful action" (V, iii, 175-178). Cynthia's welcoming of Endymion is a reaffirmation of his loyalty, not a forgiveness for disloyalty. "Persevere, Endymion, in loving me, and I account more strength in a true heart than in a walled city . . . Endymion, continue as thou hast begun" (ll. 180-186). She chides him only (in Endymion's enigmatic dream) for presuming too much on her affection.

Furthermore, the queen is not jealous. She has known for some time of Tellus' infatuation for Endymion, and appears to be no more than mildly amused about it: "What maketh you, Tellus, to be so short? The time was, Endymion only was" (III, i, 8-9). She sends Tellus into custody not because of a suspected affair with Endymion but because Tellus speaks disparagingly of Endymion in her presence. Even after the exposure of Tellus' plotting, the queen generously allows her to keep the "picture of Endymion" that Tellus has wrought in her captivity. Mrs. Bennett supposes this picture to be Oxford's illegitimate child. The unlikelihood of this supposition has been shown by G. K. Hunter, for the existence of such a child would admit Oxford's fathering of it and hence his sexual disloyalty to the queen.[22] Equally contradictory to such a reading is Cynthia's reaction. Far from being horror-stricken at what would be her first clear knowledge of Endymion's sexual transgression —an offense against both her and the moral code she enforces—Cynthia is jovial and placating. She approves of Tellus' admiration for Endymion so long as it is kept within proper bounds. The meaning of Endymion's portrait in the philosophical allegory, on the other hand, is evident. Cynthia and Tellus are to share Endymion, the one his soul and the other the mere shell or matter: "so much of Endymion as his picture cometh to, possess and play withal" (V, iii, 254-255). In harmony at last, the representatives of divine and mortal being agree that man's body must remain below while his better part is translated into eternal youth, beyond the flux of mutability.

The topical interpretation might still be conceivable if Lyly's supposed intent was to make light of an embarrassing but inescapable fact of bastardy, and to plead that during his years of estrangement from the queen Oxford had remained steadfastly loyal despite the vicissitudes of his worldly entanglement with Anne Vavasour. "With Tellus, fair Tellus, have I dissembled, using her but as a cloak for mine affections" (II, i, 22-23). Elizabeth did after all come to terms with the frailties of her courtiers, such as Oxford and Lee. To deny the queen's jealousy would both flatter Elizabeth's Olympian calm and suggest, tactfully, that a virgin queen demands affection but not absolute asceticism in her courtiers. The topical reading is nonetheless unnecessary, and contrary to the spirit of the philosophical allegory. It rests on extended analogy, and can explain no aspect of the play not incorporated successfully in a more generic meaning.

Like Venus in *Sapho*, Tellus behaves as goddess in a way that could not motivate a lady at court. She is Cynthia's foil in a cosmic struggle between chaste and earthly affection. Endymion's philosophic quest seeks a virtuous ideal beyond the mutability of worldly imperfection, a magic fusion of time and eternity that he comprehends (like the speaker of Keats's "Grecian Urn") but cannot achieve because he is mortal. Cynthia, as the moon, grows old but seems ever young; her unapproachable perfection is a mockery of Endymion's wasting, from which he seemingly cannot return. Tellus conversely is an earth goddess: "Is not my beauty divine, whose body is decked with fair flowers, and veins are vines, yielding sweet liquor to the dullest spirits; whose ears are corn to bring strength; and whose hairs are grass, to bring abundance?" All life depends on her for fleshly sustenance: "Infinite are my creatures, without which neither thou nor Endymion nor any could love or live" (I, ii, 19-26). She is the Circean temptress, plotting to turn Endymion's thoughts from honor and achievement. She speaks, that is, as an abstracted principle; no court lady would aim for the destruction of man's reason as an end in itself.

Tellus openly insists that her position is one of vice, like Mundus in the morality plays: "All his virtues will I shadow with vices. His person —ah, sweet person!—shall he deck with such rich robes as he shall forget his own person . . . The prime of his youth and pride of his time shall be spent in melancholy passions, careless behavior, untamed thoughts, and unbridled affections" (I, ii, 41-61). Accordingly, Tellus fears death not as an ordinary woman might, but as a goddess who will lose control of her victim with dissolution of the flesh (I, ii, 62-69). Her rival is the embodiment of essence and form, who governs all living things: "Your grapes would be but dry husks, your corn but chaff, and all your virtues vain, were it not Cynthia that preserveth the one in the bud and cherisheth the other in the blade, and by her influence both comforteth all things, and by her authority commandeth all creatures" (I, ii, 27-32). It is only when Tellus accepts this subservience of the chaotic elements to divine idea that the play can end happily. Similarly, English society must accept the visionary leadership of its queen; *Endymion* intends a political compliment to Elizabeth, but not in terms of specific court individuals.

Though Endymion's virtuous instincts prompt him to choose correctly between Cynthia and Tellus, his love for the queen is flawed. The hazard is not disloyalty but a coveting of her special regard to the exclusion of his rivals. Cynthia's loftiness toward Endymion is quite the opposite of jealousy: she must temper the zeal of his unquestioned devotion. "I favored thee, Endymion, for thy honor, thy virtues, thy affections. But to bring thy thoughts within the compass of thy fortunes, I have seemed strange, that I might have thee stayed" (IV, iii, 78-81). Just as God allows fleshly tribulations for his elect in order to teach them humility and dependence, the queen must discipline her courtiers with remoteness. Endymion is a mortal and imperfect, and confesses he has longed to possess Cynthia for his own, using Tellus "but as a cloak for mine affections, that others, seeing my mangled and disordered mind, might think it were for one that loveth me, not for Cynthia" (II, i, 23-25). He fears retribution not for his innocent relation to Tellus but for having concealed a blasphemous aspiring toward Cynthia herself. In Endymion's dream (V, i) a Cynthia-like figure approaches the sleeper with knife and looking-glass, about to offer violence until she perceives in the glass how ill anger becomes a lady of her quality. Accompanied by two ladies representing Anger and Mercy, the Cynthia figure eschews wrath for pity until "there appeared in her heavenly face such a divine majesty mingled with a sweet mildness that I was ravished with the sight" (ll. 97-98). The balance of rigor and forgiveness is a commonplace of divinity, and reflects Endymion's mingled fear and love toward his queen. These fantasies are the product of Endymion's guilty soul, not of Cynthia's conscious disapproval. The queen herself never gives an indication of wrath. As the generic courtier, Endymion knows his own sin to have been not infidelity but ambition.

In his dream, after having rejected "counsels" and "policies" offered him by the aged man with a book, thereby incurring the disdainful pity and wrath of the old man, Endymion is strangely prompted by curiosity to accept the third leaf of the book with its revealing "pictures." There Endymion beholds the ugly spectacle of those who presume on the queen's royal affection—the drones or beetles "creeping under the wings of the princely eagle, who, being carried into her nest, sought there to suck that vein that would have killed the eagle" (ll. 130-132). The drones are like the wolves barking at the moon, "Ingratitude with an hundred eyes gazing for benefits," treachery, envy. As in *Sapho*, these are not political rivals whom Endymion would like to see crushed for his own advancement, but the generic disturbances of court peace which he too must avoid.[23] They are enemies of the chaste affection that must prevail between a queen and all her courtiers indifferently. They emanate from man's corrupted nature, not from the queen's divinity, and are present even in Endymion's psyche as revealed by his dream. Such chimeras are sufficient to explain Endymion's fear of divine wrath. Only when he is purged of the vestiges of court rivalry can Endymion become the eternal type of true courtier.

Endymion's is the most exalted and difficult quest in love, but there are other paths. As J. A. Bryant, Jr., has shown, the types of love evolve from an artistic pattern of pairing and contrasting Endymion's love for Cynthia with other love relationships, rather than depending on vignettes of Lyly's contemporaries.[24] Eumenides' sensuous and yet virtuous love for Semele is but one momentous step below that of Endymion and Cynthia in the scale of platonic values. Womanish, resentful, waspish of tongue, Semele represents for Eumenides (as her name suggests) a temptation of excessive and ruinous physical joy. Her perverse thwarting of his pleasure is necessary "lest, embracing sweetness beyond measure, I take a surfeit without recure. Let her practice her accustomed coyness that I may diet myself upon my desires; otherwise the fulness of my joys will diminish the sweetness, and I shall perish by them before I possess them" (III, iv, 98-102). Chivalric faithfulness and chaste yet passionate womanhood can be rescued from themselves, like Scudamour and Amoret in the House of Busirane, only by the higher ideals of selfless friendship that Endymion and Cynthia perfectly enjoy. Similarly, Corsites is a fit companion for Tellus, since he is a stern and masculine person easily ensnared by beauty. He is still, however, a worthy courtier, able to see at once in the queen's presence that he has betrayed his manly self, and to rouse himself once again to proper military service. His relationship to Tellus is still basically sensual but no longer emasculating. A queen's court can accommodate all levels of love, even the lowest form comically represented by Tophas, Dipsas, and Bagoa. Tophas' lust for an older woman and his "sleeping in love" for an enchantress parody Lyly's serious interest in platonic attachments. He fancies his lower body to be animal and "the rest immortal," in a spoof of man's amphibious nature (I, iii). He boasts of Mars' strength, untouchable by Venus, but falls into an exaggerated enervation through love and turns poetaster (III, iii). Tophas is even able to produce a symbolic but meaningless dream containing the image of his mistress (III, iii). As the wooer of Geron's wife he is a would-be adulterer, and so is matched out of his social class with a servant with whom he will quarrel. In Tophas, Lyly manages at once to make fun of his own vision and to illustrate the depths of carnal mismating. Tophas certainly exists for artistic and thematic design, not for contemporary slander.

As in Lyly's earlier plays, philosophers seek a place of importance in the court of the maiden queen. On first learning of Endymion's distress, Cynthia sends to Egypt, Thessaly, and Greece for wise men to unfold the riddle of the enchanted sleep. Pythagoras and Gyptes heap praise on Cynthia for her palace "where truth is not in colors but in life, virtues not in imagination but execution" (IV, iii, 49-50), as in *Sapho*. Pythagoras and Gyptes are, however, unable to explain the enchantment, conceding "that no power can end it, till she die that did it, or the heavens show some means more than miraculous" (IV, iii, 146-148). They are powerless where the queen succeeds in restoring youth and reconverting trees into women. The philosophers are taught a higher truth, and their best reward is to be invited to "fall from vain follies of philosophers" and to stay on with Cynthia (V, iii, 285-289). This is the final capitulation of Lyly as an intellectual who once fretted about philosophic independence. He bows to a world where wise men are not ignored but are translated by Cynthia's magic into a higher realm, able to bridge the false distinction between intellectual inquiry and virtue in action. In terms of this ideal, Endymion's quest is Lyly's own.

Apart from *Endymion* and *Midas* (to be discussed in the next chapter), Lyly's later experiments with changing dramatic fashion turned away from praise of Elizabeth and then faltered. Even the comparatively early *Gallathea* (S. R., 1585), deferred for court production until 1588 seemingly because of the dissolution of the "Oxford boys" group who had performed *Campaspe* and *Sapho*,[25] is less overtly devotional. To be sure, *Sapho's* motif of a contest between Venus and Diana, so obviously flattering to Elizabeth, is consciously repeated in *Gallathea*. Cupid is taken into safekeeping "first by Sapho, now by Diana" (V, iii, 85-86). Diana's self-mastery over passion anticipates the unapproachability of Cynthia in *Endymion*. Yet in *Gallathea*, Diana's experiencing of the pangs of love results in more of a truce than chaste triumph. She must make an accommodation with Venus. This is merely a commonplace of harmony between chaste and erotic love, and does not have any obvious reference to Elizabeth. Nor is the portrait of Diana as endearing as that of Cynthia. Diana is no ruler of a court; she leads a group of nymphs but commands no courtiers. Her infatuation for a maiden disguised as a boy renders the affair innocuous but risible, certainly precluding any meaningful study of Elizabeth's relationship to her court admirers. Most of all, Diana is no mistress of learning. She fails to come in contact with the supposedly learned men present, and they are in any case a sorry lot—humbug alchemists and astronomers who can only parody the serious themes of philosophical independence or quest for scientific knowledge.

Neither *Mother Bombie* (ca. 1587-1590) nor *Love's Metamorphosis* (ca. 1589-1590) mentions performance before the queen on its title page. There were, after all, other outlets for writers of coterie plays, and sophisticated theater at the turn of the 1590's was drifting away from the queen's dominant influence. Lyly became involved in the acrid exchanges of the Martin Marprelate controversy, wherein his shrillness appears to have offended some of those he meant to please.[26] *Mother Bombie* contains no figure that could possibly resemble Elizabeth. *Love's Metamorphosis* does return to the contest between chaste and erotic love, but (as in *Gallathea*) without motives of royal flattery. The theme that Lyly created for Elizabeth has passed almost imperceptibly out of her realm.[27]

Lyly's seemingly latest play, *The Woman in the Moon* (ca. 1590-1595?), although performed before Elizabeth, is a melancholy instance of an image tarnished and a vision lost. Pandora's list of failings is almost without end. The jest is conventional and not necessarily misogynistic. Quite obviously it is no attack on Elizabeth. One cannot safely speculate that it offended politically, or contributed in any way to the fading of Lyly's hopes for the mastership of the revels.[28] Lyly was silenced perhaps not by resentment over an abortive campaign for preferment, but by becoming the "victim of fashion" in the rapidly changing drama of his time.[29] Even so, when compared with *Endymion's* queen, the emblem of Luna as fickle, slothful, and "lunatic" is no compliment to women or to the Diana into whom Pandora is transformed. Such a narrative can be safely set only in Utopia, nowhere, and can end only with the universal disclaiming of love by men and women. Whatever else the play means, it signals an end to the triumph of devotion in Elizabeth's court drama of the 1580's.

The celebration of Queen Elizabeth in the drama of the 1580's, although limited chiefly to plays at court, paralleled a movement in popular drama described earlier in the chapter on "The Elizabethan Settlement": a turning away from internal problems of religious conflict to a unifying animosity toward foreigners. As exemplified in the plays of Lupton, Wapull, the Wagers, and especially Robert Wilson, popular drama found a scapegoat in Flemish, French, and Italians for such problems as inflated rents or covetousness of the clergy. This movement naturally reached its culmination during and immediately following the crisis of the Spanish Armada (July 1588). For a brief time, this crisis produced a rare fusion of interests in private and public drama in England. Even John Lyly, concerned otherwise with the exclusive interests of court life, gave expression to the quickening tempo of patriotic fervor in his *Midas* (1589)—albeit with a tone and attitude characteristically different from that of popular jingoistic drama.

Lyly's satire of King Philip of Spain is mock-heroic and essentially tolerant, provoking laughter instead of hate. Although the great event of the Armada is unmistakably present—"Have not I made the sea to groan under the number of my ships, and have they not perished? . . .

A bridge of gold did I mean to make in that island where all my navy could not make a breach" (III, i, 31-47)—Lyly is not at all interested in slanderous personal judgments. Midas' pursuit of the chaste Celia would be laughably inept if intended to apply biographically to the compulsive ascetic who ran Spain's affairs from the gloomy Alhambra. Lyly does not defame the Spanish character indiscriminately: Celia and Midas' daughter Sophronia are models of feminine virtue, offsetting Midas' greed and lust with positive ideals of courtesy, harmony, and the softening effects of chaste womanhood. They are types created to fit the thematic antithesis of tyranny and its opposite. Nor are Midas' advisers recognizable as historical individuals. The courtier insisting on military solutions bears only the most generic relation to the Duke of Alva;[1] he and his companions urging policies of lust, war, and riches are completely schematized tempters, like Lechery, Pride, and Covetousness. Desire for gold wins the upper hand with Midas because it is the *radix malorum*, the means to buy international power and to subvert the loyalties of statesmen serving foreign princes. Hence the very legend of the golden touch is, in Lyly's witty topical reading, a commonplace emblem of tyranny applying to King Philip insofar as he uses gold to "tempt the minds of true subjects," and "draw them from obedience to treachery, from their allegiance and oaths to treason and perjury" (I, i, 59-61).

The second familiar legend, of the ass's ears, pokes fun at Philip's international embarrassment in 1588 and 1589, and moralizes on the function of satire in reforming tyrannical behavior. Palpably, Midas' expedition against Lesbos (England) has ended in failure and humiliating counterattack by the enemy (Drake's raid).[2] "All his expeditions for wars are laid in water; for now when he should execute, he begins to consult; and suffers the enemies to bid us good morrow at our own doors" (IV, iv, 11-13). As a result, even his own countrymen are whispering behind his back, yet dare not speak aloud of their king's figurative ass's ears. All tyrants object to public discussions of their failures, as the king's barber learns to his discomfiture. Such petty suppression of popular criticism cannot, however, protect the king against Apollo—the god of poets. If Apollo is also Protestant truth defying Pan's Catholicism,[3] the religious argument is extremely indirect. Midas' chief discomfiture comes at the hands of true artists, who must proclaim a king's reputation whether for good or evil. In these terms the ass's ears are the artists' black trump of fame, exemplified by Lyly's own play. Let no monarch underestimate the power of satirical laughter. Midas is completely unable to hide the shame so widely proclaimed. No barber need spill the secret, for nature itself resounds to the echo of Midas' foolish tyranny and usurpation.

Midas at least has the sense to know that he will be shamed before his neighbor kings for his military failure (IV, i). Concern for international reputation is a saving grace. It prompts Midas to heed the advice of his poet-critics, as expressed by Apollo at Delphos: leave England and her virtuous ruler alone. As soon as Midas resolves "to shake off all envies abroad, and at home all tyranny" (ll. 115-116), his ears fall from his head. Poets will stop celebrating Philip's wrongs only when he ceases to perform them. The king of Spain will perhaps learn for all time the crucial importance of celebratory poetry and so erect a statue to Apollo as Midas does. The ending of the play, with a song "to poesy's king," graphically illustrates the extent to which Lyly espouses the doctrine of art's political purpose and effectiveness. Writers can achieve what statesmen cannot, teaching kings "to make me know myself" (V, iii, 62). The solution is peaceful rather than retributive, attuned to Elizabeth's own flexible foreign policy, not deploring Catholicism as such. England's navy has repulsed the enemy; England's writers can help to make Philip a useful neighbor. Able thus to wield such power by means of satirical example, art dare not turn its back on a crisis like the Armada.

The jubilation, excitement, and open contempt for the Spanish in Robert Wilson's *The Three Lords and Three Ladies of London* (printed 1590) are perhaps closer than Lyly's attitudes to those of the average theatergoer in 1589 and of the reforming Protestants in Parliament who openly defied what they viewed as Elizabeth's dilatoriness and appeasement. Wilson belonged to the acting company of the Earl of Leicester, who aspired until his death in 1588 to be viceroy of the Netherlands, and who may have been behind the House of Commons' attempt to dictate a hard line in foreign policy. Wilson's mood of impatience with social corruptions in his earlier jeremiad, *The Three Ladies of London* (early 1580's), has given way to a mood of exuberant defiance. The act of bracing against foreign invasion leads to astounding improvements in public and private morality. The villains of yore are still present but are on the defensive, banished "out of London, and almost out of the world" (C4^v), prospering only in conservative rural areas or in Catholic countries. London is ready to meet her test of singlehanded engagement with the Spanish.

Wilson's attitudes toward war are representative of the London public theater, and differ characteristically from those of Lyly. The tone is not one of urbane satirical exposure, but of hysterical appeal to terror. "From Spain they come with engine and intent To slay, subdue, to triumph and torment" (F^v). The cool-headed Policy calculatedly whets the emotions of derision and hate in his call to arms.

> I need not tell thee, they are poor and proud,
> Vaunters, vainglorious, tyrants, truce-breakers,
> Envious, ireful, and ambitious,
> For thou hast found their facings and their brags.
> Their backs their coffers, and their wealth, their rags.   (F4^v)

The English long for bright fame and honor, which "The world shall witness by this action" (F2). Though facing "a mighty host," the Englishmen contemptuously "reck so little such a foe, Whom all the world admires, save only we" (F2-F2^v). The battle proves them right, for the Spaniards skulk away in cowardly retreat. The English are courteous, the Spanish are not. As Policy says to the Spanish herald, "Speak man, fear not; though Spain use messengers ill, 'Tis English guise to entreat them courteously" (G3). These attitudes are commonplace enough in contemporary and later English history plays like 1 Henry VI and Henry V; but it is significant to find them explicitly evoked by the great Armada in the very days when the English history play began its vogue.

Even more remote from Lyly is Wilson's bourgeois pride in London and her economic rivalries with the rest of the world. Her tireless leaders, Pomp, Policy, and Pleasure, are "Citizens born and courtiers brought up" (C3), self-made men who have become the "Lords" of London and watchdogs of her civic greatness. As types of municipal authority, they engineer a victory over Spain that is London's achievement alone, seemingly owing nothing to royal or national support. London's rivalry with other English communities such as Lincoln is parallel to her rivalry with the Armada itself. Wilson condescends to the "russet-coats" of the English countryside, who are inveterate practitioners of Catholic dissimulation and so are unworthy to share the glory of defeating the Spanish. The Lincoln lords are sent home to shoulder the heavy burdens of remorse, care, and charity, without which they cannot hope to enjoy success. Wilson speaks for an especially virulent form of chauvinism, selfishly protectionist, given to crude prejudices, blaming even inner faults on a great vague conspiracy of the entire external world. Ideologically and artistically Wilson seems unworthy of comparison with Lyly. Yet Wilson's is the milieu out of which the English history play evolved.

As a dramatic genre, *Three Lords* is ritualistic and celebratory, close to civic street pageantry in its elaborately ornate spectacle. The three Lords are identified by symbolic costume, bestiary lore, shields, lances, and mottos, all contrasted point by point with the corrupted pageantry of the Spanish lords or the Lords of Lincoln. Balanced staging and exchanged taunts reveal the influence of the big scenes of confrontation in *Tamburlaine*. The schematized motif of three is based on the truism of spirit, world, and flesh, as in *Midas*. Yet Wilson's handling of this commonplace reveals a view of the didactic function of art far different from that of Lyly. Although the two dramatists agree up to a point that art has a public commitment, especially in times of crisis, Wilson pays little attention to the essentially literary qualities of drama. He views his writing as the outgrowth of traditional folk celebrations, such as the mumming, the morality play, the street pageant, or even the victory bonfire, and he refuses to rank any one kind of public suasion above the others. All forms of spectacle and ritual are equally valid in achieving the sole criterion of success, an awakened patriotism. As Policy insists, in urging propagandistic arousing of the citizenry,

> Lord Pomp, let nothing that's magnifical
> Or that may tend to London's graceful state
> Be unperformed; as shows and solemn feasts,
> Watches in armor, triumphs, cresset-lights,
> Bonfires, bells, and peals of ordnance.
> And, Pleasure, see that plays be publishèd,
> May-games and masques with mirth and minstrelsy,
> Pageants and school-feasts, bears and puppet-plays.   (F2ᵛ)

Wilson answers not only literary purists who scoff at bear-baiting and puppet shows, but Puritans who decry the frivolity of all public entertainments.[4] Celebrations of past events are needed to reward valor and inculcate the virtues of a mighty people. Emotions are to be kept at a pitch "With pageants, plays, and what delights may be" (H2).

There is no talk, as in Lyly, of a rejuvenated Spanish conscience. Peace in Wilson's terms is to be achieved only through English might. Consequently there must be no letdown in public hatred of the Spaniard. (Even after the Armada victory, the Parliament of 1589 pressed Elizabeth to declare open war on Spain—a reckless defiance not suited to her policy.) Drama exists to enforce such feelings of national pride, in the face of not only the present Spanish threat but other traditional continental foes—French, Italians, Dutch, and Scots. Attacks on non-Spanish foreigners seem gratuitous in this play, but the continued animosity is credible enough. The suspected Catholic "league" against Protestant England justified viewing the Armada as a victory not against the Spanish alone but against all foreigners. It was in this spirit that the English history play, just coming into being, could celebrate England's great victory of 1588 with remembrances of similar triumphs over the French or Scots.[5]

In another play written to commemorate the Armada, *The Cobbler's Prophecy*, Wilson similarly insists upon the utilitarian value of a jingoistic drama created solely for the great national event at hand. Wilson's figure of the Scholar offers sobering evidence of the effeminacy into which the arts can fall when they pursue decadent courtly games. The muses of epic and tragic verse languish; only Thalia, with her estridge pen (a bird greedy and devouring, feathered but earthbound), is busied with a frivolous pageant about Pleasure's departure from the earth in disgust (ll. 449-606). Because the Scholar has abrogated his political responsibility, the gods must raise someone contemptible and vile to warn of England's appalling situation. This lower-class savior is the Cobbler, like the Peddler of the earlier *The Peddler's Prophecy* (see Chapter 10) a man of no pretense to literary excellence who can still instruct his betters in the harsh realities of international conspiracy. Speaking for Wilson as a sort of comic Jonah, the Cobbler can tell more sophisticated writers what they know to be true but have ignored in their fawning dependency on court favor. The self-educated popular dramatist can thus serve as a gadfly to prompt tragedies and histories from those who speak with Melpomene and Clio. The Cobbler's crude manifesto has its effect, for the Scholar belatedly learns the wisdom of simple men and becomes a bulwark of England's defense. The Cobbler's viewpoint is prophetic: it was through the genre of war drama that bourgeois dramatists seized the initiative in shaping popular opinion.

Although confessedly talentless himself, fulfilling a mission in default of England's nominal leaders, the Cobbler bears a divine mandate. Only he can effectively expose the malevolent Courtier and similar types close to the throne. Most astonishingly, his wife actually stabs and kills the Courtier in the Duke's presence, ridding the country of a prime traitor. The potential effrontery of such aggressive behavior must be undercut by several means. The Cobbler's wife is mad, and her husband goes briefly to jail. The Cobbler's comic bumbling and garbled allegorical prophecies make clear that he is an unwitting instrument. Even so, he is God's appointed chastiser of his social betters. Though the wife is mad, her act is nonetheless a fulfillment of divine decree. The Cobbler's perfunctory imprisonment does not nullify his role as the brash opponent of an effete aristocracy. In fact, he is soon freed with his fellow prisoners to triumph over the external Spanish enemy who are "upon your coast. They burn, waste, spoil, kill" (ll. 1370-1371). Having delivered England from her internal dangers, the Cobbler and artisans like him now man the defenses so long in disrepair. They are easily forgiven their comparatively minor sins of stealing (ll. 1450-1485); they are good-hearted and loyal, London's best hope, and they shame the upper classes. Once again, the Armada is a London citizens' victory that excludes court and countryside.

The Cobbler's Prophecy thus reveals a more ominous facet of jingoism than *Three Lords*. Wilson concentrates on treason at home, and finds ample excuse in his patriotic fervor for wholesale abuses of the upper classes (excluding the monarch). The Cobbler's partners in glory are the honest Soldier and the Duke. The Soldier has long been denied due recognition, as in Barnabe Rich's *Alarm to England* (1578).[6] The well-intentioned Duke is not to blame; he has long deplored his aristocracy's lack of concern for national defense, and he offers no objection to the stabbing of the Courtier in his presence because he knows the Courtier to have been an active traitor. The Catholic-leaning Country Gentleman deserves no greater sympathy. Such traitors crowd Charon's boat leading

193

to hell along with popes, prelates, judges, the ghost of a Gray Friar, and legions of other decadent rich (ll. 606-696). The ordinary professional soldier and the London citizen join with the monarch in mutual defiance of stay-at-home courtly politicians. *The Cobbler's Prophecy* is sturdily pro-monarchist, but only because it pleads for a realignment of power emphasizing the mutual interests of throne and commons. Wilson's tirade against entrenched authority is characteristic of much popular war drama around 1590, and is part of a broader exploitation in the drama of bourgeois attitudes (see Chapter 15). The play may well have been performed at court, though not written exclusively for it.[7] If so, Robert Wilson had his chance to tell Elizabeth who was on her side in "old London town" and whom she ought to disregard among her official advisers.

Elizabeth's attitude toward jingoistic drama, even in this period of open foreign threat, was characteristically prudent. The amount of anti-Catholic vituperation had increased alarmingly, in pamphlet as well as in play, whetted not only by the Armada but by the assassination of the Prince of Orange, the siege of Antwerp, and the Babington conspiracy. Much of the pamphleteering emanated from Calvinist centers on the continent, beyond Elizabeth's control.[8] Even at home the reaction was violent enough. Performance of a rousing play by the Earl of Nottingham's servants at Belsavage Inn, on Ludgate Hill, produced open brawling among the spectators.[9] Foreign observers naturally interpreted Elizabeth's actions in the worst light. In 1592 Verstegan wrote that England's policy was to make Philip II "odious unto the people, and to that end certain players were suffered to scoff and jest at him upon their common stages."[10] Hieronimo Lippomano, the Venetian ambassador in Spain, wrote to his Doge and Senate in 1586 that Philip was incensed at "the account of the masquerades and comedies which the Queen of England orders to be acted at his expense." Purportedly Philip was accused of "spending all his time in the Escurial with the monks of S. Jerome, attending only to his buildings, and a hundred other insolences."[11] Certainly Leicester's campaign in the Netherlands and his insolent regard for politicians at home, so akin in spirit to *The Cobbler's Prophecy*, gave foreign observers reason to complain. Yet Elizabeth tempered Leicester's warmongering stance. Even in January of 1588, Antonio de Vega was able to report that "at 11 o'clock at night, after the Queen had heard a comedy, she flew into a passion with the Earl of Leicester, who was present, and told him that it behoved her at any cost to be friendly with the King of Spain. 'Because,' she said, 'I see that he has great preparations made on all sides.' " [12] Leicester's drama was no doubt the occasion of her tirade. However much her reaction may have been play-acting to impress Spanish listeners, Elizabeth felt the need as always to restrain violence. Even if some dramatic activity was no doubt carried on with her connivance, her attitude would appear to explain the rational and even conciliatory tone of *Midas.*

Her attitude may also explain the comparative rarity of extant direct treatments of contemporary warfare, such as in *Three Lords* or *The Cobbler's Prophecy.* War plays abound in the Armada years, of course, but seldom are they overtly concerned with Philip II or Alva. The analogous method of celebrating England's past military victories offered a safer milieu in which to urge generalized lessons of readiness and valor. Current policies were touchy subjects. As the 1590's advanced, the Cecil party at court increasingly favored peace with Spain, and frowned on outspoken opposition. Direct advocacy of war with Scotland might also offend a courtly faction. With Holinshed's new edition of his *Chronicles* appropriately at hand after 1587,[13] dramatists could instead ransack the nation's annals for the commemorative triumphs of Agincourt, Crécy, or Flodden Field. The occasion of these remembrances was topical, but the analogy need not be very direct. The emphasis was on bolstering and exploiting jingoistic attitudes, not on devising ingenious parallels to contemporary campaigns. Nonetheless, because this war drama viewed itself didactically, in the spirit of Wilson's pragmatic manifestoes, it naturally took sides on the broad issues of waging war. Did true patriotism demand extremism or some moderation? How serious was the Catholic threat, and how deeply did it permeate England's ruling class? Who were the traitors at home, and who the bulwark of England's defense? Were all foreigners equally depraved? Most dramatists were fundamentalist patriots; others, especially Shakespeare, saw dangers more complex than a massive Catholic "league." Both sides spoke through historical analogy, drawing their materials from the chronicles rather than from day to day events. The English history play was the vehicle inevitably created by this need for a relevant but broadly analogous appeal to war fever.

The pre-Armada *Famous Victories of Henry V*, probably the first extant English history play, reveals how easily the nation's annals could yield through indirect analogy the same brash values of *The Cobbler's Prophecy:* contempt for foreigners (here the French), and glorification of the English lower classes in union with the king. It also reveals, in contrast to Shakespeare's later *Henry IV* and *V*, the enormous range of emotional appeal encompassed by the abstract idea of patriotism; for despite their common debt to chronicle traditions of Hal's wild youth and edifying reform, the two dramatists are worlds apart in their appreciation of defiant lawlessness and lower-class aspirations.[14] However much he is attracted by Hal's waywardness as broadening and educative, Shakespeare overtly moralizes against implications of social inversion and regicide. He attributes to Falstaff most sentiments about abolishing jails, lord chief justices, and the like, that might seem ungracious coming from the prince, and protects Hal with a disclaiming soliloquy. The anonymous playwright looks upon Hal, for a time at least, as the hero of thieves and commoners.

Famous Victories does not transfer Hal's Vice-like qualities to a companion who can at last, however reluctantly, be repudiated.[15] Hal himself robs continually and has a widespread reputation as "one of these taking fellows" (l. 151). He observes a sort of leveling doctrine in the art of robbing, like Robin Hood. Although outraged to hear of a "base-minded rascal" who has waylaid a simple common carrier (ll. 34-35), Hal readily attacks his father's royal officers, or "receivers." As instruments of a hierarchy oppressing the poor, they merit only cruel laughter. Hal is a user of women, and never condescends to his riotous companions. When they propose to "wait upon your grace," he renounces title and ceremony: "Gogs wounds, 'wait'? we will go all together; we are all fellows. I tell you, sirs, and the king my father were dead, we would all be kings" (ll. 125-128). It is his idea, not Ned's or Sir John Oldcastle's, to replace the Lord Chief Justice with a minion. When Hal delivers the Justice a box on the ear (a scene not displayed in Shakespeare), the blow is in part the act of a folk hero daring the might of administrative authority, inviting the spectator to share this sense of bravado: "By Gogs blood, it did me good to see it. It made his teeth jar in his head!" (ll. 613-614). Of course Hal must atone for these escapades, but only after the author has played to its full length the disturbing theme of regicide and anarchism. The dramatic excitement of this inversion reaches its highest pitch when Hal orders "three noise of musicians" to trouble his father's slumbers and comes to his father "with a dagger in his hand" (ll. 745-746).

As in *The Cobbler's Prophecy,* this affectionate if non-hierarchical league of prince and commoner is the source of England's strength against the hated foreigner. Young in heart and cocky, Hal and his admiring soldiers despise the authoritarian and worldly-wise French who chide Hal for his misspent youth with the tedious condescension of respectability. Hal need spend no time in justifying war against another monarch. His claim is clear and unambiguous (ll. 1043-1050), as it isn't quite even in Shakespeare's *Henry V*.[16] The French are Catholic, "open enemies to God" (l. 1406), "in league" with Scotland by a system of pensions. No Scottish soldiers join the English forces, as in *Henry V.* The French are uniformly craven; no Mountjoy redeems their national character, no Duke of Burgundy extols the French countryside yearning for peace. Even Katharine is a Frenchwoman of the most calculating sort, withholding her affection for political advantage (ll. 1810-1813).[17] Peace with France is to be had only on terms of total submission. The heroes of this triumph are the archers and infantrymen who repel the French cavalry with stakes pitched into the ground (ll. 1538-1546). England's aristocratic leaders, although present in the battle, occupy little of the action. A predominant number of speeches is given to nameless soldiers and captains, or to the comic crew of London artisans like Robin Pewterer, John Cobbler (representing the gentle craft), the Thief, and Dericke, who anticipate the knavery of Pistol and Nym and yet are the bulwark of the English army.

The Troublesome Reign of King John (ca. 1587-1591) similarly features an alliance of king and zany, outspoken commoner (the Bastard) against the purported Catholic league of French, Spanish, Danish, Germans, Austrians, and corrupt English aristocracy. Again, Shakespeare later presented this subject from a more moderate viewpoint.[18] (Shakespeare's interest in the question of obedience to a tyrant properly belongs to Chapter 16, below; solely at issue here is the expression of patriotic sentiments toward foreign enemies and domestic traitors.) Whereas Shakespeare's *King John* avoids all suggestion of moral laxity in the monasteries, and motivates the king's actions against the church exclusively on the economic basis of the church's ability to pay for England's military operations,[19] the anonymous play glorifies John as "a warlike Christian" who "set himself against the man of Rome." Whether or not he actually consulted Bale's *King John*,[20] the author of *Troublesome Reign* was obviously heir to the fanatic Protestant spirit of Bale, Polydore Vergil, and Foxe. The anonymous author refuses to question John's royal claims, because to do so would lend respectability to the baronial uprising. The proceedings against the religious houses are prompted by revenge for treason and for slothful decadence. "Now will I take no more but all they have. I'll rouse the lazy lubbers from their cells, And in despight I'll send them to the pope" (I, 1024-1026). Anyone who appeals to Rome's jurisdiction will be judged a traitor to the state (I, 1110). The Bastard gleefully anticipates his chance "To dive into the monks' and abbots' bags, To make some sport among the smooth-skin nuns, And keep some revel with the fanzen friars" (I, 1130-1132). His "sport" is presented at length in a scene of gross comedy, featuring a "Fat Franciscan" and "Alice the Nun" hiding in the abbot's treasure chest (I, 1181-1279). The monk who murders John at Swinsted Abbey is in league with the abbot, and receives absolution. (Shakespeare reports the fact that John was poisoned by a monk, but refuses to exploit any inference of ecclesiastical rancor or conspiracy.) For such treason the abbot is executed and his abbey pulled down as an emblem of shame. "This is the fruit of poperie, when true kings Are slain and shouldered out by monks and friars" (II, 1093-1094). The analogy in this statement to Elizabeth is obvious. She too had been placed under excommunication and interdiction, and was troubled by the rival domestic claim of a popular kinsman who somehow had to be eliminated. *Troublesome Reign* dwells on the unspeakable crime of Catholic-engineered deposition for its lesson of present danger to the English throne.

Shakespeare's refusal to impute the basest of motives to all of John's enemies does not mean, of course, that he was "soft" on international conspiracy. His moderate anticlericalism and acceptance of royal supremacy over the church permit occasional slurs against the "Italian priest" and "this meddling priest" (III, i, 153, 163). Shakespeare saw the dangers of Machiavellians like the French dauphin, Lewis, who stands ready to exploit English weaknesses by allying himself with a rebellious faction and then destroying his supporters after having seized the English throne. Shakespeare warns of the obvious folly of such flirtations with outside assistance. Yet he refuses to oversimplify the issues of right and wrong, or to brand all Frenchmen as villains. Because of John's tyrannical behavior and his admittedly disputed claim to Arthur's heritage, King Philip of France is in a genuine dilemma. As a man of integrity, he defends Arthur out of honorable intentions and is willing to make a sensible peace. He is greatly perplexed at the conflict between his oath to John and his obedience to the church (III, i). Lord Melun too is an individual of dignity, caught by divided loyalties. On the English side, however mistaken their attempt, the nobles are motivated by moral considerations rather than Catholic treason and are deeply troubled by their rebellion. As Salisbury confesses, "O! it grieves my soul That I must draw this metal from my side To be a widow-maker!" (V, ii, 15-17). Rebellion is not a feasible solution for political ills, but the complexity of its impulses can be appreciated.

The anonymous author's view of courtly treason at home, as in *The Cobbler's Prophecy*, leads to an indiscriminate defaming of the aristocracy. England's rebellious lords are willingly part of "A holy knot of Catholic consent" (II, 545). At their clandestine meeting in Bury St. Edmunds (alluded to but not presented by Shakespeare), they are dressed as pilgrims paying reverence to a shrine. They fret about "the pope's most dreadful curse," and must listen to the Bastard's warnings that their acts lead to perdition through espousal of a benighted faith. "Aid Lewis, leave God, kill John, please hell, Make havoc of the welfare of your souls" (II, 416, 476-477). (Shakespeare's Bastard appeals to the lords in terms of patriotism only.) Even worse, when the lords are ordered by Pandulph to lay aside their arms, they remain truculent and still prefer Lewis as their king. The act exposes the hypocrisy of their religious fervor. They are no better than traitors, and are reclaimed to English loyalty only by the revelation that Lewis will treat them worse than John has done. Plainly the author appeals to fears, endemic in Elizabeth's reign and aggravated in the late 1580's, that powerful Catholic English nobles would hearken to papal directives ordering Elizabeth's overthrow on behalf of Philip of Spain.[21]

The Bastard Falconbridge, as choral spokesman for both plays, best summarizes the contrast between complex and fundamentalist expressions of patriotism. To Shakespeare, the crux lies in defining "commodity":

at its worst, the ruthlessness and cynicism of Pandulph, Lewis, or John himself; at its best, a kind of political morality justifying rightminded expediency because politics demands effective action.[22] *Troublesome Reign's* Bastard is a simple patriot, adoring his king, pressing on in battle against impossible odds, defending his father's name, chiding the Lady Blanche for accepting a French husband, and vowing to present Lewis with "an English horn" of cuckoldry (I, 799). In his encounter with the Catholic Limoges, he has the pleasure of calling a duke "Base herdgroom, coward, peasant, worse than a threshing slave" (I, 565). Yet the Bastard is both common man and true-born nobleman, having it both ways like the later dramatic figure of Robin Hood, Earl of Huntingdon. Partly of illegitimate royal blood, he incorporates the sentimental appeals of the professional military class and the ideal English throne. Soon he is raised from his lack of status to the highest peerage, displacing the effete barons as chief counselor of the realm. The success story of his "mounting mind," expunged in Shakespeare, is a tribute to his invincible anti-Catholicism. No less than Wilson's plays and *Famous Victories, Troublesome Reign* glorifies the aspirations of its London audiences in a folk hero of uncompromising resistance to Catholic treason.

Even in his earliest history plays, and before he had met the Earl of Southampton, Shakespeare avoided the fanatic impulses of his contemporaries. His *1 Henry VI* (perhaps as early as 1590) [23] is patriotic and anticlerical without dwelling on fears of omnipresent international conspiracy. Although it depicts some highly-placed officials as corrupt, they are not all Catholic-inspired, and are counterbalanced by noblemen of complete integrity such as Gloucester. The hero Talbot is a professional soldier betrayed by the politicians at home, but he is himself impeccably well born. His many aristocratic titles are ringingly recited by Sir William Lucy at the time of Talbot's death (IV, vii). His chief associates are patriotic lords such as the Earl of Salisbury and the Duke of Bedford.

Shakespeare subjects the French not to hysterical hatred but to satiric laughter. They are not tyrants or blood-stained torturers. Some indeed are noble enough to atone for the general French character, like the intrepid and gracious Countess of Auvergne. Yet most French are inept and incurably lecherous. Even when they have managed to take Orleans, they devote the night to lovemaking and are taken in their beds, jumping ludicrously on stage "over the walls in their shirts" (II, i, 38). The wit of the Dauphin's encounters with Joan is that of the sexual double entendre, carried deliberately to outrageous lengths, as in his account of his "night watch" with Joan: "Within her quarter and mine own precinct I was employed in passing to and fro" (II, i, 68-69). Even Joan's witchcraft is amusing rather than terrifying, and her purported pregnancy is a parody of the virgin birth (V, iv, 65-66). The French are easily discouraged in battle, skeptical of their leaders, inconstant as allies. Without the English political division at home, these French would be no threat at all. Talbot, the English general, never indulges in vituperation or remorseless extermination; he is diplomatically courteous with the Countess of Auvergne and fair in his terms to the city of Bordeaux. Shakespeare's jingoism is exaggerated enough, but stays within the bounds of wholesome rivalry.

The French are never associated with Catholic repression, despite fairly recent memories of St. Bartholomew's Massacre, 1572. Except for Joan's mariolatry (I, ii), in fact, they can scarcely be identified as Catholic at all. This play illustrates the distinction between Shakespeare's anticlericalism and the "conspiracy" hypothesis of so many of his contemporaries. He freely ridicules the Bishop of Winchester for his exploitation of houses of prostitution (a condition that ended only in Henry VIII's reign, and thus the well-known subject of a near-contemporary and only mildly partisan jibe at Rome), his ambition, conniving, and vanity, his payment to Rome for a cardinal's hat (V, i), and his cynical appeasement of the French (V, iv). Gloucester and Warwick are champions because they expose such abuses. When the bishop fulminates that "Rome shall remedy this," he is suitably told to "Roam thither, then" (III, i, 51). Yet the satire, even in its defiance of the papacy, is consistent with the most moderate Anglicanism. It attacks the bishop for moral crimes and political meddling, not for doctrine. Furthermore, Romish conspiracy is no more the cause of the War of the Roses than of French resistance. Winchester is less dangerous than Richard Plantagenet or Suffolk, whose opportunism shows no religious coloration.

Anticlericalism is staple in Shakespeare's plays: Pandulph in *King John*, the prelates in the opening scene of *Henry V*, Ophelia's remark to Laertes in *Hamlet* concerning "some ungracious pastors." [24] In its historical context, however, Shakespeare's anticlericalism is notably mild.

It is certainly less malicious, for instance, than that of Marlowe's *The Jew of Malta*, with its scandalous love affairs between friars and nuns, its chortling at the avarice of two brotherhoods corruptly bidding for Barabas' wealth, its violation of the sacred oath of secret confession, and its ambiguous complacency about the double-dealing of the Catholic prince Ferneze. Shakespeare's anticlericalism in no way contradicts his generous attitude toward the old religion, or his "essentially secular, temporal, non-theological" intimacy with the essentials of Christian doctrine.[25] Shakespeare came honestly by his acquaintance with the precise liturgical phraseology of Hamlet Senior's Ghost and of Ophelia's maimed burial service.[26] Although the word "priest" is often pejorative, Shakespeare offers exceptions. Whatever may be charged against Friar Laurence in *Romeo and Juliet* or Friar Francis in *Much Ado about Nothing* as to their bumbling and extra-legal devices, they are far from the conventional stereotype of the day. If individual priests may err, the Catholic religion itself is never subjected to the indignities that were so easy and so popular on the contemporary stage. Yet Shakespeare may be equally absolved of campaigning for a return to the medieval church. In *1 Henry VI* he takes aim at Catholic meddling as a source of faction, but weighs it in the balance against other forms of opportunism.

Shakespeare's obviously didactic plea for an end to the squabbling at home, and for unified support of England's generals in the field, places him in general agreement with the party of Leicester and Essex rather than the more cautionary party of Burghley.[27] Any attempts to find specific parallels, however, meet with little success. J. Dover Wilson's quest for source material in Essex's Normandy campaign of 1591-1592, including a siege of Rouen, fails to uncover any compelling verbal echoes.[28] Sir William Lucy's prediction that Talbot's spirit will rise again to fight the French (IV, vii, 92-93) or Joan's wry comment that the typical Frenchman will "turn and turn again" (III, iii, 85) need not refer to Essex or to Henry of Navarre's abjuring of Protestantism, for the lines are plausible in context. Even less tenable is the notion of a satirical likeness between Henry VI and Elizabeth.[29] Shakespeare avoids precise analogy in the interests of exploring the larger meaning of patriotism and national unity.

Shakespeare is frequently argued to have had an important hand in the writing of *Edward III* (ca. 1590-1593).[30] Whether it was he or some unknown person, the author was clearly of Shakespeare's persuasion about the morality of warfare. The play is overtly patriotic, hoping that "many princes more" in England may be famous again for victories like Crécy and Poitiers (V, i, 220-222). Edward's defeat of the French tyrant, in the name of England's just claim to that throne, is welcomed by thoughtful French citizens as well as by the English. Yet the play eschews facile anti-Catholicism and is deeply concerned with an analysis of ethical responsibility in such a potentially aggressive war. Edward must learn to govern himself, and to maintain a proper subservience of king's law to moral law,[31] both in his private and public life. It is his moral superiority over his rival kings that alone entitles him to God's protection. He must realize that he is delivering a worthy French nation from tyranny rather than massacring a despicable foe. The author is similarly attuned to the dilemma of the well-meaning French people, faced with a rule that has *de facto* sanction even if based upon usurpation. The French peasantry wisely do not rise in arms, even though they concede the rightness of England's quarrel (III, ii). Their compassionate concern for their countryside anticipates Burgundy's eloquent plea for France's orchards, vineyards, and children in *Henry V* (V, ii). Their political leaders—Robert of Artois, Lord Mountford, Villiers, even Charles of Normandy, the king's own son—must make a more difficult choice. Although their rebellion even under such extreme circumstances raises complex issues of passive obedience to an established tyrant, it demonstrates in any event that Frenchmen of all ranks desire to live under the same rule of law as their English brethren.

Ultimately, King John of France and perhaps the Dauphin Philip are the only villains. The French are a good people misgoverned. Edward acts accordingly, sparing even the citizens of Calais who have held out against his siege (V, i). A king is nearest God in being merciful to his enemies, foreign as well as domestic. Such magnanimity on the playwright's part is truly remarkable in the genre of war plays under discussion. This playwright holds as perhaps his central thesis that the land of France ought to be incorporated for its own good under English law, but that the people are to be treated as civilized and entitled to peace. Conversely, any English monarch presuming to overthrow a neighboring kingdom must justify his acts before the world by his impeccable personal and official conduct, by his legitimate claim through primogeniture, and by his demonstration of the usurper's total unfitness. The author views the theory of international interference as an argument that can cut both ways. If Shakespeare is in part responsible for *Edward III*, the consistency of his humane qualms stands in single opposition to the bloodletting zeal of Wilson and anonymous authors of this group of plays.

No contrast between Shakespeare and the journeymen-dramatists of his time can be as surprising or meaningful, however, as that between Shakespeare and Marlowe. *The Massacre at Paris* (1593) is an appallingly savage catalogue of atrocities, committed by the Catholic Guises against the Huguenots, with no attempt to explore historical complexities or to soften the rabid prejudices of the pamphlets on which the play is based.[32] The explicit didactic lesson for English audiences is the immediate danger of a comparable outrage at the English court. Both Henry III and IV directly warn Elizabeth to expect a plot (ll. 807-808, 1208). English Catholic priests are being trained at Rheims "To hatch forth treason 'gainst their natural queen" (l. 1044). Elizabeth had, of course, come to the aid of Henry IV against the Guises and Spain in 1590. Lord Willoughby d'Eresby and Sir John Norris were in command at Dieppe. The war was immensely popular in London as a Protestant crusade, even if the queen herself was characteristically reluctant. Marlowe's timely parallel of the Catholic menace in England and France is a relentless appeal to fear and hatred.

The parallel suggests that the enemy are everywhere, and that another reactionary coup in the 1590's would be as effortless as the one so impressively engineered by the Guise. Marlowe is fascinated by the techniques of subversion: the large secret army ready to come forward at the Guise's command, the underhanded financial support from Spain, the dispensations for murder from the pope, the infiltration of the king's high command and even the royal family, the exploitation of moral weaknesses in men of authority, the hiring of political assassins. Although the analogy to England in the 1590's is deliberately imprecise, and makes no specific charges of treason at the English court, Marlowe portrays a generic counter-revolution that relies on foreign loyalties in persons of great power. The calculated effect is to engender suspicion of one's neighbors and political leaders.

The explicit warning, that such a massacre can happen in England, reaches its climax of hysteria in the series of atrocities committed on stage. The old queen of Navarre accepts a pair of poisoned gloves too late to heed the warning of the Protestant Lord High Admiral. The admiral himself is shot down in the open streets, stabbed in bed, and mangled so that his head and hands may be sent "for a present to the pope" (l. 321). Five or six Protestants at prayer are cut down by the Guise and his followers crying "*Tuez, tuez, tuez!*" (l. 539). Famous intellectuals like Ramus must suffer for their ideas. Even the spectacular deaths of the Guise and the Cardinal of Lorraine intensify rather than purge the emotions of hatred and panic. Guise's dying curse is a fearsome prophecy of retaliatory disasters.

> Ah, Sixtus, be revenged upon the king!
> Philip and Parma, I am slain for you!
> Pope, excommunicate, Philip, depose
> The wicked branch of curst Valois his line!
> *Vive la messa!*   (ll. 1022-1026)

The cardinal accurately predicts that his brother Dumaine will avenge his death on Henry III, and Henry in turn dies with the admonition to "Fire Paris, where these treacherous rebels lurk" (l. 1254). Civil peace is still far off. Yet Marlowe implicitly condones the vindictiveness of the surviving Protestants. He provides no argument, as does Shakespeare, for mutual forbearance. Navarre is unequivocally a good man—a rarity in Marlowe's plays—but his goodness must manifest itself in canny preparedness and in remorseless vengeance toward Rome. For Marlowe, war is a ceaseless condition of contemporary life.

The bluntness of Marlowe's implied comment on foreign and domestic policy can be savored by its affinity to the firebrand speeches of Protestant extremists in Parliament, notably of Job Throckmorton, a Leicester admirer. Just prior to the Armada threat, Throckmorton was punished for the unrestrained vituperation of his attacks on not only Philip of Spain, but Henry III of France, James VI of Scotland, and traitorous officials in England. Elizabeth and Burghley, anxious to retain the alliance and good will of Henry III and James, were soon frantically busy assuring various ambassadors that the eruptions in Parliament did not represent the government's attitude. Marlowe is officially correct in lauding Henry of Navarre, but his caustic appraisal of Henry III and his insinuations of the need for a witch-hunt in England are closer to the program of those reformers urging Elizabeth to accept the sovereignty of the Netherlands in open defiance of the Catholic powers.[33]

War hysteria inevitably found expression in more romantic or journalistic treatments of military glory, which borrowed aspects of historical setting but without serious historical purpose.[34] Because they were blatantly capitalizing on current vogues of exaggerated prejudice, these potboilers naturally represent the extremes of anti-foreign and anti-Catholic sentiment. Freed from much pretense of historical accuracy, able to use jest-books and ballads as well as the chronicles for source materials, these plays exploit the box-office appeal of panoramic spectacle, sensational incident, and caricature of national attitudes. Peele's *Edward I* (ca. 1590-1591) makes a large step in this direction. It is an interesting blend of romance and history, politically shallow but not entirely lacking in meaningful lessons of statecraft.[35] Its more libelous distortions of history are probably derived to some extent from the ballad of "Queen Eleanor's Confession," seemingly anterior to the play.[36]

The debate between King Edward and his Spanish wife is a patriotic and exaggerated study in contrasts between English "familiar majesty" and foreign tyranny. The spectator is asked to imagine what would happen if the Spaniard or any Catholic power came to a position of authority over the English people. In defining his conception of the ideal relationship between king and people that distinguishes a Christian principality from its enslaved neighbors, Peele overtly appeals not only to Londoners' fear of Catholic takeover, but to their insistence on citizens' prerogatives and a consequent restraint of monarchical authority. Queen Elinor is, as in the ballad version, an arrogant believer in royal whim. She attempts to corrupt decent English fashion with her sartorial vanity and her innovation of riding in a coach. She chides Edward for his over-reliance on the good will of the commons, urging that they must learn to bear "a Spanish yoke" (l. 257). She turns up her nose at a rough homespun mantle for the christening of her child offered as the ceremonial gift of Wales. Her request that all Englishmen be required to shave and all women to surrender their right breasts is intended to be a test of absolute royal supremacy over the personal lives of subjects.

Edward's answers are as the average Londoner would wish them to be. Edward relies not on oppression but on obedience yielded through loving consent of his commons, "the strength And sureness of the richest commonwealth" (ll. 252-253). He knows that his toughminded subjects are unfailingly loyal as long as (and only as long as) the king accepts the guidance of English law and custom. He is a good king because he observes and indeed approves of something approaching an unwritten constitutional framework. A king must govern by reasonable demands and by personal example, foregoing his own beard first if he is to ask others to sacrifice theirs. Even the Welsh, Catholic and treacherous for the most part, deserve respect for their local customs (ll. 1604-1605). They must be cajoled and tricked into compliance, not bludgeoned into submission. A king must be responsive to the whimsy of each infinitely varying locale in his realm.

Most of all, the English monarchy must respect the privileges of the city of London. It is no coincidence that the haughty Elinor's chief antagonist is the mayoress, wife of "sweet John Bearmber, Mayor of London" (l. 2105). Charitable toward the poor, beloved of the citizens, she is the victim of royal and foreign tyranny for which the heavens will demand the humbling of Elinor. As in *Three Lords,* London is the bulwark of England's defense against the Spanish. Yet the issue is also one of conflicting jurisdictions between city and king. Edward is a London favorite because he pointedly avoids the royal intrusions into the city's domain that Elinor so blatantly practices.

Edward not only possesses the common touch, but shares the London viewpoint on every subject. He is offhand about ceremonial distinctions, fond of English folkways yet paradoxically wedded to the mores of the city in preference to those of England's outlying territories, brashly anti-Catholic and intolerant of foreigners even though able to reform them with his affable fairness. In his resourcefulness and wit he is a folk hero: confessing his Catholic wife while disguised as a French friar, taking his pregnant wife to Wales so that their son will be king of the Welsh, having "a merry flirt" with Lluellen, who is parading as Robin Hood. The king is splendidly liberal to soldiers maimed in the wars (like Leicester, who had operated a hospital for wounded soldiers in Amsterdam, 1587),[37] and a generous patron of the universities. This portrait obviously bears little personal resemblance to Elizabeth, even less to the historical Edward I. It is London's sentimentalized projection of a king created in her own image.

Robert Greene's *James IV* (ca. 1591) is perhaps the most notorious example in its time of the romantic exploitation of fictional history. Derived chiefly from ballad and Italian novella (Cinthio's *Hecatommithi,* first novel of the third decade), it dabbles journalistically in the timely Scottish question, employing historical setting largely as a way of capitalizing on a fashionably popular theatrical genre. Viewed from this perspective, Greene's motive seems one of time-serving in the spirit of his own earlier *Spanish Masquerado* (1589), an anti-Catholic tract proffered to celebrate the defeat of the Armada.[38] More positively considered, Greene is the apostle of entertainment in literature for whom didacticism is a guise necessitated by the norms of his generation. At any rate, Greene's attempt to have it both ways—to fulfill his audience's appetite for bloodletting and yet to moralize an acceptable lesson—involves him in a critical ambiguity. Are his observations on the Scottish situation, however subordinated to purposes of entertainment, relevant to current problems? Analysis suggests that they are, and that Greene's free-wheeling alterations of history and of Cinthio were directed by considerations of analogy.[39] He offers no rational solution to problems, however, and is content to mirror the befuddlement of the ordinary London citizen toward his northern neighbor.

Although Greene's historical situation is manifestly impossible, speaking of an imaginary English king Arius and his daughter Dorothea in the supposed era of Flodden Field (1513), its "facts" are all accurate enough if taken as a medley of typical English-Scottish encounters—the king's difficulties with his refractory nobility, the penchant for Catholic league against England. In the Induction, Bohan can protest with some reason that the play is "much like our court of Scotland this day" (ll. 110-111).[40] *James IV* begins with a marriage treaty and ends with the restoration of harmony, obviously touching upon the sentiment for union of the two countries. In the 1590's this objective was equated with the likelihood of James VI's inheritance of Elizabeth's throne. James was at least no Catholic, as his mother had been. Yet the Scots were old enemies, and James himself was not popular with many Englishmen. (In 1587, as we have seen, the Parliamentary firebrand Job Throckmorton openly accused both James and France's Henry III of duplicity and vacillation, thus endangering Elizabeth's fragile negotiations to prevent reprisals for the execution of Mary; and the intrepid Peter Wentworth probably reflected a common attitude when in 1594 he reluctantly gave up his long-standing disapproval of James, endorsing the Scottish succession only in view of Mary's execution and the assurance of James's unwavering Protestantism.) Consequently, Greene's play reflects the ambivalent mentality of his auditors in a mood inclined to vindictive slaughter followed by reconciliation, crystallizing anti-Scottish sentiment even while it idealizes peaceful union.

Not all of Greene's slanders against James IV apply directly to James VI, of course. They rely heavily on truisms of tyrannous behavior: the keeping of seditious favorites, the neglect of the queen for adulterous pursuits, the refusal to heed counsel, the suppression of criticism. Melodramatic titillation is coupled with patriotic indignation at the prospect of an English princess being maltreated by Scottish royalty. The story is in part fairy tale and mere escape, and to this extent the standard moralisms about counselors "That are, or should be, eyes of commonweal" (l. 985) are dissipated into empty pieties. Yet the political context inevitably evokes anti-Scottish bias. Catholic in sympathy and led by an unattractive monarch, the Scottish must be taught a fearsome lesson. They will not reform themselves; the English King Arius must be sole and overwhelming nemesis. Only after the fantastic slaughter of seven thousand Scottish lords (far exceeding the realities of Flodden Field) can the English victors incongruously pardon James IV for a mere peccadillo. "Youth hath misled—tut, but a little fault. 'Tis kingly to amend what is amiss" (ll. 2509-2510). In this massive contrast between gory massacre and magnanimity, Greene constructs his topical if irresponsible fantasy. Union is eminently desirable: "These nations if they join, What monarch, with his liege-men, in this world, Dare but encounter you in open field?" (ll. 2529-2531). The union must be, however, on England's terms. England will stand strong against the whole world and invites a chastened Scotland to join her. The political realities of the 1590's rendered such an aggressive solution unthinkable, but no one could gainsay the appeal of a dream of glory.

In a similar fashion, Peele's *The Battle of Alcazar* (ca. 1589) combines the far-off exotic appeals of African warfare with some relevant comment on the subjugation of the Netherlands and Portugal by Spain, a power struggle with which Elizabeth's government was concerned throughout the Armada years and afterwards. Portugal's interference in the dynastic affairs of Barbary in 1578 had ended in disaster for her and a consequent danger for England. Possessed before of an immense American and Asiatic empire, but near the point of overextension and bankruptcy, Portugal was toppled politically by the death of her king and the annihilation of most of her army at Alcazar. King Sebastian's childless demise left the way open for Spain's successful takeover in 1580.[41] The shift in balance of power gave Spain an ominous initiative. Elizabeth supported the expatriate Antonio, and sent Norris and Drake on an expedition in 1589 to restore him to the Portuguese throne.

Peele's assessment of Spanish motive in the Alcazar campaign, derived from an egregiously biased account in *The Explanation of the True and Lawful Right and Title of . . . Prince Anthonie* (1585),[42] is a topical defense of popular English attitudes in 1589. Warning his audience through the choric Presenter to " 'ware ambitious wiles and poisoned eyes" (l. 756), Peele interprets the Spanish failure to deliver promised aid for Sebastian as deliberate treachery. Spain has promised to join Sebastian, in this "Catholic case" installing Muly Mahamet on the throne of Barbary, but actually will attack Flanders instead while the Portuguese enfeeble themselves at Alcazar: "all too sure, Flanders, I fear, shall feel the force of Spain" (ll. 817-818). Thereafter, the Portuguese can be easily overwhelmed. All the adventurers in this African war are unsavory types—the scheming Muly, the traitorous English Catholic Stukeley and his crew, the papal authorities who have commissioned Stukeley "To violate the Queen of Ireland's right"—but Spain is easily the most villainous of all. Once she has subdued Flanders and Portugal, her intent is of course to invade England. Thus Peele sees the Alcazar episode not as remote history but as a keystone of King Philip's tenacious plotting against Elizabeth. Peele asserts, however, that Providence will never allow such evil to reap any reward other than deserved overthrow.

> Philip, if these forgeries be in thee,
> Assure thee, king, 'twill light on thee at last,
> And when proud Spain hopes soundly to prevail,
> The time may come that thou and thine shall fail.
>
> (ll. 823-826)

The defeat of the Armada, here predicted with the vantage of hindsight, is England's retort to the Catholic enemy abroad and a triumphant affirmation of England's unassailable strength.

> T'invade the island where her highness reigns,
> 'Twere all in vain, for heavens and destinies
> Attend and wait upon her majesty.
> Sacred, imperial, and holy is her seat,
> Shining with wisdom, love, and mightiness. (ll. 675-679)

England is hemmed in by the protecting sea, "Whose raging floods do swallow up her foes, And on the rocks their ships in pieces split" (ll. 687-688), especially those of Spain. In its blustering, its hatred of all English traitors, and its theory of conspiracy threatening England from all sides, *Alcazar* is a typical war play of its period. Shakespeare's moderation is truly exceptional. So too is his avoidance of bourgeois ambitions challenging the authority of the upper classes seen in so many war plays. The related phenomenon of such restiveness in non-war plays is our next subject.

T he jingoism in several plays already examined is accompanied by an importunate claim for the role of the commons in government and national defense. This heady train of thought was natural enough in a theater created for the London bourgeoisie and lower classes in times that, however economically precarious, gave London ascendancy over the rest of the nation. The doctrine was, however, potentially offensive, and so required a self-protective disclaimer as a censorship screen. Wilson groups the professional soldier and London artisan against the aristocracy and landed gentry, who are never of any use against the Spaniard and can in fact be obliterated with no national loss; but the actual stabbing of the courtier must be inspired by a divine frenzy. Even though *Famous Victories* makes an exaggerated case for Prince Hal as a hero of the people, Hal does ultimately forswear the company of Ned and Sir John Oldcastle. Peele's *Edward I* asserts London's ancient prerogatives in dealing with royalty, but in this instance the offending royal figure is Spanish. In the earlier *The Peddler's Prophecy* (Chapter 10), the Peddler believes that poor men "ought to rail upon authority," but he protests that he is discussing the affairs of far-off Ilion and Tyre, not meddling in "the state of this region."

Similarly, Marlowe's *Tamburlaine* plays (1587-1588), with their poet-ically intoxicating appeal to the restive spirit, necessarily take place in a distant oriental setting. Tamburlaine's rise to power cannot justify English rebelliousness, because the context of his political action is so manifestly remote. Besides, Marlowe probably had no intention, even indirectly, of serving as apologist for the political ambitions of the tradesman class, as Wilson had done. As an intellectual and free spirit, Marlowe dramatized not the homely virtues of the typical London artisan, but the soul of daring in a rarely gifted individual. Yet *Tamburlaine's* immediate success on the popular stage was undoubtedly the result of its ability to stir the aspirations of the lowly born. Tamburlaine is "a lord, for so my deeds shall prove, And yet a shepherd by my parentage" (Pt. I, ll. 230-231). Baseborn and an outlaw, he aims solely at political supremacy, at "The sweet fruition of an earthly crown" (l. 880). His enemies are all potentates, and all resist him not merely to retain their own power but in aristocratic fury at the effrontery of one of such lowly stock. "What means this devilish shepherd to aspire With such a giantly presumption?" Cosroe inquires (ll. 812-813). The repeated pattern of Tamburlaine's triumphs is to "let the majesty of heaven behold Their scourge and terror tread on emperors" (ll. 1475-1476). Tamburlaine is the champion over established authority.

Marlowe is perhaps deliberately noncommital, or ambiguous, as to whether this example of worldly success should be regarded as admir-able or villainous.[1] His key purpose is to assert the fascinating reality of Tamburlaine's career, not to formulate an easy moral response of emula-tion or revulsion. He does not even flatly deny the role of providence in human affairs or the possibility of divine punishment,[2] although he allows room (especially in Part I, a separate dramatic production) for heterodox speculation. Most important, he compels admiration for a man who rises above the common reach of mortal endeavor in defiance of normal Christian values.[3] Tamburlaine is, as Eugene Waith has shown, a "Herculean hero" whose very faults are integral to his kind of heroic nature. Tamburlaine makes good his boast to be "the amazement of the world." A person of physical beauty and of indomitable godlike will even in the act of slaying his own son, he has "something of the mag-nificence and the incomprehensibility of a deity."[4] His appeal to an audience is above all that of the active life in all its contradictions of human limits and divine aspiration. Even if Tamburlaine is to be detested for it, even if his career ends vainly in death, Tamburlaine's rise illustrates the extraordinary possibilities of self-assertion.

Tamburlaine's success is possible not only because of his irresistible will but because of the universal corruption at the top of nearly every society—Persian, Turkish, and finally (in Part II) Catholic European. Protestant civilization and especially England are not included in this survey of rotten monarchies, but neither are they specifically excluded. Marlowe's implicit generalizations about royal authority clinically reveal a pattern of inescapable decay. Royal lineages are, by the very nature of their long continuance, increasingly vulnerable to their own whimsy and enervation. Marlowe's emperors are effete and witless like Mycetes, traitors against their own brothers like Cosroe, or blustering and tyrannical like Bajazeth. They worship false gods and forswear sacred promises. Regrettable or not, Marlowe drily reports, the fact is that traditional medieval kingship is vulnerable to new and revolutionary concepts of power.

Another idea that Marlowe appears to insist on as objective fact is the human typicality of Tamburlaine's quest for greatness.

> Nature, that framed us of four elements,
> Warring within our breasts for regiment,
> Doth teach us all to have aspiring minds.
>
> (Pt. I, ll. 869-871)

No man that lives can avoid the "climbing after knowledge infinite," which "Wills us to wear ourselves and never rest Until we reach the ripest fruit of all," the earthly crown. Such restiveness may be no more than the perversity of having to aim at a goal because it exists. Zenocrate interprets her husband's ambition as sinful pride, and piously prays that he may consider the lesson of the vanity of human wishes (l. 2138). For Tamburlaine, however, ambition is self-fulfillment and Promethean discovery. Although death may mock his hopes, the spirit of climbing is still unquenchable. Marlowe, obsessed by the paradox of man's potentiality and his limitations, axiomatically assumes that human life cannot cease its struggle upward—in the political arena as well as the spiritual.

The combination of these ideas—that established power tends to be corrupt and that human nature quests upward—produces a situation that is always unstable, usually explosive. *Tamburlaine's* world is tumultuous, ever changing. If Tamburlaine himself is to be overthrown in his death, the process of revolution will in all events continue. Certainly no orderly hierarchical millenium is in sight.

Demonstrably, then, whether Marlowe thinks his audiences ought in their practical lives to emulate or eschew his protagonist's example, he does expect them to identify with Tamburlaine. This theory implies that Marlowe too feels some kinship with Tamburlaine, since Marlowe is a man. No elaborate biographical hypothesis is necessary, however, to explain the author's choice of subject or its awesome success in London.[5] Marlowe's own life as a shoemaker's son on the make is but one instance of the aspiration that he assumes and exploits in his spectators. The London citizen is given a glimpse of himself heretofore denied in morality drama, for that drama always took care to provide the moral safeguards of preaching against negative example. One identifies with Moros or Worldly Man only to condemn fallen nature. *Tamburlaine* may also evoke or at least allow defensive reactions of disapproval. At the same time it compels acknowledgment that it is only human to aspire, and that climbing can lead to unbelievable power. If it has happened before, it can happen again. In this respect Tamburlaine is close to Wilson's Cobbler. Both protagonists are thrust suddenly by their daring and by a sense of divine mission into the counsels of the rich and mighty, where they prove to be wielders of human destiny. This appeal to the individual free spirit embraces no specific political analogy. The vision is escapist and dreamlike, asking the spectator to imagine himself mounted on the back of a pagan king, or in some faraway land commanding imperiously, "Holla, ye pampered jades of Asia!" The mood of self-glorification is no less inebriating because it is part fantasy.

Lack of orthodox political example in *The Jew of Malta* (ca. 1589) leaves the impression, as in *Tamburlaine*, that all governments are run on considerations of strength. Even Barabas is an effective spokesman against established order;[6] though his colossal villainy ultimately deprives him of sympathy for his aspirations, he nonetheless reveals the ruthless expediency of his political superiors. In a location remote from England, Catholic hypocrisy wages an uneasy struggle with Eastern tyranny. Neither can claim moral superiority over the other, and in the end a *realpolitik* not unlike that of the historical Machiavelli yields for Ferneze a worldly vindication. How long he will continue in power is uncertain, for the only sure thing in Mediterranean politics is constant upheaval.

Although Ferneze is no more deserving of moral sympathy than Barabas, he is at least doing what princes do. However morally indefensible may seem the exorbitant tax placed on the Jews, and the refusal to let Barabas reconsider his defiance, the tax enables Ferneze to hold off the Turk and continue his administration. In his view, the needs of the state transcend those of an alien minority. Ferneze's pursuit of the murderer Barabas is incumbent upon him as keeper of the status quo, even though Ferneze has himself goaded the Jew into revenge. It does not follow that Marlowe is defending such a governor as the ideal prince, or that Ferneze is the true Machiavellian hero in a play that destroys another supposed Machiavellian (Barabas) only to assuage conventional morality. Undeniably, however, Marlowe is describing the techniques of *realpolitik* without describing alternative political techniques. The only other choice presented is Abigail's. Her longing for the eternal verities of salvation may cast reflections on the vanity of worldly strife, but conversely her utter ineffectuality in this world would seem to confirm the dictum that might makes right (even if it should not). Her dramatic function is analogous to that of Zenocrate; both underline the ephemeral quality of worldly aspiration but do not gainsay its immediate success.

The basic drive the spectator is asked to regard as a universal human attribute is "Desire of gold" (l. 1423). The quest may be fruitless, a self-imposed treadmill, as even Barabas acknowledges. It cannot provide moral justification for personal or governmental action; but in *The Jew's* restless world it is a fact. Ferneze owes his survival to superior expertise in "policy." However distasteful the method, it alone can claim political success. Marlowe does not urge citizens to play the same game, or even to like it. He does, however, report its existence and its universal application to the art of retaining political power.

When Marlowe at last brings his scene to England in *Edward II* (1593), probably under the vogue of the history play given such impetus by Shakespeare, he naturally adopts more conventional safeguards in moral viewpoint. The choral figure of Kent directs a change in sympathy from the barons to Edward. Sententious remarks, such as the queen's confession "I feared as much; murder cannot be hid" (l. 2614), spell out edifying conclusions. Most important, young Edward III is a prince without faults: loyal to England and his father, distrustful of young Mortimer and the French. In the final judgment scene the new monarch sentences Mortimer without hesitation and is firm in sending even his mother to trial. Marlowe has finally delineated in England a rule of compassionate wisdom that gives every promise of long success.[7]

Despite these harmonies, which show that Marlowe knew well enough how to fulfill the conventional expectations of his audience, *Edward II* remains something less than orthodox. Its defense of kingship never rests on divine right, but on the inner qualities of the young prince.[8] Marlowe's preoccupation is still not with political resolution but with conflict. As a dispassionate observer of men's struggle for power, he attends less to moral truisms than to the poignancy of suffering and the resistlessness of ambition.[9] Moreover, he employs a favorite iconoclastic device by setting up conventional moral appeals in a morally indefensible context. Anti-Catholic attitudes, for instance, should presumably elicit approbation from an Elizabethan audience. Young Edward III's animus toward Catholics and French is a sure sign of his political rightmindedness, as with Duke Humphrey of *1 Henry VI* or the Bastard of *Troublesome Reign*. The moral appeal is deliberately confused, however, when (in *The Jew of Malta*) Barabas practices his villainy against corrupt friars and delights the audience by his anti-Catholic slanders, or when Dr. Faustus employs evil magical powers to embarrass the pope and his cardinals. Similarly in *Edward II* it is confusing to find the king's worst tyrannies justified in the name of royal independence from the papacy. Because the Bishop of Coventry, speaking in behalf of Rome, joins the barons in demanding Gaveston's ouster, King Edward can proclaim:

> Why should a king be subject to a priest?
> Proud Rome, that hatchest such imperial grooms,
> For these thy superstitious taper lights,
> Wherewith thy antichristian churches blaze,
> I'll fire thy crazèd buildings, and enforce
> Thy papal towers to kiss the lowly ground!   (ll. 392-397)

The sympathies thus aroused are specious, for the barons' objections to Gaveston are plausible and wholly unrelated to the Romish issue. Deplorable behavior is oddly sanctioned by patriotic commonplaces.

Again, the labels of pro- and anti-French, for obvious reasons a ready-made guide to moral character in the plays of Marlowe's contemporaries, are used in *Edward II* to blacken both sides rather than one. Gaveston is "That sly, inveigling Frenchman" (l. 263), a manifest signal of opprobrium. Yet Gaveston's antagonist the queen is called a "French strumpet" (l. 441) long before her manner betrays any duplicity. Strumpet or not, she is "the sister of the King of France" (l. 483), a foreign consort like Peele's Queen Elinor, and one who naturally turns to France for aid. As for King Edward, he regards the invasion of his Normandy by the King of France as "a trifle" (l. 812). "Tush, sib, if this be all, Valois and I will soon be friends again" (ll. 1374-1375). Standards of Italianate statecraft fail also to distinguish the two sides in the wars. Gaveston's successors, the Spencers, are master hypocrites who "now and then stab, as occasion serves" (l. 763). On the other side, young Mortimer considers early in the play "How easily might some base slave be suborned To greet his lordship [Gaveston] with a poniard" (ll. 562-563). For these reasons one cannot postulate a straightforward, edifying pattern of transferred sympathies, as in *Richard II*, by which the barons are largely in the right until they reach the point of open defiance.

Until the advent of the rightminded Edward III, then, Marlowe gives us a world like that of *Tamburlaine* or *The Jew* in which power at the top is corrupt, and in which revolutionary aspirations press from all sides. Edward II's weakness for Gaveston is hardly surprising, for moral experimentation in high places is a fact of history: "The mightiest kings have had their minions" (l. 688). Nor is it surprising that Gaveston should exploit this relationship for personal gain, offending the barons with his lowborn presumption. Sycophants have always behaved so, just as barons always react by asserting their feudal autonomy under pretext of patriotic concern. Edward II's only solution for worldly failure is that of Abigail: "Father, this life contemplative is Heaven . . . O might I never open these eyes again! Never again lift up this drooping head!" (ll. 1887-1909). Only the belated arrival of young Edward III can impose orthodoxy at last on a cutthroat and morally ambiguous world. Monarchy can succeed under a good king; but where he is absent, divine right offers no defense against anarchy.

Peele's *David and Bethsabe* (ca. 1589-1592), written under the influence of Marlowe's "mighty line," offers a similarly ambiguous treatment of rebellion. Superficially orthodox in its depiction of David's suppression of the revolt of his son, and in its use of truisms about divine right, the play nevertheless offers comfort to the disaffected by its disparaging view of kingship.[10] Such iconoclasm is all the more daring in view of the already established political analogy linking David and Absalom with Elizabeth and Mary Queen of Scots. As early as 1572, David had been held up to Elizabeth as a mirror of excessive lenity, and in 1586 Sir Christopher Hatton ended a speech to the House of Commons on Mary's crimes with the moral tag, *"Ne pereat Israel, pereat Absolom."* [11] Peele does not pursue this analogy, but he is unsparing in his depiction of David's royal faults.

However much "Elected to the heart of Israel's God" (l. 108), David is also "the tyrant of the land, Bolstering his hateful head upon the throne That God unworthily hath blessed him with," a "Foul lecher, drunkard, plague to heaven and earth" (ll. 1332-1334, 1392). His adulterous love is exploited for titillating effect in a play that is fashionably Ovidian rather than biblical in tone.[12] He is a murderer and a lecher who neglects to punish lechery in others. He provokes Absalom to rebellion, although the rebellion itself cannot be condoned for that reason. The plausibility of Absalom's motive exceeds that of the biblical account. Absalom comes forward in the name of justice and moral decency, pledging to keep God's covenants pure and redeem His people from the path of error (ll. 1218-1229).

Accordingly, when he confronts David's concubines, Absalom attacks moral enervation at the very center of power—yet he does so as a rebel. Peele deliberately crosses stock moral responses in an ironic and ambiguous situation, as Marlowe was so fond of doing. When the concubines cry out for the aid of Heaven to avenge themselves and their anointed king (ll. 1178-1183), they enunciate a sacrosanct political truism in defense of a morally reprehensible situation. David's divine right is linked with the concubines' privileges, and indeed the victory over Absalom does restore the king to his wonted lusts. Neither side has a just cause. Moreover, their struggle for power is, as in Marlowe, a typical state of human affairs. David is like other monarchs: "The best, ye see, my lords, are swift to sin" (l. 1472). David's human frailty strikes at the divinity of monarchs. Whether or not Peele condones rebellion, he is at least sympathetic to its motives. The question of what to do about an inadequate monarch remains unanswered. Absalom's rebellion cannot succeed, yet David is unfit to govern. His wisest act is to step down and invest royal power in Solomon, who like Marlowe's Edward III can begin anew without the contamination of his predecessor's reign.

These sophisticated questionings of Marlowe and Peele, with their matter-of-fact attitude toward royal corruption and the revolutionary process, represent a different sort of aspiration from that of Wilson, the author of *Famous Victories,* or Peele himself in a drama like *Edward I.* Marlowe's implied daring made a terrific hit with London audiences, but Marlowe never expressed much liking for the ordinary ingredients of popular taste: patriotism, loyalty to the king tempered by a jealous guarding of bourgeois privileges, contempt for aristocracy and landed gentry, and praise for the homely virtues of the artisan class. A fellow University Wit who more closely studied London's folkways and catered to its dream of glory was Robert Greene.

Greene, who tried almost everything, attempted to imitate the stage success of the Marlovian rebellious hero, but demonstrated that he was able only to spoof the exotic vision, for which he was temperamentally and poetically unsuited. Greene's tragic or heroic dramas lapse unpredictably into fairy tale or parody. His attitude toward Marlowe is ambivalent, servile and resentful, seeking both to capitalize on a theatrical vogue and to satirize its bombast. In these circumstances, one must question whether Greene is earnestly combatting the political heterodoxies of his model simply because he omits a consistent theory of history glorifying the will of the individual.[13] Greene's railing at the "atheist Tamburlaine" and his facile moralizing cannot make him a serious political moralist. Greene tries to construct an admirably unconventional superman, and then, falling short of convincing stature, resorts to deliberate exaggeration. The prologue to his *Alphonsus, King of Arragon* (1587-1588), for example, appeals grandly to the need for martial verse and heroic purposefulness in art. Accordingly, the hero is at first a man of Tamburlaine-like ambition for whom nothing else will "satisfy thy conquering mind Besides the crown" (ll. 498-499). Alphonsus is derided by the king he deposes as a "base brat" presuming to aspire. Alphonsus' bombastic reply would seem to exploit the emotions Marlowe had so successfully aroused. " 'Base brat,' say'st thou? as good a man as thou. But say I came but of a base descent, My deeds shall make my glory for to shine" (ll. 538-540). The joker is that Alphonsus is a prince in disguise, winning back his own title and demonstrating not that a shepherd can be an emperor but that royal blood will tell. His defiance of an entrenched monarch who "braggest so of thy birth" cannot convey any political meaning. Alphonsus' saga follows the romantic course of mistaken identities, coincidental meetings, riddling oracles, and finally winning the hand in marriage of the Great Turk's daughter. The play's evident lack of success was probably the result of its inconsistent attitude toward subject and genre. *Selimus* (1591-1592), although more denunciatory of the Marlovian hero, again loses its way between unreconciled appeals to Senecan sensationalism and to pretentious morality. Only *Orlando Furioso* (1588-1592) manages to be thoroughly engaging as parody, but the achievement is lighthearted nonsense rather than a satire of heterodoxy. At best, Greene's heroic plays reveal a frivolous mixture of titillation and partial disapproval of Marlowe's *realpolitik* that was perhaps shared by many of Greene's fellow Londoners.[14]

Although Greene was not cut out to breathe Promethean defiance of established power, he was admirably suited to reflect more cheerful and domestic fantasies of lower-class success. The remarkable appeal of *Friar Bacon and Friar Bungay* (ca. 1589) is its blend of fairy tale or pastoral with a quasi-realistic English historical setting, creating an environment in which the impossible takes on plausibility: English milkmaids marrying into the aristocracy, humble scholars affirming the glories of England in defiance of foreigners, Catholicism, and the landed gentry. The social implications of the love plot are Greene's own invention, not to be found in the chapbook *Famous History of Friar Bacon*.

Imagined marriages between princes and commoners are as old as folk literature, and were especially familiar to the Renaissance in the enduring saga of patient Griselda.[15] Greene gives new relevance to the legend, however, by stressing the unique benefits of Margaret's rustic origins. Her country honesty espouses a higher morality than that of her social betters. Her virtues are not those of nobility in disguise; she has nothing to learn from "quainter dames than she, Whose faces are enriched with honor's taint, Whose beauties stand upon the stage of fame" (ll.

69-71). Prince Edward seeks her out not simply because she is lowborn and presumably an easy prey to his importunity, but because she is refreshingly different from his usual artificial fare. This paragon of lower-class virtue is, moreover, content with her lot, even though worthy of aristocratic privilege. She happily assumes that she will be a farmer's wife, and innocently chooses the disguised Earl of Lincoln with no knowledge of his wealth. Greene's comfortable disclaimers of ambition allow his spectators to enjoy their imaginings of social acceptability without branding such thoughts as presumptuous. Neither King Henry III nor any member of his court stops to question the propriety of Margaret's sudden elevation. A double wedding is entirely appropriate. Margaret will say her vows side by side with the future king and queen of England. The court has long known of her rare virtues and has admired them as emblems of England's proud destiny. The ideal of "gentilesse," long a favorite of aristocratic writers, is now the plaything of popular romance.

Greene disavows any affront to English ladies at the court by using only Spanish women as explicit foils to Margaret. His treatment of the much-maligned Elinor of Castile is ambivalent. She is beautiful, is attracted immediately to Prince Edward, and ultimately receives his ardor in return. Nevertheless an arranged state affiance must compete with romantic infatuation, duty with passion. The Earl of Lincoln's brief engagement to a Spanish lady of Elinor's retinue echoes even more clearly the theme of English country virtue versus statecraft and Spanish pride. The earl is never interested in a Spanish match. He "is forced To love the lady by the king's command" (ll. 1539-1540). Even the King of Castile must acknowledge Margaret's excellence and support the earl's desire for English beauty and constancy.

Conversely, Margaret's unwelcome wooers are anathema to popular taste, not only as believers in arranged marriage but as representatives of the landed gentry. Older men of considerable landed wealth and social prominence, Lambert and Serlsby are traditional obstacles to romantic love. They woo Margaret by bribery and extortion, just as they always oppress their social inferiors. Ignoring her pleas that she is, as a keeper's daughter, "too base in gree To match with men accompted of such worth" (ll. 1437-1438), they ply Margaret with promises of material comfort. Their bid for purchased affection parallels the Spanish lady's contract with the earl. Failing to win her by such blandishments, Lambert and Serlsby resort to sterner economic measures. Serlsby holds Margaret's father under his thumb. "I am the lands-lord, keeper, of thy holds; By copy all thy living lies in me. Laxfield did never see me raise my due" (ll. 1400-1402). The keeper must promote Serlsby's suit to Margaret or expect reprisals. Country justices will provide no relief, for Serlsby is the squire and has strict legality on his side. Greene's hostility in this episode meaningfully reinforces the liaison between common people and monarch at the expense of the landed gentry.

In the plots both of Margaret and of Friar Bacon, humble English fare is good enough for king or emperor. Courts have long admired Margaret's reputation for virtue and Bacon's for learning. King must seek out commoner, as Alexander sought Diogenes. Although Bacon occasionally uses his magic for questionable ends, and must ultimately renounce his art as blasphemous meddling, his sin is (unlike Faustus') reversible.[16] For the most part, his displays of supernatural ability invite admiration for a patriotic power acquired through learning. Though he can imprison Prince Edward's sword in its sheath, he never acts disloyally toward Edward and his father. One of Bacon's most cherished dreams is "To compass England with a wall of brass" (l. 204)—a pertinent emblem of insular strength in the Armada years. He is also a source of England's reputation. "England and Europe shall admire thy fame" (l. 214). The Emperor of Germany seizes on the opportunity to visit Oxford and pit his magician Jacques Vandermast against Bacon. The Friar's victory expresses both national pride and confidence in the unique power of learning. "Bacon, thou hast honored England with thy skill, And made fair Oxford famous by thine art" (ll. 1284-1285). Bacon is a worthy man to fete the emperors of the world with an overwhelming banquet and courteous service such as "all the German peers Could not afford" (ll. 1366-1367). In part, then, Greene is enamored of the temporal authority that wisdom can bring a poor scholar. Quite properly the king himself defers to learning, in his insistence "that wisdom must go before majesty" (ll. 943-944). As in Wilson's *The Cobbler's Prophecy*, the invincible league of king, commons, and intelligentsia stands firm on England's shores, "whose promontory cleeves Shows Albion is another little world" (ll. 451-452).

Margaret and Bacon are also alike in their attitudes toward Rome.

Margaret's renunciation of a nun's livery, for all her previous sincerity about life's vanities, is inevitably a triumph for anti-Catholic audiences: "All the show of holy nuns, farewell! Lacy for me, if he will be my lord" (ll. 1988-1989). Bacon vows to strengthen England so by his skill "That if ten Caesars lived and reigned in Rome, With all the legions Europe doth contain, They should not touch a grass of English ground" (ll. 233-235). Between them, Margaret and Bacon possess every virtue and success that a Londoner could imagine in himself. "Thus glories England over all the West." These patriotic truisms are even more exaggerated in a sequel written perhaps by Greene, the manuscript *John of Bordeaux* or *The Second Part of Friar Bacon* (ca. 1591-1592), with its alliance of scholar and honest professional soldier against the villainous Turks and Germans.

As in Greene's heroic plays or in *James IV*, however, the suggestion of mockery through caricature is never entirely absent from the *Friar Bacon* plays. Did Greene really warm to his task in creating Margaret, or did he cater to a pipe dream that he then passed off as faintly ludicrous and ineffably bourgeois? The patriotism, the insistence on love before marriage, and the perceptions of simple beauty all seem direct enough, and yet they are the work of a man given to the most debilitating irregularity of life. One senses not that Greene was consciously cynical of his popular themes and morality, but that he concocted an unstable vision of goodness he yearned for and then mistrusted because it eluded him. Hence the occasional tendency to lay on with heavy hand, as if laughing at the excesses of his own idealized fancy. If *George a Greene* (1587-1593) is his play, it best exemplifies in Greene the dual longing to glorify the figure of the virile, bluff, typical English yeoman and yet paradoxically to exaggerate that figure to the point where the author is detached, safe from commitment.

George a Greene is certainly larger than life. He "is framed Like to the picture of stout Hercules, And for his carriage passeth Robin Hood" (ll. 857-859). George reflects all the ideals and prejudices of his class. Intensely loyal to the king, he nevertheless defends local prerogatives against even royal authority and expresses only contempt for most of the aristocracy. Fiercely hating all foreigners, especially the Scots, aided by fellow commoners such as Old Musgrove and his son, George defends England's borders far better than do those of noble birth. The treatment of the Scots, as in *James IV*, is one of overwhelming slaughter followed by peaceful union. George is a common person, like Margaret of *Friar Bacon*, whose virtues have long been admired by the royalty of several nations. Like Wilson's Cobbler, his advice to kings is homely but wise and is acted on to universal benefit. He believes in romantic love rather than arranged contracts, has no use for wealth, and actually turns down knighthood. (Many Tudor yeomen did in fact resist advancement in rank, both from a sense of class pride and from wariness of the costs and responsibilities incumbent upon the gentry. Yeomen generally lived comfortably in a period of inflated farm prices. They were often remorseless enclosers of land, and were all in all a type not to sentimentalize about.) George's inamorata, Bettris, is equally contemptuous of rank; like Margaret, she spurns the suit of two wealthy landowners who use their economic power to enforce the collaboration of her hapless father. George is both contented with his social station and insistent that he is as good a gentleman as any in England, worthy to sup with the king. To the Earl of Kendall's claiming of rights as a gentleman, George retorts, "Why sir, so may I sir, although I give no arms" (l. 503). He entertains noble and royal visitors in style, as Bacon is fond of doing.

Such a figure might easily be satirical, were it not that the play offers no alternative viewpoint to George's confident self-appraisal. The aristocrats and gentry over whom George triumphs are afforded no sympathy. Almost all of them are ambitious to seize the throne, traitorously in league with Scotland, and indifferent to the sufferings of the poor. The Earl of Warwick provides the sole and questionable exception to a picture of total depravity at court; even he, for some unexplained but presumably valid reason, has previously earned a blow from George that made his bones ache (l. 853). Faced with such universal corruption, George is renowned as a man who is utterly fearless of rank. "An earl, my lord? Nay, he will strike a king, Be it not King Edward" (ll. 855-856). Because the upper classes are so inclined to treason, George earns sympathy for his leveling sentiments uttered at their expense. When he strikes the Earl of Kendall, for instance, he can protest that his enemies are rebels first and gentlemen second: "Why, what care I? A poor man that is true Is better than an earl, if he be false" (ll. 531-532). George is punishing the "obviously" guilty, but he nevertheless makes his own extra-legal determination of guilt and proceeds to action without further ado. Though he sends the rebellious lords on to King Edward for sentencing, he has already killed one of them in hand-to-hand combat. Similarly his namecalling and humiliation of Sir Nicholas Mannering are offered as comic triumphs over a "Proud dapper Jack" (l. 99) who bears a commission signed by the Earl of Kendall. George's jest of forcing Mannering to eat the seals of this commission resembles Fluellen's treatment of Pistol and the leek in *Henry V*, with the crucial difference that Fluellen teaches manners to a rogue whereas George takes the law in his own hands to discipline a gentleman. A Justice is present in this scene who could apply legal sanctions against the rebels, but the townsfolk prefer the leadership of one of their own: "Pray let George a Greene speak for us" (l. 118). It is George who decides that the commission is treasonous; he has discretionary powers to determine whether orders of the aristocracy ought to be obeyed. Even the Prince of Wales would receive the same treatment. George owes allegiance to absolutely no one except the king.

Combating treason in the upper classes is not the sole reason for George's zealous advocacy of lower-class privilege. He is fully as defiant toward the Earl of Kendall and the rest when they appear to him in disguise, for the moment not known to be rebels. They insist on the right of their rank to feed their horses where they please, in George's own wheatfield. George inveighs not only against violation of property rights, but against the very concept of degree. He acknowledges two ranks of society, kings and non-kings. "Now, gentlemen—I know not your degrees, But more you cannot be, unless you be kings" (ll. 496-497). Furthermore, the concept of private ownership and of local custom is so sacrosanct that even the king must accede: "Were good King Edward's horses in the corn, They shall amend the scath or kiss the pound" (ll. 520-521). The weight of this dictum is borne out in the disguised Edward's later visit to Bradford, where he and King James of Scotland must "vail staff" because of "a custom kept of old" (l. 1120). Edward is surprised to hear of the custom; evidently he did not grant the town a charter for such behavior. Of course the townsfolk insist that King Edward, had he appeared in his royal person, could have taken his unique privileges: "King or kaiser, none shall pass this way, Except King Edward; No, not the stoutest groom that haunts his court" (ll. 1126-1128).

The fact remains that Edward has agreed to vail staff, and he later warmly praises such evidence of spirit in his friends of the "gentle craft" (l. 1251). Like Prince Hal in *Famous Victories*, the king of *Edward I*, and the king of the later *Shoemakers' Holiday*, Edward enjoys hobnobbing with his plainest countrymen. He rules by their consent.

Many of *George a Greene's* ideas are staple in early ballad and folk tale. Especially so are the associations of George with Robin Hood and his band.[17] In this play Robin Hood is no longer the defender of English freedoms against the Norman conqueror. He is a timeless legendary figure whose supremacy is being challenged by a new breed of popular hero. Robin and George are much alike in their social unpretentiousness, their daring, and even in their women; Maid Marian is galled by the competition of Bettris' reputation for beauty. George is the new subject of folk art; Marian reports that "I hear no songs but all of George a Greene" (l. 930). George's victory over Robin is a friendly one but still an assertion of mastery. George refuses a place in Robin's band just as he refuses knighthood and attendance on the king. He is neither courtly hanger-on nor outlaw.

George a Greene is the law. His title of pinner—especially if translated "dog-catcher"—has an inglorious ring today, but George is the local official responsible for the safekeeping of livestock and property. In his hands are the keys to the pound, which can hold human malefactors as well as stray beasts, baron as well as peasant (l. 860). As a kind of frontier sheriff he is the natural leader of a popular movement. Since he has saved the king from rebellion he feels a duty to advise the king on the disposition of the offenders. Solely on his counsel the rebel lords are to be pardoned (ll. 898-899); the upper classes are to be retained on a probationary status, thanks to the magnanimity of the yeoman class. The Scottish king is to "make good Those towns which he hath burnt upon the borders; Give a small pension to the fatherless" (ll. 1326-1328). King Edward follows these recommendations, although he would not have been so merciful at any other's behest. In sum, George lets it be known that he is not a threat to king, nobles, or gentry, but their best conscience. He must be stern, but he will be merciful. As King Edward wonderingly says of him, "I think the man striveth to be glorious."

King Edgar, the Saxon ruler of *A Merry Knack to Know a Knave*

(1592), possibly by Peele and Will Kemp, entertains an equally high regard for his yeoman adviser, named simply Honesty. This generic name, and the Saxon setting, are necessary disclaimers of contemporary satire, but the lower-class viewpoint is transparent. Honesty is, like Wilson's Cobbler, or like the outspoken author of the lost satire *The Play of the Cards*,[18] the ingenuous speaker of truth however much he may offend the court. He is "a plain man of the country" (l. 79) and a comrade of Piers Plowman. King Edgar is quick to realize that "many times such simple men as he Bewray much matter in simplicity" (ll. 119-120). The admission is magnanimous, for Honesty has dared to cry out against sin in the king himself. Edgar appreciates the candor that he cannot hope to obtain even from his best counselors, and so chooses Honesty as his special agent to detect and scourge moral decay in every level of society. Honesty has the special knack, in other words, of knowing a knave. The king's weaknesses are venial and soon conquered by self-mastery; he and the yeoman join forces to save the English nation. Honesty is commissioned to "find deceivers out, And finding them, to give us notice straight, That we may punish them for their amiss" (ll. 135-137). As in other plays, the king leaves the ceremony of his court to share briefly the life of his yeoman class, witnessing social problems from their viewpoint and profiting uniquely from this experience. He learns that there are "monstrous vipers in my land, That with their very breaths infect the air" (ll. 885-886).

The targets of this alliance of king and commoner are the familiar villains in popular London social drama: royal favorites, priests, the landed gentry, and usurers or other financial middlemen. Old traditions of hospitality among the rural squirearchy have given way to sharp practices such as foreclosing of rents and exporting of commodities in short supply. These malpractices, inveighed against decades earlier in *Respublica*, *Enough Is as Good as a Feast*, and *Three Ladies of London*, were still sufficiently rampant in 1591 to require new governmental orders against grain export to Spain and the like.[19] The Priest is seen as typically self-serving and treasonous, seeking "To carry tin, lead, wool, and broad clothes beyond seas" (l. 1785). He is, moreover, a "Precisian" or Puritan, perhaps the first so lampooned on the popular stage.[20] This savage portrait is an important reminder that the bourgeois aspirations studied in this chapter are by no means equated with Puritan goals. Robert

Wilson, after all, defended the stage in response to Puritan objections. Honesty represents a democratic force that later coalesced with religious separatism, but his class hostility is political rather than doctrinal. His principal enemy, saved for last, is the courtier Perin, who, "Unknown to your majesty," has "levied great sums of money, And bribed upon your poor commons extremely" (ll. 1829-1830). Perin is the hardest to bring to justice because of his power at court; he is also the most seditious, because his influence has been required to countenance the perpetrations of the other villains. With his arrest, the field is cleared for Honesty's supremacy in the king's regard.

The scope of Honesty's authority to expose, prosecute, and then to execute sentence on his erstwhile social superiors is ominously broad. His retributions are unremittingly vengeful in fitting the punishment to the crime. The middleman is to stand at the market-cross, "And have thy cursèd tongue pinned to thy breast . . . Till owls and night ravens pick out thy cursèd eyes" (ll. 1845-1847). The landowner will be carried to a cornfield, "and there have your legs and hands cut off, because you loved corn so well, and there rest till the crows pick out thine eyes" (ll. 1851-1853). The priest will be shot to death in Finsbury Field, and the courtier must be towed in a cart up Holborn Hill to be hanged at Tyburn in a twopenny halter. Honesty, the survivor, is invited to court, clearly to replace those whom he has violently swept away. King Edgar permits this revolution, and gives Honesty the final speech in which the events of a fictitious past are related as a blunt warning to the auditors of the 1590's. To the predominating lower-class portion of that audience, however, the lesson is not so much warning as hope for social justice. The mood is one of defiance. The time is ripe not for reconciliation with the upper classes but for enforcement of principles. The king himself is never to blame in any of these popular plays; but such loyalty is not orthodoxy when it serves as the rationalization for a general antipathy toward aristocracy and gentry. The king himself is viewed as the prisoner of a system, eager for the new order and ready to implement it with his full power.

The unrest to which Marlowe, Wilson, Peele, Greene, and others appealed was an unceasing problem throughout the 1590's. In large part this unrest was a symptom of an Elizabethan sense of national destiny, which had awakened new expectations in social groups previously accustomed to servitude.[1] Even though optimistic in flavor, the clamor was visibly unsettling. All Europe pondered the outcome of England's crisis. The Venetian ambassador in Spain noted, in 1594, "Everyone is agreed that at this juncture England is shaken by religious feuds, by plagues, and other internal troubles."[2] The Earl of Essex, with his peculiar genius for faction, was incessantly berating his rivals the Cecils as appeasers of the Spanish, frustrating the queen's wishes in Ireland, and negotiating for James VI's succession, attracting Catholic and Puritan followers alike by his religious tolerance and his political rashness. Courtiers found it impossible to remain neutral in the conflict between Essex and his foes; personal influence became the focus of politics. Standards of public morality declined markedly. Inadequate official salaries were supplemented by gratuities, by selling of bureaucratic services, and by monopolies on staple commodities that grew into a major scandal and a burden for consumers. The competition for advancement at court, although spectacularly successful for a few, required a lavish investment and exacted a heavy toll from those who failed. New peerages and knighthoods were in short supply. Even though the scramble produced no great overall change in the structure of society, individual fluctuations were painfully evident.[3]

For all classes, the long-continuing war meant heavy taxes, forced loans, ship money, and impressment for war service. Dissident returning veterans were a potential source of agitation. The harassments of tax-collectors and of purveyors for the army and the court provoked cries of bribery and corruption. Economic hardship was exacerbated by an unusually rapid inflation, by major outbreaks of the plague, by several succeeding years of bad harvest, and by a new wave of enclosures of arable land. Many of the wealthy prospered while the plight of the poor worsened; the discrepancy was especially evident in London. The astonishing fact is that there was so relatively little class warfare. Probably the credit belongs to extensive charity and to the unceasing watchfulness of the authorities. Despite these measures, in 1596 the agrarian poor of Oxfordshire began a desperate food riot, with talk of massacring the gentry and marching on London. An earlier peasant uprising of 1586 was in "all things as like unto ill May day [1517] as could be devised." In 1591 William Hackett and his associates proclaimed their notorious manifesto from a pease cart in Cheapside: Hackett, anointed by the Holy Ghost, was to replace Elizabeth as monarch.[4]

Though this event itself was somewhat freakish, official reaction was serious. A royal order of 1595 forbade "assemblies and routs compounded of sundry sorts of base people: some known apprentices such as were of base manual occupations; some others wandering idle persons, of conditions rogues and vagabonds; and some colouring their wandering by the name of soldiers returning from the wars." [5] The mood was one of political alarm, in which the natural tendency was to regard all reform movements, however moderate, as a threat. The Puritan wing of the church, having made its well-organized bid for radical reform as proclaimed in the brilliantly vituperative Martin Marprelate tracts, was on the defensive and experiencing its severest repression in Elizabeth's reign. Conservative spokesmen embarked on a propagandistic campaign of equating nonconformism with communistic Anabaptism, although in fact most Puritans were at this time wholly unsympathetic to leveling doctrines.[6] Laws of 1593 limited recusants to five miles' travel from their homes. Advice on the succession, whether from the reforming viewpoint of Peter Wentworth or the militant Catholic viewpoint of Robert Parsons, was regarded as seditious. Indeed, extremists from both ends of the religious spectrum urged limits on obedience to a tyrannical prince, and Parsons' analogies of Elizabeth to Edward II, Richard II, and Henry VI were aimed at the legitimacy of her rule. The queen was troubled both by the reformers in Parliament who posed constitutional challenges to her prerogatives, and by the ominous plotting of Spain and the papacy (continuing since the Armada) against Scotland, Ireland, and England itself. The government, concerned above all with the maintenance of political stability, was understandably wary of popular insurrection. Apprehensions of revolutionary change were topical and real enough in the 1590's, and inevitably conditioned the reaction of playgoers and playwrights dealing with the subject of political overthrow or popular restiveness.

These circumstances give valuable critical perspective to Shakespeare's famous pronouncements on order and degree, as for instance in Ulysses' address to the Grecian generals (*Troilus and Cressida*, I, iii). Without having to postulate that Shakespeare literally shared the opinions of one of his dramatic characters, one can at least sense the weightiness of the occasion for his audience and hence the force of a blatantly orthodox sentiment.[7] Although Shakespeare is less doctrinaire than some of his fellow dramatists, he does reflect a hierarchical view that in effect answers the demands of the Puritan left wing or of any disaffected faction. He heard frequently, and absorbed, the teachings of official church homilies on obedience.[8] He had sufficient reason to mistrust mob violence: Puritan antipathy to the stage, disorders in London, and his own dependency on the patronage of the nobility. He was of course no mere apologist for the administration, and increasingly displayed an interest in questions lying beyond the merely political. No playwright of the decade is less restricted by contemporary attitudes or events than Shakespeare; that is a measure of his greatness. Yet though his genius transcends the orthodoxies of his age, it never gives encouragement to dreams of political inversion. For all the complexities of his view of inequalities in law and government, he never attacks the concept of inherited rank as such, and sees little likelihood that common men such as Honesty or the Cobbler can solve problems their superiors have mishandled.

When Archbishop Whitgift and Secretary Cecil, in referring to various instances of political agitation, spoke disparagingly of "some Jack Cade or Jack Straw," [9] they testified to the currency of these chronicle subjects for topical use. The dramatists who employed such historical examples—Lodge, Shakespeare, Munday, Drayton, Thomas Heywood, and others—could not avoid the relevancy of their choice. Nor did they wish to do so. The question already introduced on the popular stage—to what extent the lower classes should be permitted to express their aspirations for power—could not go unanswered. To Shakespeare and other traditionalists fell the task of answering in kind, in the forum of the London public theater. The answer had to come from such men of modest social backgrounds, speaking not as aristocrats but as equals of their auditors. Their remarkable and peculiarly English contribution, in the midst of extremist sentiment from all sides, was to express a more or less rational appeal to the conservative instincts of men from laboring, artisan, and mercantile backgrounds. Naturally their appeals varied in degree of conservatism. *Jack Straw* is almost hysterically anti-plebeian, whereas *Thomas of Woodstock* comes dangerously close to sanctioning rebellion. Within these limits, however, many dramatic treatments of political change echo the impulse of a sober artisan class to work toward moderation.

Ironically, these dramatists ran into continual difficulties with official censorship because of the delicacy of their topics and the comparative honesty of their treatments.[10] Bureaucratic minds are too often baffled by subterfuge. How could one legislate, for example, against the subversive impulse in a play about an essentially fictitious King Edgar, or a raw dream of class fulfillment hiding behind a romantic plot in *George a Greene?* Drama about Edward IV or especially Thomas More was much closer to home. Depictions of English civil rebellion were almost certain to be censored, sometimes without much sensitivity for the viewpoint of approval or condemnation. These difficulties of misunderstanding were inevitable in questions of such emotional impact, and help explain the tendency toward explicit didacticism in writers who were trying to make themselves heard.

Apart from the earlier *Gorboduc, Horestes,* and *Jocasta,* drama of civil rebellion did not really gain currency until the Armada years. It was, like war drama, occasioned by renewed anxieties over regal succession, Catholic plotting in the 1580's, dissension over the fate of Mary Stuart, and lower-class restiveness. *The Misfortunes of Arthur*, 1588, offers a clear instance of this topical motivation (see Chapter 11). Among the pioneers of the genre was Thomas Lodge, who based *The Wounds of Civil War* (ca. 1588) on Plutarch's and Appian's Roman histories of the rivalry between Marius and Sulla (or Sylla). As its pointed title suggests, the play hammers away at the horrors of rebellion, urges a cautious approach to reform that must not challenge the existing political structure, and pleads for toleration between factions. Certain details of Sylla's tyrannical behavior, his forcing captive kings to draw him in a chariot and his treading on the neck of the Consul Carbo, are not to be found in Lodge's Roman sources and appear instead to be echoes of *Tamburlaine*.[11] If so, *Wounds* is a specific rejoinder to Marlowe's seductive heterodoxy. It should not be read, however, as an allegory of conflict between living statesmen of the time. Even if the confrontation of young and old counselors may suggest Essex's challenge to Burghley, the situation is a common one and is fully explored in Lodge's sources. More important, Lodge's play is unsparing toward both Marius and Sylla, and would flatter neither Burghley (whom Lodge admired) nor Essex if so applied.[12]

Structurally, Lodge's play is noteworthy for its anticipation of dramas like *Richard II* and *Julius Caesar* in which the political orientation shifts midway and brings about a realignment of sympathies. Sylla is at first the militaristic threat to Rome's senatorial institutions and hence is the villain of disquiet. Once he is firmly in control, however, the onus of challenge to the status quo falls on Marius and his son. Choric figures resist any new intrusion, however much they may have deplored Sylla's ascendancy to power. In death, Sylla is a dignified and thoughtful man, aware of his sins but still the unquestioned leader who is able to assure a tranquil succession to the dictator's throne. Any earlier sympathies for senatorial rule rather than absolutism are obviated by the overriding concern for order.

Sylla's armed takeover in defiance of the senate and its chosen leader, Marius, is an act deplored by choric spokesmen such as Anthony. These wars will lead to the decline of a great city "Through civil discords and domestic broils" (1. 317). Rome's institutions of government should not have to "dread for any private man" (1. 105). Sylla is a tyrant and usurper. Yet however much Anthony may prefer senatorial rule to dictatorship, his chief concern is not the form of government chosen but the preservation of existing order. He is accordingly consistent, not wavering, when he accepts the inevitable fact of Sylla's triumph and attempts to soften the impact of Sylla's wrath on those who opposed the general's entry into Rome. Even though Sylla behaves like the conventional tyrant, murdering his opposition and governing through whim rather than counsel, the moderates must offer criticism and aim for some rapprochement instead of taking to arms. The personal risk in such a mediating effort is great, as both Granius and Anthony discover, but the extreme of rebellion will only destroy what little hope remains for slow improvement and well-intended free speech.

It is for such reasons that the Mariuses' counter-rebellion, although seemingly justified by Marius' senatorial authority, represents a further assault on responsible government. " 'Twere better Sylla learnt to mend in Rome, Than Marius come to tyrannize in Rome" (ll. 869-870). Most of the rebels are "the younger citizens," hotheads, turning their "ambitious stratagem" against not only Sylla but what remains of the senate. Religious fear, the gods themselves, the counsel of age, law, and conscience are on the side of the city's defenders. Octavius emerges as the new spokesman against "a bootless war," a man as yet of no imperial ambitions but an enemy of civil disorder. He admonishes the rebel Cinna, "How darest thou press near civil government?" (1. 1410). The very arguments urged earlier against Sylla now apply without contradiction to his enemies. The fabric of the state must be preserved at all costs. The career of Marius' son, like that of Brutus and Cassius in *Julius Caesar*, can end only in suicide and a lost cause that has aggravated rather than alleviated Rome's political troubles.

Ultimately, the Mariuses must be held accountable as much as Sylla for the annihilation of the middle ground. Anthony, who has "Sealed up the mouths of false seditious men," urging allegiance to the declining state, is purged in a fury of retaliation along with forty other senators. Pompey's cry for an end to revenge, to "establish peace in Rome, And pardon these repentant citizens" (ll. 1967-1968), goes unheeded. The alternative of living under a dictatorship has manifest evils and, at its extreme, few means of redress other than patience; but rebellion itself can only worsen a bad situation. Sylla's edifying if belated self-reform illustrates that time will heal what violence cannot. Lodge's *A Looking-Glass for London and England* (ca. 1587-1590), written with Greene's assistance, is similarly orthodox in its disapproval of lower-class restiveness; the commons are, in a conventional metaphor, the "feet" of the commonwealth, and when they rebel against their head "The city's state will fall and be forlorn" (l. 1363).[13]

A still darker view of lower-class irrationality is to be found in the anonymous *The Life and Death of Jack Straw* (ca. 1587-1591), based on the chronicle accounts of Wat Tyler. Its extreme fear of popular unrest reveals the comparative calm of Lodge's and Shakespeare's first history plays. Although the rebels in *Jack Straw* behave no more ludicrously than in *2 Henry VI*, their motiveless impulse for troublemaking implies a far greater malice and instability. *Jack Straw's* commoners rebel without any general provocation from their superiors and without a corrupt example at court for them to imitate. Unlike the Duke of York and other scheming noblemen in Shakespeare's *1 and 2 Henry VI* who deliberately incite the mob to violence, no aristocrat in *Jack Straw* hopes to gain power by Wat Tyler's insurrection. However deplorable the original incident involving the insolent tax-collector and the hapless Jack, the wrongdoing is an isolated abuse. Taxation is lawful and necessary (ll. 177-195). The king, Richard II, betrays none of the weaknesses abundantly attributed to him in Holinshed's and Grafton's chronicles. *Jack Straw* absolves Richard and the nobility of all blame and ascribes the rebellion to the simple communistic aspirations of the poor. The author's one-sided defense of the administration is plainly analogous in character, vindicating Elizabeth's policies of taxation in answer to the increasingly outspoken criticism of the late 1580's and early 1590's.[14]

The author, in attempting to stress his disapproval of peasant uprisings, deprives a historical movement of any meaningful causality. Rebellion is solely a lower-class reaction, triggered not by general social injustice but by hot tempers and by the desperate rabble's alacritous exploitation of a random occasion for its own preconceived ambitions. From the first, the rebels talk not of solving inequities in taxation but of abandoning all social distinctions. The comic viewpoint at once reduces such claims to intended absurdity. Parson Ball, who is to be found "in a pulpit but twice in the year," but "forty times in the ale house tasting strong beer" (ll. 71-72), appeals to the conventional Utopian vision of Paradise "when Adam delved and Eve span," as an argument against difference in social degree. He believes in perfect communal ownership (ll. 106-107), although he will himself of course be Archbishop of Canterbury and Chancellor. Ball's hyperbole cannot be taken as a sympathetic expression of genuine peasant grievances. All lower-class spokesmen are either wholly depraved, or, like Nobs, chorically aware of the rebels' sinful delusion.

Faced with such audacity, the king is encouraged by his unceasingly watchful nobility to uphold his just principles. As "God's vicegerent here on earth," his decrees "should be irrevocable" (ll. 439-442). Unlike the self-indulgent Richard of Shakespeare or *Thomas of Woodstock*, this king represents the best of divine right. He taxes only by "general consent of either house" to conduct wars in France "For wreak and just recovery of his right" (ll. 170-172). Unnamed in the dialogue, he is a generic "true-succeeding prince" who has won the esteem of the people and Parliament "with reason and regard" (ll. 178-179). He is the soul of the commonwealth to whom all parts contribute: "the noble and the slave, And all, do live but for a commonweal, Which commonweal, in other terms, is the king's" (ll. 209-211). His nobles contemptuously regard the rebels as "The multitude, a beast of many heads, Of misconceiving and misconstruing minds" (ll. 188-189). In dealing with the rebels he ignores danger to his person, is far more clement than his advisers would have been, and is consistent in his promises. Only with the greatest reluctance does he countenance the execution of two or three leaders like Straw, Ball, and Tyler. The king acts not from considerations of prudence or policy, as in Holinshed and Grafton, but from inborn clemency. These manifest departures from the sources are the clearest indication of the author's topical motive: glorifying Elizabeth's merciful handling of both her Catholic enemies and the restive peasantry.

In sum, *Jack Straw* is a strongly propagandistic defense of hierarchy, unusual in its conservative bias even among English history plays. In its favorable analogy of Richard II and Elizabeth it is perhaps an answer to Parsons' *Leicester's Commonwealth*, implicitly denying his charges of royal favoritism and corruption at court. To be sure, the play's viewpoint is not exclusively that of the administration: *Jack Straw* was written for the London public stage, and appeals to the Londoners' fear of Kentish insurrectionists who will pillage and burn at will in the city. It identifies the cause of mayor and court. The mayor objects as much to the "foul slaughter of your noblemen" (l. 650) as to the burning of shops, and he is knighted for his service to the king. Many Londoners are presumably too prosperous to succumb to Tyler's specious definitions of "wealth and liberty." Other plays at the public theaters, including Shakespeare's 2 Henry VI, similarly imply the conservatism of London citizens in resisting agrarian movements. Despite this resemblance, however, Jack Straw is useful to illustrate the exception rather than the rule in the drama of orthodox reply. By presenting a generic king and council entirely free of blame, Jack Straw avoids the real problems of injustice under monarchical government. More than any of Shakespeare's plays, Jack Straw echoes policies of the Tudor regime, and probably exemplifies the unconvincing sort of historical whitewash that would have prevailed if Tudor censors had had the coercive power over the arts of a modern totalitarian state. Their evident lack of that absolute power is reflected in Shakespeare's conscientious and independent approach, which argues against lower-class rebellion while candidly examining the painful reasons for its existence.

The Henry VI plays are closely contemporary with Jack Straw. The Cade rebellion is also Kentish and a threat to the city of London. Shakespeare's demonstration of the origins of revolt is, however, far more complex than that of Jack Straw. Trouble begins among the aristocracy long before the people are aroused. When the retainers of Gloucester and Winchester repeatedly violate the peace, the citizens desire only civil quiet and fear for the safety of their shops. The Mayor of 1 Henry VI is, like the king, an ineffectual spokesman for keeping the peace (I, iii). Caught between the dynastic squabbles of Lancaster and York, the citizens seek proper redress from the throne, and champion the cause of Duke Humphrey of Gloucester, who increasingly identifies himself with orderly procedures of appeal. His martyrdom in 2 Henry VI, at the hands of schemers wishing to exploit or arouse the populace for ulterior motives, is a prime cause of rebellion. Without his patient intercession, allowing popular grievances to be aired within the hierarchical framework, the citizens are at the mercy of despots like Suffolk and Margaret (I, iii) and must resort finally to illegal means. Humphrey's removal as "the shepherd of the flock" (II, ii, 73) does not excuse the uprisings, but it places blame on the country's leaders.

Without Humphrey the commons are "like an angry hive of bees That want their leader" (III, ii, 125-126), and their voice is importunate. Accurately surmising that Humphrey has been "murdered By Suffolk and the Cardinal Beaufort's means" (III, ii, 123-124), the commons extract a concession from the king that Suffolk be banished. Historically, the indictment of Suffolk was an action formally undertaken by the House of Commons;[15] Shakespeare interprets it as a near riot in order to illustrate the crucial turning point between orderly appeal for redress of grievances and mob rule. Although actual violence is averted, and the king protests that "had I not been cited so by them, Yet did I purpose as they do entreat" (ll. 281-282), the commons have tasted the advantage of forceful threat.

The transition to private vengeance is almost imperceptible, and for a time still restricts itself to justifiable causes, though not to justifiable means. Suffolk is murdered by Walter Whitmore and a "jaded groom" who has held the duke's stirrup (IV, i). Motives of social inversion are reinforced by patriotic defense of England and the king, for Suffolk is an insufferable aristocrat who has practiced adultery with the queen and contributed to the loss of Anjou, Maine, Normandy, and Picardy. Nevertheless, Shakespeare clearly places Suffolk's murderers in the wrong for assuming the authority to punish even a manifest treason with their own hands. "O barbarous and bloody spectacle!" (IV, i, 144) is the choric observation of a surviving gentleman. The juxtaposition of the murder and Cade's antics in the next scene (IV, ii) reinforces the point that "justice" administered by private citizens will soon lead to anarchy.

The Cade rebellion, with its grotesque excesses, is therefore the inevitable result of oppression and lack of leadership in the ruling class. Even more directly, it stems from a Yorkist plot to foment peasant unrest in order to overthrow the existing government. York, seizing the opportunity of the Irish uprising to levy his own army, boasts in soliloquy that he has "seduced a headstrong Kentishman, John Cade of Ashford, To make commotion . . . This devil here shall be my substitute" (III, i, 356-371). In direct contrast to *Jack Straw's* fortuitous incident, Shakespeare's rebellion is blamed primarily on the ambitious aristocracy. Cade is undoubtedly a troublemaker, but he presumably would never have organized a revolt without York's rabble-mongering. Once begun, the insurrection resembles in detail that in *Jack Straw*. Shakespeare's use of the chronicles indicates his unsparing denunciation. He conflates the accounts of the Peasants' Revolt of 1381 and Cade's rebellion of 1450 to include as much violence as possible. His ridicule of Utopian communism, and his ascription to Cade of stupidity and clumsiness, are invented. He omits a list of the rebels' demands, presumably because the list contained some rational and sympathetic points. He prejudicially reports Cade's death according to Hall's version rather than Holinshed's. The clowning is Saturnalian in inspiration, viewing Cade as Lord of Misrule.[16] The agrarian commons (as differentiated from the still-loyal Londoners) are no longer capable of distinguishing good aristocrats from bad, and turn their particular wrath on Lord Say, who is Duke Humphrey's successor in the play as a man of flawless integrity. Yet the rank and file rebel only when goaded by actual oppression and incited by the nobility, and are easily pacified by Clifford's appeal to their good-humored patriotism and love of the king. Cade's rebellion is symptomatic of social disorder but is only a peripheral factor in the Lancastrian wars. It is after Cade's death that the real conflict begins.

Subsequently, the people in Shakespeare's first tetralogy are unlucky pawns in a struggle not of their own devising. Untitled persons scarcely appear in *3 Henry VI*, except as nameless fathers who have slain their own sons or sons who have slain their fathers. The keepers who arrest the fugitive King Henry have long since ceased to question the interchanges of power. They are "true subjects to the king, King Edward," but would be so again to Henry "If he were seated as King Edward is" (III, i, 94-96). Similarly in *Richard III* they are sensitive to the evils of a "giddy world," see all too plainly the dangers threatening young Edward V in the persons of his uncle Gloucester and the queen's kindred (II, iii). Their appraisals of their betters are, as in *2 Henry VI,* accurate. In the language of proverbial wisdom—"When clouds appear, wise men put on their cloaks"—they resign themselves to passive obedience. "But leave it all to god." Speech is dangerous, as the Scrivener observes of a proclamation justifying Hastings' death that was inscribed before the deed was purportedly contemplated. "Who's so gross That cannot see this palpable device? Yet who's so bold but says he sees it not?" (III, vi, 10-12). In these circumstances, the London citizens' acquiescence in Richard's skulduggery is not sheepish gullibility but the only course of survival. Richard supposes the commons to be childishly pliable and arranges elaborate deceptions for their benefit, but he misjudges the pious motive in their passivity. The citizens who are so unaffected by Buckingham's rhetoric in the Guildhall (III, vii) cannot be presumed to take seriously Richard's maidenly reluctance at Baynard's Castle. Even the mayor, in a difficult position as intermediary, says as little as possible and only what is demanded by the situation. The citizens themselves say only "Amen." Shakespeare displays no great fear of popular unrest, not because he countenances it but because he assumes a virtuous inner strength in the great mass of the English people (especially Londoners) enabling them to persevere.

As individuals, Shakespeare's citizens are capable of humanity, a sense of humor, and endless patience. Shakespeare's view is not one of antagonism or personal revulsion toward the common members of his audience. After all, Shakespeare himself had benefited from the increased social fluidity of the age.[17] To appreciate his constant and loving attention to ordinary people in his *dramatis personae,* one need only compare Shakespeare with Spenser or with dramatists of the private theater (see Chapter 17). Yet without responsible guidance, the Shakespearean citizen occasionally succumbs to mob psychology and behaves irresponsibly. Though Shakespeare is not snobbish, he is no democrat either, for "democracy" however defined must imply at least an acceptance of aggregate lower-class political action. Nor is he sympathetic with the moderate and gradual progressivism of those bourgeois spokesmen whose sentimental fondness for the monarch scarcely concealed their antipathy to feudalism and their espousal of constitutional limits on absolute power.[18] The topical force of Shakespeare's political portraiture is non-progressive. No matter how much in his later history plays he analyzes the defects of hierarchy, Shakespeare's constant motive is to preserve its true function as the only viable defense against social disintegration.

The comparative absence of bourgeois elements in Shakespeare's first tetralogy can perhaps best be seen in contrast with Thomas Heywood's dramatic treatment of the Lancastrian wars. Heywood was certainly honest in his orthodox belief that plays should strive "to teach the subjects obedience to their king, to show the people the untimely ends of such as have moved tumults, commotions, and insurrections, to present them with the flourishing estate of such as live in obedience."[19] The plays *1 and 2 Edward IV* (1594-1599), ascribed to him on convincing internal evidence,[20] amply fulfills this didactic purpose. Yet they magnify the role of the citizen in English history as Shakespeare never does. They focus chiefly on the sentimental trials of ordinary people, arguing that such lives warrant a dignified and even tragic expression. The virtuous Matthew Shore, husband of the king's mistress, displays a saintly forbearance and undeviating sense of moral principle peculiar to his class and implicitly critical of Edward's *droit du seigneur*. Shore actually refuses knighthood, in the bourgeois spirit of *George a Greene*.[21] Hobs the Tanner of Tamworth is a patriotic commoner who knows his place, accepts de facto rule in the veering political fortunes of the wars, and welcomes royal visitors to his humble abode with a proud faith in his "content sufficiency." The citizens of London, defending their city against a Kentish insurrection similar to that of "Tyler, Cade, and Straw" (A4^v), are heroes worthy to be compared with England's finest champions. They are well-disciplined soldiers, and like Robert Wilson's Londoners prevail against their country's foes "without the help either of king, Or any but of God and our own selves" (D3). Their deed ranks with Agincourt or Crécy; although they are mere prentices, "The chronicles of England can report What memorable actions we have done" (C). Even though Heywood eschews Wilson's facile derogation of the aristocracy, he still proclaims a great heritage and a momentous destiny for his artisan heroes.

Shakespeare's contrasting emphasis on true monarchy as the source of political salvation is the basis of his growing criticism of the imperfections in the system. If true monarchy is to be found, one must eschew the facile whitewash of *Jack Straw* as well as the bourgeois and superficial loyalties of Heywood and Greene. Increasingly Shakespeare reveals a fascination with the limits of divine right, and explores unattractive but necessary aspects of compromise in the art of kingship even at its best. *Richard III* offers a seeming contradiction to the lessons of the *Henry VI* plays that de facto rulers of whatever shortcomings are to be endured in passive obedience. The justifying of this particular overthrow was for obvious reasons universally allowed under the Tudor myth,[22] and Shakespeare's arguments are conventional. Richard is the scourge of God punishing a nation for its rebelliousness, and his destruction is a sign of God's appeasement. The people themselves do not rise against Richard, and even Henry Tudor's role is tactfully discreet. The event is God's alone, and cannot sanction a challenge of established rule in the 1590's. Nevertheless, a king in power has displayed qualities of despotism that, however rare perhaps in occurrence, render him unfit for rule.

The analogous dilemma in *King John* accordingly offers a searching challenge of divine right. Compared with the blatant hero-worshiping of *Troublesome Reign* (see Chapter 14), Shakespeare's analysis deliberately puts the king in as unbecoming a light as possible. Shakespeare follows the adverse historical tradition of Polydore Vergil, instead of the far more prevalent and Protestant bias of Bale and Foxe that had become equated in the popular mind with official Tudor polemicism. John's claim to the throne is dubious; he is, like Richard III, a usurper. His abuse of Arthur, whose age is reduced to increase the pathos of his suffering, gives plausible impetus to the barons' defiance.[23] These defects of monarchy are all the more disturbing because of their potential relevance to events of Elizabeth's reign. Catholics viewed Elizabeth as a usurper, and challenged her right to interfere in France. Catholic writers frequently spoke of the parallel between Arthur and Mary Stuart, both of whom were kinsmen and political prisoners of the monarchs who were reluctant to execute them. John's hesitation and remorse, not reported in the chronicles, and his attempt to carry out the deed through the suborning of Hubert, suggest Elizabeth's unhappy dealings with Secretary Davison.[24] The parallel, if intended at all, could not be stated directly, for it would imply not only Elizabeth's admission of guilt in her handling of Mary but her vulnerability to overthrow as a result. Nevertheless, Shakespeare's emphasis in this topic of common analogy exposes monarchy to an extreme test of loyalty, and asks plausibly whether tyrannical behavior and misrule should not cancel the people's obligation to obey.

Even though the problems are stated in such a way as to suggest sympathy for Catholic discontent, Shakespeare's answer is unimpeachably and genuinely loyal. In fact, the very cogency of the opposition lends ultimate strength to his rejoinder; if John's aristocrats cannot be excused for rebellion, surely Elizabeth's detractors have no case. Even Arthur's legitimate claim to the throne cannot sanction a revolt against de facto rule that will merely play into the hands of opportunists. Faulconbridge, as choric fulfillment of the audience's viewpoint, must experience all the appeals of disaffection in order to perceive their ultimate fallacy. He must show revulsion at the death of Arthur and despair at the political world of "commodity" so that he may speak convincingly not as a mouthpiece for divine right (as in *Troublesome Reign*) but as a humane and sensitive man. He must even acknowledge the impulse toward base commodity in himself in order to rise above it. More than choric spokesman, he is a mirror for the audience, teaching them to resist cynicism and self-aggrandizement. His avowal of loyalty is thus the salvation of England's political system.[25] Faulconbridge arrives ultimately at a definition of commodity in its proper context: a code of behavior applicable to politics that may involve some compromise with absolute Christian values, but that justifies itself in the name of public welfare. Political rule demands effective action. The overriding need for stability means that kings cannot be judged as other mortals are, since they must place nation and administration above friendship, blood, and the abstractions of merciful justice for each individual. Such a view does not simply reduce politics to a Machiavellian game. John remains, in Shakespeare's evaluation, one of England's most deplorable kings because his self-interested commodity is often mere ruthlessness. The solution lies, however, not in rebellion but in subtle understanding of the limits of political morality.

Shakespeare's great second historical tetralogy (ca. 1595-1599) continues to examine the paradox of effective political action and its seemingly necessary compromises. With whom are we to sympathize: the poetic, humanly attractive, and rejected figures of Richard II, Falstaff, and Hotspur, or the successful but frequently callous Henry IV and his son? [26] Disenchanted liberals such as Shaw have long decried Prince Hal's jingoistic imperialism, his specious rationalizations for warmongering, his humbug religiosity, and most of all his coldblooded denial of the companions of his youth. Yeats has eloquently contrasted the "vessel of clay," Bolingbroke, with the "vessel of porcelain," Richard II.[27] If Shakespeare can offer nothing better than Hal as his epitome of leadership, then his view of politics is a dismal one indeed—grudgingly orthodox, to be sure, but undercut by an ironical sympathy for those who dare to satirize the moral bankruptcy of public life. Historical critics like E. M. W. Tillyard and Lily Campbell, on the other hand, explain away Hal's unattractive qualities in the name of Elizabethan world order and the education of a Christian prince. Falstaff is a Vice, braggart soldier, and parasite, typifying (however engagingly) the vanities of misrule that must be overcome in a great statesman. Hal's rejection of Falstaff is not priggishness but inevitable triumph over sin, signifying an end to England's morality-like soul struggle.

The question of Shakespeare's ironic or approving attitude toward the invincible Lancastrian kings is central to his topical framework, as well as to his timeless fascination with men's struggles for power. Richard II and his immediate successors were inherently dangerous subjects because of their potential for infamous analogy. Shakespeare's choice of historical material constantly used by propagandists did not of course require him to be propagandistic also,[28] but it did impose on him the need for constant awareness of his topical milieu. If he appeared to glorify the Henries, as Essex's followers in 1601 evidently thought he had, then he might be suspected of apologizing for successful revolution. Or he might be viewed as the apostle of Machiavellian *virtù*, extolling in Bolingbroke the wary pragmatist who fully justifies the expedient approach because he succeeds where Richard has failed. Shakespeare could not be neutral in such an environment.

Shakespeare views the ethics of rebellion in much the same light as does Lodge in *The Wounds of Civil War:* challenge of established government is always to be deplored. Until Bolingbroke succeeds, he is a rebel; once he is in power, England's citizens have no responsible alternative other than to submit. Both York and Bolingbroke's own father, Gaunt, speaking in vain like Lodge's Anthony for a middle course, simultaneously rebuke Richard's oppressions and Bolingbroke's challenge. Even though Richard provokes his cousin and undercuts the premises of his own hierarchical authority by denying Bolingbroke's titles, open defiance is still the worse of two evils. As Gaunt and York foresee, Bolingbroke's first disobedience sets in motion a train of events from which neither he nor Richard can escape. Bolingbroke insists he is merely recovering what is his own, and characteristically does not look beyond the immediacy of this issue. He in fact never actually decides to be king, never allows himself to know where he is going. By imperceptible stages, his gaining of seemingly just concessions leads to the deposition and murder of Richard.[29] Rebellion must by its very nature go too far, since it lays irresistible temptations before the successful insurrectionist. When the means are at hand, why not depose a king who has proven incapable? And what is to be done, short of murder, to a living monarch in prison whose legitimate claims surpass those of the usurper? The compelling logic of Bolingbroke's silent answers portrays him as a successful man of action rather than a theorist, but scarcely ennobles his spirit. However much he may satisfy the requirements of good kingship in his maintenance of civil order,[30] Bolingbroke is knowingly guilty of a wrong for which his country must atone. If Richard's incompetence cannot ultimately divest him of true royalty, there must be some unseen quality about hereditary kingship that mere competence cannot replace.[31] Tactfully, then, Shakespeare warns both monarch and people of the dual peril attendant upon royal willfulness and rebellion. He unsparingly probes the weaknesses of monarchy, and in terms often used to criticize Elizabeth; but his sympathy for the opposition, as in *King John,* serves only to illustrate the folly of rebellion under all but the worst of conditions.

In the *Henry IV* plays (ca. 1596-1598), the rewards of Bolingbroke's competence are seen to be illusory. Even if Tudor kings had to believe that "The crown once possessed, cleareth and purifies all manner of defaults or imperfections,"[32] Bolingbroke's assumption of power by no means remedies the inescapable defect of his own disobedience. He may be skilled at suppressing revolt, but the uprisings are those which he began. No one can arbitrarily terminate a royal succession without teaching others to do so. Northumberland is the ugly symbol of this infectious character of ambition. Shakespeare deliberately blackens the earl's character, rendering him less courageous and more contemptible than he appears in Holinshed.[33] Bolingbroke's troubles are, abstractly considered, God's punishment for sin, but the workings of divine providence are humanly logical too. By its disruptive nature, rebellion always produces its own plagues.

Despite Bolingbroke's blameworthiness, however, his opponents are as guilty as were Richard's opponents. Shakespeare is consistent in resisting further challenge to established power. He refuses to espouse the claim of Mortimer, Richard's legitimate heir, just as Lodge denies to Marius the right to regain by violence the authority that was once properly his. Hotspur's gallantry and his scorn for a vile politician validly rebuke the king, but are tragically dissipated in a wrong cause. Hotspur is, like the man he detests, trapped in the fatal logic of armed resistance, and is at last betrayed by the "policy" in his own camp that he had naively believed he could transcend. Inflexible chivalric idealism is in fact the chief casualty of the civil wars, a lesson Prince Hal is not slow to learn. He must even tacitly accept the dastardly stratagem of his brother, Prince John, in voiding his promises to a dangerous enemy (2 *Henry IV*, IV, ii). To follow such a course, not unlike Elizabeth's secret policy toward the Irish, which Spenser defended in 1598,[34] is to acquiesce without enthusiasm in the necessities of modern warfare. It reflects small credit on Prince John and his father, and is an excess of expediency that Hal himself never practices. The king's own former crimes have brought him to the point of lying to his one-time allies. Politics need not always be such a dirty business, but may well be so in dilemmas growing out of usurpation.

Hotspur's idealism, however impossible, never ceases to mock the limits of Prince Hal's quest for unsullied heroism. One cannot imagine Hotspur, for instance, giving credit for victory to someone other than himself, or undertaking a great foreign war from considerations of policy, or rejecting a friend in the interests of his royal image. Hal accepts the play-acting necessities of his public role, and as the heroic image augments the man himself dwindles. However necessary his rejection of Falstaff, Hal is dehumanized by the self-imposed loss of that "genial humanity and free play of mood which the political leader inevitably foregoes when he confines himself within the restricted field of public affairs."[35] Hal must also condemn a personal friend at Southampton (*Henry V*, II, ii). These decisions are inescapable, and Shakespeare's attitude is never satirical although it is ironic. Even when the patriotic hyperboles of *Henry V's* opening chorus descend abruptly into the tarnished realities of church politics, the observation is matter-of-fact. Priests often behave so, as Shakespeare's chronicle sources attested, and glorious wars must have pragmatic support. That Hal behaves as a politician even in his wooing of Katharine illustrates merely (as King Alexander learned from Campaspe) that kings must marry in the national interest. Katharine knows this fact as well as Hal, and yet both honestly search for an enduring fondness within the limits of their public responsibilities. Hal's attempt to find real camaraderie with his soldiers eludes him because he can only act out his plebeian longings in an escapist fantasy. His firsthand knowledge of the "infinite heartsease" enjoyed by private men grows ever more distant with the encroachments of "idol ceremony." Even so, the anonymous experience among his common soldiers enriches his return to officialdom.

Hal's failures in disinterested affection, then, are imposed upon him not by inner lacks so much as by the nature of his role. In this light, Shakespeare's view of political expediency is not one of distaste for sordid realities, but compassionate admiration for self-sacrifice. Like Lyly, he applauds the ideal monarch (implicitly complimenting Elizabeth) who possesses the wisdom both to cultivate the common touch and to perceive the insuperable gulf between public and private life. The king "must bear all." Ultimately, Shakespeare's criticisms of monarchy are a part of his defense, for no good king can be otherwise than impersonal and occasionally ruthless. Hal is, to his credit, the sort of man who succeeds in public life, even if one would not wish to be like him.

The contemporary *Julius Caesar* (1599), although set in a Roman political context that avoids precise analogies to England, is still politically consistent with the themes of Shakespeare's second historical tetralogy. Shakespeare eschews the extreme interpretations that critics frequently have urged, both of Caesar as a virtuous model of "prince's power" supplanting "people's rule," and of Brutus as a tragic hero in the cause of freedom versus servitude.[36] Nor does Shakespeare offer a portrait of political ambiguity to which there can be no meaningful answer.[37] Aware of both the Plutarch tradition emphasizing Caesar's genius as soldier and statesman, and the Senecan tradition sympathizing more with Brutus,[38] Shakespeare views Caesar as a tyrant but holds as elsewhere that disruption of existing government is an evil exceeding the conditions it hopes to correct. Whatever men's commendable reasons for wishing change, the process of overthrow necessarily denies what they hope to accomplish.[39] Caesar is obsessed with his uniqueness and yet prey to many human failings of superstition, vanity, uxoriousness, deafness, and fever. He has dared to "press near civil government," like Sylla in *The Wounds of Civil War*. He is not a king sanctioned by divine right; Cassius insists correctly that he and Caesar were born social equals. Caesar appears less and less willing to heed counsel, especially from those who represent the traditions of senatorial authority. Removal cannot be gradual or constitutional: "It must be by his death." Yet Caesar tempers his ambition with a sense of public responsibility. Given his need to retain power, his ruthlessness and inflexible resolution are as incumbent on him as they were on Bolingbroke. Caesar is unquestionably another example of the man who is born to be a politician.

Brutus, contrastingly, is victimized by the unshakable flaw of rebellion. It must force aside the very institutions of legitimate power that it had hoped to preserve. Men must replace the tyrants they destroy, and as men they are prone to the temptations of power. The conflict between idealistic principles and sordid conspiracy produces in Brutus a fatal division of personality; the gentle friend of Caesar and the assassin cannot understand one another.[40] Although Brutus searches his motives for the deed, he never begins to suspect the extent to which he resembles Caesar: the pride that grudges partnership in greatness, the unilateral overriding of the objections of his fellow-conspirators, the unconscious susceptibility to Cassius' flattery. " 'Brutus' and 'Caesar.' What should be in that 'Caesar'? Why should that name be sounded more than yours?" (I, ii, 142-143). Brutus is presumably startled to be greeted by the plebeians with "Let him be Caesar," and "Caesar's better parts Shall be crowned in Brutus" (III, ii, 56-57), but the surprise is to be found less in the mob's changeability than in the ironic confirmation of Brutus' own unacknowledged ambition. His desire, as the scion of a proud old family, to be the savior of Rome is hardly different from that of the popular general he has killed.

Once in office, Brutus fails to comprehend the pragmatic necessities of power that might in time have justified his de facto rule. His divisions of authority and his acceding to the making of rabble-rousing speeches, however humanely motivated, are too permissive in this hour of crisis. Abler and more ruthless politicians fill the vacuum with expedient action. Antony and Octavius are at least as ruthless as Caesar was: too cunning in their manipulation of public emotion, too quick to cut off the legacies promised in Caesar's will (IV, i) and to proscribe the lives of even their close relatives for the cause of security. They know how to "use" weak men like Lepidus. They lack the trusting, visionary quality that both ennobles Brutus' character and disqualifies him as an efficient politician. The paradox is that "the noblest Roman of them all" cannot command a noble revolution. Violent overthrow merely creates an environment in which opportunistic men further suppress civic liberties, and deliberately unleash mob violence to secure their own ends. "Now, let it work," says Antony. "Mischief, thou art afoot. Take thou what course thou wilt" (III, ii, 265-266). The unstable commons are not fomenters of rebellion themselves, but are a dangerous force in the hands of a demagogue. Antony's extremes are nonetheless ultimately plausible and defensible in context. The times have proven Plutarch's contention that "the state of Rome (in my opinion) . . . could no more abide to be governed by many lords, but required one only absolute governor." [41] To acknowledge the necessity is not, however, to rejoice at it. Both Shakespeare and Lodge permit eloquent spokesmen to regret the passing of institutions in which wise men may speak well-considered judgments of their government. Yet both playwrights foresee that revolution inevitably hastens rather than retards the process. Temperate, innocent men such as Cicero or Cinna the poet are senselessly sacrificed. Disorder, and then tyranny, are the only victors. Both poets agree, also, that another country, such as England, need not embroil itself in Rome's impasse if it will heed the warning in time and eschew political innovation.

Shakespeare's and Lodge's conservatism, more thoughtful and temperate than that of *Jack Straw*, is plainly more loyal to the crown than that of the anonymous manuscript play *Thomas of Woodstock* (ca. 1591-1594). Indebted to *2 Henry VI* and influencing in turn Shakespeare's later *Richard II*, *Woodstock* is deeply involved in the period of English history which the opposition literature of the time used to castigate Elizabeth. *Woodstock's* topical bias is evident in its thematic alteration of historical dates and personalities. The title figure, uncle of Richard II, bears no resemblance to Holinshed's portrait of a vengeful, seditious plotter who was executed for his treasonable designs on the king and for his policy of war with France. Instead, "plain Thomas" is another good Duke Humphrey, obviously modeled on Shakespeare's hero and like him a champion of orderly redress for the commons' grievances. His brothers, Lancaster and York, are also defenders of English liberties, although in a more ominously violent manner. *Woodstock* conflates several incidents of strife between Richard and his uncles, and thereby clusters together an overwhelming and unhistorical array of royal favorites depending upon the king.[42] The effect is to exaggerate Richard's depravity and to unify and ennoble the baronial opposition. To the extent that the play's heroes are noblemen who believe in rank, *Woodstock* is hierarchically orthodox. Far from indulging in the anti-aristocratic jibes of *George a Greene* or *The Cobbler's Prophecy*, *Woodstock* upholds an ideal of old-fashioned nobility as England's best hope for justice. No Cade or Tyler spouts leveling doctrines. In its use of metaphor, *Woodstock* views the universe itself as one of order and degree. Yet, under the extremities of royal abuse, armed resistance by the aristocracy may be necessary. As A. P. Rossiter observes, the author had read *How Superior Powers Ought to be Obeyed,* or had thought that for himself.[43]

Woodstock is naturally reluctant to espouse a cause of rebellion. The hero, like Duke Humphrey and perhaps even more like the York of *Richard II,* bravely reprimands both sides in the struggle. He berates the king in plainspoken terms and urges a parliament at which the knights and burgesses may present petitions, and conversely employs all his eloquence in urging passive resistance. "I must tell them plain We are all struck, but must not strike again" (III, ii, 112-113). As he assures the virtuous queen, aware that her riotous husband is to blame for widespread poverty, "Fear not that, madam, England's not mutinous. 'Tis peopled all with subjects, not with outlaws . . . none dares rob him of his kingly rule" (II, iii, 38-42). Woodstock's death is, like Duke Humphrey's, a double tragedy: it confirms the extent of duplicity at court, and it removes the one public figure with sufficient stature to avert bloodshed.

Even Woodstock concedes, however, that passive obedience has its limits of endurance. He fully sympathizes with those who refuse to sign Lord Tresilian's blank charters for arbitrary taxation: "Afore my God I cannot blame them for it . . . I speak but what I fear, not what I wish. This foul oppression will withdraw all duty" (III, ii, 82-87). The only way he and the other lords can see to quiet the commons is to promise reform of the tax. "Ancient liberties Recorded and enrolled in the king's crown-office" impose constitutional limits on the king's authority. England's citizens are "free-born," and although they owe him "what we best may spare," the king may not "force it from our hands" (IV, iii, 34-38). Taxation cannot be permitted without some sort of representation to ensure willingness to pay and to determine how much may be spared—particularly through knights and burgesses in Parliament or through such lords as Woodstock and Lancaster.

This issue of parliamentary interest in taxation clearly had repercussions in the 1590's; the Parliament of 1593, for instance, questioned the subsidy on the grounds that war with Spain had not been officially declared. Repeatedly throughout the reign, the reformers in Parliament coupled the issue of taxation with attempted assaults on the royal prerogative, as in their insistence that Elizabeth correct the abuses of the much-hated royal purveyors (in 1589) and the monopoly-holders (1597-1598, 1601). Elizabeth's strategy in such confrontations was to accept petitions but repudiate directives. She invited House members to conferences altering the regulations of the purveyors, and herself repealed the most obnoxious monopolies, but insisted that the authority for reform in matters of the royal household (and of religion) was hers alone. Thus she preserved the principle of royal prerogative while conceding the substance of some requests.[44] Her prolonged struggle with Parliament over this vital issue, of parliamentary right of initiative versus the paternalistic royal acceptance of an orderly petition, is central to the roles of Woodstock, Duke Humphrey, and York as would-be mediators.

Equally timely was the issue of free speech. Protestant reformers in Parliament, in 1584-1585 and afterwards, were understandably worried that bills nominally aimed at curbing seditious Catholic utterances might apply equally to the religious left. Indeed, Whitgift's increasing phobia for Puritanism led in the early 1590's to severe repression under an efficient intelligence-gathering network. *Woodstock's* most biting satire is directed toward a country "so full of intelligencers that two men can scarce walk together but they're attached for whisperers" (III, iii, 161-163). The atmosphere of hysteria is such that even whistlers are arrested for "a piece of treason that flies up and down the country in the likeness of a ballad" (III, iii, 230-231). The authorities' paranoiac suspicion of all criticism forces the nation's writers to resort to parables. The Schoolmaster, for instance, composes verses that "run o'er all the flatterers i'the court" with allusions to "green" poison, "bushy" fagots, and the like, and then concludes with the pious disclaimer "God bless my Lord Tresilian" (III, iii, 171-195). The author of *Woodstock*, hinting at a similar ulterior meaning in his own play, lampoons the mood of fear and repression that has driven him to speak in "a kind of equivocation." In its view of taxation and of criticizing the government for manifest abuses, *Woodstock* is an outspoken defense of the rights of free men within the existing social order.

Civil war, however reluctantly arrived at, is at last an unavoidable necessity. Ultimate failure at conciliation must rest solely on the king's decision to close Parliament without redress of grievances. Lancaster, and even the conservative York, are up in arms with the commons. When the ghosts of the Black Prince and Edward III appear to Woodstock urging him to "Go join with them: prevent thy further harms" (V, i, 101), there can be no doubt of the authorial viewpoint condoning violence. Unlike the rebellion in Shakespeare's *Richard II*, the commencement of open defiance does not bring with it an orthodox shift of sympathy away from the rebels. Although Woodstock goes to his death still wishing Richard's safety, his brothers evidently (although the manuscript is imperfect) extort from Richard some of the conditions for which they have fought.

Lancaster and his allies never aim at replacing Richard himself. This seemingly important disclaimer of regicide offers little consolation to the orthodox, however, for every major rebellion of the sixteenth century protested its loyalty to the crown. *Woodstock's* civil war is in fact politically close to the aims of the Pilgrimage of Grace (1536), the Western Rising of 1549, or the Northern Rebellion of 1569, with their reverence for the conservative nobility, their sympathy for the oppressions of the peasantry, and their longing to disencumber the monarch of upstart favorites. To this older form of protest is added a radical interest in plain dress, free speech, and constitutional safeguards—a coalescing of extremist dissidence in the 1590's increasingly associated with the erratic leadership of Essex.[45] Such a political alignment explains how *Woodstock* can be at once old-fashioned in its social values and unorthodox regarding Tudor monarchism. *Woodstock* is relevant to the current discussion because it prefers orderly redress through the hierarchical middle course so eloquently argued by Thomas; but the tendency toward polarization of extremes is alarmingly evident.

Another public figure who grows to heroic stature as intermediary between an angry people and their monarch is the title figure of *Sir Thomas More* (ca. 1593-1601). The play exists only as a manuscript and quite possibly was never performed; for, despite some blatantly orthodox sentiments, its subject was simply too controversial to be dramatized at all. Especially if written late in Elizabeth's reign, when Essex's popularity in London was at its height,[46] the play could scarcely leave the Master of the Revels, Sir Edmund Tilney, with any other choice than to excise "the insurrection wholly and the cause thereof." Thomas More, as a darling of the populace and a heretic slain by Elizabeth's father, was too close for objective appraisal. However much the authors might subordinate the Catholic element in More's struggle with King Henry, the cause for which More died was notorious. Moreover, the actual presentation of a London riot, as differentiated from the peasant uprisings of 2 *Henry VI*, *Jack Straw*, and *Edward IV*, was cause for official concern. The "ill May day" (1517) of which the play treats had become, in the analogous parlance of the time, a synonym for recent disturbances in the 1580's and 1590's.[47] Perhaps the contributing authors, Munday, Chettle, and Dekker, were innocent in intent but found themselves overwhelmed by the onrush of Essex's turbulent career. One plausible theory of composition holds that Shakespeare was called in to bolster the orthodoxies of a play fighting for its life.[48] The passages ascribed to Shakespeare are, under the presumed circumstances, understandably more official in substance than anything else he wrote. Even his ministrations could not, however, dispel the troublesome implications surrounding this hero of the people.

Because he is not a nobleman but a Londoner, More is especially able to sympathize with popular distress and channel it into orderly procedures of law. He rebukes the rebels not for their aims but for their methods, and he succeeds in forestalling violence because he offers a surer way of righting their wrongs. He need not counsel passive obedience to tyranny in this case, for he has the king's ear and the king is amenable to just appeal. More is above all a leader with the common touch—at ease with the common players, generous to servants, evenhanded in dispensing justice to rich and poor alike. Like Thomas of Woodstock, though less nobly born, More resists the temptations of prideful dress and extravagant life. He praises God alone "That I from such an humble bench of birth Should step as 'twere up to my country's head" (Addition III, ll. 6-7). More is the only member of the Establishment able to win the commons' unhesitating support, since he looks at things their way.

The authors of *Sir Thomas More* show sympathy for London's complaints, although not for the rising itself. The abuses suffered are undeniable and must be remedied. Wise observers agree that the king is overly clement to the insolent Lombards and other alien extortionists only because he "Is not informèd of this base abuse," and hence "his gracious wisdom Would soon redress it" if presented with an orderly petition (ll. 382-385). There is considerable sentiment among the Londoners themselves for peaceful appeal. The issue is really a narrowly-defined one of procedure. Goaded as they are by daily outrages, most citizens are aware that they "must be bridled by law," that redress of "yours and mine own is a matter beyond all our abilities" (ll. 52-60). Accordingly, even though John Lincoln and his fellow radicals are successful in starting a riot, they are in a minority. The mob itself is not basically irresponsible as in 2 *Henry VI* or *Jack Straw* and is ready to listen to More's reasonable persuasions.

More is able to be perfectly orthodox without alienating himself from the crowd or denying its legitimate aspirations. His argument is not to give over the complaint, but to choose the easy path to success: "to calm our private foes With breath of gravity, not dangerous blows" (Addition II, ll. 119-120). Even the extremist leaders are glad to hear him speak, and acknowledge that they have sinned against the Gospel "urging obedience to authority." They see that challenge to order produces only anarchy. Lincoln actually goes to his death confessing "it was not fit That private men should carve out their redress" (ll. 622-623). The rest are pardoned and are all rehabilitated citizens. This understanding treatment of even the rebel leaders suggests that the London populace is able to control itself. More is, after all, one of their own. The citizens are entitled to enumerate their just grievances, and the authorities are willing to listen. In orthodox fashion, but with a strong awareness of London's prerogatives, *Sir Thomas More* offers a mirror not only to the citizens but to the king. It does not allow rebellion under any circumstances, but it stresses the way in which trouble can be forestalled through royal generosity and it glorifies the role of the popular London leader who brings about social amelioration.

More's doctrinal beliefs are of course virtually eliminated. His reasons for refusing to subscribe to the king's articles are never explained, other than as an abstract matter of "conscience." The king is never called a tyrant for executing him. More is not a martyr of the old faith. His own actions, in fact, have shown him to be no advocate of corrupt privilege enjoyed by an international church: he has sentenced Faulkner, a ruffian dependent on the Bishop of Winchester, despite Faulkner's pleading of ecclesiastical shielding from the law. No rebuttal is allowed to the position of secular supremacy over the church. Even More's friends at court think it strange for a chancellor to "refuse The duty that the law of God bequeathes Unto the king" (ll. 1276-1278). However puzzling the choice, More's integrity in refusing remains an admirable trait of character throughout. The poor grieve at his death. The underlying argument seems to be that, within the orthodox limits of obedience to the king as head of the church, a man's private opinions are his own. In understated fashion, *Sir Thomas More* illustrates the inevitable relationship in the 1590's between issues of private conscience and obedience to the Tudor state. More himself is no rebel. Yet the very magnanimity of his spirit eloquently indicates his willingness to suffer for an inner faith. His stance, since it is not labeled Catholic, appeals to all those who are troubled in their religious allegiances. The answer is staunchly orthodox, in that it absolutely forbids any compromising of duty toward the state in matters of social injustice or doctrine; but it plainly views sympathetically the Londoners' plea for some official forbearance in return for their loyalty.

The political lesson of *1 Sir John Oldcastle* (1599) is virtually identical. Written by Anthony Munday (probably the chief author of *Sir Thomas More*) in collaboration with Michael Drayton, Thomas Hathaway, and Robert Wilson,[49] *Oldcastle* is the moderate Puritans' warning to extremists of their own party. Yet the play also hopes to achieve gains in personal religious freedom under a tolerant king, and it breathes defiance of the old guard who persecute true believers. It was, appropriately, a play for the Admiral's men, whose dominant audience of respectable Puritan citizens inclined to old-fashioned, unsophisticated morality and anti-Catholic ridicule. Munday, a well-known controversialist, was the leader of a last-ditch effort to make the theater attractive to the Puritans; his own defection from the theater in 1602 was an ominous portent.[50] *Oldcastle's* valiant efforts at reconciliation of the extremists should be read in the light of a rapidly approaching religious impasse.

The religious crisis in 1599 also illuminates *Oldcastle's* feud with Shakespeare's *Henry IV* plays at Chamberlain's. The rivalry was of course partly economic, but the figure of Sir John Oldcastle had become as polemical in Reformation England as that of King John. Historically a Lollard nobleman who was hanged as a traitor and burned as a heretic under Henry V, Oldcastle (Lord Cobham) was vilified by the Catholics Fabyan and Harpsfield and then apotheosized into Protestant martyrdom by Tyndale, Bale, and Foxe. *Oldcastle* propagandistically follows the spirit of the Protestant tradition.[51] Shakespeare's treatment of Falstaff, on the other hand, whom he had originally named Oldcastle in recollection of the anonymous *Famous Victories of Henry V*, was negligent toward a revered saint. However much Shakespeare played down the Puritan mannerisms, and used Falstaff to underscore a higher political morality, the affront was manifest to the literal-minded. *Oldcastle* is piously shocked at the "pampered glutton" and "agèd counselor to youthful sin" of *Henry IV*, and undertakes above all to reclaim the reputation of "A valiant martyr and a virtuous peer" who expressed true faith and loyalty "Unto his sovereign and his country's weal" (Prologue). This defense of Oldcastle by the Admiral's men also had in mind the living Lord Cobham, Puritan descendant of Oldcastle, whose relations with the Chamberlain's men were none too cordial.

The play's hero is yet another in the imposing list of victimized intermediaries urging a moderate and lawful course of popular reform— Duke Humphrey, Thomas of Woodstock, Thomas More. As a believer in the reformed religion and an opponent of violent change, Oldcastle is slanderously misinterpreted by Catholic reactionaries and Lollard extremists alike, and is presumably destroyed by them in the play's sequel (now lost). Catholics brand him a heretic, Lollards naturally wish to claim him for one of their own. *Oldcastle's* voice is shrill in depicting both dangers. The Catholic menace, comparable also to that of Whitgift's conservative Anglicanism in the 1590's, is one of repression of all moderate reform and individual conscience. The Bishop of Rochester (a familiar and hated name to *Oldcastle's* Puritan audience) [52] insists on ancient prerogatives of trying heretics, and manages to goad even the pious Henry V into a Protestant-like resentment of the church's jurisdiction over civil matters. Henry and Oldcastle are thus as one in their belief that the church must be subjected to royal authority and reformed under the king's direction.

The opposite danger of reform through insurrection is equally unpalatable to king and heroic moderate. Despite its Puritan leanings, *Oldcastle* follows the official government line of equating Puritan radicalism with communistic Anabaptism.[53] It is wary of the people. Wherever "the vulgar sort Sit on their ale-bench, with their cups and cans," all discussion of politics and religion is to be forbidden by governmental action (ll. 136-137). Revolution inevitably aims not only at religious freedom but at social leveling, as in the brewer William Murley's fantasies of knighthood and a colonel's uniform (ll. 1194f). Violent religious change also offers a fatal opportunity to traitors and foreign enemies, such as the three aristocrats planning to assassinate King Henry with French aid. They are not Wyclifites themselves, but hope to profit from the prevailing anarchy, and suppose that Oldcastle will join them because of his persecutions by the clergy. Radical overthrow not only destroys itself, but gives unintended assistance to the forces of reaction.

For both king and champion of moderate reform, the obvious bulwark against radicalism and reaction is the throne. Neither the people nor the established church must be allowed ultimate authority in determining the course of religious settlement. In a time of impending rebellion, royal power must deal harshly with civil liberties. All gentlemen, mayors, and sheriffs are ordered "to have care For the suppressing of all mutinies, And all assemblies, except soldiers' musters" (ll. 119-121). Conventicles are to be disbanded. Oldcastle himself must agree to avoid all group activities with his co-religionists, and must not "suffer any meetings to be had Within your house, but to the uttermost Disperse the flocks of this new gathering sect" (ll. 861-863). No virtuous character in the play takes exception to these restrictive measures. Oldcastle himself sees no contradiction in being forbidden to proselytize others to the faith for which he would lay down his life. Belief is a matter of conscience; recruitment is a matter of political activity. *Oldcastle* is close to *Sir Thomas More* in acknowledging integrity of conscience as long as individual attitude is severely distinguished from all corporate aspects of nonconformism.

These repressive tactics of the government do not mean, however, that the cause of religious reform is to stand still. Henry insists only that it is his sole prerogative to direct that reform. Unhistorically, he is fully inclined in that direction. He respects conscience, and "would be loath to press our subjects' bodies, Much less their souls" (ll. 856-857). As long as the reformers acknowledge that conscience binds them to king and country as well as to religion, they are encouraged to press for religious reform through proper channels: "Make known their grief And pray amendment, not enforce the same, Unless their king were tyrant" (ll. 1662-1664). Henry is not insensitive to the failings of the established church. He welcomes the loyal Oldcastle as his assistant in uncovering the enormities of church abuse. Together they will remedy evil in the name of supreme civil authority. Henry is, then, despite his nominal Catholicism, a Protestant in matters of church government. As an ideal prince he offers a mirror to Elizabeth. She must acknowledge (and in fact Elizabeth was responsive to this point) that a ruler who allows some toleration of conscience will earn the loyalty of an important segment of her people. The plea is notably moderate in comparison with the militance of the Parliament of 1584-1585; then the Puritans, pressing for basic revision of the episcopal structure, had insisted on forcing their initiative in defiance of Elizabeth's stern guarding of her prerogative. *Oldcastle,* by conceding Elizabeth's position that the monarch acts with unchallenged authority upon the petitions of her loving people, and by disclaiming conventicles (as the moderate reformers in Parliament had done in 1589), reflects the decline of the Puritan "classical" movement and the effectiveness of Whitgift's no-nonsense discipline.[54] To be sure, the mood is unmistakably one of mistrusting the bishops in Convocation to accept any thorough alteration without royal urging. The reformers have just grievances, and the hour is late. They must learn from their past, however, that moderates can win a more lasting triumph for truth than those who flout their duty to the state.

T he political debate in later Elizabethan drama was, as we have
seen, chiefly a product of the public theaters. This was in part attributable
to the obvious fact that the boys' companies were closed during most
of the 1590's. Yet there were also basic differences in political viewpoint
separating public and private theaters. The entire absence of English
history plays from the elite repertory cannot be attributed to mere accident.[1] Blatant appeals to anti-foreign sentiment, belief in continental
Catholic conspiracy, and glorification of the sturdy English citizen did
not suit the taste of the more cosmopolitan courtly and intellectual circle.
Rather than argue, as Shakespeare did, for a middle position of patriotism without extremes, private dramatists tended to view the debate
itself as unsophisticated. Their reactions were similar toward avowedly
homiletic defenses of hierarchy and public authority. Leaving to public
dramatists the task of inculcating the great commonplaces of Elizabethan world order, private dramatists concentrated on satirical exposure
of hypocrisy in all ranks of society. Increasingly they ridiculed ambitious
shopkeepers, Puritans, parvenu knights, complacent patrons of the arts,
and busybody public officials stifling their pungent criticisms.

However genuinely motivated by a desire to renovate the society in which they lived, the satirists were bound to be misunderstood by the spokesmen of bourgeois and lower-class opinion. In a time of civil restiveness, threat of invasion, and uncertain royal succession, satire seemed to many a frivolous luxury at best, a carping about minutiae. To others, satirical writing was unregenerately subversive, embodying the treasonous Italianate dilettantism and immorality at court insinuated by many antiaristocratic popular plays. This harsh view had some official support, as is evidenced by the closing of the boys' theaters in the early 1590's and by Archbishop Whitgift's ban on satire in 1599. The broad issue, of artistic free speech versus the needs of a troubled state for enforced orthodoxy, was obscured by mutual invective. Public moralists perhaps overestimated the dangers to the state; the satirists perhaps underestimated the need for accommodation of viewpoint in an era of political transition. The result was unfortunately symptomatic of, and no doubt contributory to, the ever-widening antipathy between courtly society and London populace.

With the reactivation of the boys' companies in 1599, contrasting attitudes toward public authority in the adult and boys' theaters were sharply joined. Observers did not fail to note the social and political ramifications of the rivalry. Public dramatists saw their primary cause as one of defending law and order. As Common Sense laments in *Lingua* (published in 1607, written by 1603), "O times! O manners! when boys dare to traduce men in authority; was ever such an attempt heard?" Even though classical times sanctioned the practice, present-day critics are clearly going too far: "In those days it was lawful, but now the abuse of such liberty is insufferable." At any rate, all debaters agree on the extensiveness of the current vogue. One character observes drily, "Think what you will of it. I think 'tis done" (II, iv). Heywood, in his *Apology for Actors* (1610), is equally disturbed at the disrespectful trend of coterie playwriting. "Now, to speak of some abuse lately crept into the quality, as an inveighing against the state, the court, the law, the city, and their governments, with the particularizing of private men's humors (yet alive), noblemen and others: I know it distastes many; neither do I any way approve it, nor dare I by any means excuse it." [2] Conversely, Heywood idealizes the public dramatist as a man of sober responsibility, aware that "the broad eye of the world" will closely judge his deportment: "Many among us I know to be of substance, of government, of sober lives, and temperate carriages, housekeepers, and contributary to all duties enjoined them." [3]

Similarly, the 1610 edition of *Mucedorus* adds a timely warning to its epilogue, satirizing the envious dramatist "Whose jaws swell to his eyes with chawing malice," who composes such dark and slanderous comedies that the magistrate "cannot but make complaint" and so restrains the acting profession. The spirit of true Comedy has his righteous answer: "This is a trap for boys, not men." Adult actors and writers are "Especially desertful in their doings, Whose staid discretion rules their purposes. I and my faction do eschew those vices" (ll. 34-56).[4] Hamlet's uneasiness about the "little eyases" who "cry out on the top of question" (II, ii, 353-354) is tactfully noncommittal as to their abuses; but Shakespeare was evidently considered to be, with his company, wary of satirists like Ben Jonson. Will Kemp, speaking in *2 Return from Parnassus* (1601-1602), notes with satisfaction that Jonson wanted to give the public dramatists a pill but instead "our fellow Shakespeare hath given him a purge" (IV, iii). Kemp probably had in mind *Satiromastix,* not actually by Shakespeare but presented by his company.[5]

Before we examine the so-called War of the Theaters alluded to by Kemp, we need to survey the evolution of the private theater's attitudes toward law and order. The growth of such attitudes is evident not only in satire, but, as a corollary process, in heroic drama and tragedy. Throughout the Elizabethan period, England's more sophisticated artists inevitably took the lead in importing neoclassical literary forms. Translations from Ariosto, Garnier, Seneca, and others were eagerly sought after, as Sir Thomas Hoby phrased it, so "that we alone of the world may not be still counted barbarians in our tongue, as in time out of mind we have been in our manners." [6] Yet this culturally liberating force was looked upon by many ordinary Englishmen as Italianate and suspect, to be expurgated or modified by English ethical standards if tolerated at all. The inveterate didacticism of the English approach to art required that continental literature, with its unfamiliar ideas about man in society or in the cosmos, be appraised in terms of the "mirror" it offered to English civilization. From this parochial viewpoint, the new fascination among the cognoscenti for non-English mores implied criticism of conventional values. Indeed, Plutarch and Ovid offered liberating views not only of personal conduct but of aristocratic superiority and distaste for ordinary law enforcement. The great truisms of political stability, divine right, and the like occupy positions of lesser importance in courtly neoclassical drama because these elements are obviously missing in the continental milieu from which such drama emerged. Furthermore, it seems likely that courtly society accepted at least in part the "mirror" thesis of art, and did in fact welcome continental vogues as a means of exploring iconoclastic attitudes toward law enforcement. Although they did not consciously model their lives on neoclassical stage conventions, patrician audiences responded instinctively to a fictional world of upper-class immunity from and indifference to mundane civil restraints.

This tendency is apparent in Elizabethan heroic drama and "regular" tragedy, and anticipates the growth of such genres in seventeenth-century select drama. Even in the 1580's, this theater proclaimed its exclusiveness. *The Wars of Cyrus* (1576-1580), probably by Richard Farrant for the Chapel children, shuns the predilections of both the vulgar and the "virtuous"—that is, those inclining to Puritanism.[7] Robert Wilmot's *Tancred and Gismond,* published 1591, reflects with pleasure that its printed record "shall be safe from the tragedian tyrants of our time." Samuel Daniel's *Cleopatra,* a strictly Senecan drama, is offered to the Countess of Pembroke as poetry in a higher strain "To chase away this tyrant of the north, Gross barbarism." Similarly remote from popular tastes are Thomas Kyd's translation of *Cornelia,* Marlowe's *The Tragedy of Dido,* and probably such lost plays as *Iphigenia and Alcmaeon* and *Timoclea at the Siege of Thebes.*[8] Part of the exclusiveness is of course literary—the decorums of single tragic action and classical chorus, the elevated diction—but the fictional appeal is, in terms of social organization, uniformly chivalric. Aristocratic persons live in the wealthy environment to which they are entitled without visible means of support, and settle their tragic differences by resort to patrician codes of death before dishonor and self-mastery in love. The king's tyranny in *Tancred and Gismond,* for example, raises no timely issues of passive obedience; the crisis is one of manners rather than administration of justice, and the ultimate appeal is to a courtesy-book tradition of princely behavior. *Soliman and Perseda* (ca. 1590), probably by Kyd and seemingly elite in its auspices,[9] regards dueling as a proper chivalric reprisal for a deed of dishonor—in contrast to a parallel incident in Shakespeare's *Romeo and*

Juliet, where the vendetta of the Capulets and Montagues necessitates the intervention of the state. "Mercy but murders, pardoning those that kill" (III, i, 202), proclaims Prince Escalus; he alone may pass sentence on homicide.[10] On the whole, then, the appeal of courtly heroic and tragic drama is backward-turning. Chivalric drama answers a craving for a disappearing world in which courtly manners alone define the greatness of a civilization.

In revenge tragedy as well, themes of an aristocratic code transcending civil authority struck a responsive note in drama for the private theaters. Again, this stage convention was in no way a realistic portrait of Elizabethan life,[11] but a fictional world made attractive by its relevance to chivalric ideals no longer easily adhered to. Dueling and private vengeance were still endorsed by many noblemen as an expression of their onetime feudal right to settle differences by personal honor rather than by the state's authority. Notorious continuing instances of vendetta at court required the monarchy to invoke religious teaching (Romans 12) and arguments of royal supremacy against "a kind of wild justice," even in cases where the magistrate could not or would not act.[12] The public theater was by no means free of the revenge spirit, as is evidenced for example in Kyd's *The Spanish Tragedy* (ca. 1584-1589) and Chettle's *The Tragedy of Hoffman* (1602-1603). Elizabethans of all classes were of divided minds concerning revenge, and had not completely disavowed the ritual of private feud derived from primitive and Anglo-Saxon society.[13] Murder was still considered an injury to the victim's nearest relatives, imposing on them the duty of indicting the offender but not of punishing him. Even if revenge tragedy flourished in both public and private theaters, however, the emphases were characteristically different. The sobering consideration that private revenge was, officially speaking, an assault on the centralized power of the state prompted at least some public dramatists to weigh the issues accordingly. Bourgeois chronicles of crime and punishment, such as *Arden of Feversham* (1585-1592), *Two Lamentable Tragedies* (1594-1601), and *A Warning for Fair Women* (ca. 1598-1599) eschew entirely the Italianate setting and the human revenger's repertory of ingenious methods. Taken from actual case histories of murder,[14] these homiletic tragedies offer "simple truth" in unadorned style, and greatly emphasize the role of God as the operative avenger. His vengeance prevails not only through providential miracle and individual conscience but through human legal institutions; police procedures in *A Warning* are meticulously and respectfully detailed.

Even *The Spanish Tragedy* concedes that the proceedings of Hieronimo and Bel-Imperia are of disastrous consequence to the body politic, although Kyd does not imply a simple condemnation of revenge on these grounds.[15] In the ironic impasse of public and private aims, Bel-Imperia's quest for romantic love undoes a state marriage arranged by the well-intending Spanish king to ease the afflictions of senseless war between two kingdoms; and Hieronimo's slaying of Don Cyprian ends the life of the king's brother "and the whole succeeding hope That Spain expected after my decease" (ll. 3190-3191). A lasting peace that seems so near, and yet is doomed from the start, provides a chief motive for suspense in this sensational play. The state is not one-sidedly in the wrong, and suffers grievous injury. Though Kyd's resolution is far from orthodox, he does not pretend that considerations of national security are irrelevant. Shakespeare, too, in *Titus Andronicus* (1594), is constantly aware of the menace to Rome engendered by Titus' vindictive sacrifice of Tamora's eldest son and its gruesome aftermath. The hero and nemesis, Lucius, commands at last a state assented to by "the common voice" (V, iii, 140) in which faction and civil disobedience are severely punished.

The underlying assumption of much private revenge drama is subtlely but importantly different. Here the act of revenge is integral to the patrician attitude of regarding civil law as a debased and contentious form of justice, suitable only for those mortals who are too ignoble to govern themselves in virtuous living.[16] As enunciated by Chapman and Marston, this idea is not a mere selfish upper-class defense of inherited prerogative, but a serious rationale for educated men ideally too wise to need external restraint. Yet the implications for state authority were unsettling in an Elizabethan context. The revenger in Marston's *Antonio's Revenge* (1600-1601), for instance, does not pause to consider whether he has authority to murder a wicked prince, or whether the state will survive his challenge. Antonio is a protagonist of superior moral and intellectual powers, alienated from a hostile society, who is entitled to impose his own higher code on that society by extra-legal standards. The only criterion of right conduct by which Marston permits criticism of his hero is that of neo-Stoic philosophy. Antonio is perhaps more engaged in the world than a true critic ought to be; Pandulpho's near invulnerability to the buffets of fortune is a goal worth striving for.[17] Such a course of inner serenity has no relation, however, to orthodox passive resistance. The neo-Stoic laughs at a king's tyrannies not because God will dispose but because the neo-Stoic is truly indifferent to the world's vanities. Once revenge becomes necessary despite these prompt-ings of disengagement, Antonio proceeds to a ritual barbarism assented to by the entire nation. The only revenger in Elizabethan or Jacobean drama to escape death, he is instead offered public honor by a grateful people (ll. 2132-2133). Yet he prefers to retire from the world, in a final affirmation of the Stoical higher truth that spurns the mundane affairs of government.[18] He is too rare a spirit to content himself with the daily operation of civil justice.

In comedy as well, a distinction between public and private theaters can be discerned in their respective handling of satire directed at law and the state. Shakespeare consistently modifies the Italianate frame-work of his sources to fit the norms of English jurisprudence. Even an early Plautine farce like *The Comedy of Errors* (ca. 1593) is not con-tent to leave justice in the hands of witty manipulators, and offers some pointedly admiring remarks about those who wish to stop "the mortal and intestine jars" between Ephesus and Syracuse (I, i, 11).[19] *The Merchant of Venice* studies the paradoxical conflict between inflexible statute law and equity, evidently a timely issue to many Elizabethans who regarded the Chancery court as a great public defender against remorseless forfeiture of bond.[20] However ironical Portia's observation that Shylock has legal right on his side, and that the state may not "do a little wrong" in this instance without establishing a precedent for sub-version of established decrees (IV, i, 216-220), Portia does not threaten the great conserving principle of a law humanely administered in accord with divine precept. She wittily outmaneuvers an overly literal law with one of its own maxims in order to demonstrate the ascendancy of true justice over the spirit of vengeance.

Similarly in *Much Ado about Nothing* (1598), one of Shakespeare's unique contributions to his continental sources is a story of simple English public law enforcement forestalling crime. However ludicrous in their bumbling, Dogberry's recognizably contemporary night-watchmen pre-serve a festive spirit of comedy by preventing the intrusion of serious crime. The arrest of Hero's slanderers coincides with the announcement of their hateful plan, so that a happy outcome is never in doubt even though it is farcically delayed.[21] No matter how pompous and inefficient their master, the watchmen display some constabulary alacrity in discerning "some treason" and "the most dangerous piece of lechery that was known in the commonwealth" (III, iii). Condescended to by their rank-conscious captain and scoffed at even by the villains they have taken captive, they see the business through. Even Dogberry's bureaucratic passion for proceeding through channels cannot delay indefinitely the report that he doggedly insists on conveying to higher authority. This is a wry comment on the absurdities often contained in legal process, as in *The Merchant of Venice,* but without satire of human institutions of justice as such. Shakespeare has dared, through the actions of pitiable men, to affirm the principle that law stumbles across more truth than it manages to overlook. The gentlemanly code of personal vengeance, as evidenced by the chivalric challenges interchanged among Don Pedro, Claudio, Leonato, Antonio, and Benedick, represents a potentially more serious threat to comic resolution.

The role of Escalus in *Measure for Measure* (1603-1604) offers yet another lesson in practical law enforcement, which, even though it cannot entirely solve the more complex dilemmas of justice posed by Angelo's transgression, is a bulwark against social decay. Escalus' dispensing of equity is immediately effective, though limited in scope, because it acknowledges the compromises involved in human imperfection. Police law can induce a degree of reform in some men—even the seemingly incorrigible Pompey—by forcibly restraining them from vice. Escalus is, like the criminal types with whom he deals, recognizably English in character, a justice of the peace making the best of a difficult situation.[22] His sanity and loyal performance offset to no small degree both the inflexibility and the corruption of Angelo. When overruled by Angelo on the issue of Claudio's fornication, Escalus wisely submits in passive obedience to his superior and turns to matters he can remedy. The ironic injustice with which the play opens, compelling the comparatively innocent Claudio to suffer imprisonment while Mistress Overdone, Pompey, Froth, and Lucio thrive in their lust, does not long remain in force. Escalus patiently attends to the rambling court testimony that Angelo finds so exasperating, and is not unduly discouraged by the incompetence of his police officer, Elbow. Though Pompey and Froth have out-witted Elbow for the present, the rioters receive stern warnings and the police force is systematically overhauled. No longer will appointees to the constabulary be permitted to pay poor Elbow to take their places; Escalus will select new officers who are "the most sufficient of your parish," and will patiently instruct the unlearned but good-hearted men who must perform the job. Elbow will do better next time; in fact it is he who apprehends Pompey redhanded for theft and commits him to prison (III, i). By keeping a file on suspected criminals and by using underworld connections as informants, Escalus builds a sufficient case against Mistress Overdone and against Lucio for his breach of promise of marriage to Kate Keepdown. Escalus believes in capital punishment, although he prefers to restore men to social usefulness. "Mercy is not itself, that oft looks so; Pardon is still the nurse of second woe" (II, i, 297-298). His words echo those of his namesake in *Romeo and Juliet*. Escalus' brand of law is thus circumscribed but not invalidated by the more complex problems of divine justice found in this play.

To move from these romantic comedies of Shakespeare to neoclassical satire is to enter a world in which law enforcement is almost always irrelevant and is not infrequently itself the subject of laughter. Like private revenge tragedy, satire exists apart from the mundane restrictions of English society, and handles its own highly idiosyncratic problems of justice according to an elite code. To be sure, the law is treated with respect in some early satires with a marked English flavor. *Gammer Gurton's Needle* (S. R., 1563), which assimilates neoclassical character types into a native tradition of humor, provides a sympathetic choral role for Master Baily. As an official and respected member of the community, he projects a spirit of tolerance and amity. Yet Baily's major service as magistrate is to disclaim any interest of the law in these farcical proceedings. To Dr. Rat's entreaty that Diccon of Bedlam be fettered in chains, Baily rejoins, "Master Doctor, there is no remedy; I must entreat you, needs, Some other kind of punishment" (V, ii, 238-239). Since the whole affair is "a sport alone," punishment must be "in no wise so great"; it is to be a slapstick penance. Legal justice is thus irrelevant, but the social norms of order and officialdom are decorously upheld. Similarly, in dramas of the "Christian Terence" tradition, such as *Misogonus* (ca. 1560-1577) and George Gascoigne's *The Glass of Gov-*

ernment (printed 1575), neoclassical appeals to social inversion are transformed into homiletic affirmations of Christian morality and obedience to civil authority. Offenses against the established Protestant religion by the graceless Misogonus require stern reprisals in the name of "conscience, and duty, and laws of the king" (I, i, 147-148). Gascoigne's compendious and nontheatrical tract urges obedience to God, king, magistrates, country, and parents; those who obey succeed, and those who rebel are destroyed. Neither play sympathizes with clever servants or hedonistic young men endeavoring to outwit careful fathers.

Early translations of Italianate comedy, on the other hand, although infused with an English comic spirit in the choice of language, make no effort to alter the setting or values of the original. *Bugbears* (1563-ca. 1565), taken from Grazzini's *La Spiritata* for boys' performance,[23] takes place "here in Italy" (III, iii, 139) in a thoroughly cosmopolitan and Catholic environment that indulges in anticlerical humor without abusing the church itself. The Plautine character types are not adapted to English social norms. Entirely absent are any impartial figures representing law. As in Plautus, the young hero and his companions both control the audience's viewpoint and engineer (with the aid of clever servants) the awarding of punishments according to the decorums of satire. The Plautine generic plot of a "trick to catch the old one," also used in *Supposes* (1566), is implicitly hostile to authoritarian figures. Cleander in *Supposes* is not simply the "humorous" type of impotent rich suitor, but a lawyer representing the learned professions and social respectability. Cantalupo in *Bugbears* is a similar figure. Amedeus, the churlish father of *Bugbears,* is "hellishly bent On the muck of this world, on his pelf and his dross" (I, ii, 50-51). In punishing such a sin, the young men are performing unilaterally a role normally undertaken by religious teaching or by the force of respectable society at large. In fact they perpetrate a religious hoax, posing as "bugbears" or disembodied spirits of divine vengeance. They have usurped the function of correction and yet can claim the audience's moral approval for what they do. Their extra-legal act of larceny is justified by the criterion of satirical "sport." The implication is not merely that small matters ought to be handled out of court, but that society in its normal hierarchy is incapable of correcting itself since the patriarchs enjoy an entrenched and undeserved privilege of authority. They must be taught by the young who, lacking the power of recognized position, have to capitalize on their own wit.

A major theme of *Supposes*, omitted entirely in the anonymous *The Taming of a Shrew* and in Shakespeare's *The Taming of the Shrew* (1594), is the satiric treatment of lawyers. Gascoigne makes much of this in his marginal notes. Shakespeare's Gremio has acquired his grasping habits as a wealthy landowner; his profession is of less importance than his generic qualities of aged miserliness. Cleander in *Supposes* follows the law, and has used it to pervert justice for his own ends. "The trade of law doth fill the boist'rous bags; They swim in silk, when others roist in rags" (I, ii, 60-61). Corruption afflicts judges as well as lawyers. When Erostrato's Sicilian father, barred from seeing his son, proposes to seek remedy at law, he is warned of the harsh realities: "Sir, he that will go to the law must be sure of four things: first, a right and a just cause; then, a righteous advocate to plead; next, favor *coram judice;* and, above all, a good purse to procure it" (IV, viii, 42-45). Favor with the judge may involve political connections and outright bribery, whereby even an untenable suit can be delayed until the opponent is wearied into surrender. The father concedes that he has no alternative but to play this unsavory game. "Then shall I give myself, as it were, a prey to the lawyers, whose unsatiable jaws I am not able to feed . . . if I do not continually feed them, as the crow doth her brats, twenty times in an hour, they will begin to wax cold and to find cavils in my cause" (ll. 58-66). Cleander is the obvious choice to represent him, since Cleander is unscrupulous, is Erostrato's angry rival in love, and ironically enjoys a reputation as "one of the excellentest doctors in our city." This satire clarifies the reason for excluding law enforcement from the play's denouement. It is not that the issues are too trivial to be brought before a judge—Erostrato's father clearly feels that judging is called for—but that the machinery of law is decayed throughout. The elderly Damon similarly would hasten to the "potestates" with a complaint against the supposed Dulippo for seducing Damon's daughter, were it not that Damon would have to "publish mine own reproach to the world" (III, iii, 30). Satire of law is an integral part of *Supposes'* attack on nominally respectable authority. The joke is of course largely inbred for Inns of Court men, who were themselves training not so much for the legal profession as for courtly advancement.[24] As one of Gascoigne's marginalia comments, "Lawyers are never weary to get money" (V, v).

It is thus paradoxical, but fully credible, that the men who wrote or saw *Gorboduc* also delighted in *Supposes* and its superbly irreverent dismissal of the law. Asked what to do with his bolts and fetters of imprisonment (V, x, 44), Nevola is instructed: "Marry, I will tell thee, Nevola. To make a right end of our supposes, lay one of those bolts in the fire, and make thee a suppository as long as mine arm." The audience, in its final "suppose," is left to imagine what Nevola is then to do with the iron arm of justice.

In the later Elizabethan period, George Chapman and Ben Jonson are most notable for their efforts to "show an image of the times" by focusing Plautine types upon recognizable social groups of London and the court. Even in his plays for the public theater, Chapman explored the appeals of legal irresponsibility. *The Blind Beggar of Alexandria* (Admiral's men, 1596) is an irrepressible spoof of the Marlovian lower-class hero who rises to fantastic power.[25] Chapman's tone is one neither of orthodox disapprobation nor of Promethean incitement, but of wrily amused detachment. Irus the beggar, with his ingenious disguises, his bigamy, his slaying of the crown prince of Egypt, and his usurious subverting of the king's justice, outstrips the mighty Tamburlaine in his series of outrages upon respectable society. This popular travesty of themes treated elsewhere in drama with serious consideration (as, for example, in *The Merchant of Venice*) is conveyed throughout in an engagingly bantering spirit of *commedia dell' arte*.[26] *A Humorous Day's Mirth* (1597), also seemingly written for the Admiral's men (who frequently catered to Puritan-leaning tastes), is surprisingly and hedonistically irreverent in its view of Puritan "preciseness." Chapman predictably soon transferred his energies to the more congenial atmosphere of the newly reopened boys' theater. *Sir Giles Goosecap* (1601-1603), almost certainly his offering for the Chapel children,[27] studies the ideal love relationship of its ratiocinative and self-possessed hero and heroine. They are cultivated arbiters of good taste who require no external guidance and are themselves satiric judges of social presumption in other less gifted mortals.

Inevitably in Chapman's world of genteel intellectuals who fashion their own higher standards of morality, law officers cut a ridiculous figure. In *May-Day* (1601-1602?),[28] performed by the Chapel children, the venerable public official Lorenzo acts as ludicrous wooer rather than as judge. A "magnifico of the city, and one of the senate" (II, i, 395-

396), Lorenzo is enticed into the filthy disguise of a chimney sweep in order that he may defend the lady's reputation while he pursues an extramarital amour. (In Chapman's source, Piccolomini's *Alessandro,* the disguise is the less humiliating one of a locksmith.) [29] Social inversion is complete when the actual chimney sweep, Snail, is dressed as a magnifico to see how he will fare with the ladies (V, i). Lorenzo is fair game for the wits not because his affair is immoral, but because he is a respectable public man leading a life of hypocrisy. His brutish transformation is symbolic of his having renounced the benefits of a humanistic education: "an old senator, one that has read *Marcus Aurelius, Gesta Romanorum, The Mirror of Magistrates,* etc., to be led by the nose like a blind bear that has read nothing. Let [any] man read how he deserves to be baited" (III, i, 58-62). It is obvious that Lorenzo cannot find a remedy in the law he embodies, even though he rashly sends for a provost at one point and exclaims self-righteously, "justice cries out on't in the streets, and I will see it punished!" (IV, ii, 64-65).

All Fools (1599-1604) [30] embodies a device similar to that in Jonson's *Volpone* (1605-1606); the use of two plots, one conducted strictly according to the code of satirical exposure, the other committed to the process of law. In both plays, the contrast emphasizes the total inadequacy of legal machinery in coping with human failings, however grave they may be. Rinaldo's astute machinations to further the love matches of Fortunio and Valerio in defiance of over-careful fathers bring harm to no one, and fittingly invite the dictatorial old Gostanzo to gull himself. Valerio's plot to undo the suspicious husband Cornelio and to "turn his wife divorced loose" among the gallants of Florence, on the other hand, is sordidly commensurate with Cornelio's insane jealousy. This plot, unlike the Terentian intrigues of Rinaldo,[31] has no source in ancient Roman comedy, and is plainly indebted to contemporary observation for its acrid view of the law courts. Valerio has nothing but contempt for lawyers, and relishes an open brawl in which he puts down their "ravished declarations, replications, Rejoinders and petitions, all their books And writings torn and trod on" (II, i, 329-331). Accordingly, he views Cornelio's legalistic preparations for a formal divorce (IV, i) as an affront to gentlemanly behavior. Cornelio insists on publicity, making "a trumpet of your own horns"—a capital offense against the satirical code. He employs a notary and parchment, insisting that the wording be "strong in law," with "egress and regress in," all *"forma juris"* according to precedents in "Butiro and Caseo, in Butler and Cason's case, *decimo sexto* of Duke Anonimo." The language of the divorce document is fraught with the technical diction of "sundry weighty and mature considerations," "aforesaid," and repetitive lists such as "divide, disjoin, separate, remove, and finally eloign, sequester, and divorce" (IV, i, 283-315). The mockery of legal jargon here is pointedly different from the detailed and respectful police reporting of *A Warning for Fair Woman*. However much he has been goaded by his wife's behavior, Cornelio has chosen an opprobrious method of reprisal; and in penance he must reclaim his tarnished wife and listen to Valerio's concluding mock oration in praise of the horn. Chapman's purpose is not to glorify adultery as such, for the main plot offers a more wholesome alternative. Chapman seems serious, however, in regarding the law as a contemptible means of resolving marital strife.

The Gentleman Usher (ca. 1602-1604), at times closer to tragicomedy than satire, contains Chapman's most eloquent statement in comedy of the inadequacy of formal justice. Lacking Roman sources found in most of his other comedies, this play seems particularly expressive of Chapman's deeply held convictions. Like the later tragedies, it analyzes the origins of law and of monarchical power, and espouses a Homeric golden-age vision of the gentleman-philosopher who does not need to be forcibly restrained from evil as do ordinary sinners, and who is therefore a law unto himself.[32]

> And what's a prince? Had all been virtuous men,
> There never had been prince upon the earth,
> And so no subject; all men had been princes:
> A virtuous man is subject to no prince,
> But to his soul and honor, which are laws
> That carry fire and sword within themselves,
> Never corrupted, never out of rule.   (V, iv, 56-62)

Certain reservations are of course inescapable in accommodating this Homeric principle to the realities of modern life. The virtuous and self-governing man does not attempt to overthrow his prince, although he may (like Strozzo) teach the prince to renounce tyranny. Chapman is not in the least interested in defending political revolution in the usual sense. His definition of the "virtuous man" is patrician, and anathematizes popular unrest. Nevertheless, Chapman's doctrine is implicitly an assault on Tudor ideas of order as enunciated in the public theaters. His rarefied kindred spirits, conforming to their own gentlemanly concepts of morality, are entitled to perform deeds exceeding the reach of ordinary justice. As Bussy Dambois urges his king in a later play, "Let me be king myself (as man was made), And do a justice that exceeds the law." [33] Revenge may not be visited on a king, but it may otherwise be justifiable. Chapman's theory of freedom from social and political norms for the chosen few is in fact a restatement of the doctrine of the Renaissance gentleman, which had always tended to regard civil law as applicable only to those who lack the virtuous power of self-government.

Chapman's manner of selecting his chosen few is not based on aristocratic birth alone. Still, his spokesmen tend to represent the social as well as intellectual elite. Strozzo is a lord of the court; the seriously philosophical lovers Vincentio and Margaret are the children respectively of a duke and an earl. By contrast, the villain Medice is the embodiment of ungentlemanly behavior: a parvenu and enemy of learning whose gypsy childhood and lack of decent parentage merely prove to the offended aristocrats that blood will tell. So, too, the gentleman-usher Bassiolo is an absurd example of social pretentiousness, probably modeled on Shakespeare's Malvolio but viewed with a more studiously patrician condescension. In contrast to Shakespeare's forgiving Countess Olivia, Chapman's Vincentio deliberately baits a subordinate into disrespectful utterances toward the duke and uncouth familiarity toward the prince. It is at Vincentio's express invitation that the usher uses the name "Vince" and embraces his master. Bassiolo is not the humorless antagonist of below-stairs revelers like Sir Toby and Sir Andrew, but the object of exclusively aristocratic scorn. He lacks the instinct to refuse improper associations with his betters. His love advice to Vincentio, employed briefly for the sake of a jest, prompts Margaret to laugh incredulously, "What villainous stuff is here?" (IV, ii, 104). Bassiolo thus deserves no better than to be used callously by two members of the elite for their sport and convenience.

Chapman does not task this pair with hardheartedness. They are his models of true virtue, and possess within them the strength to supplant legal custom among ordinary men. Their view of marriage parallels that of obedience to a prince. Since they are forbidden to marry by the tyrant duke who represents justice in its normal imperfection, they will couple in a higher union.

> Are not the laws of God and Nature more
> Than formal laws of men? Are outward rites
> More virtuous than the very substance is
> Of holy nuptials solemnized within?
> Or shall laws made to curb the common world,
> That would not be contained in form without them,
> Hurt them that are a law unto themselves? (IV, ii, 134-140)

Their mutual vow, without witnesses, "is enough, and binds as much as marriage," enjoining them to sexual fidelity just as mutual agreement dictated their abstention from "untried nuptials" until this ritual moment. Higher morality of an unorthodox cast similarly prompts Strozzo to vow a pilgrimage on foot to Rome in celebration of his miraculous cure, not as a deed of Romish superstition but as "a right use." "No act is superstitious that applies All power to God, devoting hearts through eyes" (V, ii, 43-44). Chapman undertakes no defense of Catholicism as an international league potentially dangerous to English politics; dismissing such considerations, he asserts the right of his *übermensch* to transcend religious law as well as social. In the play's happy ending, which is more than a conventional untangling of romantic complications, Chapman's spokesmen have convinced the duke of the need for emancipation of the elite. The philosopher-gentleman is to be the ultimate arbiter of justice in Chapman's new society.

A recurring type in private drama after 1599 is the merry magistrate who prefers satirical exposure to the legal machinery of which he is nominal representative. One such instance is to be found in *Blurt Master-Constable* (Paul's boys before 1602),[34] featuring in its title figure an incompetent police officer obviously inspired by Shakespeare's Dogberry and anticipatory of Elbow but without their naive penchant for stumbling onto social correction. Blurt is totally ineffectual in razing his city's houses of prostitution; they remain standing with the duke's implied blessing, while the resourceful and ingratiating Madame Imperia flourishes as chief architect of the play's extra-legal solutions of conflict.

275

The genial duke never attempts to reform the police; instead, he applauds Imperia's witty discomfiture of the fops who frequent her house, and with tongue in cheek orders them to marry their whores for penance. Similarly, he approves Imperia's resolution of the love quarrels afflicting Fontinell and the kindred of Violetta, who have contentiously demanded rigorous legal punishment. The duke invites Imperia to a banquet in celebration of her ability to settle matters out of court. He is merely amused that she has hoodwinked the constabulary into making false arrests of her customers. To be sure, the duke will not condone violence in the streets, but he avoids harsh judicial pronouncements in dealing with the lesser follies of mankind.

The merry judge is something of a hallmark in Jonson's earlier comedies. Justice Preamble of *A Tale of a Tub* (ca. 1596-1597),[35] in partnership with an equally gay vicar, Sir Hugh, contrives a series of outlandish and illegal ruses to secure the hand in marriage of Audrey Turfe. Preamble's methods are clearly an abuse of his office, but are never regarded as such from the Saturnalian viewpoint of this comedy. His hapless victims, High Constable Tobias Turfe and other ingenuous pillars of the community, are, like Constable Blurt, subjected to unmitigated scorn. Preamble orders his own police officer to raise a hue and cry after the purported felon for a purely fictitious crime, and mockingly threatens the constable with every conceivable action at law when Turfe both loses track of his prisoner and fails to uncover the supposedly missing money. "Yes, I will have sir what the law will give me . . . your carelessness in the pursuit Argues your slackness and neglect of duty, Which ought be punished with severity" (IV, i, 45-50). Further warnings of court action, and of attendant frustrations and costly attorney's fees, blackmail Turfe into a forfeiture of one hundred pounds. Preamble not only sends his own police officer on a wild goose chase and countenances impersonation and perjury, but receives stolen goods. Small wonder that the citizens of Finsbury call the judge "Bramble" for his prickly approach to the law, and vow to "triumph Over this justice, as becomes a constable" (III, vi, 1-2). They are sensible of his contempt for "the incorrigible Knot-headed beast, the clowns, or constables" (I, v, 21-22). Ultimately all are looking for "a jest to twit the justice with" (IV, iii, 15). The justice and vicar, for their parts, are constantly having to concoct "another quaint devisèd drift," "such a

new and well-laid stratagem As never yet your ears did hear a finer"
(III, vii, 66-71). The law may be used as an instrument of wit, never
as a means of protecting the innocent.

The judge figure of *Every Man in His Humor* (1598) is less of a
rogue than Preamble, but is no less contemptuous of recourse to law
enforcement in dealing with men's foibles. Perhaps because Jonson was
writing at this time for a public company, he treats a public official
with admiration. Yet Clement is no ordinary magistrate. His role is
essentially extra-legal, both in the original quarto version and in the
Folio revision (1616) with its Anglicized setting.[36] He is the quixotic
resolver of strife, and despite his office he is bored and outraged by the
endless succession of lawsuits brought to his attention. Cob would enjoin
Bobadilla to keep the peace, by means of a written warrant. Bobadilla
and Matheo hope to prefer charges against Giuliano (Downright), Giuliano against Stephano for filching his coat, Thorello (Kitely) against
his wife and vice versa, Cob against his wife and vice versa, and old
Lorenzo (Knowell) against his son. Mere cowardice and not concern
for public safety prompts Bobadilla to plead a "warrant of the peace"
as his excuse for avoiding a manly duel. Such resorts to the law are an
affront to the gentlemanly code. Clement counsels, shames, and reconciles; his only sentences are mocking ones to frighten would-be litigants,
and the only penance he assigns (to the most incorrigible gulls) is to
mourn at the market cross in sackcloth and motley and "sing some
ballad of repentance very pitiously" (V, iii, 363-364). His renowned
calculated whimsy ("They say he will commit a man for taking the
wall of his horse") is not simple idiosyncrasy but satirical exaggeration,
for purging effect, of the lawsuits endlessly appearing before him as
judge. Clement is thus like the duke in the later *Blurt Master-Constable*,
a worthy public officer who is worthy precisely because he always avoids
legal process. He is a learned man and a satirist, ready to defend other
worthy practitioners of satire as the guardians of society (V, iii). He
differs from Jonson himself only in holding public office, and that office
is largely tangential to his practical function. Like any other satirist,
Clement varies his approach according to the subject, dealing calmly
with nearly sane men like old Lorenzo and using comic exposure solely
for the incorrigible. He countenances a series of legal impersonations
by the ingenious servant Musco (Brainworm), who, with his serving of

warrants and his mocking arrests, engineers a salubrious exposure of the costliness and acrimony of most legal process.

Clement's most nearly official action is to burn the plagiarized verse found in Matheo's pockets. Yet it is as guardian of true poets that Clement applies the torch, not as protector of the regime against seditious libel. The distinction is crucial, and looks forward to Jonson's attitude concerning the rights of artists under Elizabethan government. Jonson allows censorship only when conducted by an intellectual elite rather than by state power. Jonson minimizes Clement's official position to urge a very real control over social behavior by the man of learning. The Jonsonian hero is not merely an arbiter of taste, he is a leader obviating the necessity of institutional law. Chapman gives to his hero the freedom to be a law to himself; Jonson insists on an authority over all men that is non-institutional but still potent.

The difficulty with Justice Clement as a Jonsonian hero is that he is not typical. The genial judge is seemingly only a concession to public morality, and is not continued in Jonson's later plays. In *Every Man In,* Clement looks toward the same ends as his admiring friends Prospero and young Lorenzo. Later comedies tend increasingly to displace and ridicule the justice figure, leaving the operation of satirical exposure to genteel wits or to manipulators outside the law. The Avocatori of *Volpone* (1606) are fatuous and corrupt; their confusion of the issues and near punishment of Bonario and Celia contrast unhappily with Peregrine's smooth exposure of Sir Politic Would-Be in the subplot.[37] Voltore's machinations in the courtroom are an indictment of the process that must deal so arbitrarily and unsatisfactorily with the crimes of Volpone and Mosca. In *The Alchemist* (1610), performed after the King's men had acquired Blackfriars, Justice Clement has been supplanted as nemesis by Lovewit, gentlemanly connoisseur of sport. The unanswerable conflicts of public justice in *Volpone* are avoided by a private (and technically illegal) accounting. *Epicoene* (1609), in the friendly atmosphere of the private theaters, leaves all satirical punishment in the hands of Dauphine and his well-bred companions. *Bartholomew Fair* (1614) treats Justice Overdo to the ignominy of the public stocks, while the role of nemesis passes to his demented alter ego, Trouble-all. In Jonson's final vision, law enforcement is nothing other than madness.

The exploration of these satirical attitudes toward law inevitably produced a misunderstanding between spokesmen for public and private theaters. However much the so-called "War of the Theaters" or Poetomachia has been blown out of proportion by its historians to include almost every living writer at the turn of the century,[38] the issues of the exchange were substantive. The personal animosities that flared briefly in Marston and Dekker's *Satiromastix* and in Jonson's *The Poetaster* were quickly smoothed over. Yet even in these two focal plays of the outburst, the authors were committed to propositions far more essential than the fleeting notoriety of a name-calling contest. Nor do the purely commercial aspects of a theatrical rivalry explain away the basic dividing issue of the proper role of satire in a commonwealth shaken by religious and dynastic uncertainties. To what extent is the satirical exposure of public officialdom consistent with the preservation of civil order? Jonson saw the argument in terms of art's public responsibility, and created in his "comical satires"[39] a series of idealized poet figures whose virtues represent not so much Jonson's vain appraisal of himself as his conception of the free intellectual critic. His main opponent, Dekker, answered in much the same terms as Thomas Heywood and other public moralists, attacking Jonson as an abettor of those who would inveigh against "Court, city, country." (Marston probably had little to do with the writing of *Satiromastix*, though he encouraged the project.)[40] The debate was real enough, a sudden eruption of uneasy feeling that had existed even in the days of the Marprelate controversy around 1590, and was reawakened in 1599 by Archbishop Whitgift's actions against satirical verses and by the reopening of the boys' theater. Our purpose here is to survey briefly the events leading up to and including the Poetomachia, not in terms of personal rivalry but in the context of the poet and the state.

Marston's frontal assault on the public companies in *Histriomastix or the Player Whipped* (Paul's boys before 1600) reveals his essential agreement with the position of Jonson despite their occasional quarreling. Marston rejects the argument of public dramatists that they are the chief defenders of hierarchy and law. Sir Oliver Owlet's public actors, and their scribbler Posthaste, are symptomatic of a profound social decay affecting the entire nation. Their vapid popular entertainment contributes, in Marston's exaggerated view, to class conflict, civil rebellion, foreign invasion, Poverty, Famine, Sickness, Bondage, and Sluttishness.

Because they consume the largess of well-to-do patrons, worthy poets must go begging. The players whet popular appetites for war and social inversion. Even the satiric philosopher Chrisoganus is blighted by the enervation and moral decay. He becomes, in response to the social abnormality of the time, an unattractive railer and tedious pedant whose rancor has ulcerated his scholarly genius.[41] Yet his venom is justly provoked, and does not gainsay the accuracy of his bleak vision. The choice between his leadership and that of Posthaste is of profound consequence to England's upper-class society. Marston in fact consciously revives the outmoded morality play, with its soul struggle, to dramatize the spiritual seriousness of the choice. Several critics have supposed that Marston revised an old play perhaps reflecting the rivalry of poets and actors in which Robert Greene took so active a part; [42] even if so, the morality plot is consistent with Marston's theme. Equally unnecessary and inconclusive are hypotheses that Posthaste represents Anthony Munday or Shakespeare, and that Chrisoganus is Jonson or Marston himself.[43] The two figures are social types, in company with abstractions such as Peace, Plenty, and Pride, and are contestants for the very soul of England. Chrisoganus, with all his crabbed flaws, is the virtuous counselor who eventually guides his wayward charges to penance and restoration. The tempter is at last driven off to perdition: Sir Oliver's men are finally exposed as cowards, tax evaders, and keepers of punks, and are hounded back to the menial trades from which they had so rebelliously erupted.

Jonson's growing hostility toward public values is scarcely less concealed in his *Every Man out of His Humor* (Chamberlain's, 1599), despite its having been written for a public company. In place of the jovial Clement in *Every Man In,* Jonson chooses as nemesis a railing satirist. Asper represents Jonson's ideal of the dispassionate critic, but Asper is too free from rancor for the evil times in which he finds himself. He must adopt the mask of Macilente, sadistically discomfiting those he envies.[44] His milieu is the "Fortunate Isle," a mocking reference to Erasmus' land of fools and folly.[45] As the depraved and unsavory scourge who must accomplish the satirist's ends, Macilente goes beyond Clement in his extra-legal manipulation of the law. He taunts the uxorious London citizen Deliro and his socially aspiring wife Fallace (who is enamored of the fashion-mongering courtier Fastidious Brisk) by encouraging these gulls to seek actions of law against one another—not to confirm public decency but contrarily as a means of inflaming the class conflict inherent in the affair. Similarly he tricks the witless constabulary into falsely arresting the parvenu Fungoso, in order to teach this innocent the folly of his social climbing. Macilente's handling of the fatuous wagers of Puntarvolo (IV, iii) is a parody of legal machinery involving a notary, indentures, and endless provisos. As in *Blurt Master-Constable* or Chapman's *All Fools*, legal duress is a weapon ingeniously employed by the satirist to award satiric penalties according to a code of poetic justice. The law repeatedly accosts the wrong man, but satire is served. Jonson's hypocritical London types, especially the uxorious citizen and his ambitious, adulterous wife, set a fashion for later private drama in its baiting of the bourgeoisie.[46] All of this in a merry spirit of misrule is admirably suited for Inns of Court readers (to whom the play was later dedicated).

Like Chrisoganus, Macilente is exalted to a position of moral judge by default of the nation's political leadership. Macilente flatteringly bestows on Elizabeth (in a court version of the play) the supreme power of quelling envy and dissimulation, but only as a flowery gesture to signify what Macilente has already accomplished in his own right as satirist. He is the guardian of her realm, displacing public and collective forms of authority. The witty chorus figures of *Every Man Out*, Cordatus and Mitis, are constantly aware of the play's controversial nature —perhaps in recollection of the government's crackdown on satirists only a few weeks before the play was performed.[47] Cordatus and Mitis view the play as experimental, and justifiably wonder on several occasions if Jonson's outspokenness will not offend his popular audience.

Jonson's transfer to the private theater in *Cynthia's Revels, or The Fountain of Self-Love* (Chapel children, 1600-1601) provided the opportunity for an even more defiant attack on "popular applause, Or foamy praise that drops from common jaws," and a corresponding elevation of the role of the laureate satirist at court. Even if his hero Crites (or Criticus) is not exclusively a self-portrait, the equation was close enough to invite disapproving comparison by Jonson's contemporaries. The idealized role of intellectual counselor and writer of masques for Queen Cynthia (obviously Elizabeth) is one to which Jonson himself aspired. Accordingly, the moral authority granted Crites is ominous. At the stern behest of the gods, he must scourge the court of folly. He is fearsome,

Olympian, calmly indifferent to the slanders heaped upon him by envious men. He does not ask for legal power, which he considers ineffective in any case. As the conscience of the English court, he will be something much greater than a lawmaker; for the court is the source of all lasting wisdom, and its spokesman enjoys a leadership second only to the queen's.

Crites is indeed the exponent of divine harmony among men. In his masque, the factious persons of the court must learn to move in sympathy. At Cynthia's express command, Crites is to become the godlike ordainer of pattern, "as Hermes' wand Charms the disorders of tumultuous ghosts, And as the strife of Chaos then did cease When better light than Nature's did arrive" (V, v, 15-18). The masque is, like Jonson's later presentations for King James, no transitory device or exercise in flattery but a serious contribution to the schooling of princes.[48] Its genre is akin to classical tragedy, which, as Sidney argued, "maketh kings fear to be tyrants." Failure to reconcile the warring elements at court would be to leave England without direction from its political head. "For, in troth, not so T'incorporate them could be nothing else Than like a state ungoverned, without laws, Or body made of nothing but diseases" (V, v, 28-31). It is in accord with this exalted poetic credo that Cynthia's courtiers must be induced to abandon their vapid parlor games of "substantives and adjectives" (IV, iii) and recognize that court entertainment contains the soul of a nation's greatness. Even Cynthia must be chastised, albeit indirectly through mythological guise, for her unintentional countenancing of dissipation. The maligners have crept in "in this licentious time, against her knowledge; and, like so many meteors, will vanish when she appears" (II, iv, 110-111). Still, it is Crites who alerts her to the danger, and so deserves to be her agent of reform. He is deputized to "Impose what pains you please; Th' incurable cut off, the rest reform" (V, xi, 96-97). Crites is plainly worthy of such authority: temperate, judicious, truly learned without affectation, valorous but offering no injury, indifferent to fortune. Arete commends Crites to Cynthia "Without hyperbole" as one "studious of deserving well, And, to speak truth, indeed deserving well" (V, vi, 84-86). Whether Jonson implicitly applies this praise to himself is less to the point here than his abstract conception of the laureate's role. Such a man is clearly England's greatest hope and the chief support of her queen.

Jonson was evidently not guilty of attacking Marston and Dekker personally in *Cynthia's Revels;* he did not start the naming of names.[49] The affront that provoked *Satiromastix* was more essential than that of personal animosity. Jonson had asserted positions that both men found intolerable. If they overlooked Jonson's higher purpose of defending the civilizing power of art, they nevertheless answered less as wronged individuals than as spokesmen for London citizens and for courtly society. Appropriately, then, *Satiromastix, or the Untrussing of the Humorous Poet* (Chamberlain's and Paul's, 1600) was a rejoinder from both public and private stages. Marston reacted more perhaps as a fellow satirist appalled by the claims of sole supremacy as court laureate, and by the license given Jonson's invincible Crites to punish his enemies. Elsewhere, in *Jack Drum's Entertainment* (1599-1600) and *What You Will* (ca. 1601), Marston caricatured self-appointed literary dictators breezily dismissing the merits of all competitors and attacking the innocent hedonism of the court.[50] Whether or not these vignettes contributed directly to the Poetomachia is a matter of dispute,[51] but they establish clearly enough Marston's viewpoint in the sponsorship of *Satiromastix*. Marston would want to rub in the fact that Horace's (Jonson's) plays had been misliked at court, and would delight in snubbing Jonson as an upstart. His sophisticated attitude prevails too in that *Satiromastix* fights fire with fire, dealing with Jonson according to his own satiric code of exposure.

Yet certain basic attitudes are those of the public companies. Crispinus and his journeyman dramatist Demetrius are proud of their standing as professional writers. Although they unseat Horace, they are not so presumptuous as to take his place of unwarranted authority over the court. They act not vengefully or privately but as rescuers of the court from one who would subvert its prerogatives. Wherever the satiric references to Jonson are most specific, they attack him for his superciliousness toward the London public. Horace quotes himself, for instance, in a passage from the prologue to *Cynthia's Revels:* "But to the vulgar and adulterate brain, Should loath to prostitute our virgin strain" (II, ii, 58-59). What to Jonson is a defense of his higher purpose in art is to Dekker mere pretentious snobbery, along with the self-glorifying cant of muses, prophecy, and inspiration. Jonson's view of himself as a dangerous man with many enemies is parodied into bullying and paranoia. Horace is ridiculous because he presumes, with divine sanction (a blasphemy in Dekker's view), to act as arbiter of public morality, to set himself up as judge and thereby supplant all who would judge in his stead. Horace puts on himself "The office of an executioner, Only to strike off the swolne head of sin Where ere you find it standing." He is guilty of covert libeling: "your dastard wit will strike at men In corners and in riddles fold the vices Of your best friends." Unoffending men, whether "A gentleman, or an honest citizen" (IV, ii, 52), must live in fear of having their private lives "satired and epigrammed upon" in such plays as "*Every Gentleman out on's Humor*." Horace places himself above all segments of society and none must reply. "Court, city, country, friends, Foes, all must smart alike; yet court, nor city, Nor foe, nor friend, dare winch at you; great pity" (I, ii, 219-237). No offense is too petty, or too heinous, to escape his purview.

Dekker insists that he is not apologizing for lawlessness in attacking this self-proclaimed moralist. The sympathetic Demetrius pointedly defines law as "Our kingdom's golden chain," and he castigates Horace's usurpation of that institution (I, ii, 239). So too does Tucca in justifying his opposition to Horace's writings.

> I'll tell thee why, because th'ast entered actions of assault and battery against a company of honorable and worshipful fathers of the law. You wrangling rascal, law is one of the pillars a'th land, and if thou beest bound to't (as I hope thou shalt be), thou't prove a skip-Jack, thou't be whipped . . . I'll tell thee why, because thou cryest ptrooh at worshipful citizens, and call'st them flat-caps, cuckolds, and bankrupts, and modest and virtuous wives punks and cockatrices. I'll tell thee why, because th'ast arraigned two poets against all law and conscience; and not content with that, hast turned them amongst a company of horrible black friars.   (IV, iii, 184-199)

Such undermining of the integrity of magistrates and ordinary citizens promotes disobedience and class hatred, and is best answered by institutional reproof. Art may of course comment on matters of public interest, but may not supplant law itself.

The exposing of Jonson's purported theory of the dictatorial power of art leads Dekker into the question of Jonson's personal motive for such claims. The answer is not flattering. Horace is viewed as a social climber whose origins, like Jonson's, include those of bricklaying and public acting.[52] Crispinus and Demetrius plan to bring Horace's "life and death upon'th stage like a bricklayer in a play" (I, ii, 138-139). The emphasis on this repeated detail seems vindictive; yet it is relevant to Dekker's larger theme, and does not necessarily look down on brick-laying even though it does look down on Jonson. The idiosyncratic Welsh-man Sir Vaughan ap Rees, for instance, queries Horace: "how chance it passes, that you bid God boygh to an honest trade of building symneys, and laying down bricks, for a worse handicraftness, to make nothing but rails?" (IV, iii, 156-159). The implication is that a decently-born Lon-doner, of proud calling, has been disloyal to his own people and disrup-tive of orderly hierarchy. The condescension toward bricklaying is Horace's own. Similarly, the references to Jonson's having killed a fellow player in a duel (IV, ii, 61-62; IV, iii, 105) suggest that one who has arrogantly displayed his own contempt for law enforcement ought not to offer his own rule of authority in continued defiance of public responsi-bility.

Forewarned of *Satiromastix*, Jonson managed with unusual speed to anticipate his critics in *The Poetaster, or His Arraignment* (Chapel, 1601). Since they offered personal satire, he felt justified in lampooning them directly. The verses of Crispinus and Demetrius are obviously in-tended for Marston and Dekker.[53] Jonson later told Drummond that he directed his *Poetaster* against Marston. All recent critics agree, however, that Jonson's interest in individual satire is only peripheral. He explores a far more serious charge against his detractors: that they are conspiring to muzzle free artistic expression.[54] From base motives of commercialism, envy, and ignorance, the common players and even some sophisticated writers are in cynical league with an oppressive governmental bureauc-racy to enforce conformity. Jonson's answer goes to the heart of the political issue, for he interprets the "orthodoxy" of the public theater as mere toadying to the administration. Even the monarch, he claims, has been deceived by this campaign of censorship parading in the guise of respect for public order. The respectability is only a sham, for although the common players pretend to avoid "humors, revels, and satires, that gird and fart at the time," they specialize in obscenity and hence con-tribute to moral decay. As one player explains, the satirists "are on the other side of Tiber"—that is, in the private theaters of the city. Bank-side actors "have as much ribaldry in our plays as can be, as you would wish, captain; all the sinners i' the suburbs come and applaud our action daily" (III, iv, 190-196). Furthermore, they are ready to slander poets like Horace for financial profit. "O, it will get us a huge deal of money, captain, and we have need on't; for this winter has made us all poorer than so many starved snakes" (III, iv, 327-329). Their reasons for collaborating with the government are craven, not public-spirited.

The government, for its part, is convulsed by hysterical fears of sedition. Asinius Lupus, a magistrate with the self-imposed crusade of protecting national security, is a new and sinister type in Jonson's satirical comedies. Unlike the dilettante courtiers of *Cynthia's Revels*, he is an administrative official whose legal power must be challenged directly by the satirist. As an old foe of the drama, Lupus retails the very charges being prepared by Dekker, Heywood, and other public moralists. Disruptive players, he warns, "will rob us, that are magistrates, of our respect, bring us upon their stages, and make us ridiculous to the plebeians" (I, ii, 40-41). He countenances an alliance with the public players not out of any genuine fondness but because their vindictiveness toward Horace and their financial need happen to play into Lupus' hands. Jonson's chief purpose in *The Poetaster* is to expose and punish the hypocrisy of such officious busybodies who "vomit forth Their own prodigious malice; and pretending To be the props and columns of [the prince's] safety, The guards unto his person and his peace, Disturb it most, with their false, lapwing cries" (IV, vii, 49-53).

Jonson's *Aeropagitica* was heartfelt. His own challenges to political authority were to result in the suppression of *The Devil Is an Ass* and of the prologue to *The Poetaster*. He was later in trouble with the Privy Council for *Sejanus* and for *Eastward Ho*. Accordingly, the banishment of Ovid dramatizes Jonson's ridicule of censorship and its fatuous misunderstanding of art's true purpose. Ovid is suitably contemptuous of the law to which his father would apprentice him. Whatever his fleshly limitations when compared with Virgil and Horace, Ovid is not a satirical type but a martyr. Less sympathetic interpretations of Ovid's banishment were current in the Renaissance; Jonson's defense is one of conscious choice.[55] Ovid's masque is utterly nonpolitical, but Lupus and the spying player Histrio twist its meaning into treason and blasphemy. To Horace and Mecaenas [sic], Lupus' exposure of a "dangerous plot" is a bitter farce, a wolfish preying on "the life of innocent mirth And harmless pleasures, bred of noble wit" (IV, vii, 48-49). Ovid's banishment is a warning of what intelligent artists may expect from a court grown too powerful in silencing free expression, and from a public theater anxious to suppress competition by whatever means necessary.

Caesar's part in countenancing the banishment is not a glorious one, and his failure must serve as a warning to all rulers faced with a similar choice. "Princes that will but hear, or give access To such officious spies, can ne'er be safe. They take in poison with an open ear, And, free from danger, become slaves to fear" (IV, vii, 64-67). Jonson's fable does not accuse Elizabeth of wrongdoing, but it bids her be on her guard. The ideal prince is like the reformed Caesar of the play's ending, who eloquently greets poesy as the prime source of Rome's greatness, showers praise on Horace's "free and wholesome sharpness," and listens in rapt attention to Virgil's recital from the *Aeneid*. Such friendship "pleaseth Caesar more than servile fawns" (V, i, 95). These men typify their exalted calling, in Elizabethan England as in Rome, and need not portray living poets of Jonson's time.[56] Horace is closest to Jonson in the context of the Poetomachia, but Virgil and Ovid too in their varying ways defend Jonson's concept of the artist in the state.

As in *Cynthia's Revels,* the true prince not only supports great artists but yields to them decisive power in punishing offenders close to the throne. Caesar is not to be fooled a second time by Lupus and his base informant Aesop, who as a public actor has brought to light another purported conspiracy against Caesar.[57] Lupus' tactics are even more outrageous than before: he has filched documents from Horace's house and has distorted them into perverse political meaning by "The senseless rigor of the wrested laws, Or the red eyes of strained authority" (V, iii, 66-67). With grasping motive he hopes to share the forfeiture of Horace's lands. For such presumption, the informant player is to be whipped, and Lupus fitted with a pair of ass's ears. The right of satire to examine large questions of state, in a spirit of "wholesome sharp morality," is upheld. Caesar asks Horace and his friends to act as his scourges. Jonson has thus triumphed over an authority representing the Privy Council itself. He will not of course become a magistrate in Lupus' stead. Jonson is a social conservative, defending the ideal of courtly society and interesting himself but little in economic problems. In fact his very contempt for law is patrician in viewpoint; distrusting systems, he refuses to consider ways of altering institutions of government because those institutions can never hope to ameliorate the human condition. The artist will always be a more effective guide than the politician. It is in the name of learning that Jonson demands the role of moral dictator.

Perhaps the most sobering topical lesson to be drawn from the Poetomachia is the evidence of misunderstanding and rigidity on all sides. Personal rivalries passed quickly, but the underlying issues were not so easily reconciled. Despite Jonson's eloquent defense of poetry as a moral art, his own superciliousness toward citizenry and court served merely to increase the artist's estrangement from the society he would guide. As protest became more and more equated with lawlessness in the public mind, the sophisticated poet gravitated to hostility and exile. A graphic appraisal of this extremist trend is to be found in the anonymous *Parnassus* trilogy (1598-1601), written and performed at St. John's College, Cambridge. Its student heroes find themselves increasingly alienated from the law, pursued by officers, and evicted from gainful employment in the professions and the public theaters. On the one hand, citizen culture demands of them an inflexible set of attitudes including hostility to Spain and the Catholic Church, automatic respect for minor law-enforcement officials and the trades, and literature devoid of "that writer Ovid, and that writer *Metamorphoses*." On the other hand, well-to-do patrons promote only "safe" university men who cravenly acquiesce in the patron's warning "to abstain from controversies; secondly, not to gird at men of worship, such as myself, but to use your wit discreetly" (*2 Return*, ll. 1137-1139). Respectable men "hate a scholar because he decries your ass's ears" (ll. 1655-1656). Accordingly, the University Wits are left ultimately with no recourse but to rant at all respectability in their colorful billingsgate and retreat to the impoverished contentment of country life. Their impotent defiance has no curative value; it is a massive venting of spleen, a telling-off of officialdom by disenfranchised, fugitive men. Leading as it does to no triumph other than verbal, the volley of epithets appeals exclusively to a violently anti-authoritarian sense of released resentment. The ending is more world-weary than Jonson's angry assertion of the need for intellectual supremacy. In *Parnassus*, the battle has been relinquished. Entrenched privilege is an unassailable fort, law enforcement a weapon of extortion to be used by the fortunate few. Plebeian culture is as rigid in its own dogmatism as that of the elite, and the gap between the two cultures can no longer be bridged. Decay and conflict are inevitable. The satirist is no longer a health-giving critic of society, but an embattled stranger.

Elizabeth's last years were characterized by a sense of foreboding. The optimism of rising social and economic expectations among a fortunate minority of Londoners was tempered by a growing mood of imminent confrontation and impasse. The queen's great compromise, tenuously holding political and religious forces in check by a dynamic balancing of opposites, seemed on the verge of dissolution.[1] Puritan leaders in Parliament, repressed by the perennially suspicious Archbishop Whitgift, were frustrated by the retrograde movement of the reformation they so ardently desired to complete. Under James, they would soon renew their strident demands for religious freedom at the Hampton Court Conference, only to be answered with the famous rebuff: "No bishop, no king." In foreign affairs, France's peace with Spain in 1597 compelled the English court to consider following suit, to the vocal dismay of the militantly Protestant war party. Extremists of Catholic and Puritan persuasion gravitated to Essex, who was dickering with James concerning the succession. Elizabeth was continually harassed by the earl's feuding with the Cecils and the Lord Admiral, his foolhardy expedition to Ireland in 1599 ending in the appeasement of Tyrone, and his desperate thoughts of a sudden return to purge the queen of "her enemies." Although the city would not rise with Essex in 1601, it continued to applaud his anti-Spanish attitudes to the last. The actors were generally his friends, and gave the administration plausible grounds for worrying about propagandizing in the drama. Essex himself acknowledged that as the focus of war sentiment and disaffection he was an inevitable subject for the stage.[2]

To a dispassionate theater-goer around the year 1600, it must have seemed as though the English Reformation, and the long years of Elizabeth's reign, had settled nothing. Discussions of royal succession, obedience to authority, the efficacy of public justice, and the dangers of religious civil war were central to most plays one could see, public or private. War plays whetted popular appetites for a hysterical hatred of foreigners and stay-at-home politicians, as in post-Armada jingoistic drama. Shakespeare's *Henry V*, to be sure, struck a note of patriotism without undue vindictiveness. If, as seems plausible, he offered praise of "the general of our gracious emperess . . . from Ireland coming" (Prologue to Act V) to Lord Mountjoy rather than to Essex,[3] Shakespeare bypassed a malcontent for one who had abstained from sedition and had gone on to genuine triumphs against the Irish. Shakespeare's humorous exasperation with Irish, Scottish, and Welsh types in *Henry V* does not conceal his admiration for a British union transcending proud local customs.[4] The lost *England's Joy* (1602 at the Swan) was evidently also generous in its praise of Mountjoy's temperate but firm stance in Ireland and the Netherlands.[5] *The Trial of Chivalry* (Derby's, 1599-1600) looks forward approvingly to an end of the civil wars in France. Yet even these comparatively moderate plays supported continued military action in Ireland and on the continent.

More representative of Essex's extremist support, although the earl's name is never mentioned, is *A Larum for London, or the Siege of Antwerp*. Entered in the Stationer's Register in 1600 "provided that it be not printed without further authority," it finally appeared in quarto in 1602. The authorities had good reason to be uneasy about the play while Essex was still alive. Like *The Massacre at Paris* it is based on raw pamphlet and ballad accounts of a continental atrocity against Protestants, with open warnings to London of a similar fate.[6] Once again the Enemy are everywhere, and easily exploit the craven effeminacy and appeasing tactics of the city's burgesses. Military preparedness has been neglected: the heroic professional soldier has been fobbed off with little pay and less recognition. Now he savagely greets the sack of modern Babylon as the welcome vengeance of the Almighty. No vision of worldly regeneration is possible. The play's victimized spokesman epitomizes the alliance between the Puritan extremist and the professional soldier, both armed in God's name against the Catholic international menace, the corruptions of peace, and the mercantile bureaucracy of London. The alliance was a dangerous one, ready to applaud Essex's crusade in Ireland or his call to action in the city.

Similarly, the anonymous manuscript *Edmond Ironside* (ca. 1590-1600) appears to have offended the censor because of its analogous theme of Catholic betrayal at court permitting successful invasion of England (ll. 377-380), and its glorification of the military leader who is a friend of the poor and the common soldier.[7] *The Life and Death of Thomas Stukeley*, to which Heywood may have contributed, is an updating (ca. 1599) of earlier dramatic accounts of the title figure, probably to commemorate the exploits of Essex. When the Irish rebels are defeated and the bloody head of O'Neill is sent "To that most noble English deputy That ministers justice as he were a god, And guerdons virtue like a liberal king" (ll. 1257-1259), London audiences would no doubt equate this deputy with their favorite.[8] Outspoken defiance of the Spanish in Ireland and Portugal would thus offer a timely rebuke in 1599 to England's peacemongers. Popular dramatists might show some relenting toward the French during these years, but they were adamant toward Spain; in *The Weakest Goeth to the Wall* (Oxford's boys, ca. 1599-1600), Spanish conspiracy is a deplorable threat to France as to other civilized countries. Chauvinism was also staple in the anti-foreign humor of popular plays, as for instance in *Englishmen for My Money* and *Grim the Collier of Croydon* (Admiral's, 1598 and 1600).

Especially unsettling during the first years of the seventeenth century is the tendency of normally moderate dramatists to abandon their middle course. Dekker, for example, reveals an increasing hostility toward both Catholic and Puritan dangers under the stresses of extremist sentiment. A genial man, he did not readily adopt Jonson's asperity in caricaturing speech patterns of the Puritans. His portrait of Margery Eyre in *The Shoemakers' Holiday* (Admiral's, 1599) is sympathetic if humorous, and is akin to his amused tolerance of immigrant Dutch laborers in London. Even though he supports patriotic war against the French, Dekker "does not claim all virtues exclusively for England." [9] Similarly, in his early plays he eschews inflammatory sentiments; a seeming reference in *Old Fortunatus* (1601) to Essex, flying like Daedalus "against the sun of majesty," was perhaps only a fortuitous allusion, excised by a prudent stationer after the event of rebellion had demanded special caution.[10] Dekker remained a conservative social critic, believing in law, social degree, and the Anglican church. His *Whore of Babylon* (ca. 1605), an account of Elizabeth's reign, genuinely admires her policies and leadership. Yet, under the pressure of growing antagonisms, the play is virulently anti-Catholic. Dekker's anger at Puritan separatists, in *If This Be Not a Good Play, the Devil Is In It*, is no less forthright.[11] Extremism calls forth bitter denunciation from the center, adding to the sense of crisis and misunderstanding. The threat to the moderate position is so galling that the moderate himself is tempted into radical means to gain his conservative ends.

This disturbing trend toward extremism is perhaps most evident in *The Famous History of Sir Thomas Wyatt* (1602), written by a team of writers probably including Dekker, Webster, Heywood, and Chettle.[12] Wyatt's noble rebellion against the threat of Spanish rule could scarcely avoid topical application in 1600-1602. The Essex faction openly accused Cecil, Cobham, Ralegh, and others of preparing for an actual landing on English shores of the Spanish Infanta. This danger was the critical issue of the hour, and had to be answered. Whether the play also objects by extension to other foreign princes such as the Protestant James of Scotland, and urges the native "Suffolk claim," is debatable; the primary issue is that of Spanish succession.[13] On this score, however, the response is radical. A Spanish claimant is to be rejected by whatever means necessary. In this sole extreme, passive resistance must yield to justified violence.

Sir Thomas Wyatt is an unwilling rebel. He makes no objection to Mary Tudor's Catholic faith because she is the legal heir to the throne, and he in fact carries the day against the Dukes of Northumberland and Suffolk who would supplant Mary with the Protestant Lady Jane Grey and her husband. He sympathizes with the patriotic motives of the dukes and pities the innocent Jane, but honors his sacred oath to

Henry "to maintain his seed" (I, vi, 69-73). The issue is one of primo-geniture and orderly succession. The turning point, however, is Mary's marriage to Philip of Spain. Whatever Mary's motives, Philip's are clearly those of territorial ambition. Wyatt concedes that Henry VIII negotiated marriages with children of neighboring princes, but not when the throne of England itself might pass to a foreign king. The distinction justifies Wyatt in mustering the men of Kent, not against their sovereign but against Spanish invasion and slavery. When royal opposition forces him to turn against English troops and against London, Wyatt reluctantly accepts the challenge as a "true friend" of England. Unlike the rebels of 2 *Henry VI* or *Jack Straw*, Wyatt's rebels are reasonable at all times. They remain fixed in their single objection to Spanish rule. Even at his death, Wyatt is anti-Spanish and no more. "But now King Philip enters through my blood" (V, ii, 37). This lack of revolutionary fervor makes him totally acceptable as the play's hero and martyr. Yet Wyatt, as a commoner, has presumed to tell the throne exactly how far it may go in foreign entanglements. A native Catholic monarch may be endured, but a foreign Catholic must not. Furthermore, this people's leader defies the police-state authority of treasonable counselors who turn monarchs' whims to their own advantage. The hated name of Gardiner, Catholic Bishop of Winchester, embodies the institutional power of the episcopacy that hunts the Protestants Wyatt, Lady Jane, and Guildford to their unjust deaths.

Similarly, *Thomas Lord Cromwell* (ca. 1597-1602), written perhaps for the Chamberlain's men in response to the Admiral's *Oldcastle* plays, glorifies the cause of religious reform with none of *Oldcastle's* orthodox warnings against Puritan excess (see Chapter 16). The title figure is beloved by the commons and the king, though hated by most of the corrupt aristocracy, and is executed only because King Henry's pardon fails to arrive in time. This biased interpretation of Cromwell as a hero of the reformers, for daring to cross Bishop Gardiner on the confiscation of abbey lands, was accessible in Foxe's *Acts and Monuments*. Further-more, Cromwell's grandson (also named Thomas Cromwell) had been a staunch defender of Puritanism in Parliament from 1571 to 1589. *Cromwell* is thought by some critics to have been an Essex play, chiefly on the grounds that Cromwell himself had received the earldom of Essex and had been supported by Southampton's grandfather. The play does not mention these facts, but the association of the earldom with Cromwell was evidently commonplace in radical circles; as late as 1647, it was noted by the Levelers.[14] Although the analogy to Essex is perhaps only coincidental, Cromwell is himself the foe of Catholic conspiracy at court and hence an appealing figure for the more daring reformers of the early 1600's.

As in the Armada years, popular sentiment feared that much of the court was drifting back toward religious conservatism or outright Catholicism. Indeed, as courtly drama withdrew into its own precincts, it afforded a haven for heterodox religious belief that could not be tolerated publicly. Ben Jonson became a Catholic, and although he never defended his religion in the drama he grew increasingly sarcastic about Puritanism. Chapman spoke openly in defense of pilgrimages to Rome (*The Gentleman Usher*) and later praised the characters of the Duke of Guise and Philip of Spain.[15] William Percy's *The Cuck-Queans and Cuckolds Errant* (1601), seemingly privately acted, manages to be flippant even about the threat of a Spanish invasion of English shores, regarding one side as being as benighted as the other: "If you be taken by Spaniards, you shall show them your Lady Matins; if by the English, you shall produce them your Geneva Psalms" (IV, x). If a version of *The Noble Spanish Soldier* was acted before 1603,[16] its sympathetic treatment of the role of the Catholic Church (including the monastic establishment) in defying royal tyranny would have argued the right of Catholic free speech and protest short of armed rebellion—the position of the so-called English Catholic "Appellants" in their answer to Robert Parsons' endorsement of the Spanish succession. The moderate center was on the defensive and losing ground.

For their part the Puritans, hampered by censorship and denied a voice, were falling away to the left. The great London public was reluctant to abandon the theater as a forum in which to express its political and religious aspirations, but accommodation with playwrights like Jonson and Chapman seemed no longer possible. Such a reformer as Munday, who still clung to the public stage as an outlet for his moderate but Puritan-leaning views (as in *Sir John Oldcastle* and *Sir Thomas More*), was about to retire from the scene.[17] Even the comparatively early *A Knack to Know an Honest Man* (Admiral's, late 1594), written seemingly in response to the anti-Puritan *A Knack to Know a*

Knave, appeals to ideas of conscience above law and of retreat from the norms of decadent society. The play's heroes are "honest men" who place virtue above loyalty to the state and so act unilaterally against moral crime when the prince proves negligent. Forced to operate outside the law, they justify their deeds by an appeal to Christian divine law rather than to revenge codes of honor.

Perhaps the Admiral's men's most ambitious efforts to give sympathetic expression to the Puritan viewpoint are to be found in their popular Robin Hood series, 1598-1601: *The Downfall of Robert Earl of Huntingdon, The Death of Robert Earl of Huntingdon,* and *Look About You.* Like that of Cromwell, the name of Huntingdon had compelling topical associations for the English elect: the third Earl of Huntingdon had been, as a candidate for succession to the throne during the 1560's, the hope of many ardent Protestants fearful of Elizabeth's untimely death, and his brothers had served the Puritan cause in Parliament throughout the reign.[18] The plays were a collaborative effort, involving Chettle and perhaps Wadeson and Dekker, but the serious conception of the first play is the work of Munday. The plethora of plot and humorous incident, especially in the disguise motif of *Look About You,* is illustrative of the kind of innocuous and old-fashioned horseplay with which the Admiral's men hoped to avoid giving offense. The drama, the authors suggest, can still be jolly, innocent fun devoid of spleen or scabrousness.

Munday's first play, however, speaks more forcefully to the conditions of a people who were on the verge of quitting the theaters. *Downfall* is his urgent attempt to justify, in the legend of Robin Hood, the resistance to oppressive authority of a misunderstood people. His didactic intention self-proclaimedly transcends mere entertainment, and will not be content with "pleasant skippings up and down the wood." The theme is political and religious injustice: "Our play expresses noble Robert's wrong; His mild forgetting treacherous injury; The abbot's malice, raked in cinders long" (*Downfall,* ll. 2226-2228). The whole series is an elaborate fable of an oppressive administration and church, which drive all well-intentioned men into outlawry. Robert, or Robin, as the Earl of Huntingdon and King Richard's most loyal supporter, has previously worked for reform within the political structure; but after the departure of Richard for the Holy Land, the atmosphere of the court becomes too poisoned to permit the continued redress of grievances by legal means. This turning point symbolically justifies the retreat from law of well-meaning men in times of unmanageable oppression, and it does so without directly confronting royal authority (since the absent Richard is ignorant of wrongs done in his place). The recourse to extra-legality of Robin and his men is therefore not their fault but that of the age. In their exile, the outcasts form a nearly Utopian society while they await the return of justice to this earth. They renounce all rank, discover the virtues of abstinence, and band together against clericalism and sophisticated learning. All social forms in the forest are extra-legal; Robin and Marian are technically not even married, since they are under sentence of excommunication. The forest life is regenerative enough to exert a beneficent effect on even the villains who come into its precinct. Robin is a Christian hero, forgiving his vindictive enemies such as Justice Warman (explicitly referred to as Judas, l. 345), reforming a bad world by the example of his forbearance, ascetic discipline, and martyrdom. The true king himself, Richard, learns to improve himself by the rule of the exiled saints.

This Puritan world in exile is not one of revolutionary activity. The forest life is one of passive obedience, waiting for a delivery that God will surely provide. Although the Earl of Leicester does rise against the usurper John and actually strips him of scepter and crown (l. 2026), and although Robin Hood foretells John's violent death as guerdon for lust, Robin asks only that he be allowed to live in charity with his separated brethren. Munday thus appeals to the more respectable element of the Puritan wing. Yet in accepting the necessity of withdrawal, he undercuts the validity of public institutions of law and social organization. Similarly, the 1600 production at the Admiral's of *The Blind Beggar of Bednal Green*, perhaps by Day, Chettle, and Houghton, sympathizes with the estrangement of Momford, a professional military man, and the yeoman Strowds of Norfolk, who are forced into exile and disguise by the villainous Sir Robert Westford, a landed gentleman and justice of the peace. Even King Henry VI finally discerns the justice of their claims against their oppressors, and so pardons the exiles and reclaims them for society. Though such a reconciliation is still ideally possible in the Puritan-leaning drama around 1600, the hour is late and success must depend on the willingness of the administration to endorse the cause of the moderate elect.

Shakespeare's awareness of and concern with the widening split between the private theater and the Puritan-leaning citizenry are tactfully evident in such plays as *Twelfth Night* (1600-1601) and *As You Like It* (1599-1600). At issue was not only the preservation of the religious and social structure but the very continuance of a truly national theater. Shakespeare alludes to the antagonism, but without mockery; his forbearance is notably greater than that of Dekker or other moderates. His Saturnalia in *Twelfth Night* justifies release, but in proper balance with social norms and the "grace of community" that must always restrain license.[19] Although he concedes that some observers may classify Malvolio as "a kind of Puritan" (II, iii, 151-152), Shakespeare refuses to stereotype him as such, and indeed never disparages collectively a people who played such an influential part in London's attitude toward the drama. Yet if Malvolio is identified with no group, he obviously embodies hostile attitudes toward holiday that must be answered. Although Shakespeare does not satirize a religious position, he deplores a fetish of austerity and fervently hopes that it will not prevail among any faction. The concern was timely and prophetic, as C. L. Barber observes, for the spirit of Malvolio was ultimately to be revenged on the whole pack of them, in the closing of the theaters in the 1640's.[20] Shakespeare's intent is to avert such a catastrophe, not by driving extreme Puritanism underground but by appealing to sanity. At the same time he points to the opposite danger of excessive indulgence.

In its gentle satire of the pastoral tradition, *As You Like It* takes aim at the courtly vogue for genteel escapism—as exemplified in the contemporary *The Thracian Wonder* and *The Maid's Metamorphosis* (1600), with their obvious debt to Spenser and Lyly, their debates on the nature of love, their lords and ladies fleeing in rustic disguise from an envious court, and their involvement of the pagan gods. The pastoral here has become a plaything of the elite, artificial, detached, requiring no involvement. Similarly, in Jaques, Shakespeare seems to laugh at the malcontent satirist of the private theater, who denounces rather than cures, with his exaggerated pessimism, his sadistic raillery, his affectation for traveling and Italianate culture.[21] The nihilism of Jaques' "seven ages" speech is clearly not Shakespeare's view of life, but a form of disavowal that must be answered in Orlando's commitment to love and charity. Yet Shakespeare avoids the opposite attraction of Puritan renunciation; he does not speak in behalf of the authors of the Earl of

Huntingdon plays.[22] However much Sherwood Forest may offer a refuge for "co-mates and brothers in exile" who have renounced the "painted pomp" of the "envious court" to "live like the old Robin Hood of England . . . and fleet the time carelessly as they did in the golden world" (I, i, 122-125; II, i, 1-17), Shakespeare's forest dwellers are obviously no apologists for the elect. They concede that the forest has its inequities and its savagery, to which man can all too readily succumb; and though the court is indeed an envious place, even its envy of Orlando and Duke Senior bespeaks a longing to be better.

Shakespeare insists, in other words, on the fallacy of oversimplifying the appeal of withdrawal, whether to courtly artifice or to ascetic plainness. The world to which Orlando and Duke Senior must return, once Orlando has learned from Rosalind the realities of marital affection and the graces of civilized manners, is a world of "better days" that they have known before—a world where they "have with holy bell been knolled to church, And sat at good men's feasts" (II, vii, 120-123). Man cannot turn his back on social rituals of legal contract, hierarchy, and divine worship. The appearance of the outcast Orlando in the forest prompts Duke Senior to think not of society's ingratitude, but of their joint need for the dignified forms of civilization that must be reclaimed. Even though Jaques may dismiss the pattern of human social activity as "mere oblivion," even though the forest may preach that "Most friendship is faining, most loving mere folly," Duke Senior knows that he is still the nobleman he was born to be and that he must return. "I am the duke That loved your father," he tells Orlando. Jaques is the only courtier to remain in the forest. However uncertain the hope for accommodation may have seemed in 1600, Shakespeare could not surrender to the alternatives pressing from both sides.

Throughout the Tudor period, we have seen a pattern of many-sided debate in political dramaturgy. Although this drama was habitually propagandistic in its heated emotions over divisive issues and its tendency to exaggerate for polemical effect, the drama was never for any extended period under the monolithic control of state power. Today we generally regard propagandistic drama with mistrust, probably in reaction to the efficiency of totalitarian ideological persuasion. We tend in fact to see polemicism in art as an inherently corrupting force, and a distinguishing feature between free and enslaved societies. President Kennedy, for example, reflected such an absolute distinction when he insisted, "In free society art is not a weapon and it does not belong to the sphere of polemics and ideology. Artists are not the engineers of the soul . . . In serving his vision of the truth, the artist best serves his nation." [23] Even protest is taboo: Arthur Miller's allusions to McCarthyism in *The Crucible* proved offensive and had to be expunged. Although one finds a strong element of protest in contemporary British and French drama, the American theater remains cautious. Political commitment in art somehow means loss of freedom.

Perhaps the Tudor drama can offer us assurances that political dramaturgy need not be equated with official propaganda. In that era, at any rate, the state lacked sufficient coercive power to insist on predetermined formulas. Tudor kingship did not have the financial resources and standing army to run every aspect of corporate life; it had to rely on amateur civil servants and local governments, and to promote its own concept of centralized authority by playing off one social group or faction against another. Accordingly, the church was enabled, in a play like *Wisdom Who Is Christ*, to assert its own repugnance to the system of promoting churchmen to high non-ecclesiastical office—despite Henry VII's reliance on the system to lessen the feudal autonomy of the barons. Conversely, Henry Medwall was emboldened in his *Fulgens and Lucrece* to plead the virtues of the new Tudor aristocracy, in the very presence of the conservative nobles who stood most to lose by the challenge of the new men. Skelton, perhaps under the patronage of the old families, dared to upbraid a warmongering king and his conniving favorites with unavoidable application to the affairs of Henry VIII and Wolsey. Although polemical and biased in their views of political organization, such offerings were the brave utterances of men deeply concerned about the schooling of magistrates. Members of the Thomas More circle cautioned against factionalism at court, or speculated among themselves about radical alternatives such as the abolishing of inheritance rights or the election of rulers. Early Tudor political drama was thus in ferment. Although it was frequently obsessed with ideology it did not cater exclusively to the government, and did not see a conflict between art and didactic purpose.

The protracted and deadly battle over England's Reformation did have the effect of narrowing the issues and of increasing penalties for nonconformity to the ascendant dogma of the moment. The government certainly learned, through the tactics of men like Cranmer and Cromwell, to wield opinion as an instrument of nationalistic purpose. Yet even here the dramatists were a fiercely independent lot. Whatever else may be charged to Bale, he was a man of compulsive integrity, fully capable of belaboring his Protestant superiors for slackening in zeal. The Catholic apologist of *Respublica* was aware of divisive issues at court and argued temperance in the restoration of old practices. Elizabeth's reforming dramatists soon found themselves absorbed in a host of social problems such as usury and inflationary rent prices.

Nothing, however, better illustrates the diversity of political expression in Tudor drama than the rising voice of bourgeois and lower-class criticism during Elizabeth's reign. Moralists expounded in their analogous fables the limits of obedience to tyranny, or proferred advice to Elizabeth on her marriage problem and the Catholic menace. War plays increasingly glorified the role of the commons in England's defense against Spain, and went further to insinuate that most aristocratic society at court could be dispensed with in England's dynamic future. When other public dramatists responded to this challenge with exhortations of hierarchical obedience to law, they did so not as mere apologists for the administration but as spokesmen for an important segment of the great London populace debating its own role in the nation's destiny. The opposite challenge, in the private theaters, of aristocratic superiority to law enforcement and the great Elizabethan verities, similarly prompted a rejoinder in the name of a moderate consensus. That consensus was indeed coming to an end, but not without the honest soul-searching of artists who spoke for themselves rather than for the Establishment.

Because Tudor political drama reflected the multiform development of England's political life, it was itself capable of experiment and growth. Dramaturgically, the arena of politics offered a constant incentive for the discovery of new literary techniques. As we have seen, the self-effacing comedy and second plot of *Fulgens and Lucrece* emerged from the delicacy of Medwall's situation at court: he urged the barons to laugh at their own political aspirations through the medium of a farcical *reductio ad absurdum*. John Heywood mastered a similar mock-heroic device in his *Play of the Weather*. Historical analogy in Bale's *King John* introduced new complexities in the creation of the author's persona, drawn variously in this instance from King John, King Henry VIII, and most of all from Bale himself. From the use of extended biblical analogy in such plays as *Godly Queen Hester* or *Jacob and Esau,* dramatists learned control of structure in a sustained comparison of simultaneous narratives. In Elizabeth's early reign, considerations of tactful disclaimer in dealing with this sensitive monarch obliged playwrights to exchange overt forms of allegory for the more indirect "mirror" play; the quest for edifying historical illustrations led to interest in Cambises, Dionysius, Orestes, Creon, Alexander, and other great figures from the past. The Tudor uses of history were such that the influx of historical material into the English drama was almost invariably motivated by the search for a contemporaneously applicable example. A similar need prompted an exploration of legendary history, myth, and romance, as in the stories of Gorboduc, Patient Griselda, Appius and Virginia, and Endymion.

It was a matter of crucial importance for the development of this politically-minded drama that it be independent of its contemporary subject, both ideologically and artistically. As this drama served no single master, it also refused to limit itself to the issues and personalities of the moment. Treatment of controversial subjects was almost invariably generic: not simply whether Elizabeth should marry Leicester or the Duke d'Alençon, but whether the type of bountiful prince can ignore the dangers of unsettled succession. Because dramatists looked beyond immediacies to principles, they sought the perspectives of historical pattern. However much they subordinated history to the uses of the present, and wrenched the bias of "fact" to suit their themes, a historical subject gave them a distance in their art that blatant apologetics for the present could not provide. We have seen repeatedly that, in characterization, these playwrights virtually never copied directly from individuals of their own times, even when (as in *Respublica*) they could have satirized with impunity.

Similarly, in the years of the Armada, dramatists preferred to invoke memories of Crécy and Agincourt rather than deal face-to-face with the Armada victory itself. Such avoidance of literalism helped create the dramatic genre that most forcefully represents the culmination of Tudor political drama: the English history play. What gave focus to this drama was neither an impartial interest in English history nor a narrowly polemical controversy over the respective merits of Leicester,

Burghley, or Essex, but a broad examination of England's military stance respecting Catholicism and of the commons' role in England's political structure. Although its voice was raw and hysterical in many instances, this drama possessed the vitality of independent expression stemming from the aspirations of a large and toughminded social group.

As supreme exemplar of this dramatic genre, Shakespeare best understood its inherent limitations as well as its usefulness. He towered above his contemporaries partly because he was able to be so much more than polemical. Yet he endorsed the opportunities for didactic statement, and counseled a political moderation more sensitive and humane than that of his peers. In Shakespeare's hands, the English history play amply demonstrated that political drama could make a surpassing contribution to literary excellence. For a brief time, ideology and art became one.

ABBREVIATIONS

BJRL	*Bulletin of the John Rylands Library*
BUSE	*Boston University Studies in English*
ELN	*English Language Notes*
HLQ	*Huntington Library Quarterly*
JEGP	*Journal of English and Germanic Philology*
JHI	*Journal of the History of Ideas*
LTLS	*London Times Literary Supplement*
MLN	*Modern Language Notes*
MLQ	*Modern Language Quarterly*
MLR	*Modern Language Review*
MP	*Modern Philology*
N & Q	*Notes and Queries*
PQ	*Philological Quarterly*
RenP	*Renaissance Papers*
RES	*Review of English Studies*
SEL	*Studies in English Literature, 1500-1900*
SJ	*Shakespeare-Jahrbuch*
SP	*Studies in Philology*
SQ	*Shakespeare Quarterly*
SR	*Sewanee Review*
UTQ	*University of Toronto Quarterly*
UTSE	*University of Texas Studies in English*

TEXTS OF THE PLAYS

The following list enumerates only those editions referred to by line, scene, or page number in the preceding chapters. Insofar as possible, the accuracy of quotations has been checked against original editions of the plays. Spelling, however, has been altered as follows for the convenience of the reader. Prior to John Lyly, I have used the modern font throughout, finding equivalents for thorns and other obsolete characters, substituting "i" for "j," "u" for "v," "i" for "y," and expanding ampersands and other contractions of an orthographic nature. In addition I have excised some final "e's" where they appear to be fortuitous or haphazard. Beginning with John Lyly I have used modern spelling throughout. The point of demarcation is arbitrary in a sense, but it occurs at a time when the transition will be scarcely noticeable to the reader. Modern spelling cannot be used throughout the entire Tudor period without markedly distorting texts of the early years.

COLLECTIONS CITED

Adams — Joseph Q. Adams, ed. *Chief Pre-Shakespearean Dramas.* Boston, 1924.

Baskervill — Charles R. Baskervill, Virgil B. Heltzel, and Arthur H. Nethercot, eds. *Elizabethan and Stuart Plays.* New York, 1934.

Bond — R. Warwick Bond, ed. *Early Plays from the Italian.* Oxford, 1911.

Cunliffe — John W. Cunliffe, ed. *Early English Classical Tragedies.* Oxford, 1912.

EETS — Early English Text Society. London, 1864——.

MSR — Malone Society Reprints. London, 1907——.

Manly — John M. Manly, ed. *Specimens of the Pre-Shaksperean Drama.* 2 vols. Boston, 1897.

Materialien — Materialien zur Kunde des älteren Englischen Dramas. W. Bang, gen. ed. Louvain, 1902-1914.

TFT — Tudor Facsimile Texts, issued by John S. Farmer. 1907-1914.

STANDARD EDITIONS OF MAJOR AUTHORS

George Chapman. *The Plays and Poems of George Chapman,* ed. Thomas M. Parrott. 2 vols. London, 1910-1914.

Thomas Dekker. *The Dramatic Works of Thomas Dekker,* ed. Fredson Bowers. 4 vols. Cambridge, Eng., 1953-1961. (Includes *Satiromastix* and *Sir Thomas Wyatt.*)

Robert Greene. MSR editions. (Includes *George a Greene* and *John of Bordeaux.*)

Ben Jonson. *Ben Jonson,* ed. C. H. Herford and Percy Simpson. 11 vols. Oxford, 1925-1952.

John Lyly. *The Complete Works of John Lyly,* ed. R. Warwick Bond. 3 vols. Oxford, 1902.

Christopher Marlowe. *The Works of Christopher Marlowe*, ed. C. F. Tucker Brooke. Oxford, 1910.

George Peele. *The Arraignment of Paris* and *David and Bethsabe* in MSR editions. All others in *The Life and Works of George Peele*, gen. ed. Charles T. Prouty. New Haven, 1961.

William Shakespeare. *Shakespeare: The Complete Works*, ed. G. B. Harrison. New York, 1948.

INDIVIDUAL PLAYS LISTED ALPHABETICALLY

Albion Knight, anon. MSR.

All for Money, by Thomas Lupton. Ed. Ernst Vogel, *SJ*, 40:129-186 (1904).

Antonio's Revenge, by John Marston. MSR.

Appius and Virginia, by R[ichard] B[ower?]. MSR.

Arden of Feversham, anon. MSR.

The Blind Beggar of Bednal Green, by Henry Chettle. Materialien, 1902.

Blurt Master-Constable, anon. 1st edition, London, 1602.

The Book of Sir Thomas More, anon. MSR.

The Bugbears, by John Jeffere (?). Bond.

Calisto and Melibea, by John Rastell (?). MSR.

Cambises, by Thomas Preston. Baskervill.

The Castle of Perseverance, anon. *The Macro Plays*, ed. Frederick J. Furnivall and Alfred W. Pollard. EETS Extra Series, 91. London, 1904.

Cleopatra, by Samuel Daniel. *The Complete Works in Verse and Prose of Samuel Daniel*, ed. Alexander B. Grosart. 5 vols. London, 1885-1896.

The Cobbler's Prophecy, by Robert Wilson. MSR.

The Comedy of Patient and Meek Grissell, by John Phillip. MSR.

The Comedy of the Most Virtuous and Godly Susanna, by Thomas Garter. MSR.

The Conflict of Conscience, by Nathaniel Woodes. MSR.

Cuck-Queans and Cuckolds Errant, by William Percy. J. Haslewood, introd. London: Roxburghe Club, 1824.

Damon and Pythias, by Richard Edwards. MSR.

The Downfall of Robert Earl of Huntingdon, by Anthony Munday and others. MSR.

Edmond Ironside, anon. MSR.

Edward III, anon. Ed. G. C. Moore Smith. London, 1897.

Edward IV, Parts 1 and 2, by Thomas Heywood (?). Facsimile reprint, ed. Seymour de Ricci. Philadelphia, 1922.

Enough Is as Good as a Feast, by William Wager. Ed. Seymour de Ricci. Huntington Facsimile Reprints. New York, 1920.

Everyman, anon. Materialien, 1904.

The Famous Victories of Henry V, anon. Adams.

The Four PP, by John Heywood. Adams.

Fulgens and Lucrece, by Henry Medwall. Ed. F. S. Boas and A. W. Reed. New York, 1926.
Gammer Gurton's Needle, by W. Stevenson (?). Baskervill.
Gismond of Salerne, by R. Wilmot and others. Cunliffe.
Gorboduc, by Thomas Norton and Thomas Sackville. Cunliffe.
Hickescorner, anon. Manly I.
Histriomastix, by John Marston. *The Plays of John Marston,* ed. H. Harvey Wood. 3 vols. London, 1934-1939.
Horestes, by John Pickering. MSR.
Impatient Poverty, anon. Materialien, 1911.
Jack Juggler, anon. MSR.
Jacob and Esau, anon. MSR.
Jocasta, trans. George Gascoigne and F. Kinwelmerche. Cunliffe.
John John the Husband, by John Heywood. Adams.
John the Evangelist, anon. MSR.
King John, by John Bale. MSR.
A Knack to Know a Knave, anon. MSR.
A Knack to Know an Honest Man, anon. MSR.
A Larum for London, anon. MSR.
Liberality and Prodigality, anon. MSR.
The Life and Death of Jack Straw, anon. MSR.
The Life and Death of Thomas Stukeley, anon. *The School of Shakspere,* ed. Richard Simpson. 2 vols. New York, 1878.
The Life and Repentance of Mary Magdalene, by Lewis Wager. Ed. F. I. Carpenter. Chicago, 1902.
Like Will to Like, by Ulpian Fulwell. TFT.
Lingua, by Thomas Tomkis. TFT.
The Longer Thou Livest the More Fool Thou Art, by William Wager. Ed. Alois Brandl, SJ, 36:1-64 (1900).
A Looking Glass for London and England, by Thomas Lodge and Robert Greene. MSR.
Lusty Juventus, by R. Wever. TFT.
Magnificence, by John Skelton. Ed. Robert L. Ramsay. EETS Extra Series, 98. London, 1908.
Mankind, anon. *The Macro Plays,* ed. Furnivall and Pollard. EETS Extra Series, 91. London, 1904.
Mary Magdalene (Digby MS), anon. *The Digby Plays,* ed. F. J. Furnivall. EETS Extra Series, 70. London, 1896.
The Misfortunes of Arthur, by T. Hughes and others. Cunliffe.
Misogonus, anon. Bond.
Mucedorus, anon. Baskervill.
Mundus et Infans, anon. Manly I.
Nature, by Henry Medwall. TFT.
The Nature of the Four Elements, by John Rastell. TFT.
New Custom, anon. TFT.

Nice Wanton, anon. Manly I.

The Noble Spanish Soldier, by Thomas Dekker (?). TFT.

Of Gentleness and Nobility, by John Rastell (?). MSR.

The Pardoner and the Friar, by John Heywood. TFT.

The *Parnassus* Trilogy, anon. *The Three Parnassus Plays (1598-1601),* ed. J. B. Leishman. London, 1949.

The Peddler's Prophecy, anon. MSR.

The Play of Love, by John Heywood. TFT.

The Play of the Sacrament, anon. *The Non-Cycle Mystery Plays,* ed. Osborn Waterhouse. EETS Extra Series, 104. London, 1909.

The Play of the Weather, by John Heywood. Adams.

Promos and Cassandra, by George Whetstone. *Narrative and Dramatic Sources of Shakespeare,* ed. Geoffrey Bullough. London, 1957——.

Ralph Roister Doister, by Nicholas Udall. MSR.

The Rare Triumphs of Love and Fortune. anon. MSR.

Respublica, anon. Ed. Leonard A. Magnus. EETS Extra Series, 94. London, 1905.

1 Sir John Oldcastle, by Anthony Munday and others. MSR.

Soliman and Perseda, by Thomas Kyd (?). *The Works of Thomas Kyd,* ed. Frederick S. Boas. Oxford, 1901.

The Spanish Tragedy, by Thomas Kyd. MSR.

Supposes, by George Gascoigne. Bond.

Thersites, by Nicholas Udall (?). TFT.

Thomas Lord Cromwell, anon. *The Shakespeare Apocrypha,* ed. C. F. Tucker Brooke. Oxford, 1908.

Thomas of Woodstock, anon. Ed. A. P. Rossiter. London, 1946.

Three Ladies of London, by Robert Wilson. TFT.

Three Lords and Three Ladies of London, by Robert Wilson. TFT.

The Tide Tarrieth No Man, by G. Wapull. Ed. Ernst Rühl, SJ, 43:1-52 (1907).

The Tragedy of Hoffman, by Henry Chettle. MSR.

The Trial of Chivalry, anon. *Old English Plays,* ed. Arthur H. Bullen. New Series. 4 vols. New York, 1964.

The Trial of Treasure, anon. TFT.

The Troublesome Reign of King John, anon. *Narrative and Dramatic Sources of Shakespeare,* ed. Geoffrey Bullough. London, 1957——.

Two Lamentable Tragedies, by Robert Yarington (?). TFT.

A Warning for Fair Women, anon. *The School of Shakspere,* ed. Richard Simpson. 2 vols. New York, 1878.

The Wars of Cyrus, by R. Farrant (?). Ed. James P. Brawner. Urbana, Ill., 1942.

Wealth and Health, anon. MSR.

Wisdom, Who Is Christ, anon. *The Macro Plays,* ed. Furnivall and Pollard. EETS Extra Series, 91. London, 1904.

The Wounds of Civil War, by Thomas Lodge. MSR.

Acheson, Arthur. *Shakespeare's Lost Years in London, 1586-1592.* New York, 1920.

Adams, Joseph Quincy, ed. *Chief Pre-Shakespearean Dramas.* Boston, 1924.

Albright, Evelyn May. *Dramatic Publication in England, 1580-1640.* New York, 1927.

———"Shakespeare's *Richard II* and the Essex Conspiracy," *PMLA,* 42:686-720 (1927).

Allen, Morse. *The Satire of John Marston.* Columbus, Ohio, 1920.

Anglo, Sidney. "The Court Festivals of Henry VII: A Study Based upon the Account Books of John Heron, Treasurer of the Chamber," *BJRL,* 43:12-45 (1960).

Armstrong, William A. "The Authorship and Political Meaning of *Cambises,*" *English Studies,* 36:289-299 (1955).

———"The Elizabethan Conception of the Tyrant," *RES,* 22:161-181 (1946).

———"Elizabethan Themes in *The Misfortunes of Arthur,*" *RES,* N.S., 7:238-249 (1956).

———"The Topicality of *The Misfortunes of Arthur,*" *N & Q,* N.S., 2:371-373 (1955).

Baker, George P., ed. *Endymion,* by John Lyly. New York, 1894.

Barber, C. L. *Shakespeare's Festive Comedy.* Princeton, 1959.

Baskervill, C. R. "On Two Old Plays," *MP,* 14:16 (1916).

———V. B. Heltzel, and A. H. Nethercot, eds. *Elizabethan and Stuart Plays.* New York, 1934.

Bennett, Josephine Waters. "Oxford and *Endimion,*" *PMLA,* 57:354-369 (1942).

Berringer, Ralph W. "Jonson's *Cynthia's Revels* and the War of the Theatres," *PQ,* 22:1-22 (1943).

Bevington, David M. *From "Mankind" to Marlowe.* Cambridge, Mass., 1962.

Bindoff, S. T., et al., eds. *Elizabethan Government and Society.* Essays Presented to Sir John Neale. London, 1961.

Bond, R. Warwick, ed. *The Complete Works of John Lyly.* 3 vols. Oxford, 1902.

Bowers, Fredson T. *Elizabethan Revenge Tragedy, 1587-1642.* Princeton, 1940.

Bradbrook, M.C. *The Growth and Structure of Elizabethan Comedy.* London, 1955.

Brie, Friedrich. "Skelton-Studien," *Englische Studien,* 37:1-86 (1906).

Calendar of Letters, Despatches, and State Papers, Relating to the Negotiations between England and Spain, ed. G. A. Bergenroth et al. London, 1862———. Also, the *Calendars of State Papers, Venetian, Domestic, and Scotland.*

Cameron, Kenneth W. *Authorship and Sources of "Gentleness and Nobility."* Raleigh, N.C., 1941.

Campbell, Lily B. *Shakespeare's "Histories": Mirrors of Elizabethan Policy.* San Marino, Calif., 1947.

——"The Use of Historical Patterns in the Reign of Elizabeth," *HLQ*, 1:135-167 (1938).

Campbell, Oscar J. *Comicall Satyre and Shakespeare's Troilus and Cressida.* San Marino, Calif., 1938.

——"The Dramatic Construction of *Poetaster*," *Huntington Library Bulletin*, 9:37-62 (1936).

Caputi, Anthony. *John Marston, Satirist.* Ithaca, N.Y., 1961.

Cartwright, Robert. *The Footsteps of Shakspere.* London, 1862.

——*Shakspere and Jonson: Dramatic versus Wit-Combats.* London, 1864.

——"Shakspeare, Sidney, and Essex," *N & Q*, 3rd ser., 3:82-84, 103-106, 124-126 (1863).

Chambers, E. K. *The Elizabethan Stage.* 4 vols. Oxford, 1923.

——*The Mediaeval Stage.* 2 vols. Oxford, 1903.

Clapham, Sir John. *A Concise Economic History of Britain from the Earliest Times to 1750.* Cambridge, Eng., 1949.

Clark, Eleanor. *Ralegh and Marlowe.* New York, 1941.

Clough, Wilson O. "The Broken English of Foreign Characters of the Elizabethan Stage," *PQ*, 12:255-268 (1933).

Cole, Douglas. *Suffering and Evil in the Plays of Christopher Marlowe.* Princeton, 1962.

Collins, Arthur, ed. *Letters and Memorials of State . . . Written and Collected by Sir Henry Sidney, Sir Philip Sidney, Robert Earl of Leicester, and Viscount Lisle (Sidney Papers).* 2 vols. London, 1746.

Craik, T. W. "The Political Interpretation of Two Tudor Interludes: *Temperance and Humility* and *Wealth and Health*," *RES*, N.S., 4:98-108 (1953).

Creizenach, Wilhelm. *The English Drama in the Age of Shakespeare*, trans. from *Geschichte des neueren Dramas.* London, 1916.

Cunliffe, John W., ed. *Early English Classical Tragedies.* Oxford, 1912.

De Groot, John. *The Shakespeares and "The Old Faith."* New York, 1946.

Dodds, Madeleine H. "Early Political Plays," *The Library*, 3rd ser., 4:393-408 (1913).

Dunbabin, R. L. "Notes on Skelton," *MLR*, 12:129-139, 257-265 (1917).

Edgerton, William L. "The Apostasy of Nicholas Udall," *N & Q*, 195:223-226 (1950).

——"The Date of *Roister Doister*," *PQ*, 44:555-560 (1965).

Elton, G. R. *Henry VIII: An Essay in Revision.* London, 1962.

——*The Tudor Revolution in Government.* Cambridge, Eng., 1959.

Farnham, Willard. *The Medieval Heritage of Elizabethan Tragedy.* Berkeley, 1936.

Feuillerat, Albert. *John Lyly.* Cambridge, Eng., 1910.

—————Documents Relating to the Office of Revels in the Time of Queen Elizabeth. Louvain, 1908.

Fisher, F. J. "Commercial Trends and Policy in Sixteenth-Century England," The Economic History Review, 10:95-117 (1940).

Fleay, Frederick G. A Biographical Chronicle of the English Drama, 1559-1642. 2 vols. London, 1891.

Furness, H. H. " 'Hamlet and the Mystery of Amy Robsart': A Reply," North American Review, 216:357-363 (1922).

Furnivall, F. J., and Alfred W. Pollard, eds. The Macro Plays. EETS Extra Series, 91. London, 1904.

Gairdner, James. The English Church in the Sixteenth Century, in A History of the English Church, ed. W. R. W. Stephens and William Hunt, vol. 4. London, 1902.

Gardiner, Harold C., S.J. Mysteries' End: An Investigation of the Last Days of the Medieval Religious Stage. New Haven, 1946.

Gayley, C. M., ed. Representative English Comedies. 2 vols. New York, 1903.

Gilbert, Allan H. "The Function of the Masques in Cynthia's Revels," PQ, 22:211-230 (1943).

Gildersleeve, Virginia C. Government Regulation of the Elizabethan Drama. New York, 1908.

Graves, T. S. "Some Allusions to Religious and Political Plays," MP, 9:545-554 (1912).

—————"The Political Use of the Stage During the Reign of James I," Anglia, 38:137-156 (1914).

Gray, Austin K. "The Secret of Love's Labour's Lost," PMLA, 39:581-611 (1924).

Greg, W. W., ed. Godly Queen Hester. Louvain, 1904.

Griffin, William J. "Notes on Early Tudor Control of the Stage," MLN, 58:50-54 (1943).

Hall, Edward. The Union of the Two Noble and Illustre Families of Lancastre and York. London, 1550.

Halpin, Rev. N. J. Oberon's Vision. London, 1843.

Hankins, John E. The Character of Hamlet and Other Essays. Chapel Hill, N.C., 1941.

Harbage, Alfred. "Love's Labor's Lost and the Early Shakespeare," PQ, 41:18-36 (1962).

—————Shakespeare and the Rival Traditions. New York, 1952.

Harris, Jesse W. John Bale, A Study in the Minor Literature of the Reformation. Urbana, Ill., 1940.

Harris, William O. Skelton's Magnyfycence and the Cardinal Virtue Tradition. Chapel Hill, N.C., 1965.

—————"Wolsey and Skelton's Magnyfycence: A Re-evaluation," SP, 57:99-122 (1960).

Harrison, G. B. The Life and Death of Robert Devereux, Earl of Essex. London, 1937.

————"Shakespeare's Topical Significances," *LTLS*, Nov. 13, 1930, p. 939, and Nov. 20, 1930, p. 974.

Hart, Alfred. *Shakespeare and the Homilies*. Melbourne, 1934.

Heffner, Ray. "Shakespeare, Hayward, and Essex," *PMLA*, 45:754-780 (1930).

Heiserman, Arthur. *Skelton and Satire*. Chicago, 1961.

Herford, C. H., and Percy Simpson, eds. *Ben Jonson*. 11 vols. Oxford, 1925-1952.

Hexter, J. H. *Reappraisals in History*. London, 1961.

Heywood, Thomas. *An Apology for Actors*. London, 1612. Ed. Richard H. Perkinson. New York, 1941.

Hillebrand, Harold N. *The Child Actors*. University of Illinois Studies in Language and Literature, No. 11. Urbana, Ill., 1926.

Hogrefe, Pearl. *The Sir Thomas More Circle*. Urbana, Ill., 1959.

Hook, Frank S., ed. *Edward I*, in *The Life and Works of George Peele*, gen. ed. Charles T. Prouty, vol 2. New Haven, 1961.

Huhner, Max. "Shakspere's Conception of the Clergy," *Shakespeare Association Bulletin*, 11:161-170 (1936).

Hunter, G. K. *John Lyly: The Humanist as Courtier*. London, 1962.

————"Shakespeare's Politics and the Rejection of Falstaff," *Critical Quarterly*, 1:229-236 (1959).

Huppé, Bernard F. "Allegory of Love in Lyly's Court Comedies," *ELH*, 14:93-113 (1947).

Jorgensen, Paul A. "Moral Guidance and Religious Encouragement for the Elizabethan Soldier," *HLQ*, 13:241-259 (1950).

————*Shakespeare's Military World*. Berkeley and Los Angeles, 1956.

————"Theoretical Views of War in Elizabethan England," *JHI*, 13:469-481 (1952).

Kelso, Ruth. *The Doctrine of the English Gentleman in the Sixteenth Century*. University of Illinois Studies in Language and Literature, No. 14. Urbana, Ill., 1929.

Kendall, Paul M. *Richard the Third*. New York, 1955.

Kernan, Alvin. *The Cankered Muse: Satire of the English Renaissance*. New Haven, 1959.

Kimbrough, Robert. *Shakespeare's Troilus and Cressida and Its Setting*. Cambridge, Mass., 1964.

Kocher, Paul H. "The Development of Marlowe's Character," *PQ*, 17:331-350 (1938).

Lamond, Elizabeth, ed. *A Discourse of the Common Weal of This Realm of England*. Cambridge, Eng., 1893, reprinted 1929.

LeComte, Edward S. "The Ending of *Hamlet* as a Farewell to Essex," *ELH*, 17:87-114 (1950).

Lee, Sidney L. "The Topical Side of the Elizabethan Drama," *Transactions of the New Shakspere Society*, ser. 1, no. 11 (1887), pp. 1-35.

Letters and Papers, Foreign and Domestic, of the Reign of Henry VIII, ed. J. S. Brewer et al. London, 1862-1910.

Lindabury, Richard V. *A Study of Patriotism in the Elizabethan Drama.* Princeton, 1930.

Lowers, James K. *Mirrors for Rebels: A Study of Polemical Literature Relating to the Northern Rebellion, 1569.* Berkeley, 1953.

MacCaffrey, Wallace T. "Place and Patronage in Elizabethan Politics," in *Elizabethan Government and Society,* ed. S. T. Bindoff et al. London, 1961.

McManaway, James, et al., eds. *Joseph Quincy Adams Memorial Studies.* Washington, D.C., 1948.

Magnus, Leonard A., ed. *Respublica.* EETS Extra Series, 94. London, 1905.

Mallory, Herbert S., ed. *Poetaster,* by Ben Jonson. New York, 1905.

Matthews, Arthur D., and Clark M. Emery, eds. *Studies in Shakespeare.* Coral Gables, Fla., 1953.

More, Thomas. *Utopia,* ed. Edward Surtz, S.J., and J. H. Hexter, in the Yale Edition of the Complete Works of St. Thomas More. New Haven, 1965.

Myers, Aaron M. *Representation and Misrepresentation of the Puritan in Elizabethan Drama.* Philadelphia, 1931.

Neale, John E. *Elizabeth I and Her Parliaments.* 2 vols., 1559-1581 and 1584-1601. New York, 1958.

———*The Elizabethan House of Commons.* New Haven, 1950.

———*Essays in Elizabethan History.* London, 1958.

———*Queen Elizabeth I.* New York: Doubleday, 1957.

Nelson, William. *John Skelton, Laureate.* New York, 1939.

Nichols, John, ed. *The Progresses and Public Processions of Queen Elizabeth.* 3 vols. London, 1823.

Palmer, John L. *Political and Comic Characters of Shakespeare.* London, 1948.

Paradise, N. Burton. *Thomas Lodge: The History of an Elizabethan.* New Haven, 1931.

Parrott, Thomas M., ed. *The Plays and Poems of George Chapman.* 2 vols. London, 1910-1914.

Penniman, Josiah H. *The War of the Theatres.* Boston, 1897.

Phillips, G. W. *Lord Burghley in Shakespeare—Falstaff, Sly, and Others.* London, 1936.

Phillips, James E. *Images of a Queen.* Berkeley and Los Angeles, 1964.

Pollard, Alfred W. "John Heywood: Critical Essay," in *Representative English Comedies,* ed. C. M. Gayley, vol. 1. New York, 1903.

Prescott, H. F. M. *Mary Tudor.* New York: Macmillan, 1962.

Prouty, Charles T., gen. ed. *The Life and Works of George Peele.* New Haven, 1961.

Ramsay, Robert L., ed. *Magnyfycence,* by John Skelton. EETS Extra Series, 98. London, 1908.

Ramsey, Peter. *Tudor Economic Problems.* London, 1963.

Read, Conyers. "William Cecil and Elizabethan Public Relations," *Elizabethan Government and Society,* ed. S. T. Bindoff et al. London, 1961.

Reed, Arthur W. *Early Tudor Drama: Medwall, The Rastells, Heywood, and the More Circle*. London, 1926.
Reese, Gertrude. "Political Import of *The Misfortunes of Arthur*," *RES*, 21:81-91 (1945).
———"The Question of the Succession in Elizabethan Drama," *UTSE*, 22:59-85 (1942).
Reese, M. M. *The Cease of Majesty*. New York, 1961.
Ribner, Irving. *The English History Play in the Age of Shakespeare*, rev. ed. New York, 1965.
Rickert, Edith. "Political Propaganda and Satire in *A Midsummer Night's Dream*," *MP*, 21:53-87, 133-154 (1923).
Rosenberg, Eleanor. *Leicester, Patron of Letters*. New York, 1955.
Rossiter, A. P., ed. *Woodstock—A Moral History*. New York, 1946.
Rowse, A. L. *William Shakespeare—A Biography*. New York, 1963.
Sharpe, Robert B. *The Real War of the Theaters*. Boston, 1935.
Sibley, Gertrude M. *The Lost Plays and Masques, 1500-1642*. Ithaca, N.Y., 1933.
Sidney Papers. See Collins, Arthur.
Siegel, Paul. *Shakespearean Tragedy and the Elizabethan Compromise*. New York, 1957.
Simpson, Richard. "The Political Use of the Stage in Shakspere's Time," *Transactions of the New Shakspere Society*, ser. 1, pt. 2 (1874), pp. 371-395.
———"The Politics of Shakspere's Historical Plays," *Transactions of the New Shakspere Society*, ser. 1, pt. 2 (1874), pp. 396-441.
———ed. *The School of Shakspere*. 2 vols. New York, 1878.
Small, Roscoe A. *The Stage-Quarrel between Ben Jonson and the So-Called Poetasters*. Breslau, 1899.
Smart, Walter K. *Some English and Latin Sources and Parallels for the Morality of Wisdom*. Menasha, Wis., 1912.
Spivack, Bernard. *Shakespeare and the Allegory of Evil*. New York, 1958.
Steane, J. B. *Marlowe: A Critical Study*. Cambridge, Eng., 1964.
Steele, Mary S. *Plays and Masques at Court during the Reigns of Elizabeth, James, and Charles*. New Haven, 1926.
Stevenson, Robert. *Shakespeare's Religious Frontier*. The Hague, 1958.
Stirling, Brents. "Anti-Democracy in Shakespeare: A Re-Survey," *MLQ*, 2:487-502 (1941).
———*The Populace in Shakespeare*. New York, 1949.
Stoll, E. E. *Shakespeare Studies, Historical and Comparative in Method*. New York, 1942.
Stone, Lawrence. *The Crisis of the Aristocracy, 1558-1641*. Oxford, 1965.
Strachey, Lytton. *Elizabeth and Essex*. New York, 1928.
Studies in Shakespeare. See Matthews, Arthur D.
Talbert, Ernest W. "The Interpretation of Jonson's Courtly Spectacles," *PMLA*, 61:454-473 (1946).

————"The Purpose and Technique of Jonson's *Poetaster*," *SP*, 42:225-252 (1945).

Thaler, Alwin. "The Original Malvolio?" *Shakespeare Association Bulletin*, 7:57-71 (1932).

Thompson, E. N. S. *The Controversy between the Puritans and the Stage*. New York, 1903.

Thompson, J. W. "Hamlet and the Mystery of Amy Robsart," *North American Review*, 215:657-672 (1922).

Tillyard, E. M. W. *Shakespeare's History Plays*. London, 1944.

Tolman, Albert H. "Is Shakespeare Aristocratic?" *PMLA*, 29:277-298 (1914).

Tucker, William J. "Shakespeare, a Catholic?" *Catholic World*, 176:14-19 (1952).

Tupper, Jr., Frederick. "The Shaksperean Mob," *PMLA*, 27:486-523 (1912).

Turner, Julia Celeste. *Anthony Mundy, An Elizabethan Man of Letters*. Berkeley, 1928.

Waggoner, G. R. "An Elizabethan Attitude toward Peace and War," *PQ*, 33:20-33 (1954).

Wallace, Charles W. *The Evolution of the English Drama up to Shakespeare*. Berlin, 1912.

Waller, Evangelia H. "A Possible Interpretation of *The Misfortunes of Arthur*," *JEGP*, 24:219-245 (1925).

Watson, Sara R. "*Gorboduc* and the Theory of Tyrannicide," *MLR*, 34:355-366 (1939).

White, Helen C. *Social Criticism in Popular Religious Literature of the Sixteenth Century*. New York, 1944.

Wickham, Glynne. *Early English Stages, 1300 to 1660*. London, 1959————.

Williams, Charles. *Henry VII*. London, 1937.

Wilson, Elkin C. *England's Eliza*. Cambridge, Mass., 1939.

Wilson, John Dover, ed. *The First Part of King Henry VI*. Cambridge, Eng., 1952.

————*The Essential Shakespeare*. Cambridge, Eng., 1932.

————ed. *Hamlet*. Cambridge, Eng., 1934.

Wine, Celesta. "Nathaniel Wood's *Conflict of Conscience*," *PMLA*, 50:661-678 (1935).

Winstanley, Lilian. *Hamlet and the Scottish Succession*. Cambridge, Eng., 1921.

————*Macbeth, King Lear, and Contemporary History*. Cambridge, Eng., 1922.

Wright, Louis B. "Social Aspects of Some Belated Moralities," *Anglia*, 54:107-148 (1930).

————"A Political Reflection in Phillip's *Patient Grissell*," *RES*, 4:424-428 (1928).

Young, Karl. *The Drama of the Medieval Church*. 2 vols. Oxford, 1933.

Zeeveld, W. Gordon. *Foundations of Tudor Policy*. Cambridge, Mass., 1948.

1. INTRODUCTION: SOME APPROACHES TO TOPICAL MEANING

1. N. J. Halpin, *Oberon's Vision* (London, 1843); Robert Cartwright, *The Footsteps of Shakspere* (London, 1862) and *Shakspere and Jonson: Dramatic versus Wit-Combats* (London, 1864).

2. A. C. Swinburne, *A Study of Shakespeare* (London, 1880), pp. 277-278.

3. Baldwin Maxwell, "The Original of Sir John Falstaff—Believe It or Not," *SP*, 27:230-232 (1930).

4. "Oxford and *Endimion*," *PMLA*, 57:354-369 (1942).

5. Edith Rickert, "Political Propaganda and Satire in *A Midsummer Night's Dream*," *MP*, 21:53-87, 133-154 (1923), p. 136.

6. Evangelia H. Waller, "A Possible Interpretation of *The Misfortunes of Arthur*," *JEGP*, 24:219-245 (1925); Robert B. Sharpe, *The Real War of the Theaters* (Boston, 1935); Richard Simpson, "The Political Use of the Stage in Shakspere's Time," *Transactions of the New Shakspere Society*, ser. 1, pt. 2 (1874), pp. 371-395.

7. H. H. Furness, " 'Hamlet and the Mystery of Amy Robsart': A Reply," *North American Review*, 216:357-363 (1922); Alfred Harbage, "*Love's Labor's Lost* and the Early Shakespeare," *PQ*, 41:18-36 (1962).

8. E. E. Stoll, *Shakespeare Studies, Historical and Comparative in Method* (New York, 1942), pp. 78-84.

9. *The Populace in Shakespeare* (New York, 1949), pp. 3-11.

10. W. B. Yeats, "On Being Asked for a War Poem," from *The Wild Swans at Coole*, in *The Variorum Edition of the Poems of Yeats*, ed. Peter Allt and Colonel Alspach (New York, 1957), p. 359; W. H. Auden, "In Memory of W. B. Yeats," in *Collected Shorter Poems, 1927-1957* (London, 1966), pp. 141-142.

11. P. B. Shelley, *A Defence of Poetry*, in *The Complete Works of Percy Bysshe Shelley*, ed. Roger Ingpen and Walter E. Beck, 10 vols. (London, 1930), VII, 118.

12. *The History of England from the Accession of Edward VI to the Death of Elizabeth*, vol. 6 in *The Political History of England*, ed. William Hunt and Reginald L. Poole (London, 1910), p. 440. See Lily B. Campbell, "The Use of Historical Patterns in the Reign of Elizabeth," *HLQ*, 1:135-167 (1938).

13. C. F. Tucker Brooke, *Shakespeare of Stratford* (New Haven, 1926), p. 150.

14. Eleanor Rosenberg, *Leicester, Patron of Letters* (New York, 1955), pp. 3-18.

15. Willard Thorp, *The Triumph of Realism in Elizabethan Drama, 1558-1612* (Princeton, 1928), p. viii and *passim*.

16. Lily B. Campbell, *Shakespeare's "Histories": Mirrors of Elizabethan Policy* (San Marino, Calif., 1947), pp. 3-116; M. M. Reese, *The Cease of Majesty* (New York, 1961), pp. 1-19; Louis B. Wright, *Middle-Class Culture in Elizabethan England* (Chapel Hill, N.C., 1935), pp. 297-338.

17. Reese, *Cease of Majesty*, p. 2; Celeste T. Wright, "The Queen's Husband: Some Renaissance Views," *BUSE*, 3:133-138 (1957); Elkin C. Wilson, *England's Eliza* (Cambridge, Mass., 1939); James E. Phillips, *Images of a Queen* (Berkeley and Los Angeles, 1964), p. 328 and *passim*.

18. Glynne Wickham, *Early English Stages, 1300 to 1660* (London, 1959———), I, 64-78, 197-209.

19. Enid Welsford, *The Court Masque* (Cambridge, Eng., 1927), pp. 120-121, 125; Sidney Anglo, "The Court Festivals of Henry VII: A Study Based upon the Account Books of John Heron, Treasurer of the Chamber," *BJRL*, 43:12-45 (1960).

20. Edward Hall, *The Union of the Two Noble and Illustre Families of Lancastre and York* (London, 1550), "The xiiii yere of King Henry the VIII," fol. lxxxviii-lxxxix. Hall's report is amplified by a letter of Martin de Salinas, ambassador of Archduke Ferdinand, who accompanied Charles to England; *Calendar of Letters, Despatches, and State Papers, Relating to the Negotiations between England and Spain*, ed. G. A. Bergenroth et al. (London, 1862———), II (1509-1525), pp. 444-445. See Sidney Anglo, "William Cornish in a Play, Pageants, Prison, and Politics," *RES*, N.S., 10:347-360 (1959).

21. Hall, *Union*, "The xix yere of King Henry the VIII," fol. clxvi. *Calendar of State Papers, Spanish*, III, pt. 2 (1527-1529), p. 458, gives the account of Don Iñigo de Mendoça, Imperial Ambassador in England. *Letters and Papers, Foreign and Domestic, of the Reign of Henry VIII*, ed. J. S. Brewer et al. (London, 1862-1910), IV, pt. 2 (1526-1528), pp. 1605-1606, gives the Revels account. See T. S. Graves, "Some Allusions to Religious and Political Plays," *MP*, 9:545-554 (1912), pp. 552-553.

22. *Calendar of State Papers, Venetian*, IV (1527-1533), p. 117. See Madeleine H. Dodds, "Early Political Plays," *The Library*, 3rd ser., 4:393-408 (1913), p. 401.

23. Hall, *Union*, "The xviii yere of King Henry the VIII," fol. cliiii.

24. *Letters and Papers of Henry VIII*, XII, pt. 1 (1537), pp. 557, 585.

25. *Letters and Papers of Henry VIII*, VIII (1535), p. 373. See Dodds, "Early Political Plays," *Library*, 3rd ser., 4:401-402; and C. R. Baskervill, "Some Evidence for Early Romantic Plays in England," *MP*, 14:229-251 and 467-512 (1916), p. 480. For the French quotation, see A. Hamy, *Entrevue de François Premier avec Henry VIII* (Paris, 1898), doc. ccclxxviii.

26. *Calendar of State Papers, Spanish*, N.S., I (1558-1567), pp. 367-368, 404-405, 633. See Mary S. Steele, *Plays and Masques at Court during the Reigns of Elizabeth, James, and Charles* (New Haven, 1926), pp. 15-16, 33.

27. Sir John Harington, *A Tract on the Succession to the Crown (A.D. 1602)*, ed. Clements R. Markham (London, 1880), p. 40.

28. Rowland Whyte to Sir Robert Sidney, Nov. 22, 1595, in *Letters and Memorials of State . . . Written and Collected by Sir Henry Sidney, Sir Philip Sidney, Robert Earl of Leicester, and Viscount Lisle (Sidney Papers)*, ed. Arthur Collins, 2 vols. (London, 1746), I, 362. For the Burghley letter see Rickert, "Political Propaganda and Satire," *MP*, 21:148.

29. J. W. Cunliffe, "The Queenes Majesties Entertainment at Woodstocke," *PMLA*, 26:92-141 (1911), p. 93.

30. Rickert, "Political Propaganda and Satire," *MP*, 21:137-138; Thomas Churchyard, *Churchyard's Challenge* (London, 1593), in the prefatory material; on the visit to Burghley, John Nichols, ed., *The Progresses and Public Processions of Queen Elizabeth* (London, 1823), III, 241-245; and on Essex's pageant, Collins, ed., *Sidney Papers*, I, 362, and Nichols, ed., *Progresses of Elizabeth*, III, 371-372.

31. Harbage, "*Love's Labor's Lost* and Early Shakespeare," *PQ*, 41:19-20. See Robert Kimbrough, *Shakespeare's Troilus and Cressida and Its Setting* (Cambridge, Mass., 1964), p. 21.

32. Quoted by Ray Heffner, "Shakespeare, Hayward, and Essex," *PMLA*, 45:754-780 (1930), p. 776.

33. Letter of Dr. Edward Stanhope to his brother, *Calendar of State Papers, Domestic*, V (1598-1601), p. 365.

34. Quoted by Simpson, "Political Use of the Stage," *New Shakspere Society Transactions* (1874), p. 379.

35. Quoted in Reese, *Cease of Majesty*, p. 160.

36. Cf. C. A. Greer, "The Play Performed at the Globe on 7 February, 1601," *N & Q*, 197:270-271 (1952).

37. See G. B. Harrison, *The Life and Death of Robert Devereux, Earl of Essex* (London, 1937), p. 214; and Reese, *Cease of Majesty*, p. 161.

38. *Calendar of State Papers, Domestic*, V (1598-1601), p. 227. See Conyers Read, "William Cecil and Elizabethan Public Relations," in *Elizabethan Government and Society*, essays presented to Sir John Neale, ed. S. T. Bindoff et al. (London, 1961), pp. 21-55.

39. Quoted by Sidney Lee, "The Topical Side of the Elizabethan Drama," *Transactions of the New Shakspere Society*, ser. 1, no. 11 (1887), pp. 1-35.

40. T. S. Graves, "The Political Use of the Stage During the Reign of James I," *Anglia*, 38:137-156 (1914), p. 151.

41. *Calendar of State Papers, Scotland*, II, 749.

42. Edward S. LeComte, "The Ending of *Hamlet* as a Farewell to Essex," *ELH*, 17:87-114 (1950), p. 111; Evelyn May Albright, "Shakespeare's *Richard II* and the Essex Conspiracy," *PMLA*, 42:686-720 (1927), pp. 719-720.

43. Kathleen Tillotson, "Drayton and Richard II: 1597-1600," *RES*, 15:172-179 (1939).

44. E.P. Kuhl, "Contemporary Politics in Elizabethan Drama: Fulke Greville," *PQ*, 7:299-302 (1928).

318

45. The citations from Jonson, Breton, and Nashe are to be found in Phoebe L. Sheavyn, *The Literary Profession in the Elizabethan Age* (Manchester, 1909), pp. 57-58. See also Eleanor Clark, *Ralegh and Marlowe* (New York, 1941), pp. 42-53.

46. Thomas Nashe, *A Countercuffe Given to Martin Junior* (1589), in Ronald B. McKerrow, ed., *The Works of Thomas Nashe*, rev. ed. by F. P. Wilson (Oxford, 1958), I, 63; *Christ's Tears over Jerusalem*, II, 182; and *Lenten Stuff*, III, 213.

47. E. P. Kuhl, "The Earl of Essex and Liberalism," *PQ*, 24:187-190 (1945).

48. Simpson, "Political Use of the Stage," *New Shakspere Society Transactions* (1874), pp. 384, 382-383, 387.

49. Albright, "Shakespeare's *Richard II* and Essex," *PMLA*, 42:686; G. W. Phillips, *Lord Burghley in Shakespeare—Falstaff, Sly, and Others* (London, 1936), pp. 67-94.

50. "C," "Shakspeare, Sidney, and Essex," *N & Q*, 3rd ser., 3:82-84, 103-106, 124-126 (1863). Mr. "C" was Robert Cartwright, author of *The Footsteps of Shakspere* and *Shakspere and Jonson*.

51. J. Dover Wilson, ed., *The First Part of King Henry VI* (Cambridge, Eng., 1952), pp. xiv-xxi.

52. Marion A. Taylor, "Lord Cobham and Shakespeare's Duchess of Gloucester," *Shakespeare Association Bulletin*, 9:150-156 (1934).

53. Harbage, "*Love's Labor's Lost* and Early Shakespeare," *PQ*, 41:26.

54. Austin K. Gray, "The Secret of *Love's Labour's Lost*," *PMLA*, 39:581-611 (1924); Arthur Acheson, *Shakespeare's Lost Years in London, 1586-1592* (New York, 1920), pp. 166-171; "C," "Shakspeare, Sidney, and Essex," *N & Q*, 3rd ser., 3:124-125; Muriel C. Bradbrook, *The School of Night* (Cambridge, Eng., 1936), pp. 1-26, 153-178; Frances A. Yates, *A Study of Love's Labour's Lost* (Cambridge, Eng., 1936), pp. 20-26 and *passim*. On the lack of textual support for the "school of night" theory, see Ernest A. Strathmann, "The Textual Evidence for 'The School of Night,'" *MLN*, 56:176-186 (1941).

55. A. L. Rowse, *William Shakespeare—A Biography* (New York, 1963), pp. 211-220; Rupert Taylor, *The Date of Love's Labour's Lost* (New York, 1932), p. 35.

56. Oscar J. Campbell, "*Love's Labour's Lost* Re-Studied," in *Studies in Shakespeare, Milton, and Donne* (University of Michigan, 1925), pp. 3-45; John Phelps, "The Source of *Love's Labour's Lost*," *Shakespeare Association Bulletin*, 17:97-102 (1942); Harbage, "*Love's Labor's Lost* and Early Shakespeare," *PQ*, 41:18-36.

57. Rickert, "Political Propaganda and Satire," *MP*, 21:147, discounts the competition as a draw. Paul N. Siegel, "*A Midsummer Night's Dream* and the Wedding Guests," *SQ*, 4:139-144 (1953) sees the play "as part of the festivities for some aristocratic wedding," but does not identify. C. L. Barber, *Shakespeare's Festive Comedy* (Princeton, 1959), pp. 121-122, supposes the play a courtly entertainment, but argues that no one has ever demonstrated any refer-

ence to court intrigue. Rowse, *Shakespeare*, pp. 203-205, prefers the wedding of Sir Thomas Heneage and the Countess of Southampton; see E. K. Chambers, *William Shakespeare: A Study of Facts and Problems* (Oxford, 1951), I, 358. W. J. Lawrence, "The Date of *A Midsummer Night's Dream*," *LTLS*, Dec. 9, 1920, p. 826, dismisses the idea of a wedding altogether.

58. Gray, "Secret of *Love's Labour's Lost*," *PMLA*, 39:611n23; C. C. Stopes, *William Hunnis and the Revels of the Chapel Royal* (Louvain, 1910), p. 243; E. K. Chambers, *The Elizabethan Stage* (Oxford, 1923), I, 124.

59. Rickert, "Political Propaganda and Satire," *MP*, 21:53-87, 133-154. Phillips, *Lord Burghley in Shakespeare*, pp. 155-169, argues irresponsibly that Bottom is Lord Burghley.

60. Rowse, *Shakespeare*, pp. 220-226.

61. "C," "Shakspeare, Sidney, and Essex," *N & Q*, 3rd ser., 3:125-126.

62. Lilian Winstanley, *Hamlet and the Scottish Succession* (Cambridge, Eng., 1921), pp. 11-14; Albright, "Shakespeare's *Richard II* and Essex," *PMLA*, 42:687; Rowse, *Shakespeare*, pp. 227-228.

63. Norman Nathan, "Is Shylock Philip Henslowe?" *N & Q*, 193:163-165 (1948).

64. John de Groot, *The Shakespeares and "The Old Faith"* (New York, 1946), pp. 180-223; Acheson, *Shakespeare's Lost Years*, pp. 133-149.

65. Sharpe, *Real War of the Theaters*, p. 186; Rowse, *Shakespeare*, pp. 236-239.

66. Albright, "Shakespeare's *Richard II* and Essex," *PMLA*, 42:686-720. See also Clark, *Ralegh and Marlowe*, pp. 116-144.

67. Robert B. Sharpe, "We Band of Brothers," *SP*, 26:166-176 (1929); LeComte, "The Ending of *Hamlet*," *ELH*, 17:113; J. Dover Wilson, ed., *The First Part of the History of Henry IV* (Cambridge, Eng., 1946), p. 120; Edward S. LeComte, "Shakspere, Guilpin, and Essex," *Shakespeare Association Bulletin*, 23:17-19 (1948); Campbell, *Shakespeare's "Histories,"* p. 287. See Irving Ribner, *The English History Play in the Age of Shakespeare*, rev. ed. (New York, 1965), p. 186.

68. Heffner, "Shakespeare, Hayward, and Essex," *PMLA*, 45:754-780.

69. Warren D. Smith, "The *Henry V* Choruses in the First Folio," *JEGP*, 53:38-57 (1954).

70. G. B. Harrison, "Shakespeare's Topical Significances," *LTLS*, Nov. 13, 1930, p. 939, and Nov. 20, 1930, p. 974; Lytton Strachey, *Elizabeth and Essex* (New York, 1928), p. 113.

71. James K. Lowers, *Mirrors for Rebels: A Study of Polemical Literature Relating to the Northern Rebellion, 1569* (Berkeley, 1953), pp. 13-16; Campbell, *Shakespeare's "Histories,"* pp. 229-237; Richard Simpson, "The Politics of Shakspere's Historical Plays," *Transactions of the New Shakspere Society*, ser. 1, pt. 2 (1874), pp. 396-441. Cf. Ribner, *English History Play*, p. 182.

72. Letter of Rowland Whyte to Sir Robert Sidney, Jan. 21, 1597/8, *Sidney Papers*, ed. Collins, II, 83-84. See Alwin Thaler, "The Original Malvolio?" *Shakespeare Association Bulletin*, 7:57-71 (1932).

73. Sharpe, *Real War of the Theaters,* pp. 122-123; Rowse, *Shakespeare,* p. 301.

74. Sharpe, *Real War of the Theaters,* pp. 166-167; Cartwright, *Shakspere and Jonson,* p. 25.

75. Cf. Frederick Tupper, Jr., "The Shaksperean Mob," *PMLA,* 27:486-523 (1912), p. 491.

76. J. W. Thompson, "Hamlet and the Mystery of Amy Robsart," *North American Review,* 215:657-672 (1922).

77. Furness, "A Reply," *North American Review,* 216:357-363 (1922).

78. Winstanley, *Hamlet and Scottish Succession,* pp. 7-10, 41-45, 109-128, 167-180, and *passim;* John E. Hankins, *The Character of Hamlet and Other Essays* (Chapel Hill, 1941), pp. 95-114; Phillips, *Images of a Queen.*

79. James T. Foard, "The Genesis of Hamlet," *Manchester Quarterly,* 8:1-31, 122-152, 220-247 (1889); J. Dover Wilson, ed., *Hamlet* (Cambridge, Eng., 1934), p. lxvi; LeComte, "The Ending of Hamlet," *ELH,* 17:87-114; Richard H. Rupp, "Hamlet and the Politics of Providence," *Xavier University Studies,* 4:155-167 (1965).

80. Thompson, "Hamlet and Amy Robsart," *North American Review,* 215:658; Winstanley, *Hamlet and Scottish Succession,* pp. 109-128; Simpson, "Political Use of the Stage," *New Shakspere Society Transactions* (1874), p. 393; Lily B. Campbell, "Polonius: The Tyrant's Ears," *Joseph Quincy Adams Memorial Studies,* ed. McManaway et al. (Washington, D.C., 1948), pp. 295-313; Rowse, *Shakespeare,* p. 323; Phillips, *Lord Burghley in Shakespeare,* pp. 125-139; J. Dover Wilson, *The Essential Shakespeare* (Cambridge, Eng., 1932), p. 104.

81. Rowse, *Shakespeare,* p. 318; Tupper, "The Shaksperean Mob," *PMLA,* 27:491; Hankins, *The Character of Hamlet,* p. 113.

82. "C," "Shakspeare, Sidney, and Essex," *N & Q,* 3rd ser., 3:82-84, 103-105. For a comprehensive review of topical theories of *Hamlet* in the nineteenth and early twentieth centuries, see Ernest Jones, *Hamlet and Oedipus* (London, 1949), pp. 24-25.

83. E. A. J. Honigmann, "The Politics in *Hamlet* and 'The World of the Play,'" *Stratford upon Avon Studies V* (London, 1963), pp. 129-147; A. P. Stabler, "Elective Monarchy in the Sources of *Hamlet,*" *SP,* 62:654-661 (1965). Cf. J. D. Wilson, *What Happens in Hamlet,* 3rd ed. (Cambridge, Eng., 1951), pp. 35-38; and Wilson, ed., *Hamlet,* pp. liv-lvi.

84. Wilson, *The Essential Shakespeare,* pp. 100-102; Rowse, *Shakespeare,* pp. 340-345; Harrison, "Shakespeare's Topical Significances," *LTLS,* Nov. 20, 1930, p. 974; Sharpe, *Real War of the Theaters,* p. 204. Cf. Oscar J. Campbell, *Comicall Satyre and Shakespeare's Troilus and Cressida* (San Marino, Calif., 1938), pp. 218-223; Kimbrough, *Shakespeare's Troilus and Cressida,* pp. 2-3.

85. Rowse, *Shakespeare,* pp. 350-354; Acheson, *Shakespeare's Lost Years,* pp. 194f. See Sharpe, *Real War of the Theaters,* pp. 123-124.

86. Rowse, *Shakespeare,* pp. 360-362; Ernest Schanzer, *The Problem Plays of Shakespeare* (London, 1963), pp. 121-125; Josephine W. Bennett, *Measure*

for Measure as Royal Entertainment (New York, 1966); J. W. Lever, "The Date of *Measure for Measure*," *SQ*, 10:381-388 (1959). Cf. David L. Stevenson, "Design and Structure in *Measure for Measure*: A New Appraisal," *ELH*, 23:256-278 (1956).

87. Henry N. Paul, *The Royal Play of Macbeth* (New York, 1950). See also J. Q. Adams, ed., *Macbeth* (Boston, 1931), pp. 235-251; Lilian Winstanley, *Macbeth, King Lear, and Contemporary History* (Cambridge, Eng., 1922), pp. 37-137; Lily B. Campbell, "Political Ideas in *Macbeth* IV. iii," *SQ*, 2:281-286 (1951).

88. For refutations of excessively narrow readings of the play, see William A. Armstrong, "The Elizabethan Conception of the Tyrant," *RES*, 22:161-181 (1946); and Irving Ribner, "Political Doctrine in *Macbeth*," *SQ*, 4:202-205 (1953).

89. Winstanley, *Macbeth, Lear, and Contemporary History*, pp. 138-222.

90. Tupper, "The Shaksperean Mob," *PMLA*, 27:491; Cartwright, *Shakspere and Jonson*, p. 25; Dixon Wecter, "Shakespere's Purpose in *Timon of Athens*," *PMLA*, 43:701-721 (1928); Clark, *Ralegh and Marlowe*, pp. 137-144.

91. Leslie Hotson, *Shakespeare versus Shallow* (Boston, 1931), refuted by John E. Hannigan, "Shakespeare *versus* Shallow," *Shakespeare Association Bulletin*, 7:174-182 (1932); Thaler, "The Original Malvolio?" *Shakespeare Association Bulletin*, 7:57-71; Acheson, *Shakespeare's Lost Years*, pp. 181-222; Chambers, *Elizabethan Stage*, III, 249; Denver E. Baughan, "A Compliment to Sidney in *Hamlet*," *N & Q*, 177:133-136 (1939); Halpin, *Oberon's Vision*, pp. 74-75; Richard Simpson, ed., *The School of Shakspere* (New York, 1878), II, 373f.

2. THE WORLDLY CHURCH AND COURT POLITICS

1. Karl Young, *The Drama of the Medieval Church* (Oxford, 1933), II, 392-396; Arthur Heiserman, *Skelton and Satire* (Chicago, 1961), p. 83.

2. F. J. Furnivall and Alfred W. Pollard, eds., *The Macro Plays*, EETS Extra Series, 91 (London, 1904). All line references are to this edition. For editions used in other plays throughout this book, see "Texts of the Plays," above.

3. Walter K. Smart, *Some English and Latin Sources and Parallels for the Morality of Wisdom* (Menasha, Wis., 1912), pp. 78-80.

4. Paul M. Kendall, *Richard the Third* (New York, 1955), pp. 280-284; Lawrence Stone, *The Crisis of the Aristocracy, 1558-1641* (Oxford, 1965), pp. 199-203; G. R. Elton, *The Tudor Revolution in Government* (Cambridge, Eng., 1953), pp. 19f.

5. Robert L. Ramsay, ed., *Magnyfycence*, EETS Extra Series, 98 (London, 1908), p. clxxxii.

6. *Ibid.*, pp. cvi-cxxviii.

7. Smart, *Sources and Parallels for Wisdom*, pp. 82-84; E. N. S. Thompson,

"The English Moral Plays," *Transactions of the Connecticut Academy of Arts and Sciences*, 14:291-414 (1910), pp. 338-340.

8. Willard Farnham, *The Medieval Heritage of Elizabethan Tragedy* (Berkeley, 1936), pp. 196-197.

9. Rev. John J. Molloy, *A Theological Interpretation of the Moral Play, Wisdom, Who Is Christ* (Washington, D.C., 1952), pp. 198-215, xiii. Molloy argues that the play was not written exclusively for those in the religious state.

10. Heiserman, *Skelton and Satire*, pp. 99-101.

11. See W. W. Greg, ed., *Everyman* (Louvain, 1910), pp. 62-69.

12. I am indebted for this information to two able graduate students at New York University summer school, 1963, Father Louis Gioia and Mr. Foster Gilece.

13. Cf. Joseph Q. Adams, ed., *Chief Pre-Shakespearean Dramas* (Boston, 1924), pp. 54n1, 262; Young, *Drama of the Medieval Church*, II, 247-248.

14. Harold C. Gardiner, S.J., *Mysteries' End: An Investigation of the Last Days of the Medieval Religious Stage* (New Haven, 1946), p. 55. Father Gardiner urges cogently that the comparative lack of miracle plays in England is probably the result of the loss of the monasteries.

15. Jesse W. Harris, *John Bale, A Study in the Minor Literature of the Reformation* (Urbana, Ill., 1940), p. 20. On the possibility of other plays dealing with Jewish conversions, and associated with Corpus Christi day, see V. A. Kolve, *The Play Called Corpus Christi* (Stanford, Calif., 1966), pp. 47-48.

16. W. K. Smart, "Some Notes on *Mankind*," *MP*, 14:45-58, 293-313 (1916); Furnivall and Pollard, eds., *Macro Plays*, pp. xi-xii.

17. Mabel M. Keiller, "The Influence of *Piers Plowman* on the Macro Play of *Mankind*," *PMLA*, 26:339-355 (1911); W. Roy MacKenzie, "A New Source for *Mankind*," *PMLA*, 27:98-105 (1912).

3. CHAPLAIN MEDWALL AND THE NEW TUDOR RULING CLASS

1. J. H. Hexter, *Reappraisals in History* (London, 1961), pp. 45-116; Wallace T. MacCaffrey, "Place and Patronage in Elizabethan Politics," in *Elizabethan Government and Society*, ed. Bindoff et al., pp. 95-126; Stone, *Crisis of the Aristocracy*, pp. 5-36 and *passim;* Elton, *Tudor Revolution in Government*, pp. 33-34.

2. *Answer Made by the Kinges Highnes to the Petition of the Rebelles in Yorkshire* (1536). See Kenneth W. Cameron, *Authorship and Sources of "Gentleness and Nobility"* (Raleigh, N.C., 1941), p. 30.

3. Hexter, *Reappraisals in History*, pp. 71-116; MacCaffrey, "Place and Patronage in Elizabethan Politics," pp. 95-100; Stone, *Crisis of the Aristocracy*, pp. 5-56.

4. Fritz Caspari, *Humanism and the Social Order in Tudor England* (Chicago, 1954), pp. 1-5; Paul N. Siegel, "English Humanism and the New Tudor

Aristocracy," *JHI*, 13:450-468 (1952), and *Shakespearean Tragedy and the Elizabethan Compromise* (New York, 1957), p. 4. Cf. R. H. Tawney, *The Agrarian Problem in the Sixteenth Century* (London, 1912), pp. 177f.

5. James K. Lowers, "High Comedy Elements in Medwall's *Fulgens and Lucres*," *ELH*, 8:103-106 (1941); Louis B. Wright, "Notes on *Fulgens and Lucres:* New Light on the Interlude," *MLN*, 41:97-100 (1926).

6. Charles Williams, *Henry VII* (London, 1937), p. 212.

7. Arthur W. Reed, *Early Tudor Drama: Medwall, the Rastells, Heywood, and the More Circle* (London, 1926), pp. 94-147.

8. Charles R. Baskervill, "Conventional Features of Medwall's *Fulgens and Lucres*," *MP*, 24:419-442 (1927).

9. Worcester was known as "the butcher of England" during the Lancastrian-Yorkist wars; see Joseph Haslewood, ed., *Mirror for Magistrates* (London, 1815), II, 201-209, and H. B. Lathrop, "The Translations of John Tiptoft," *MLN*, 41:496-501 (1926).

10. Eugene M. Waith, "*Controversia* in the English Drama: Medwall and Massinger," *PMLA*, 68:286-303 (1953).

11. Ramsay, ed., *Magnyfycence*, pp. lxxviii-lxxix; Friedrich Brie, "Skelton-Studien," *Englische Studien*, 37:1-86 (1906), p. 40. See also the first part of the Digby *Mary Magdalene* for a satire of exaggerated sleeves, false hair, etc., in the character of Curiosity or Pride (ll. 491-506).

12. Williams, *Henry VII*, pp. 166-168, 178.

13. F. S. Boas and A. W. Reed, eds., *Fulgens & Lucres. A Fifteenth-Century Secular Play* (London, 1926), pp. xix-xx.

14. Anne Righter, *Shakespeare and the Idea of the Play* (London, 1962), pp. 37-40.

15. Heiserman, *Skelton and Satire*, pp. 91-92.

4. SKELTON AND THE OLD ARISTOCRACY

1. Elton, *Tudor Revolution in Government*, pp. 62-63; Stone, *Crisis of the Aristocracy*, pp. 59-60.

2. On Skelton's humanistic achievement, see William Nelson, *John Skelton, Laureate* (New York, 1939), pp. 40-58, 75-76; on Skelton and the More circle, see Pearl Hogrefe, *The Sir Thomas More Circle* (Urbana, Ill., 1959), pp. 311-313.

3. R. L. Dunbabin, "Notes on Skelton," *MLR*, 12:129-139, 257-265 (1917). Cf. Brie, "Skelton-Studien," *Englische Studien*, 37:80; Arno Thümmel, *Studien über John Skelton* (Leipzig, 1905), p. 19; W. H. Williams, ed., *A Selection from the Poetical Works of John Skelton* (London, 1902), p. 7.

4. George L. Frost and Ray Nash, "*Good Order:* A Morality Fragment," *SP*, 41:483-491 (1944); *Malone Society Collections*, IV (1956), pp. 33-39.

5. Ramsay, ed., *Magnyfycence*, p. cxxv.

6. William Nelson, "Skelton's Quarrel with Wolsey," *PMLA*, 51:377-398 (1936).

7. Ramsay, ed., *Magnyfycence*, pp. xxi-xxv.

8. F. M. Salter, ed., "Skelton's *Speculum Principis*," *Speculum*, 9:25-37 (1934). See Nelson, *John Skelton*, pp. 75-76.

9. Heiserman, *Skelton and Satire*, pp. 75-87; Ramsay, ed., *Magnyfycence*, p. lxxv; Farnham, *Medieval Heritage*, pp. 216-217, 223.

10. William O. Harris, "Wolsey and Skelton's *Magnyfycence*: A Re-evaluation," *SP*, 57:99-122 (1960), and *Skelton's Magnyfycence and the Cardinal Virtue Tradition* (Chapel Hill, N.C., 1965), pp. 12-45. E. S. Hooper, "Skelton's *Magnyfycence* and Cardinal Wolsey," *MLN*, 16:426-429 (1901), unwisely suggested that Magnificence is to be equated with Wolsey.

11. Heiserman, *Skelton and Satire*, pp. 81-82.

12. On Thomas More's wary appraisal of Henry VIII in 1516, see Edward Surtz, S.J., and J. H. Hexter, eds., *Utopia*, in the Yale Edition of the Complete Works of St. Thomas More (New Haven, 1965), pp. lxxxi-lxxxvi.

13. Ramsay, ed., *Magnyfycence*, pp. cxix-cxx.

14. Harris, "Wolsey and *Magnyfycence*," *SP*, 57:99-122, and *Magnyfycence and the Cardinal Virtue Tradition*, pp. 14-15, 33-44.

15. Brie, "Skelton-Studien," *Englische Studien*, 37:9.

16. Kendall, *Richard the Third*, p. 377.

17. Letter from Wolsey to Fox, Sept. 30, 1512, in *Letters and Papers of Henry VIII*, I (1509-1514), p. 420.

18. Francis Hackett, *Henry the Eighth* (Garden City, N.Y., 1929), p. 76.

19. Nelson, *John Skelton*, pp. 210-211.

20. Ramsay, ed., *Magnyfycence*, pp. xlviii-l.

21. H. L. R. Edwards, *Skelton, the Life and Times of an Early Tudor Poet* (London, 1949), p. 177; Dodds, "Early Political Plays," *Library*, 3rd ser., 4:394; and Anglo, "Court Festivals of Henry VII," *BJRL*, 43:12-26, esp. p. 20.

22. Ramsay, ed., *Magnyfycence*, p. lxxxi.

23. G. R. Elton, *Henry VIII: An Essay in Revision* (London, 1962), p. 10, underscores "the relative ease with which this powerful and personal monarch could be manipulated by those who knew how to play on his prejudices, fears and suspicions."

24. Harris, *Magnyfycence and the Cardinal Virtue Tradition*, *passim*.

5. HEYWOOD'S COMIC PLEADING FOR RECONCILIATION

1. T. S. Graves, "The Heywood Circle and the Reformation," *MP*, 10:553-572 (1913); Reed, *Early Tudor Drama*, pp. 29-71.

2. Alfred W. Pollard, "John Heywood: Critical Essay," in C. M. Gayley, ed., *Representative English Comedies* (New York, 1903), I, 10.

3. Harold N. Hillebrand, "On the Authorship of the Interludes Attributed to John Heywood," *MP*, 13:267-280 (1915).

4. Kenneth W. Cameron, *John Heywood's "Play of the Wether,"* A Study in Early Tudor Drama (Raleigh, N.C., 1941). See also Hogrefe, *The More Circle*, pp. 305-309.

5. David M. Bevington, *From "Mankind" to Marlowe* (Cambridge, Mass., 1962), pp. 40-41.

6. E. K. Chambers, *The Mediaeval Stage* (Oxford, 1903), I, 336-371.

7. T. W. Craik, "Experiment and Variety in John Heywood's Plays," *Renaissance Drama*, 7:6-11 (1964).

8. More, *Utopia*, ed. Surtz and Hexter, p. 63. For the ending of *Calisto and Melibea*, see Chapter 6 below.

9. Emile Legouis and Louis Cazamian, *A History of English Literature*, rev. ed. (New York, 1935), p. 243. Cf. Hogrefe, *The More Circle*, pp. 290-293.

10. Charles W. Wallace, *The Evolution of the English Drama up to Shakespeare* (Berlin, 1912), p. 52.

11. Reed, *Early Tudor Drama*, pp. 139-144.

6. SPECULATIONS IN DEMOCRATIC IDEALISM

1. Cameron, *Gentleness and Nobility*, pp. 9-13; G. R. Owst, *Literature and Pulpit in Medieval England* (Cambridge, Eng., 1933), Chapter V: "The Preaching of Satire and Complaint"; Ruth Kelso, *The Doctrine of the English Gentleman in the Sixteenth Century*, Univ. of Illinois Studies in Language and Literature, No. 14 (Urbana, Ill., 1929), pp. 18-41 and *passim;* Ruth Kelso, "Sixteenth Century Definitions of the Gentleman in England," *JEGP*, 24:370-382 (1925); Ruth Mohl, *The Three Estates in Medieval and Renaissance Literature* (New York, 1933), pp. 20f, 197-229, and *passim*.

2. David M. Bevington, "The Dialogue in *Utopia*: Two Sides to the Question," *SP*, 58:496-509 (1961).

3. Erasmus, *Institutio Principis Christiani* (1516). See Frederic Seebohm, *The Oxford Reformers*, 3rd ed. (London, 1887), pp. 365-378.

4. Hogrefe, *The More Circle*, p. 287.

5. Thomas Starkey, *A Dialogue Between Cardinal Pole and Thomas Lupset*, in *England in the Reign of King Henry the Eighth*, ed. Sidney J. Herrtage, EETS Extra Series, 32 (London, 1878), pp. 104-116, 131-132, 159, 167, 185; Helen C. White, *Social Criticism in Popular Religious Literature of the Sixteenth Century* (New York, 1944), pp. 62-73, 110-131. See Cameron, *Gentleness and Nobility*, p. 33. *A Discourse of the Common Weal of this Realm of England*, ed. Elizabeth Lamond (Cambridge, Eng., 1893, reprinted 1929), is, as Miss White observes, a more pragmatic analysis of England's social ills of 1549, concentrating on trenchant description rather than on philosophic speculation.

6. John Rastell, *Abridgement of the Statutes* (London, 1527), "Prohemium," sig. A1.

7. Reed, *Early Tudor Drama*, pp. 1-28.

8. W. Gordon Zeeveld, *Foundations of Tudor Policy* (Cambridge, Mass., 1948), p. 204.

9. Favoring Heywood's authorship are C. F. Tucker Brooke, "*Gentleness and Nobility;* The Authorship and Source," *MLR*, 6:458-461 (1911); J. E. Bernard, Jr., *The Prosody of the Tudor Interlude* (New Haven, 1939), p. 54; and Cameron, *Gentleness and Nobility*, pp. 59-92. Favoring Rastell's authorship are Reed, *Early Tudor Drama*, pp. 104-117; Esther C. Dunn, "John Rastell and *Gentleness and Nobility*," *MLR*, 12:266-278 (1917); and Pollard, "Heywood," in *Representative English Comedies*, ed. Gayley, I, 8-9.

10. C. R. Baskervill, "John Rastell's Dramatic Activities," *MP*, 13:557-560 (1916).

11. Cameron, *Gentleness and Nobility*, pp. 36-58.

12. Pollard, "Heywood," in *Representative English Comedies*, ed. Gayley, I, 8-9. On the absorption of bourgeois land-purchasers into the landed aristocracy, see Hexter, *Reappraisals in History*, pp. 91-93, and Stone, *Crisis of the Aristocracy*, pp. 27-28.

13. Cameron, *Gentleness and Nobility*, pp. 59-92; Hogrefe, *The More Circle*, pp. 337-346.

14. Bevington, "*Mankind*" to Marlowe, p. 45.

15. Hogrefe, *The More Circle*, pp. 343-345; Reed, *Early Tudor Drama*, pp. 113-117. See also H. Warner Allen, ed., *Celestina, or the Tragi-Comedy of Calisto and Melebea*, by de Rojas, trans. James Mabbe (London, 1923).

16. More, *Utopia*, ed. Surtz and Hexter, p. 103.

7. ROYAL DIVORCE AND SUPPRESSION OF THE MONASTERIES

1. Zeeveld, *Foundations of Tudor Policy*, pp. 201-202. See *Letters and Papers of Henry VIII*, XII, pt. 1 (1537), pp. 284, 519.

2. Hogrefe, *The More Circle*, pp. 230-238, 334-337.

3. Roy was a friar observant of the Franciscan house at Greenwich; see W. W. Greg, ed., *Godly Queen Hester* (Louvain, 1904), p. xi. Katharine was especially close to this religious house; but Roy became, like Bale, a notorious renegade, preaching against Latin scriptures, the mass, and monasticism itself. He was a collaborator with Tyndale before the presumed date of *Hester*.

4. Wickham, *Early English Stages*, I, 70-71. See Chapter 1 above, n. 20 and accompanying text.

5. *Letters and Papers of Henry VIII*, XII, pt. I (1537), pp. 462-464. See J. E. Neale, *Elizabeth I and Her Parliaments*, 2 vols., 1559-1581 and 1584-1601 (New York, 1958), I, 277-278.

6. Vulgate: "nec habebat potestatem ad regem ultra redeundi nisi voluisset

rex, et eam venire iussisset ex nomine." For English text I use the Coverdale translation of 1535. Although it was not in print in 1527-1529, it represents a closely contemporary translation from the Vulgate. The author of *Hester* unquestionably used the Vulgate. His spellings of characters' names are those of early Tudor Vulgate editions: Assuerus, Hester, Aman, Mardocheus. Coverdale, translating chiefly from the Vulgate, has Ahasuerus, Hester, Mardocheus, Aman. The Wyclifite texts of the late fourteenth century, also derived from the Vulgate, have Assuer or Assuerus, Ester or Hester, Mardoche or Mardochee, Aaman or Aman. The Authorized Version of James' reign departs somewhat from the Vulgate: Ahasuerus, Esther, Mordecai, Haman. For the convenience of the modern reader I have keyed chapter and verse citations to the Authorized Version.

7. Dodds, "Early Political Plays," *Library*, 3rd ser., 4:398.

8. Bernard Spivack, *Shakespeare and the Allegory of Evil* (New York, 1958), pp. 256-259.

9. Dunbabin, "Notes on Skelton," *MLR*, 12:258.

10. James Gairdner, *The English Church in the Sixteenth Century*, in *A History of the English Church*, ed. W. R. W. Stephens and William Hunt, vol. 4 (London, 1902), p. 81.

11. Harris, "Wolsey and *Magnyfycence*," *SP*, 57:102; John M. Berdan, "The Dating of Skelton's Satires," *PMLA*, 29:499-516 (1914), pp. 509-510.

12. Greg, ed., *Godly Queen Hester*, p. x.

13. Vulgate: "et decem millia talentorum appendam arcariis gazae tuae."

14. See Chambers, *Elizabethan Stage*, III, 25-27.

15. Madeleine H. Dodds, "The Date of *Albion, Knight*," *The Library*, 3rd ser., 4:157-170 (1913). Cf. Gwen Ann Jones, "The Political Significance of the Play of *Albion Knight*," *JEGP*, 17:267-280 (1918), who dates the play 1559-1566 on slender evidence.

16. Gardiner, *Mysteries' End*, pp. 46-57.

17. Dodds, "Early Political Plays," *Library*, 3rd ser., 4:403.

8. HENRY VIII AND HIS SON AS PROTESTANT SAINTS

1. *Letters and Papers of Henry VIII*, XII, pt. 1 (1537), pp. 557, 585. See Chapter 1 n. 24, above. John Hazel Smith, ed. and trans., *A Humanist's "Trew Imitation": Thomas Watson's Absalom* (Urbana, Ill., 1964), argues entirely without substantiation that Watson's *Absalom* contains topical passages in which this Catholic humanist complained of Henry VIII's rash divorce and his Royal Injunctions of 1530. See pp. 37, 100-101, 170-171.

2. T. W. Craik, "The Political Interpretation of Two Tudor Interludes: *Temperance and Humility* and *Wealth and Health*," *RES*, N.S. 4:98-108 (1953). As to date, W. W. Greg, ed., *Malone Society Collections*, I, pt. 3, pp.

243-246, believes the printer to have been De Worde, Pynson, or Skot, all of whom were dead by 1536.

3. *Letters and Papers of Henry VIII*, XII, pt. 1 (1537), p. 244. See Gertrude M. Sibley, *The Lost Plays and Masques, 1500-1642* (Ithaca, N.Y., 1933), p. 3.

4. Chambers, *Mediaeval Stage*, II, 217-218; Gardiner, *Mysteries' End*, pp. 51-53; Dodds, "Early Political Plays," *Library*, 3rd ser., 4:407.

5. Harris, *John Bale*, pp. 67-74.

6. *Ibid.*, pp. 20-23.

7. Virginia C. Gildersleeve, *Government Regulation of the Elizabethan Drama* (New York, 1908), p. 6.

8. Harris, *John Bale*, pp. 96-98.

9. Edwin S. Miller, "The Roman Rite in Bale's *King John*," *PMLA*, 64:802-822 (1949).

10. Ribner, *English History Play*, p. 35; Honor McCusker, *John Bale, Dramatist and Antiquary* (Bryn Mawr, Pa., 1942), pp. 90-93.

11. Arnold Edinborough, "The Early Tudor Revels Office," *SQ*, 2:19-25 (1951); also see Alfred Harbage, *Annals of English Drama, 975-1700*, rev. S. Schoenbaum (Philadelphia, 1964), pp. 26-31.

12. Frederick S. Boas, "*The Four Cardynal Vertues*, A Fragmentary Moral Interlude," *Queen's Quarterly*, 58:85-91 (1951). William Middylton, the printer, was active from 1541 to 1549. W. W. Greg, *Malone Society Collections*, IV, 41-54, speculates that the play may be related somehow to *Temperance and Humility* (ca. 1535), but the political and religious attitudes of the two are different. See above, this chapter. See also Harris, *Magnyfycence and the Cardinal Virtue Tradition*, pp. 157-168.

13. LeRoy Merrill, ed., *The Life and Poems of Nicholas Grimald* (New Haven, 1925), pp. 57-215.

14. William J. Griffin, "Notes on Early Tudor Control of the Stage," *MLN*, 58:50-54 (1943).

15. Dodds, "Early Political Plays," *Library*, 3rd ser., 4:408; Chambers, *Mediaeval Stage*, II, 221-222.

16. Wickham, *Early English Stages*, II, pt. 1, pp. 15-16, 63.

17. Griffin, "Early Tudor Control of the Stage," *MLN*, 58:51-52.

18. See Albert Feuillerat, ed., *Documents Relating to the Revels at Court in the Time of King Edward VI and Queen Mary* (Louvain, 1914), pp. 5, 20, 26, 255-256, 266.

19. Wickham, *Early English Stages*, II, pt. 1, pp. 65-66, citing Raphael Holinshed, *The Chronicles of England, Scotland, and Ireland* (London, 1586-1587), III, 1028.

20. Gildersleeve, *Government Regulation of the Drama*, pp. 8-10; Lamond, ed., *Discourse of the Common Weal*, pp. xii-xiii.

21. Gardiner, *Mysteries' End*, pp. 58-60.

22. Albert Feuillerat, "An Unknown Protestant Morality Play," *MLR*, 9:94-96 (1914); C. R. Baskervill, "On Two Old Plays," *MP*, 14:16 (1916).

23. *Malone Society Collections,* I, 17-25. The date may also be early Eliza-bethan, although restriction on drama during this later period was notably more stringent than in 1547-1549. Anabaptism was clearly a recognized threat in midcentury England. See Chambers, *Elizabethan Stage,* IV, 28-29. Leah Scragg, "'Love Feigned and Unfeigned': A Note on the Use of Allegory on the Tudor Stage," *ELN,* 3:248-252 (1966), believes the play was probably performed between 1540 and 1560. Cf. E. Beatrice Daw, *"Love Feyned and Unfeyned* and the English Anabaptists," *PMLA,* 32:267-291 (1917), who argues unwisely for seventeenth-century composition.

24. William L. Edgerton, "The Apostasy of Nicholas Udall," *N & Q,* 195:223-226 (1950). Cf. A. R. Moon, "Was Nicholas Udall the Author of *Thersites?" The Library,* 4th ser., 7:184-193 (1926), who argues that the references to Purgatory are Lutheran.

25. Heywood played an interlude with his children before Princess Mary in 1538; see also Arthur Brown, "Two Notes on John Redford," *MLR,* 43:508-510 (1948).

26. Wallace, *Evolution of English Drama,* p. 101, proposes Udall as author of *Jacob and Esau.* For confirmation see Leicester Bradner, "A Test for Udall's Authorship," *MLN,* 42:378-380 (1927).

27. The author of *Jacob and Esau* probably used Cranmer and Cromwell's *"Great" Bible,* first published in 1539. Its circulation was restricted somewhat during the retrenchment years of 1540-1546, but it was universally available thereafter.

28. *The Merchant of Venice,* I, iii, 72-97. See Leah W. Wilkins, "Shylock's Pound of Flesh and Laban's Sheep," *MLN,* 62:28-30 (1947).

29. Licensed to the printer in 1560, *Nice Wanton* concludes with a conven-tional flattering of Elizabeth; but the rhyming on two occasions of "queens" with "things" suggests a simple alteration of the original "kings" written before the death of Edward VI. See John M. Manly, ed., *Specimens of the Pre-Shaksperean Drama* (Boston, 1897), p. 479n2.

9. ENGLAND RETURNS TO CATHOLICISM: HOW FAR?

1. H. F. M. Prescott, *Mary Tudor* (New York: Macmillan paperbacks, 1962), p. 196.

2. W. C. Hazlitt, ed., *The English Drama and Stage under the Tudor and Stuart Princes, 1543-1644* (London, 1869), pp. 15-18.

3. John Strype, ed., *Historical Memorials, Ecclesiastical and Civil, of Events under the Reign of Queen Mary I* (London, 1721), III, 297, Chapter XXXVIII, April 30, 1556. The Council's letter is quoted by Rickert, "Political Propa-ganda and Satire," *MP,* 21:137.

4. Leonard A. Magnus, ed., *Respublica,* EETS Extra Series, 94 (London, 1905), p. xxv. On the inflation and mismanagement of 1541-1547, see Elton,

Henry VIII, pp. 8-15, and *Tudor Revolution in Government*, pp. 63-98; Sir John Clapham, *A Concise Economic History of Britain from the Earliest Times to 1750* (Cambridge, Eng., 1949), p. 187.

5. Magnus, ed., *Respublica*, p. xxvi.

6. *Ibid.*, p. xxv, and note to line 847. For contemporary observations on the evils of exporting strategic metals and devaluating the coinage, see Lamond, ed., *Discourse of the Common Weal*, pp. 35, 79.

7. F. J. Fisher, "Commercial Trends and Policy in Sixteenth-Century England," *The Economic History Review*, 10:95-117 (1940); Peter Ramsey, *Tudor Economic Problems* (London, 1963), pp. 24-47; Clapham, *Concise Economic History of Britain*, pp. 210-211; Stone, *Crisis of the Aristocracy*, p. 48.

8. Sibley, *Lost Plays and Masques*, p. 8; G. C. Moore Smith, *College Plays Performed in the University of Cambridge* (Cambridge, Eng., 1923), p. 107. See also Albert Feuillerat, "Performance of a Tragedy at New College, Oxford, in the Time of Queen Mary," *MLR*, 9:96-97 (1914). On the date of *Impatient Poverty*, see Ronald B. McKerrow, ed., *Impacyente Pouerte* (Louvain, 1911), pp. v-xv, 46n253.

9. See, for example, Ewald Flügel, "Nicholas Udall: Critical Essay," in *Representative English Comedies*, ed. Gayley, I, 89-104; and Muriel C. Bradbrook, *The Growth and Structure of Elizabethan Comedy* (London, 1955), p. 37.

10. John W. Hales, "The Date of 'The First English Comedy,'" *Englische Studien*, 18:408-421 (1893); Chambers, *Mediaeval Stage*, II, 215-216; A. W. Reed, "Nicholas Udall and Thomas Wilson," *RES*, 1:275-283 (1925). The date of the third edition of *The Rule of Reason* is January "1553"; the new style of dating (which would indicate 1553 instead of 1554) is conceivable here, especially in a printed book, despite the custom of employing the legal calendar in legal and religious documents. See William L. Edgerton, "The Date of *Roister Doister*," *PQ*, 44:555-560 (1965), and *Nicholas Udall* (New York, 1965), pp. 89-92, who argues for a date of composition in late 1552. *A Pore Helpe* has been shown to be of little value in dating Udall's play; see Cathleen H. Wheat, "*A Pore Helpe, Ralph Roister Doister*, and *Thre Laws*," *PQ*, 28:312-319 (1949), who confutes T. W. Baldwin and M. Channing Linthicum, "The Date of *Ralph Roister Doister*," *PQ*, 6:379-395 (1927), and M. Channing Linthicum, "*A Pore Helpe* and Its Printers," *The Library*, 4th ser., 9:169-183 (1928).

11. See William Peery, "The Prayer for the Queen in *Roister Doister*," *UTSE*, 27:222-233 (1948).

12. Prescott, *Mary Tudor*, p. 98.

13. A. W. Plumstead, "Satirical Parody in *Roister Doister*: A Reinterpretation," *SP*, 60:141-154 (1963). Edgerton, "The Date of *Roister Doister*," *PQ*, 44:555-560, overstresses the Protestant aspect of Udall's career, especially around 1552-1553. Even if written in 1552, *Roister Doister* could scarcely have been presented before Edward VI's Protestant court. The burlesque of

the Burial for the Dead is too loving and familiar, not satirical enough for Edwardian drama.

14. Edwin S. Miller, "Roister Doister's 'Funeralls,'" *SP*, 43:42-58 (1946); Edgerton, "The Apostasy of Udall," *N & Q*, 195:223-226.

15. On date, see Alois Brandl, ed., *Quellen des weltlichen Dramas in England vor Shakespeare* (Strassburg, 1898), p. lxxi, and Chambers, *Mediaeval Stage*, II, 457-458. The printed book of *Jack Juggler* was evidently in existence before the S. R. entry of 1562; see W. W. Greg, "Some Notes on the Stationers' Register," *The Library*, 4th ser., 7:376-386 (1926).

16. Bartlett J. Whiting, *Proverbs in the Earlier English Drama* (Cambridge, Mass., 1938), pp. 198-201. Cf. R. Marienstras, "*Jack Juggler*: Aspects de la conscience individuelle dans une farce du 16ᵉ siècle," *Etudes Anglaises*, 16: 321-330 (1963), and Jacques Voisine, "A propos de *Jack Juggler*," *Etudes Anglaises*, 18:166 (1965), who assume that the epilogue is by the author of the play. For an untenable autobiographical interpretation, see W. H. Williams, "The Date and Authorship of *Jacke Jugeler*," *MLR*, 7:289-295 (1912), and Williams, ed., *Jacke Jugeler* (Cambridge, Eng., 1914), pp. x-xvi. Williams speculates that Udall alludes to his alleged robbing of silver plate in 1542, insinuating that he was forced to confess a crime not committed.

10. THE ELIZABETHAN SETTLEMENT

1. Letter of Il Schifanoya to Castellan of Mantua, *Calendar of State Papers, Venetian*, VII (1558-1580), p. 11. See also Neale, *Elizabeth I and Her Parliaments*, I, 42, for a related episode, 1559, in which Elizabeth, met by an abbot and monks bearing torches, exclaimed, "Away with those torches, for we see very well."

2. Wickham, *Early English Stages*, II, pt. 1, p. 75.

3. *Calendar of State Papers, Spanish*, N.S., I (1558-1567), p. 62.

4. *Calendar of State Papers, Venetian*, VII (1558-1580), pp. 80-81.

5. *Calendar of State Papers, Spanish*, N.S., I (1558-1567), p. 247.

6. M. A. Tierney, ed., *Dodd's Church History of England from the Commencement of the Sixteenth Century to the Revolution in 1688* (London, 1839-1843), II, 149-150. On Elizabeth's policy of tolerance, see Neale, *Elizabeth I and Her Parliaments*, I, 61-62, 121, 191-192, 216, 233, 262-263, 370, 390-391, II, 52, and *passim*. The quotation on causes of conscience and faction is the observation of Sir Francis Bacon, ca. 1588-1589; see *ibid.*, I, 391.

7. *Calendar of State Papers, Spanish*, N.S., I (1558-1567), p. 405.

8. Chambers, *Elizabethan Stage*, I, 244.

9. Celesta Wine, "Nathaniel Wood's *Conflict of Conscience*," *PMLA*, 50:661-678 (1935); Louis B. Wright, "Social Aspects of Some Belated Moralities,"

Anglia, 54:107-148 (1930), p. 114. On the intensity of reforming Protestant pressures in the Parliament of 1571, when many zealous churchmen were going to jail for their sentiments on images and vestments, see Neale, *Elizabeth I and Her Parliaments*, I, 177-181.

10. Celesta Wine, "Nathaniel Woodes, Author of the Morality Play *The Conflict of Conscience*," *RES*, 15:458-463 (1939).

11. Wine, "*Conflict of Conscience*," *PMLA*, 50:673.

12. Leslie M. Oliver, "John Foxe and *The Conflict of Conscience*," *RES*, 25:1-9 (1949).

13. Spivack, *Shakespeare and Allegory of Evil*, p. 260.

14. Leslie M. Oliver, "John Foxe and the Drama *New Custom*," *HLQ*, 10:407-410 (1947), argues that an episode of *New Custom* may also have been revised after 1570, using amplified details from Foxe of a martydom incident not as fully reported in the earlier edition of *The Book of Martyrs*. Frederick G. Fleay, *A Chronicle History of the London Stage, 1559-1642* (London, 1890), pp. 64-65, believes an earlier edition of the play to have existed in Edward VI's reign. Both theories are possible.

15. Rainer Pineas, "The English Morality Play as a Weapon of Religious Controversy," *SEL*, 2:157-180 (1962).

16. Alois Brandl, ed., "*The Longer Thou Livest the More Fool Thou Art*," *SJ*, 36:1-64 (1900), pp. 1-2.

17. Wright, "Social Aspects of Belated Moralities," *Anglia*, 54:112.

18. Craik, "Political Interpretation of *Temperance and Humility* and *Wealth and Health*," *RES*, N.S., 4:98-108, makes a rather flimsy case for dating this play during Mary's reign, identifying Remedy as Cardinal Pole. Rainer Pineas, "The Revision of *Wealth and Health*," *PQ*, 44:560-562 (1965), argues that the play was originally Catholic polemic, but was then revised in Elizabeth's reign with the Protestant Vices easily changed into Catholic Vices. Pineas disputes the identification of Remedy as Cardinal Pole. Mark Hunter, "Notes on the *Interlude of Wealth and Health*," *MLR*, 3:366-369 (1908), speculatively would place the drama as early as the *Intercursus Malus* of 1506. In its revised and garbled state, the text is apparently not suited for a detailed and consistent analysis of political intent.

19. William Cunningham, *The Growth of English Industry and Commerce in Modern Times: The Mercantile System* (Cambridge, Eng., 1912), pp. 75-82; Fisher, "Commercial Trends and Policy," *Economic History Review*, 10:95-117; Ramsey, *Tudor Economic Problems*, pp. 51-78; Clapham, *Concise Economic History of Britain*, pp. 225, 241-251; Lamond, ed., *Discourse of the Common Weal*, pp. 63-67. See also Wright, "Social Aspects of Belated Moralities," *Anglia*, 54:115, and Richard V. Lindabury, *A Study of Patriotism in the Elizabethan Drama* (Princeton, 1930), pp. 105-119.

20. Wright, "Social Aspects of Belated Moralities," *Anglia*, 54:124; Celeste T. Wright, "Some Conventions Regarding the Usurer in Elizabethan Litera-

ture," *SP*, 31:176-197 (1934); Philip Stubbes, *The Anatomy of Abuses* (London, 1583), "Covetousness in Ailgna," and "Great Usury in Ailgna."

21. Cf. Raymond M. Alden, *The Rise of Formal Satire in England* (Philadelphia, 1899), pp. 228f.

22. Celeste T. Wright, "The Usurer's Sin in Elizabethan Literature," *SP*, 35:178-194 (1938).

23. Neale, *Elizabeth I and Her Parliaments*, II, 335-351; Ramsey, *Tudor Economic Problems*, pp. 152-155, 171.

24. Wright, "Social Aspects of Belated Moralities," *Anglia*, 54:120.

25. George L. Kittredge, "The Date of *The Pedlers Prophecie*," *Harvard Studies and Notes in Philology and Literature*, 16:97-118 (1934). Kittredge believes the play too early to have been Robert Wilson's. On the similarity of this play to the program of the radical reformers of midcentury, see White, *Social Criticism in Popular Religious Literature*, pp. 110-131.

26. Wright, "Social Aspects of Belated Moralities," *Anglia*, 54:131.

27. *Ibid.*, p. 130.

28. *Henry IV Part II*, IV, v, 214-215. See G. R. Waggoner, "An Elizabethan Attitude toward Peace and War," *PQ*, 33:20-33 (1954).

29. William Ringler, "The First Phase of the Elizabethan Attack on the Stage, 1558-1579," *HLQ*, 5:391-418 (1942).

11. UNWELCOME ADVICE ON THE SUCCESSION

1. Stone, *Crisis of the Aristocracy*, pp. 206-220, 250-256; J. E. Neale, "The Accession of Queen Elizabeth I," in *Essays in Elizabethan History* (London, 1958), pp. 45-58.

2. J. E. Neale, *Queen Elizabeth I* (New York: Doubleday, 1957), pp. 148-151, and *Elizabeth I and Her Parliaments*, I, 129-176.

3. John H. Pollen, *Mary Queen of Scots and the Babington Plot* (Edinburgh, 1922), p. xiii. See Waller, "The Misfortunes of Arthur," *JEGP*, 24:234.

4. Rickert, "Political Propaganda and Satire," *MP*, 21:138. For considerable information on Norton as a "Parliament man" and pamphleteer against Mary and the Northern Rebellion, see index entries to "Norton" in Neale, *Elizabeth I and Her Parliaments*, vols. 1 and 2, and *The Elizabethan House of Commons* (New Haven, 1950); also Read, "William Cecil and Elizabethan Public Relations," in *Elizabethan Government and Society*, ed. Bindoff et al., p. 31.

5. Sara R. Watson, "*Gorboduc* and the Theory of Tyrannicide," *MLR*, 34:355-366 (1939); S. A. Small, "The Political Import of the Norton Half of *Gorboduc*," *PMLA*, 46:641-646 (1931).

6. Howard Baker, *Induction to Tragedy* (University, La., 1939), pp. 28-29, and Ribner, *English History Play*, p. 41, argue also that I, i is by Sackville. The perils of determining authorship by internal evidence alone are examined by Paul Bacquet, *Un contemporain d'Elisabeth I: Thomas Sackville, l'homme*

et l'oeuvre (Geneva, 1966), pp. 229-230; reviewed in *LTLS*, July 14, 1966, p. 614.

7. See John W. Cunliffe, ed., *Early English Classical Tragedies* (Oxford, 1912), p. 306; and Gertrude C. Reese, "The Question of the Succession in Elizabethan Drama," *UTSE*, 22:59-85 (1942), pp. 62-63.

8. Leonard H. Courtney, "The Tragedy of *Ferrex and Porrex*," *N & Q*, 2nd ser., 10:261-263 (1860); Homer A. Watt, *Gorboduc: or, Ferrex and Porrex* (Univ. of Wisconsin, 1910), pp. 33-45.

9. Neale, *Elizabeth I and Her Parliaments*, I, 109, 145-164, and II, 44-48. Cf. Watson, "*Gorboduc* and Theory of Tyrannicide," *MLR*, 34:355-366, who argues too heretical a position for Norton.

10. Louis B. Wright, "A Political Reflection in Phillip's *Patient Grissell*," *RES*, 4:424-428 (1928); Reese, "Question of the Succession," *UTSE*, 22:65-66.

11. Greg, ed., *Godly Queen Hester*, p. viii.

12. Rickert, "Political Propaganda and Satire," *MP*, 21:148.

13. On Phillip's indebtedness to Chaucer, see Wright, "Political Reflection in *Patient Grissell*," *RES*, 4:424.

14. Neale, *Elizabeth I and Her Parliaments*, I, 109, 125, 147.

15. On performance at court, see Bevington, "*Mankind*" *to Marlowe*, p. 61. Cf. Cunliffe, ed., *English Classical Tragedies*, p. lxx; and Albert Feuillerat, ed., *Documents Relating to the Office of Revels in the Time of Queen Elizabeth* (Louvain, 1908), p. 449, who argue that the play was too crude for performance at court. On Scotland, see James E. Phillips, "A Revaluation of *Horestes* (1567)," *HLQ*, 18:227-244 (1955), and *Images of a Queen*, pp. 45-48.

16. Neale, *Queen Elizabeth*, pp. 157-166.

17. Farnham, *Medieval Heritage*, p. 259.

18. H. Oskar Sommer, ed., *The Recuyell of the Historyes of Troye* (London, 1894), II, 685.

19. E. B. de Chickera, "Horestes' Revenge—Another Interpretation," *N & Q*, N.S., 6:190 (1959).

20. Cf. Phillips, *Images of a Queen*, p. 46.

21. *Ibid.*, pp. 45-48, 55-60; Neale, *Elizabeth I and Her Parliaments*, I, 250.

22. Waller, "The Misfortunes of Arthur," *JEGP*, 24:228-245.

23. Armstrong, "Elizabethan Conception of the Tyrant," *RES*, 22:161-181.

24. Gertrude Reese, "Political Import of *The Misfortunes of Arthur*," *RES*, 21:81-91 (1945); William A. Armstrong, "The Topicality of *The Misfortunes of Arthur*," *N & Q*, N.S., 2:371-373 (1955); Armstrong, "Elizabethan Themes in *The Misfortunes of Arthur*," *RES*, N.S., 7:238-249 (1956).

25. Armstrong, "*The Misfortunes of Arthur*," *RES*, N.S., 7:248.

26. Ribner, *English History Play*, pp. 234-235.

27. Neville Williams, *Thomas Howard:Fourth Duke of Norfolk* (New York, 1965), pp. 252 and *passim*. Quotation from Neale, *Elizabeth I and Her Parliaments*, I, 270.

28. Reese, "*The Misfortunes of Arthur*," *RES*, 21:89.

12. THE QUESTION OF OBEDIENCE TO A TYRANT

1. Rosenberg, *Leicester*, pp. 192-193.
2. William A. Armstrong, "The Authorship and Political Meaning of *Cambises*," *English Studies*, 36:289-299 (1955); Stone, *Crisis of the Aristocracy*, p. 30.
3. Richard Taverner, *The Second Book of the Garden of Wisdom* (London, 1539), fol. 21.
4. Boswell's *Life of Johnson*, Johnson's conversation with Dr. Adam Fergusson, March 31, 1772.
5. William A. Armstrong, "The Background and Sources of Preston's *Cambises*," *English Studies*, 31:129-135 (1950); Don Cameron Allen, "A Source for *Cambises*," *MLN*, 49:384-387 (1934).
6. Wilson, *England's Eliza*, p. 71; Armstrong, "Political Meaning of *Cambises*," *English Studies*, 36:289-292. Cf. Chambers, *Elizabethan Stage*, III, 469; C. R. Baskervill, V. B. Heltzel, and A. H. Nethercot, eds., *Elizabethan and Stuart Plays* (New York, 1934), p. 143; and Adams, ed., *Pre-Shakespearean Dramas*, p. 638.
7. See More, *Utopia*, ed. Surtz and Hexter, p. 87. For other influences on Edwards' thought, especially Plutarch's *Life of Dion*, Cicero's *Tusculan Disputations*, Elyot's *Governor*, Book II, Chapter xi, Aristotle's *Nichomachean Ethics*, and Diogenes Laertius' *Lives of the Philosophers*, see Claude M. Newlin, "Some Sources of Richard Edwards's *Damon and Pythias*," *MLN*, 47:145-147 (1932); Laurens J. Mills, *Some Aspects of Richard Edwards' Damon and Pythias*, Indiana University Studies, No. 75 (Bloomington, Ind., 1927), pp. 3-11; William A. Armstrong, "The Sources of *Damon and Pythias*," *N & Q*, N.S., 3:146-147 (1956); and Leicester Bradner, *The Life and Poems of Richard Edwards* (New Haven, 1927), pp. 58-73.
8. William A. Armstrong, "*Damon and Pythias* and Renaissance Theories of Tragedy," *English Studies*, 39:200-207 (1958), compares Edwards' *ars poetica* with Sidney's later *Defense of Poesy*.

13. THE TRIUMPH OF DEVOTION

1. Josephine W. Bennett, "Churchyard's Description of the Queen's Entertainment at Woodstock in 1592," *MLN*, 55:391-393 (1940); E. K. Chambers, *Sir Henry Lee: An Elizabethan Portrait* (Oxford, 1936), pp. 145-162.
2. E.g., Feuillerat, ed., *Documents Relating to Revels of Elizabeth*, pp. 145, 238.
3. *M. S. R. Collections*, I, pt. 2 (London 1908), pp. 144-148.
4. Wright, "Social Aspects of Belated Moralities," *Anglia*, 54:144. *Liberality and Prodigality* may also have been performed in 1575 and as a revival in 1601 or 1602, shortly before its belated publication, in which case a seeming

allusion to Essex's Irish campaigns and pleas for Elizabeth's support may have provided a piquancy not intended by the original author (probably Sebastian Westcote). See Harold N. Hillebrand, "Sebastian Westcote, Dramatist and Master of the Children of Paul's," *JEGP*, 14:568-584 (1915), and *The Child Actors*, University of Illinois Studies in Language and Literature, No. 11 (Urbana, Ill., 1926), pp. 128-131; Wright, "Social Aspects of Belated Moralities," *Anglia*, 54:146; and Sharpe, *Real War of the Theaters*, p. 183.

5. Baskervill et al., eds., *Elizabethan Plays*, p. 205; John D. Reeves, "The Judgment of Paris as a Device of Tudor Flattery," *N & Q*, N.S., 1:7-11 (1954); Inga-Stina Ekeblad, "On the Background of Peele's *Araygnement of Paris*," *N & Q*, N.S., 3:246-249, 456 (1956). Carter Daniel, "Patterns and Traditions of the Elizabethan Court Play to 1590," unpub. diss., University of Virginia, 1965, has found a painting of "Queen Elizabeth Confounding Juno, Minerva, and Venus" in 1569, by Hans Eworth.

6. R. Warwick Bond, ed., *The Complete Works of John Lyly* (Oxford, 1902), II, 306-309.

7. John L. Lievsay, "Some Renaissance Views of Diogenes the Cynic," in *J. Q. Adams Memorial Studies*, ed. J. F. McManaway et al., pp. 447-455.

8. G. K. Hunter, *John Lyly: The Humanist as Courtier* (London, 1962), pp. 1-35.

9. Simpson, "Political Use of the Stage," *New Shakspere Society Transactions* (1874), p. 381.

10. George P. Baker, "John Lyly: Critical Essay," in *Representative English Comedies* ed. Gayley, I, 265-276.

11. Bond, ed., *John Lyly*, II, 364-367.

12. Frederick G. Fleay, *A Biographical Chronicle of the English Drama, 1559-1642* (London, 1891), II, 40, equates Pandion with Lyly.

13. Bernard F. Huppé, "Allegory of Love in Lyly's Court Comedies," *ELH*, 14:93-113 (1947), p. 98.

14. Albert Feuillerat, *John Lyly* (Cambridge, Eng., 1910), pp. 108-118; Felix Schelling, *Elizabethan Drama, 1558-1642* (Boston, 1908), I, 127; Bond, ed., *John Lyly*, II, 366.

15. Frederick S. Boas, *Queen Elizabeth in Drama, and Related Studies* (London, 1950), pp. 20-21.

16. Reese, "Question of the Succession," *UTSE*, 22:75.

17. Hunter, *John Lyly*, pp. 174-175.

18. Halpin, *Oberon's Vision*, pp. 49-78; Bond, ed., *John Lyly*, II, 259 and III, 9-10, 81-103; George P. Baker, ed., *Endymion* (New York, 1894), pp. xliii-lxxxi.

19. Percy W. Long, "The Purport of Lyly's *Endimion*," *PMLA*, 24:164-184 (1909).

20. Feuillerat, *John Lyly*, pp. 141-190. See Percy W. Long, "Lyly's *Endimion*: An Addendum," *MP*, 8:599-605 (1911).

21. Bennett, "Oxford and *Endimion*," *PMLA*, 57:354-369.

22. Hunter, *John Lyly*, p. 188.

23. Huppé, "Allegory of Love in Lyly," *ELH*, 14:105.

24. J. A. Bryant, Jr., "The Nature of the Allegory in Lyly's *Endymion*," *RenP* 1956, pp. 4-11. For numerous speculations on topical identifications of the secondary characters, such as Gabriel Harvey for Sir Tophas, see *passim* in Halpin, *Oberon's Vision*, Feuillerat, *John Lyly*, the editions of Bond and Baker, and John D. Peter, *Complaint and Satire in Early English Literature* (Oxford, 1956), p. 199.

25. Hunter, *John Lyly*, p. 76; Hillebrand, *The Child Actors*, pp. 137-143.

26. Aaron M. Myers, *Representation and Misrepresentation of the Puritan in Elizabethan Drama* (Philadelphia, 1931), p. 29; Frederick W. Fairholt, ed., *The Dramatic Works of John Lilly* (London, 1892), I, xxii; Hunter, *John Lyly*, p. 80.

27. Cf. Paul E. Parnell, "Moral Allegory in Lyly's *Loves Metamorphosis*," *SP*, 52:1-16 (1955); cf. also Bond, ed., *John Lyly*, II, 259. Parnell conjectures that the figure of Ceres alludes to England's fecund prosperity; Bond sees in Erisicthon the ungrateful design of Essex against Elizabeth, 1599.

28. Chambers, *Elizabethan Stage*, I, 96-97, and III, 412-414; Warren B. Austin, "John Lyly and Queen Elizabeth," *N & Q*, 176:146-147 (1939).

29. Hunter, *John Lyly*, p. 83.

14. WAR FEVER

1. Hunter, *John Lyly*, pp. 180-181; cf. Halpin, *Oberon's Vision*, p. 104, and Bond, ed., *John Lyly*, III, 108-110. Halpin further identifies Motto as Antonio Perez, Sophronia as the Infanta Isabella, Martius as the Duke of Medina Sidonia, and Eristus as Ruy Gomez de Libra.

2. Bond, ed., *John Lyly*, I, 47.

3. Halpin, *Oberon's Vision*, p. 104.

4. Muriel C. Bradbrook, *The Rise of the Common Player: A Study of Actor and Society in Shakespeare's England* (London, 1962), pp. 184-189.

5. Lindabury, *Patriotism in Elizabethan Drama*, p. 67.

6. See Wright, "Social Aspects of Belated Moralities," *Anglia*, 54:127.

7. Chambers, *Elizabethan Stage*, III, 516.

8. Leicester Bradner, "Poems on the Defeat of the Spanish Armada," *JEGP*, 43:447-448 (1944).

9. Winifred Smith, "Anti-Catholic Propaganda in Elizabethan London," *MP*, 28:208-212 (1930). According to Miss Smith, Paulo Lardi's description of this anti-Catholic propagandistic event may possibly refer to *Dr. Faustus*. If so, then the play was at one time more rampantly anti-Catholic than it now appears.

10. Simpson, "Political Use of the Stage," *New Shakspere Society Transactions* (1874), p. 374.

11. *Calendar of State Papers, Venetian*, VIII (1581-1591), p. 182.

12. *Calendar of State Papers, Spanish,* N.S., IV (1587-1603), p. 191.

13. E. M. W. Tillyard, *Shakespeare's History Plays* (London, 1944), p. 101.

14. For the untenable theory that Shakespeare wrote *Famous Victories* as a way of apologizing for his own youth, see Seymour M. Pitcher, *The Case for Shakespeare's Authorship of "The Famous Victories"* (Albany, N.Y., 1961), pp. 113-114 and *passim.* For an equally untenable allegorization of the play as reflecting the Earl of Oxford's escapades around 1573, see Bernard M. Ward, *"The Famous Victories of Henry V:* Its Place in Elizabethan Dramatic Literature," *RES,* 4:270-294 (1928).

15. On the relationship of Falstaff to Dericke and Oldcastle in *Famous Victories,* see James Monaghan, "Falstaff and His Forebears," *SP,* 18:353-361 (1921).

16. Allan Gilbert, "Patriotism and Satire in *Henry V,*" *Studies in Shakespeare,* ed. Arthur D. Matthews and Clark M. Emery (Coral Gables, Fla., 1953), pp. 40-64.

17. Wilson O. Clough, "The Broken English of Foreign Characters of the Elizabethan Stage," *PQ,* 12:255-268 (1933).

18. The hypothesis of E. A. J. Honigmann, ed., *King John,* Arden Shakespeare (London, 1954), that *Troublesome Reign* is a bad quarto of *King John* has been universally rejected. See, for instance, Robert A. Law, "On the Date of *King John,*" *SP,* 54:119-127 (1957); Reese, *Cease of Majesty,* p. 265; and Arthur Freeman, "Shakespeare and *Solyman and Perseda,*" *MLR,* 58:481-487 (1963).

19. Shakespeare, *King John,* I, i, 48-49, III, iii, 7-10. See Ribner, *English History Play,* pp. 121-122; Sharpe, *Real War of the Theaters,* pp. 54-55; Tillyard, *Shakespeare's History Plays,* p. 215f; de Groot, *"The Old Faith,"* pp. 180-223; and William J. Tucker, "Shakespeare, a Catholic?" *Catholic World,* 176:14-19 (1952).

20. Mrs. Martin Le Boutillier, "Bale's *Kynge Johan* and *The Troublesome Raigne,*" *MLN,* 36:55-57 (1921); W. W. Greg, "Bale's *Kynge Johan,*" *MLN,* 36:505 (1921); Harris, *John Bale,* pp. 93-94; John Elson, "Studies in the King John Plays," *J. Q. Adams Memorial Studies,* pp. 183-197.

21. Ribner, *English History Play,* pp. 78-79.

22. Reese, *Cease of Majesty,* p. 285.

23. *1 Henry VI* is now generally thought to be Shakespeare's own work, and perhaps the earliest written of his first tetralogy; see John B. Henneman, "The Episodes in Shakespeare's *I. Henry VI,*" *PMLA,* 15:290-320 (1900); Leo Kirschbaum, "The Authorship of *1 Henry VI,*" *PMLA,* 67:809-822 (1952); and Andrew S. Cairncross, ed., *The First Part of King Henry VI,* Arden Shakespeare (London, 1962), Introduction, pp. xxviii-xxxviii.

24. Max Huhner, "Shakspere's Conception of the Clergy," *Shakespeare Association Bulletin,* 11:161-170 (1936); Robert Stevenson, *Shakespeare's Religious Frontier* (The Hague, 1958), pp. 1-51; Wilhelm Creizenach, *The English Drama in the Age of Shakespeare,* trans. from *Geschichte des neueren*

Dramas (London, 1916), pp. 101-103; Simpson, "Politics of Shakspere's Historical Plays," *New Shakspere Society Transactions* (1874), pp. 438-439.

25. Roland M. Frye, *Shakespeare and Christian Doctrine* (Princeton, 1963), pp. 3-12.

26. De Groot, "*The Old Faith*," pp. 159-180; M. J. Quinlan, "Shakespeare and the Catholic Burial Services," *SQ*, 5:303-306 (1954); Tucker, "Shakespeare, a Catholic?" *Catholic World*, 176:14-19. On Friar Laurence and Friar Francis, see Stevenson, *Shakespeare's Religious Frontier*, pp. 25-47; and Huhner, "Shakspere's Conception of the Clergy," *Shakespeare Association Bulletin*, 11:166-170.

27. Paul A. Jorgensen, "Theoretical Views of War in Elizabethan England," *JHI*, 13:469-481 (1952).

28. Wilson, ed., *Henry VI Part I*, pp. xiv-xxi.

29. Simpson, "Politics of Shakspere's Historical Plays," *New Shakspere Society Transactions* (1874), pp. 419-423.

30. See, for instance, Robert M. Smith, "*Edward III*, A Study of the Authorship," *JEGP*, 10:90-104 (1911); Alfred Hart, *Shakespeare and the Homilies* (Melbourne, 1934), 219-241; Kenneth Muir, "A Reconsideration of *Edward III*," *Shakespeare Survey*, 6:39-48 (1953); Ribner, *English History Play*, pp. 142-150; Arthur Platt, "*Edward III* and Shakespeare's Sonnets," *MLR*, 6:511-513 (1911); MacD. P. Jackson, "*Edward III*, Shakespeare, and Pembroke's Men," *N & Q*, N.S., 12:329-331 (1965); Inna Koskenniemi, "Themes and Imagery in *Edward III*," *Neuphilologische Mitteilungen*, 65:446-480 (1964); and Kenneth Muir, *Shakespeare as Collaborator* (London, 1960), pp. 31-55.

31. Ribner, *English History Play*, pp. 144-150.

32. Paul Kocher, "François Hotman and Marlowe's *The Massacre at Paris*," *PMLA*, 56:349-368 (1941), and "Contemporary Pamphlet Backgrounds for Marlowe's *The Massacre at Paris*," *MLQ*, 8:151-173, 309-318 (1947).

33. Neale, *Elizabeth I and Her Parliaments*, II, 169-177. For understanding interpretations of Elizabeth's foreign policy in the Armada years, see R. B. Wernham, "Elizabethan War Aims and Strategy," in *Elizabethan Government and Society*, ed. Bindoff et al., pp. 340-368; and Neale, "Elizabeth and the Netherlands, 1586-7," in *Essays in Elizabethan History*, pp. 170-201. On Marlowe's favorable depiction of Navarre, see J. B. Steane, *Marlowe: A Critical Study* (Cambridge, Eng., 1964), pp. 236-246.

34. Ribner, *English History Play*, p. 25.

35. Frank S. Hook, ed., *Edward I*, in *The Life and Works of George Peele*, gen. ed. Charles T. Prouty (New Haven, 1961), II, 9-23, 46-60.

36. Holger Nørgaard, "Peele's *Edward I* and Two Queen Elinor Ballads," *English Studies*, 45:Supplement, pp. 165-168 (1964), argues that another ballad, "The lamentable fall of Queene Elnor," is based on the play; cf. Frank S. Hook, "The Ballad Sources of Peele's *Edward I*," *N & Q*, N.S., 3:3-5 (1956). For text, see Hook, ed., *Edward I*, pp. 206-211.

37. Hook, ed., *Edward I*, pp. 4-5; Ribner, *English History Play*, p. 89.

38. Waldo F. McNeir, "Robert Greene and *John of Bordeaux*," *PMLA*, 64:781-801 (1949); Anthony Esler, "Robert Greene and the Spanish Armada," *ELH*, 32:314-332 (1965).

39. Ruth Hudson, "Greene's *James IV* and Contemporary Allusions to Scotland," *PMLA*, 47:652-667 (1932). For a contrary view, see J. Churton Collins, ed., *The Plays and Poems of Robert Greene* (Oxford, 1905), II, 80.

40. Thomas H. Dickinson, ed., *Robert Greene*, Mermaid Series (London, 1904), p. xlvii, suggests a possible parallel to Elizabeth in the lines "Shall never Frenchman say an English maid Of threats of foreign force will be afraid" (ll. 1695-1696).

41. Thorleif Larsen, "The Historical and Legendary Background of Peele's *Battle of Alcazar*," *Transactions of the Royal Society of Canada*, ser. 3, vol. 33, sec. 2, pp. 185-197 (1939).

42. John Yoklavich, ed., *The Battle of Alcazar*, in *The Life and Works of Peele*, ed. Prouty, II, 276-278. For other sources, see Warner G. Rice, "A Principal Source of *The Battle of Alcazar*," *MLN*, 58:428-431 (1943).

15. VOX POPULI

1. See Paul H. Kocher, "The Development of Marlowe's Character," *PQ*, 17:331-350 (1938), and *Christopher Marlowe: A Study of His Thought, Learning, and Character* (Chapel Hill, N.C., 1946), pp. 69-103; Harry Levin, *The Overreacher: A Study of Christopher Marlowe* (Cambridge, Mass., 1952), pp. 30-54; cf. Roy W. Battenhouse, *Marlowe's Tamburlaine: A Study in Renaissance Moral Philosophy* (Nashville, Tenn., 1941), pp. 248-253 and *passim*.

2. Cf. Irving Ribner, "Marlowe and Machiavelli," *Comparative Literature*, 6:348-356 (1954), and *English History Play*, pp. 61-62.

3. Steane, *Marlowe*, pp. 62-116.

4. Eugene M. Waith, *The Herculean Hero in Marlowe, Chapman, Shakespeare, and Dryden* (New York, 1962), pp. 68, 60-87. See also Douglas Cole, *Suffering and Evil in the Plays of Christopher Marlowe* (Princeton, 1962), pp. 90-92, 110.

5. The latest autobiographical interpretation is that of A. L. Rowse, *Christopher Marlowe: A Biography* (London, 1964), pp. 50-59. For an untenable theory that Tamburlaine represents not only Marlowe but Sir Walter Ralegh, with his "school of night" and his longing for empire, yielding his rich spoils to Queen Elizabeth (Zenocrate), see Clark, *Ralegh and Marlowe*, pp. 390-413.

6. Kocher, "Development of Marlowe's Character," *PQ*, 17:339. Clark, *Ralegh and Marlowe*, pp. 414-459, would unwisely associate Barabas and his daughter with Philip II of Spain and the Spanish Infanta.

7. For a questionable theory of analogy to the Scottish situation, in defense of James VI's hopes of the English succession, see J. M. Berdan, "Marlowe's

Edward II," PQ, 3:197-207 (1924). The only evidence is extended analogy, and Baines's accusation that Marlowe was pro-Jamesian.

8. Ribner, *English History Play*, pp. 129-132.

9. Clifford Leech, "Marlowe's *Edward II:* Power and Suffering," *Critical Quarterly*, 1:181-196 (1959).

10. Cf. Carolyn Blair, "On the Question of Unity in Peele's *David and Bethsabe*," *Studies in Honor of Hodges and Thaler*, ed. Richard B. Davis and John L. Lievsay (Knoxville, 1961), pp. 35-41, who views the play as a rebuttal of the Marlovian superman.

11. Armstrong, "Topicality of *The Misfortunes of Arthur*," *N & Q*, N.S., 2:371-373; Neale, *Elizabeth I and Her Parliaments*, I, 270, and II, 107.

12. Inga-Stina Ekeblad, "*The Love of King David and Fair Bethsabe:* A Note on George Peele's Biblical Drama," *English Studies*, 39:57-62 (1958).

13. Cf. Irving Ribner, "Greene's Attack on Marlowe: Some Light on *Alphonsus* and *Selimus*," *SP*, 52:162-171 (1955).

14. Cole, *Suffering and Evil in Marlowe*, pp. 99-100. See also F. P. Wilson, *Marlowe and the Early Shakespeare* (Oxford, 1953), pp. 40-41.

15. Daniel Seltzer, ed., *Friar Bacon and Friar Bungay* (Lincoln, Nebraska, 1963), Introduction, pp. xvii-xviii. For an unlikely topical interpretation of a similar play, *Fair Em, The Miller's Daughter of Manchester* (ca. 1589-1591), as dealing with Shakespeare's company, see Simpson, ed., *The School of Shakspere*, II, 373-375. For a refutation, see Alwin Thaler, "*Fair Em* (and Shakespeare's Company?) in Lancashire," *PMLA*, 46:647-658 (1931).

16. Robert West, *The Invisible World: A Study of Pneumatology in Elizabethan Drama* (Athens, Ga., 1939), p. 3. Cf. Frank Towne, "'White Magic' in *Friar Bacon and Friar Bungay?*" *MLN*, 67:9-13 (1952), answered by West on pp. 499-500.

17. On the relation of *George a Greene* to ballad tradition, see Malcolm A. Nelson, "The Sources of *George a Greene, The Pinner of Wakefield*," *PQ*, 42:159-165 (1963).

18. See Steele, *Plays and Masques*, p. 85.

19. Wright, "Social Aspects of Belated Moralities," *Anglia*, 54:130, 142-143.

20. Mary G. M. Adkins, "The Genesis of Dramatic Satire against the Puritan, as Illustrated in *A Knack to Know a Knave*," *RES*, 22:81-95 (1946); Myers, *Representation of the Puritan in Drama*, pp. 21-22, 115; E. N. S. Thompson, *The Controversy between the Puritans and the Stage* (New York, 1903), p. 200.

16. ORTHODOX REPLY

1. Alfred Harbage, *Shakespeare and the Rival Traditions* (New York, 1952), pp. 266-267.

2. *Calendar of State Papers, Venetian*, IX (1592-1603), p. 119.

3. Neale, "The Elizabethan Political Scene," in *Essays in Elizabethan History*, pp. 59-84; MacCaffrey, "Place and Patronage in Elizabethan Politics," in *Elizabethan Government and Society*, ed. Bindoff et al., pp. 101-126; Stone, *Crisis of the Aristocracy*, pp. 208-211, 426-434.

4. Clough, "Broken English of Foreign Characters," *PQ*, 12:255; Tupper, "The Shaksperean Mob," *PMLA*, 27:490; Stirling, *Populace in Shakespeare*, pp. 102-103. See Neale, *Elizabeth I and Her Parliaments*, II, 335-337; and Ramsey, *Tudor Economic Problems*, pp. 113-122.

5. Quoted by Tupper, "The Shaksperean Mob," *PMLA*, 27:491.

6. Stirling, *Populace in Shakespeare*, pp. 105-107; Neale, *Elizabeth I and Her Parliaments*, II, 251-297.

7. Brents Stirling, "Anti-Democracy in Shakespeare: A Re-Survey," *MLQ*, 2:487-502 (1941), p. 501.

8. Hart, *Shakespeare and the Homilies*, pp. 9-76; Tillyard, *Shakespeare's History Plays*, pp. 18-20.

9. *Calendar of State Papers, Domestic*, V (1598-1601), p. 352.

10. E.g., on the "staying" of *The Merchant of Venice*, 1598, see Ernest P. Kuhl, "Shakespeare and Hayward," *SP*, 25:312-315 (1928). On censorship in *2 Henry IV*, see L. L. Schücking, "The Quarto of *King Henry IV., Part II*," *LTLS*, Sept. 25, 1930, p. 752; Hart, *Shakespeare and the Homilies*, pp. 154-218.

11. Chambers, *Elizabethan Stage*, III, 410; William A. Armstrong, "*Tamburlaine* and *The Wounds of Civil War*," *N & Q*, N.S., 5:381-383 (1958). Cf. N. Burton Paradise, *Thomas Lodge: The History of an Elizabethan* (New Haven, 1931), pp. 128-138, who argues that *Wounds* was written in 1586 prior to *Tamburlaine*.

12. Paradise, *Thomas Lodge*, pp. 141-142. Cf. Simpson, "Political Use of the Stage," *New Shakspere Society Transactions* (1874), p. 392.

13. *King Leir* (ca. 1588-1594), to which Lodge may have contributed, is a sentimental romance with surprisingly little awareness of the problems of kingship or political division; see Ribner, *English History Play*, p. 247. *Locrine*, perhaps by Greene, bears several resemblances to *King Leir*, and its warnings against would-be invaders and negligent politicians at court seem largely conventional.

14. Albright, "*Richard II* and Essex," *PMLA*, 42:693; Mary G. M. Adkins, "A Theory about *The Life and Death of Jack Straw*," *UTSE*, 28:57-82 (1949); Simpson, "Political Use of the Stage," *New Shakspere Society Transactions* (1874), pp. 385-386; Stirling, *Populace in Shakespeare*, pp. 136-137, 149; Ribner, *English History Play*, pp. 71-76. Cf. Evelyn May Albright, *Dramatic Publication in England, 1580-1640* (New York, 1927), pp. 104-105, who argues without sufficient proof that the play aims covertly to arouse sentiment against oppressive taxes.

15. According to Hall's *Union;* see A. P. Rossiter, ed., *Woodstock—A Moral History* (London, 1946), pp. 32, 55.

16. Lucille King, "*2 and 3 Henry VI*—which Holinshed?" *PMLA*, 50:745-752 (1935); Stirling, *Populace in Shakespeare*, pp. 22-25; Tupper, "The Shaksperean Mob," *PMLA*, 27:501; Barber, *Shakespeare's Festive Comedy*, p. 29.

17. A. C. Bradley, *Shakespearean Tragedy*, 2nd ed. (New York, 1905), p. 326n1; Tupper, "The Shaksperean Mob," *PMLA*, 27:487; Alwin Thaler, *Shakespeare and Democracy* (Knoxville, Tenn., 1941), pp. 42-44; Harbage, *Shakespeare and Rival Traditions*, pp. 266-267. Cf. Ernest Crosby, "Shakespeare's Attitude to the Working Classes," in *Tolstoy on Shakespeare*, trans. V. Tchertkoff (New York, 1907), pp. 127-165; and Albert H. Tolman, "Is Shakespeare Aristocratic?" *PMLA*, 29: 277-298 (1914).

18. Stirling, *Populace in Shakespeare*, pp. 79-99.

19. Thomas Heywood, *An Apology for Actors* (1612), ed. Richard H. Perkinson (New York, 1941), Book III, sig. F3ᵛ.

20. Otelia Cromwell, *Thomas Heywood: A Study in the Elizabethan Drama of Everyday Life* (New Haven, 1928), pp. 154-162.

21. Ribner, *English History Play*, p. 274.

22. Campbell, *Shakespeare's "Histories,"* pp. 320-334; Ribner, *English History Play*, p. 117. For the relation of *Richard III's* political stance to that of *The True Tragedy of Richard III* and *Richardus Tertius*, see Robert J. Lordi, "The Relationship of *Richardus Tertius* to the Main Richard III Plays," *BUSE*, 5:139-153 (1961). For a plausible political allusion in *Richard III*, see Lewis F. Mott, "A Political Allusion in Shakespeare's *Richard III*," *Todd Memorial Volumes* (New York: Columbia University Press, 1930), II, 41-44.

23. John R. Elliott, "Shakespeare and the Double Image of King John," *Shakespeare Studies*, 1:64-84 (1965); Ribner, *English History Play*, pp. 121-122; Reese, *Cease of Majesty*, pp. 263-272.

24. Harrison, "Shakespeare's Topical Significances," *LTLS*, Nov. 13, 1930, p. 939; Campbell, *Shakespeare's "Histories,"* pp. 142-162; Ribner, *English History Play*, pp. 80-81.

25. Adrien Bonjour, "The Road to Swinstead Abbey: A Study of the Sense and Structure of *King John*," *ELH*, 18:253-274 (1951); James L. Calderwood, "Commodity and Honour in *King John*," *UTQ*, 29:341-356 (1960); Reese, *Cease of Majesty*, p. 285.

26. G. K. Hunter, "Shakespeare's Politics and the Rejection of Falstaff," *Critical Quarterly*, 1:229-236 (1959); Jonas Barish, "The Turning Away of Prince Hal," *Shakespeare Studies*, 1:9-17 (1965).

27. W. B. Yeats, "At Stratford-on-Avon," in *Ideas of Good and Evil*, collected in *Essays and Introductions* (New York, 1961), p. 108. See A. P. Rossiter, "Ambivalence: The Dialectic of the Histories," in *Talking of Shakespeare*, ed. John Garrett (London, 1954), pp. 149-171; John C. McCloskey, "The Mirror of All Christian Kings," *Shakespeare Association Bulletin*, 19:36-40 (1944); and Paul A. Jorgensen, "Accidental Judgments, Casual Slaughters, and Purposes Mistook: Critical Reactions to Shakspere's *Henry the Fifth*," *Shakespeare Association Bulletin*, 22:51-61 (1947).

28. Ernest Talbert, *The Problem of Order: Elizabethan Political Commonplaces and an Example of Shakespeare's Art* (Chapel Hill, N.C., 1962), pp. 123-129; Campbell, *Shakespeare's "Histories,"* pp. 168-212.

29. Brents Stirling, "Bolingbroke's 'Decision,'" *SQ*, 2:27-34 (1951); John L. Palmer, *Political and Comic Characters of Shakespeare* (London, 1948), pp. 118-179, esp. pp. 136f; Reese, *Cease of Majesty*, pp. 228-230.

30. Irving Ribner, "The Political Problem in Shakespeare's Lancastrian Tetralogy," *SP*, 49:171-184 (1952); and *English History Play*, p. 160.

31. Reese, *Cease of Majesty*, p. 253.

32. Campbell, *Shakespeare's "Histories,"* p. 156.

33. Sarah Dodson, "The Northumberland of Shakespeare and Holinshed," *UTSE*, 19:74-85 (1939).

34. Paul A. Jorgensen, "The 'Dastardly Treachery' of Prince John of Lancaster," *PMLA*, 76:488-492 (1961).

35. Palmer, *Political Characters*, pp. 187-188, 197-218. See also C. L. Barber, "The Saturnalian Pattern in Shakespeare's Comedy," *SR*, 59:593-611 (1951), pp. 606-609; and H. B. Charlton, *Shakespeare, Politics, and Politicians*, English Association Pamphlet No. 72 (1929). Cf. Herbert M. McLuhan, "*Henry IV*, A Mirror of Magistrates," *UTQ*, 17:152-160 (1948).

36. On *Julius Caesar* as pro-Caesar, see James E. Phillips, Jr., *The State in Shakespeare's Greek and Roman Plays* (New York, 1940), pp. 172-188; Tolman, "Is Shakespeare Aristocratic?" *PMLA*, 29:285-287; and Sir Mark Hunter, "Politics and Character in Shakespeare's *Julius Caesar*," *Transactions of the Royal Society of Literature of the United Kingdom*, N.S., 10:109-140 (1931). On *Julius Caesar* as pro-Brutus, see J. Dover Wilson, ed., *Julius Caesar* (Cambridge, Eng., 1949), p. xxv; John E. Uhler, "Julius Caesar—A Morality of Respublica," *Studies in Shakespeare*, ed. Matthews and Emery (1953), pp. 96-106; and G. B. Shaw, *Three Plays for Puritans* (New York, 1900, 1906), p. xxx.

37. Cf. Ernest Schanzer, "The Problem of *Julius Caesar*," *SQ*, 6:297-308 (1955); Vernon Hall, Jr., "*Julius Caesar*: A Play without Political Bias," *Studies in the English Renaissance Drama in Memory of Karl Julius Holzknecht*, ed. Josephine W. Bennett et al. (New York, 1959), pp. 106-124; Thomas M. Parrott, ed., *Shakespeare* (New York, 1938), p. 633; Hazelton Spencer, *The Art and Life of William Shakespeare* (New York, 1940), p. 229; and Mildred E. Hartsock, "The Complexity of *Julius Caesar*," *PMLA*, 81:56-62 (1966).

38. Irving Ribner, "Political Issues in *Julius Caesar*," *JEGP*, 56:10-22 (1957).

39. Harley Granville-Barker, *Prefaces to Shakespeare* (Princeton, N.J., 1946-1947), II, 351; R. A. Foakes, "An Approach to *Julius Caesar*," *SQ*, 5:259-270 (1954).

40. Robert Ornstein, "Seneca and the Political Drama of *Julius Caesar*," *JEGP*, 57:51-56 (1958); Norman Rabkin, *Shakespeare and the Common Understanding* (New York, 1967), pp. 105-119; L. C. Knights, "Shakespeare and

Political Wisdom: A Note on the Personalism of *Julius Caesar* and *Coriolanus*," *SR*, 61:43-55 (1953).

41. Plutarch, "The Life of Julius Caesar," *Plutarch's Lives of the Noble Grecians and Romans*, trans. Sir Thomas North (1579), in Geoffrey Bullough, ed., *Narrative and Dramatic Sources of Shakespeare* (London, New York, 1964), V, 127.

42. Rossiter, ed., *Woodstock*, pp. 18-23.

43. *Ibid.*, p. 32; Ribner, *English History Play*, p. 141.

44. Neale, *Elizabeth I and Her Parliaments*, II, 94-95, 207-215, 298-300, 376-388.

45. Lowers, *Mirrors for Rebels*, p. 31. See Albright, "*Richard II* and Essex," *PMLA*, 42:695-697, for a hypothesis of the importance of Essex's descent from Thomas of Woodstock.

46. Those who see reflections of Essex include D. C. Collins, "On the Date of *Sir Thomas More*," *RES*, 10:401-411 (1934). Cf. J. M. Nosworthy, "Shakespeare and *Sir Thomas More*," *RES*, N.S., 6:12-25 (1955); and I. A. Shapiro, "Shakespeare and Mundy," *Shakespeare Survey*, 14:25-33 (1961).

47. Clough, "Broken English of Foreign Characters," *PQ*, 12:255; Julia Celeste Turner, *Anthony Mundy, An Elizabethan Man of Letters* (Berkeley, 1928), pp. 108-112.

48. The extensive literature on Shakespeare's hand in *Sir Thomas More* has been comprehensively reviewed by R. C. Bald, "*The Booke of Sir Thomas More* and Its Problems," *Shakespeare Survey*, 2:44-61 (1949). See also Ribner, *English History Play*, p. 215.

49. Percy Simpson, ed., *The Life of Sir John Oldcastle*, Malone Society Reprints (London, 1908), pp. v-vi. This Wilson is probably the author of *The Cobbler's Prophecy, Three Ladies of London*, etc., in the Armada years. Even in the bourgeois *Three Lords of London*, Wilson's defense of popular dramatic art is an answer to the Puritans (see Chapter 14 above). On the "Two-Wilsons" controversy, see Chambers, *Elizabethan Stage*, II, 349-350; and H. S. D. Mithal, "The Two-Wilsons Controversy," *N & Q*, N.S., 6:106-109 (1959).

50. Sharpe, *Real War of the Theaters*, pp. 19-21; Turner, *Anthony Mundy*, pp. 132-143.

51. Mary G. M. Adkins, "Sixteenth-Century Religious and Political Implications in *Sir John Oldcastle*," *UTSE*, 22:86-104 (1942); Rudolph Fiehler, "How Oldcastle Became Falstaff," *MLQ*, 16:16-28 (1955); Ribner, *English History Play*, pp. 200-205.

52. Sharpe, *Real War of the Theaters*, pp. 144-145, argues that *Oldcastle* chose the hated John Young, Bishop of Rochester, as its target, because Archbishop Whitgift was simply too powerful a figure to be attacked. Oldcastle's original enemy, according to Bale, was the Archbishop of Canterbury.

53. Stirling, *Populace in Shakespeare*, pp. 105-107.

54. Ribner, *English History Play*, pp. 203-205; Neale, *Elizabeth I and Her Parliaments*, II, 60-78, 236.

17. SATIRE AND THE STATE

1. Harbage, *Shakespeare and the Rival Traditions*, p. 260.
2. Heywood, *An Apology for Actors*, Book III, sig. G3ᵛ.
3. *Ibid.*, Book II, sig. E3.
4. See Bradbrook, *Growth and Structure of Comedy*, p. 101.
5. Marjorie L. Reyburn, "New Facts and Theories about the Parnassus Plays," *PMLA*, 74:325-335 (1959).
6. Sir Thomas Hoby, trans., *The Courtier*, by Castiglione, in Hyder E. Rollins and Herschel Baker, eds., *The Renaissance in England* (Boston, 1954), p. 523.
7. James P. Brawner, ed., *The Wars of Cyrus*, Univ. of Illinois Studies in Language and Literature, No. 28 (Urbana, Ill., 1942), Introduction, p. 18.
8. James P. Brawner, "Early Classical Narrative Plays by Sebastian Westcote and Richard Mulcaster," *MLQ*, 4:455-464 (1943).
9. W. J. Lawrence, "Soliman and Perseda," *MLR*, 9:523-525 (1914).
10. Lodwick Hartley, " 'Mercy but Murders': A Subtheme in *Romeo and Juliet*," *Papers on English Language and Literature*, 1:259-264 (1965). Cf. John W. Draper, "Shakespeare's 'Star-Crossed Lovers,' " *RES*, 15:16-34 (1939). On the topical relevance of *Romeo and Juliet* to some famous Elizabethan quarrels, see Neale, *Elizabethan House of Commons*, p. 25.
11. See Stoll, *Shakespeare Studies*, pp. 71-78.
12. Lily B. Campbell, "Theories of Revenge in Renaissance England," *MP*, 28:281-296 (1931); Lewis Einstein, *Tudor Ideals* (New York, 1921), pp. 63-75, 121-123; Herbert F. Schwarz, ed., *Alphonsus, Emperor of Germany* (New York, 1913), pp. v-xxxv; M. C. Bradbrook, "Authority, Truth, Justice in *Measure for Measure*," *RES*, 17:385-399 (1941); Stone, *Crisis of the Aristocracy*, pp. 223-247; Hexter, "Storm over the Gentry," in *Reappraisals in History*, pp. 146-147. See *The Charge of Sir Francis Bacon, Knight, His Majesty's Attorney-General, Touching Duels* (London, 1614), pp. 12-13 and *passim*.
13. Fredson T. Bowers, *Elizabethan Revenge Tragedy, 1587-1642* (Princeton, 1940), esp. pp. 3-36.
14. Lee, "Topical Side of Elizabethan Drama," *New Shakspere Society Transactions* (1887), pp. 22-32; Henry H. Adams, *English Domestic or Homiletic Tragedy, 1575 to 1642* (New York, 1943), pp. 100-125.
15. Ernst de Chickera, "Divine Justice and Private Revenge in *The Spanish Tragedy*," *MLR*, 57:228-232 (1962); William H. Wiatt, "The Dramatic Function of the Alexandro-Villuppo Episode in *The Spanish Tragedy*," *N & Q*, N.S., 5:327-329 (1958).
16. Kelso, *Doctrine of the English Gentleman*, pp. 99, 70-110.
17. Anthony Caputi, *John Marston, Satirist* (Ithaca, N.Y., 1961), pp. 147-152.
18. Bowers, *Revenge Tragedy*, pp. 118-125.
19. Reese, *Cease of Majesty*, p. 120n1.
20. Maxine MacKay, "*The Merchant of Venice*: A Reflection of the Early

Conflict between Courts of Law and Courts of Equity," *SQ*, 15:371-375 (1964). For a theory that Shylock's preciseness, Old Testament morality, and pharisaical contempt for merry-making are an oblique reference to Puritanism, see Paul N. Siegel, "Shylock and the Puritan Usurers," *Studies in Shakespeare*, ed. Matthews and Emery (1953), pp. 129-138.

21. Bertrand Evans, *Shakespeare's Comedies* (Oxford, 1960), pp. 77-79. Cf. John W. Draper, "Dogberry's Due Process of Law," *JEGP*, 42:563-576 (1943), who finds the constable scenes "unnecessary," added for mere travesty of legal parlance and procedure.

22. Wilbur Dunkel, "Law and Equity in *Measure for Measure*," *SQ*, 13:275-285 (1962); John W. Dickinson, "Renaissance Equity in *Measure for Measure*," *SQ*, 13:287-297 (1962); Mary Lascelles, *Shakespeare's Measure for Measure* (London, 1953), pp. 61-63.

23. R. Warwick Bond, ed., *Early Plays from the Italian* (Oxford, 1911), p. lxvii.

24. Charles T. Prouty, *George Gascoigne, Elizabethan Courtier, Soldier, and Poet* (New York, 1942), p. 144; Harry Ransom, "Some Legal Elements in Elizabethan Plays," *UTSE*, 16:53-76 (1936).

25. Ennis Rees, "Chapman's *Blind Beggar* and the Marlovian Hero," *JEGP*, 57:60-63 (1958); Sharpe, *Real War of the Theaters*, pp. 50, 89-90. Sharpe's hypothesis of an allusion to Essex and Elizabeth in the affair of Cleanthes and Aegiale is extremely dangerous and unlikely; it would imply sexual indiscretion and political conniving of a most indelicate sort.

26. Helen A. Kaufman, "*The Blind Beggar of Alexandria*: A Reappraisal," *PQ*, 38:101-106 (1959); Sharpe, *Real War of the Theaters*, p. 50.

27. Thomas M. Parrott, ed., *The Plays and Poems of George Chapman* (London, 1910-1914), II, 889-897; George L. Kittredge, "Notes on Elizabethan Plays," *JEGP*, 2:7-13 (1898).

28. On dating, see Parrott, ed., *George Chapman*, II, 731-737; Chambers, *Elizabethan Stage*, III, 256. The echo of Dekker's *Gull's Hornbook* (1607) could have been added in a revision of *May-Day*.

29. A. L. Stiefel, "George Chapman und das italienische Drama," *SJ*, 35:180-213 (1899).

30. On the choice of date between 1599 and 1604, see Parrott, ed., *George Chapman*, II, 701-702; and Chambers, *Elizabethan Stage*, III, 252. If written originally for the Admiral's men, the play may have been revised for performance at Blackfriars.

31. Max Stier, *Chapmans "All Fools" mit besonderer Berücksichtigung seiner Quellen* (Halle, 1904), pp. 8-19; Elisabeth Woodbridge, "An Unnoted Source of Chapman's *All Fools*," *JEGP*, 1:338-341 (1897).

32. Charles W. Kennedy, "Political Theory in the Plays of George Chapman," in *The Parrott Presentation Volume*, ed. Hardin Craig (Princeton, 1935), pp. 73-86; Henry M. Weidner, "The Dramatic Uses of Homeric Idealism: The Significance of Time and Design in George Chapman's *The Gentleman Usher*," *ELH*, 28:121-136 (1961).

33. *Bussy D'Ambois,* II, i, 198-199.

34. Recent scholarship tends to favor Dekker as author of *Blurt Master-Constable* rather than Middleton, but the external evidence is as yet very slight. See S. Schoenbaum, "*Blurt, Master Constable:* A Possible Authorship Clue," *Renaissance News,* 13:7-9 (1960); and Juliette Gowan, "*Edward Pudsey's Booke* and the Authorship of *Blurt Master Constable,*" *Research Opportunities in Renaissance Drama,* 8:46-48 (1965).

35. On the likelihood of early date, see C. R. Baskervill, *English Elements in Jonson's Early Comedy,* Univ. of Texas Bulletin No. 178 (1911), pp. 76-89. The play was later revised to satirize Inigo Jones.

36. On Jonson's revisions, see Henry H. Carter, ed., *Every Man in His Humor* (New Haven, 1921), pp. xxxi-lvii; J. A. Bryant, Jr., "Jonson's Revision of *Every Man in His Humor,*" *SP,* 59:641-650 (1962); and Arthur Sale, "Introduction to *Every Man in His Humour,*" in *Ben Jonson: A Collection of Critical Essays,* ed. Jonas Barish (Englewood Cliffs, N.J., 1963), pp. 75-81. My textual references are to the 1598 quarto in C. H. Herford and Percy Simpson, eds., *Ben Jonson* (Oxford, 1925-1952), vol. III.

37. Jonas A. Barish, "The Double Plot in *Volpone,*" *MP,* 51:83-92 (1953); S. L. Goldberg, "Folly into Crime: The Catastrophe of *Volpone,*" *MLQ,* 20:233-242 (1959).

38. The worst offenders are E. Hermann, *Shakespeare der Kämpfer* (Erlangen, 1879) and *Weitere quellenmässige Beiträge zu Shakespeares literarischen Kämpfen* (Erlangen, 1881); Cartwright, *Shakspere and Jonson;* Fleay, *Biographical Chronicle of Drama,* s.v. Jonson and Marston; and Josiah H. Penniman, *The War of the Theaters* (Boston, 1897). Most of the excesses have been successfully refuted by Roscoe A. Small, *The Stage-Quarrel between Ben Jonson and the So-Called Poetasters* (Breslau, 1899). At the opposite extreme are recent critics arguing that the Poetomachia was only a hoax to attract customers; see Morse Allen, *The Satire of John Marston* (Columbus, Ohio, 1920), pp. 51-66; W. L. Halstead, "What 'War of the Theaters'?" *College English,* 9:424-426 (1948); and Robert Withington, "What 'War of the Theaters'?" *College English,* 10:163-164 (1948).

39. The term "comical satires" is defined in Campbell, *Comicall Satyre, passim.*

40. Allen, *John Marston,* pp. 66-74; Chambers, *Elizabethan Stage,* III, 293, 428.

41. Alvin Kernan, *The Cankered Muse: Satire of the English Renaissance* (New Haven, 1959), pp. 143-148.

42. Chambers, *Elizabethan Stage,* IV, 17-18; Allen, *John Marston,* pp. 23-24. Cf. Alvin Kernan, "John Marston's Play *Histriomastix,*" *MLQ,* 19:134-140 (1958).

43. Simpson, "Political Use of the Stage," *New Shakspere Society Transactions* (1874), p. 391; Chambers, *Elizabethan Stage,* III, 445; Penniman, *War of the Theatres,* pp. 33-43; Allen, *John Marston,* pp. 23-34.

44. Kernan, *Cankered Muse,* pp. 137-138, 156-162.

45. W. W. Main, "'Insula Fortunata' in Jonson's *Every Man out of His Humour*," *N & Q*, N.S., 1:197-198 (1954).

46. Harbage, *Shakespeare and the Rival Traditions*, p. 274. On Jonson's anti-Puritan position as a Catholic, see Theodore A. Stroud, "Ben Jonson and Father Thomas Wright," *ELH*, 14:274-282 (1947).

47. Campbell, *Comicall Satyre*, pp. 54-63.

48. Allan H. Gilbert, "The Function of the Masques in *Cynthia's Revels*," *PQ*, 22:211-230 (1943); Ernest W. Talbert, "The Classical Mythology and the Structure of *Cynthia's Revels*," *PQ*, 22:193-210 (1943); Talbert, "The Interpretation of Jonson's Courtly Spectacles," *PMLA*, 61:454-473 (1946).

49. See Ralph W. Berringer, "Jonson's *Cynthia's Revels* and the War of the Theatres," *PQ*, 22:1-22 (1943), for a careful refutation of the theory equating Hedon and Anaides with Marston and Dekker, as maintained even by such careful scholars as Small, *Stage Quarrel*, pp. 61f, and Chambers, *Elizabethan Stage*, III, 363-364.

50. Allen, *John Marston*, pp. 45-51; Caputi, *John Marston*, p. 157.

51. On *Jack Drum's Entertainment*, see Small, *Stage-Quarrel*, p. 127; Alexander C. Judson, ed., *Cynthia's Revels* (New York, 1912), pp. xliv-lvii; Allen, *John Marston*, pp. 34-40; and Chambers, *Elizabethan Stage*, IV, 21. On *What You Will* see Campbell, *Comicall Satyres*, pp. 166-181; Berringer, "*Cynthia's Revels* and War of Theatres," *PQ*, 22:20-22; and Eric Linklater, *Ben Jonson and King James* (New York, 1931), p. 85. On the unsuitability of the hypothesis that Shakespeare's *Troilus and Cressida* is also an answer to Jonson and Marston, see John S. P. Tatlock, "The Siege of Troy in Elizabethan Literature, Especially in Shakespeare and Heywood," *PMLA*, 30:673-770 (1915), pp. 726-734.

52. On *Satiromastix* and the evidence of Jonson as an actor, see Fredson T. Bowers, "Ben Jonson the Actor," *SP*, 34:392-406 (1937).

53. Herford and Simpson, eds., *Ben Jonson*, I, 423-425; Berringer, "*Cynthia's Revels* and War of Theatres," *PQ*, 22:2; Oscar J. Campbell, "The Dramatic Construction of *Poetaster*," *Huntington Library Bulletin*, 9:37-62 (1936); John J. Enck, *Jonson and the Comic Truth* (Madison, Wis., 1957), p. 71.

54. Ernest W. Talbert, "The Purpose and Technique of Jonson's *Poetaster*," *SP*, 42:225-252 (1945).

55. Gilbert, "The Masques in *Cynthia's Revels*," *PQ*, 22:229; Talbert, "Purpose and Technique of *Poetaster*," *SP*, 42:226-232; Ralph Nash, "The Parting Scene in Jonson's *Poetaster* (IV, ix)," *PQ*, 31:54-62 (1952). For the unlikely identification of Ovid as Donne, see Fleay, *Biographical Chronicle of Drama*, I, 367. Cf. Campbell, "Dramatic Construction of *Poetaster*," *Huntington Library Bulletin*, 9:41-42, and *Comicall Satyre*, pp. 113-115, who sees Ovid as the enervating type of libertine poet in the 1590's.

56. For the identification of Virgil as Shakespeare or Chapman, see Herbert S. Mallory, ed., *Poetaster* (New York, 1905), pp. lxxxiv-xcvi.

57. On attempts to identify Aesop as Shakespeare or Heminges, and to

identify no less than seven members of the Chamberlain's company, see T. W. Baldwin, *The Organization and Personnel of the Shakespearean Company* (Princeton, 1927), pp. 232-234; Henry David Gray, "The Chamberlain's Men and the *Poetaster*," *MLR*, 42:173-179 (1947); Percy Simpson, "A Modern Fable of Æsop," *MLR*, 43:403-405 (1948); and Henry David Gray, "Shakespeare or Heminge? A Rejoinder and a Surrejoinder," *MLR*, 45:148-151, 151-152 (1950). On the unconvincing identification of Histrio as Shakespeare, see Henry Wood, "Shakespeare, Burlesqued by Two Fellow-Dramatists," *American Journal of Philology*, 16:273-299 (1895). Cf. Mallory, ed., *Poetaster*, pp. xxxviii-xcvi, esp. lvi-lxi.

18. LAST YEARS

1. Siegel, *Shakespearean Tragedy and Elizabethan Compromise*, pp. 25-40 and *passim*.

2. Laura H. Cadwallader, *The Career of the Earl of Essex from the Islands Voyage in 1597 to His Execution in 1601* (Philadelphia, 1923), pp. 74-75; Harrison, *Essex*, p. 277; a letter from Essex to the queen, May 12, 1600, *Calendar of State Papers, Domestic*, V (1598-1601), p. 435.

3. See Chapter 1 above, n. 73.

4. See J. Le Gay Brereton, "Shakespeare's Wild Irishman," *MLR*, 12:350 (1917); Creizenach, *English Drama*, pp. 135-136; and Paul A. Jorgensen, *Shakespeare's Military World* (Berkeley and Los Angeles, 1956), pp. 72-81. Cf. Campbell, *Shakespeare's "Histories,"* pp. 295-305.

5. A plot summary of *England's Joy* exists in *The Harleian Miscellany: A Collection of Scarce, Curious, and Entertaining Pamphlets and Tracts*, ed. Thomas Park et al. (London, 1808——), X, 198-199. See Lee, "Topical Side of Elizabethan Drama," *New Shakspere Society Transactions* (1887), pp. 13-16; and Albright, *Dramatic Publication in England*, p. 108.

6. S. M. Pratt, "Antwerp and the Elizabethan Mind," *MLQ*, 24:53-60 (1963); Waggoner, "Elizabethan Attitude toward Peace and War," *PQ*, 33:30; Jorgensen, "Theoretical Views of War," *JHI*, 13:470-471; Jorgensen, "Moral Guidance and Religious Encouragement for the Elizabethan Soldier," *HLQ*, 13:241-259 (1950); Fernando Ferrara, "Barnabe Riche, difensore del soldato inglese e autore di *A Larum for London*," *English Miscellany*, 8:21-54 (1957); A. Bronson Feldman, "The Rape of Antwerp in a Tudor Play," *N & Q*, N.S., 5:246-248 (1958).

7. Eleanore Boswell, ed., *Edmond Ironside*, Malone Society Reprints (Oxford, 1927), p. xi. Madeleine H. Dodds, "*Edmond Ironside* and *The Love-Sick King*," *MLR*, 19:158-168 (1924), and Ribner, *English History Play*, p. 241, prefer a date in the early 1590's.

8. Simpson, ed., *The School of Shakspere*, I, 209n2. See Joseph Q. Adams, Jr., "Captaine Thomas Stukeley," *JEGP*, 15:107-129 (1916), for a carefully

reasoned theory of revision. See also John M. Yoklavich, *"Captain Thomas Stukeley," N & Q,* N.S., 10:96-98 (1963).

9. Mary L. Hunt, *Thomas Dekker* (New York, 1911), pp. 23-24.

10. Fredson T. Bowers, "Essex's Rebellion and Dekker's *Old Fortunatus*," *RES,* N.S., 3:365-366 (1952). Cf. Simpson, "Political Use of the Stage," *New Shakspere Society Transactions* (1874), p. 394, who views *Old Fortunatus* as an Essex play throughout.

11. Mary G. M. Adkins, "Puritanism in the Plays and Pamphlets of Thomas Dekker," *UTSE,* 19:86-113 (1939); Kate L. Gregg, *Thomas Dekker: A Study in Economic and Social Backgrounds* (University of Washington, 1924), pp. 92-104.

12. Mary F. Martin, *"If You Know Not Me You Know Nobodie,* and *The Famous Historie of Sir Thomas Wyat," The Library,* 4th ser., 13:272-281 (1932); Mary F. Martin, "Stow's *Annals* and *The Famous Historie of Sir Thomas Wyat," MLR,* 53:75-77 (1958); Phillip Shaw, "Sir Thomas Wyat and the Scenario of *Lady Jane," MLQ,* 13:227-238 (1952).

13. Cf. Sharpe, *Real War of the Theatres,* p. 194; Reese, "Question of the Succession," *UTSE,* 22:73-75; and Ribner, *English History Play,* p. 217.

14. Simpson, "Political Use of the Stage," *New Shakspere Society Transactions* (1874), p. 388; Sharpe, *Real War of the Theaters,* p. 193; Ribner, *English History Play,* p. 205. See Gairdner, *English Church in Sixteenth Century,* p. 215. Also see index entry under "Cromwell, Thomas" in Neale, *Elizabeth I and Her Parliaments,* vols. I and II.

15. Clermont in *The Revenge of Bussy D'Ambois,* II, i, 200-234, and Byron in *The Tragedy of Byron,* IV, ii, 115-155. See Parrott, ed., *George Chapman,* I, 687.

16. On date, see W. W. Greg, ed., *Henslowe's Diary* (London, 1904-1908), II, 220; and Baskervill, "On Two Old Plays," *MP,* 14:16. Cf. Gerald E. Bentley, *The Jacobean and Caroline Stage* (Oxford, 1941——), III, 257-260, who prefers a later date. For an account of the English Catholic "Appellants" of the "Archpriest controversy," see Joel Hurstfield, "The Succession Struggle in Late Elizabethan England," in *Elizabethan Government and Society,* ed. Bindoff et al., pp. 369-396.

17. Turner, *Anthony Mundy,* p. 143. For evidence that the break between Puritans and the theater did not come as early in the sixteenth century as many critics have supposed, see William Ringler, *Stephen Gosson: A Biographical and Critical Study* (Princeton, 1942), pp. 53-82.

18. On the question of dates and precedence in the series, see Fred L. Jones, *"Look About You* and *The Disguises," PMLA,* 44:835-841 (1929); and Malcolm A. Nelson, *"Look About You* and the Robin Hood Tradition," *N & Q,* N.S., 9:141-143 (1962). On the historical earl and his family, see index entry under "Hastings" in Neale, *Elizabeth I and Her Parliaments,* vols. I and II, and *Elizabethan House of Commons.*

19. Morris P. Tilley, "The Organic Unity of *Twelfth Night," PMLA,* 29:550-

566 (1914); John Hollander, "*Twelfth Night* and the Morality of Indulgence," *SR*, 67:220-238 (1959); Barber, *Shakespeare's Festive Comedy*, pp. 240-261; Myers, *Representation of the Puritan in Drama*, pp. 32-33; L. G. Salinger, "The Design of *Twelfth Night*," *SQ*, 9:117-139 (1958). Cf. Robert A. Law, "Two Shakespearean Pictures of Puritans," *UTSE*, 13:78-83 (1933); and Donald J. McGinn, "The Precise Angelo," *J. Q. Adams Memorial Studies*, pp. 129-139.

20. Barber, *Shakespeare's Festive Comedy*, p. 257.

21. Z. S. Fink, "Jaques and the Malcontent Traveler," *PQ*, 14:237-252 (1935); Oscar J. Campbell, "Jaques," *Huntington Library Bulletin* 8:71-102 (1935), and *Comicall Satyre*, p. 185; Kernan, *Cankered Muse*, pp. 132-134.

22. Bradbrook, *Growth and Structure of Comedy*, p. 120; P. V. Kreider, "General Literary Satire in the Forest of Arden," *Shakespeare Association Bulletin*, 10:212-231 (1935).

23. John F. Kennedy, speaking at Amherst College, 1963; quoted in Arthur M. Schlesinger, Jr., *A Thousand Days* (Boston, 1965), p. 923.

Anonymous plays are listed by title.
All others will be found under their authors' names.

and Medwall's plays, 43, 44, 45, 48, 49, 50, 52, 53
Henry VIII, 28, 43, 134; and Shakespeare, 16–17, 18, 23; and Skelton, 54–63, 299; and John Heywood, 64–65, 70, 71; and *Godly Queen Hester*, 86–93, 94–95; and Protestant drama, 6, 7, 8, 96–97; and Bale, 98, 99–105, 301; late reign, 105–106, 107, 108, 109, 121; and *Gorboduc*, 141–142, 143, 146; and later drama, 116, 117, 158, 254, 255, 293
Henslowe, Philip, 18
Herodotus, 6
Hertford, Earl of (Edward Seymour), 16–17, 143
Hester, Queen, see *Godly Queen Hester*
Heywood, John, 109; *Play of the Weather*, 49, 64–70, 71, 72, 73, 74, 88, 118, 300; *Four PP*, 70–73, 74; other plays, 73–76; and Rastell, 76, 77, 79, 80, 81, 82
Heywood, Thomas, 14, 233, 279, 286; *1 and 2 Edward IV*, 241–242, 254; *Apology for Actors*, 261–262; *Sir Thomas Wyatt*, 292
Hickescorner, 40–41
Hoby, Sir Thomas, 262
Hoccleve, Thomas, 56
Holinshed, Raphael, 195, 236, 237, 240, 246, 250
Howards, family of (Dukes of Norfolk and Earls of Surrey), 86, 87, 155; and Skelton, 54–63
Hunsdon, first Baron (Henry Carey), 11
Huntingdon, third Earl of (Henry Hastings), 142, 295. See also Munday, Anthony

Impatient Poverty, 121, 125
Iphigenia and Alcmaeon, 263
Ireland, 12, 14, 20, 103, 232, 247, 289–291

Jack Juggler, 124–126
Jack Straw, The Life and Death of, 233, 236–238, 239, 242, 250, 254, 255, 293
Jacob and Esau, 109–113, 124, 125, 157–158, 301
James VI of Scotland, later James I of England, 12, 14, 205, 230, 289; and Shakespeare, 17, 21–22, 23–24; and *Horestes*, 150; and *The Misfortunes of*

Arthur, 154; and Lyly, 178; and Greene, 208–209; and later plays, 282, 292, 341n7
Jocasta, see Gascoigne, George
John, King, 4, 98–105. *See also* Bale, John; Shakespeare, William; *Troublesome Reign of King John*
John the Evangelist, 41
Jonson, Ben, 3, 4, 271, 279, 280, 288, 291, 294; *A Tale of a Tub*, 276–277; *Every Man in His Humor*, 277–278, 280; *Every Man Out of His Humor*, 280–281, 284; *Cynthia's Revels*, 281–283, 286, 287; *The Poetaster*, 13, 279, 285–287; *Sejanus*, 13, 286; *Volpone*, 13, 272, 278; *Epicoene*, 278; *The Alchemist*, 278; *Bartholomew Fair*, 101, 278

Katharine of Aragon, 22, 49, 95, 119, 123, 147; and *Godly Queen Hester*, 87–93
Kempis, Thomas à, 36–37, 38
Kenilworth, the entertainment of, 9, 16, 169
Kett's Rebellion, 106
King Darius, 130, 151
King Leir, 343n13
Kirchmayer, Thomas (*Pammachius*), 97, 105
Knack to Know a Knave, A Merry, 227–229, 233, 294–295
Knack to Know an Honest Man, A, 294–295
Knollys, Sir Francis, 11, 22
Knollys, Lettice, Countess of Essex, 22
Knox, John, 111, 157
Kyd, Thomas: *Cornelia*, 263; *Soliman and Perseda*, 263–264; *The Spanish Tragedy*, 264, 265

Langton, Stephen, 99, 103, 104
Larum for London, A, 290–291
Lee, Sir Henry, 169, 178, 180
Leicester, Earl of, *see* Dudley, Lord Robert
Leicester's Commonwealth, see Parsons, Robert
Leicester's men, 138, 158, 189
Liberality and Prodigality, 169–170, 336n4 (of Chap. 13)
Lindsay, Sir David (*Satire of the Three Estates*), 119
Lingua, 261
Livy (Titus Livius), 161

357